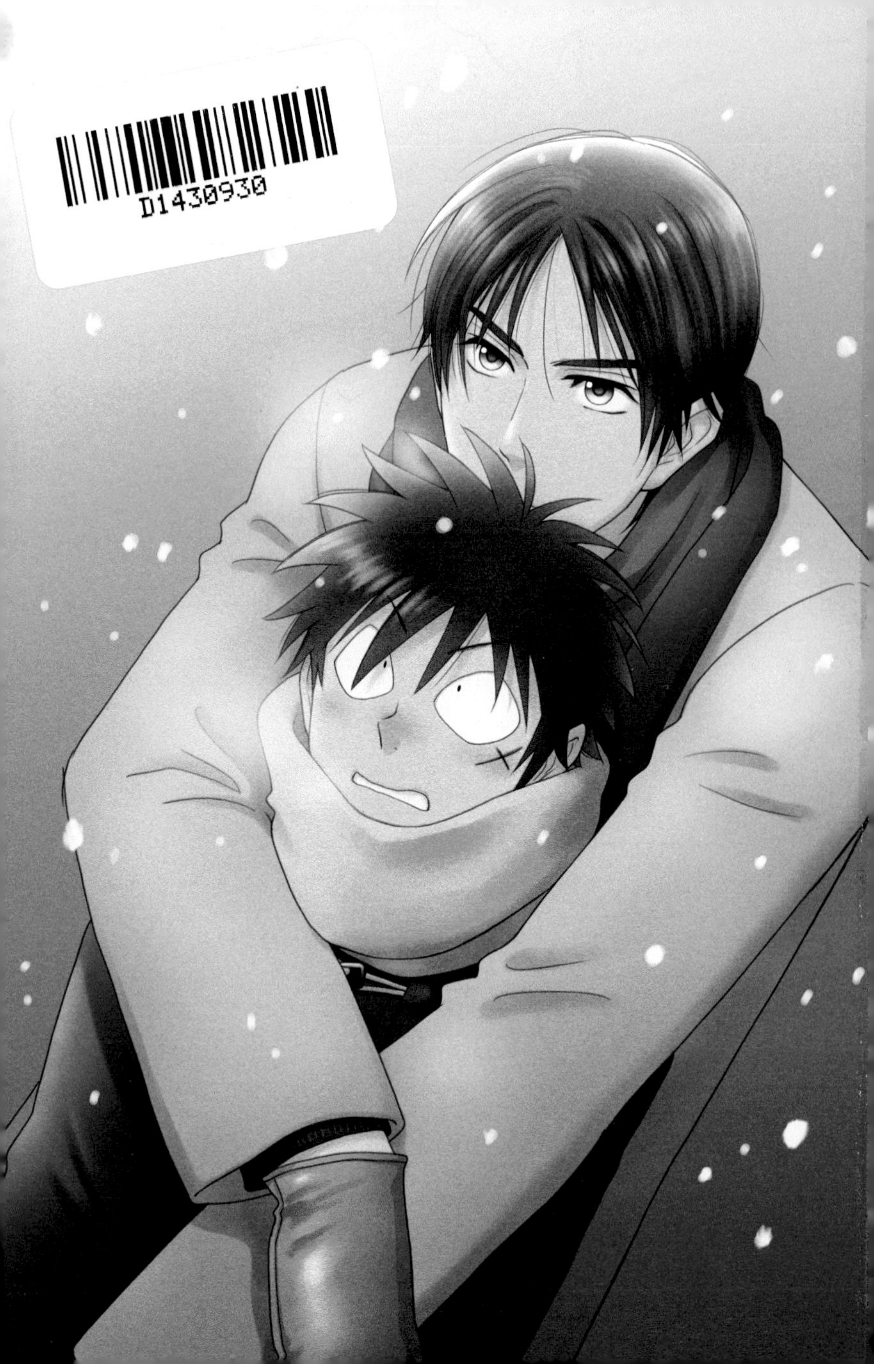

His Favorite

Story and Art by Suzuki Tanaka volume 12

CONTENTS

SUBLIME
SuBLimeManga.com

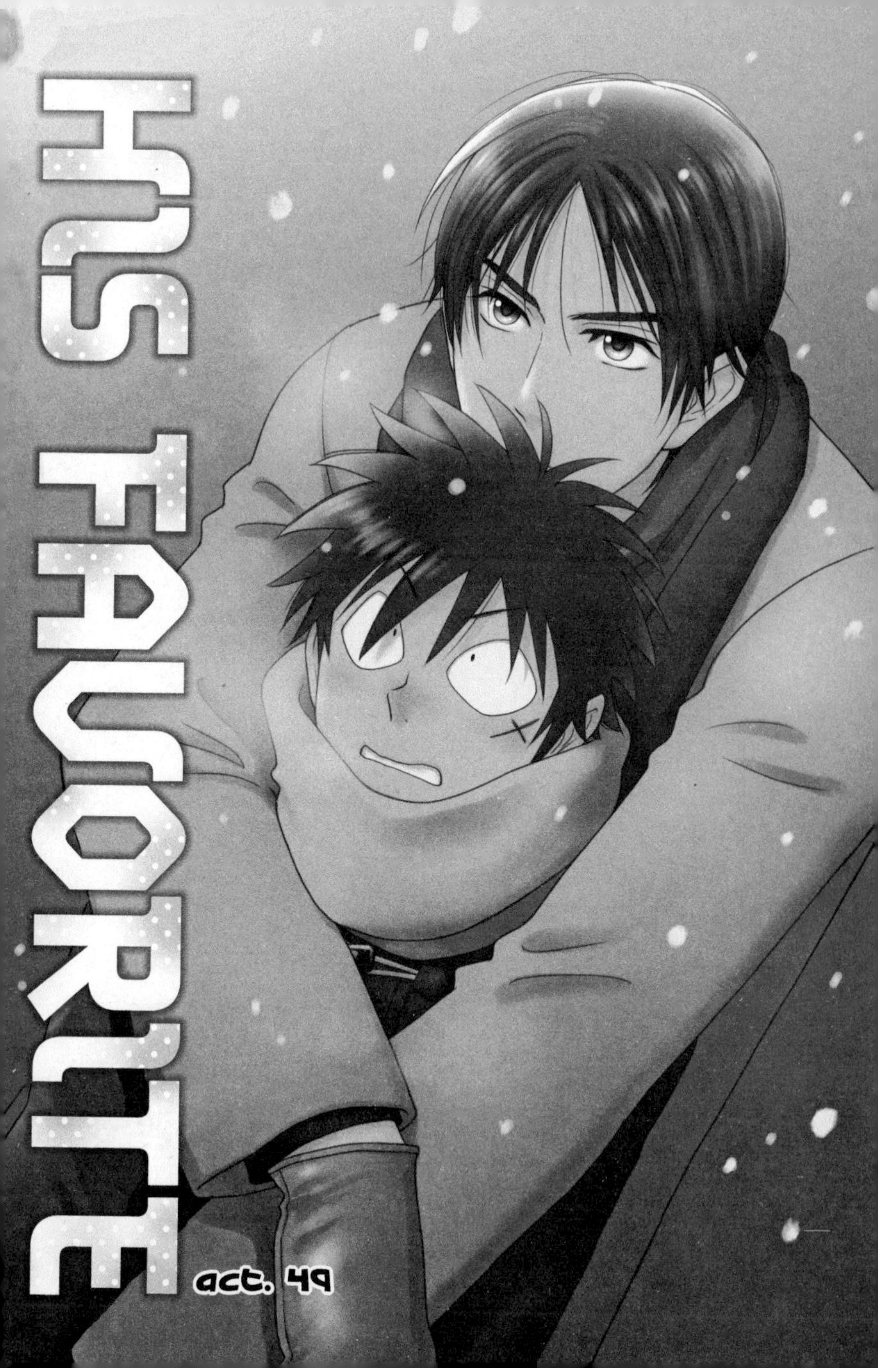
HIS FAVORITE
act. 49

HIS
FAVORITE

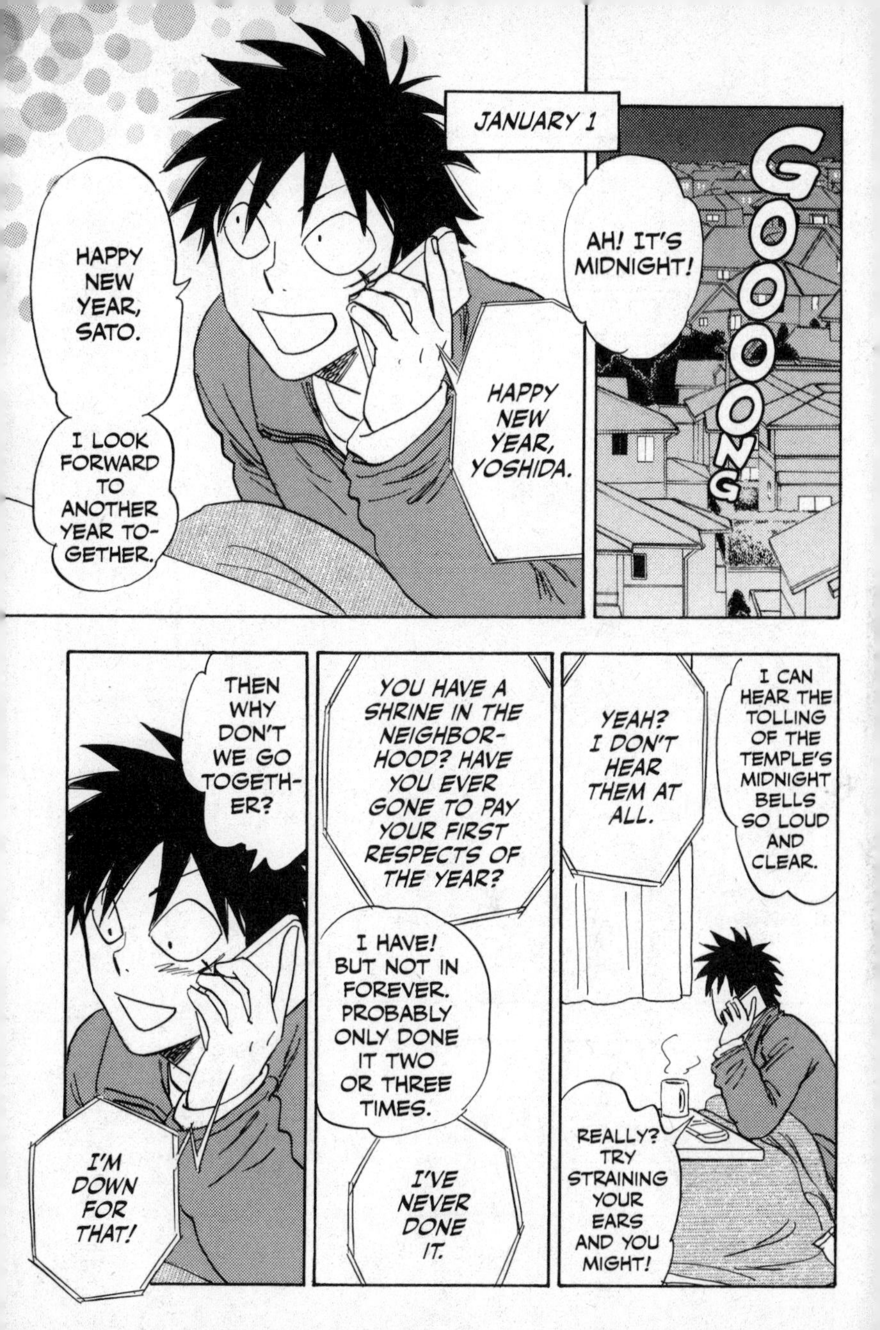
JANUARY 1
AH! IT'S MIDNIGHT!
GOOOONG
HAPPY NEW YEAR, YOSHIDA.
HAPPY NEW YEAR, SATO.
I LOOK FORWARD TO ANOTHER YEAR TO-GETHER.
I CAN HEAR THE TOLLING OF THE TEMPLE'S MIDNIGHT BELLS SO LOUD AND CLEAR.
YEAH? I DON'T HEAR THEM AT ALL.
REALLY? TRY STRAINING YOUR EARS AND YOU MIGHT!
YOU HAVE A SHRINE IN THE NEIGHBOR-HOOD? HAVE YOU EVER GONE TO PAY YOUR FIRST RESPECTS OF THE YEAR?
I HAVE! BUT NOT IN FOREVER. PROBABLY ONLY DONE IT TWO OR THREE TIMES.
I'VE NEVER DONE IT.
THEN WHY DON'T WE GO TOGETH-ER?
I'M DOWN FOR THAT!

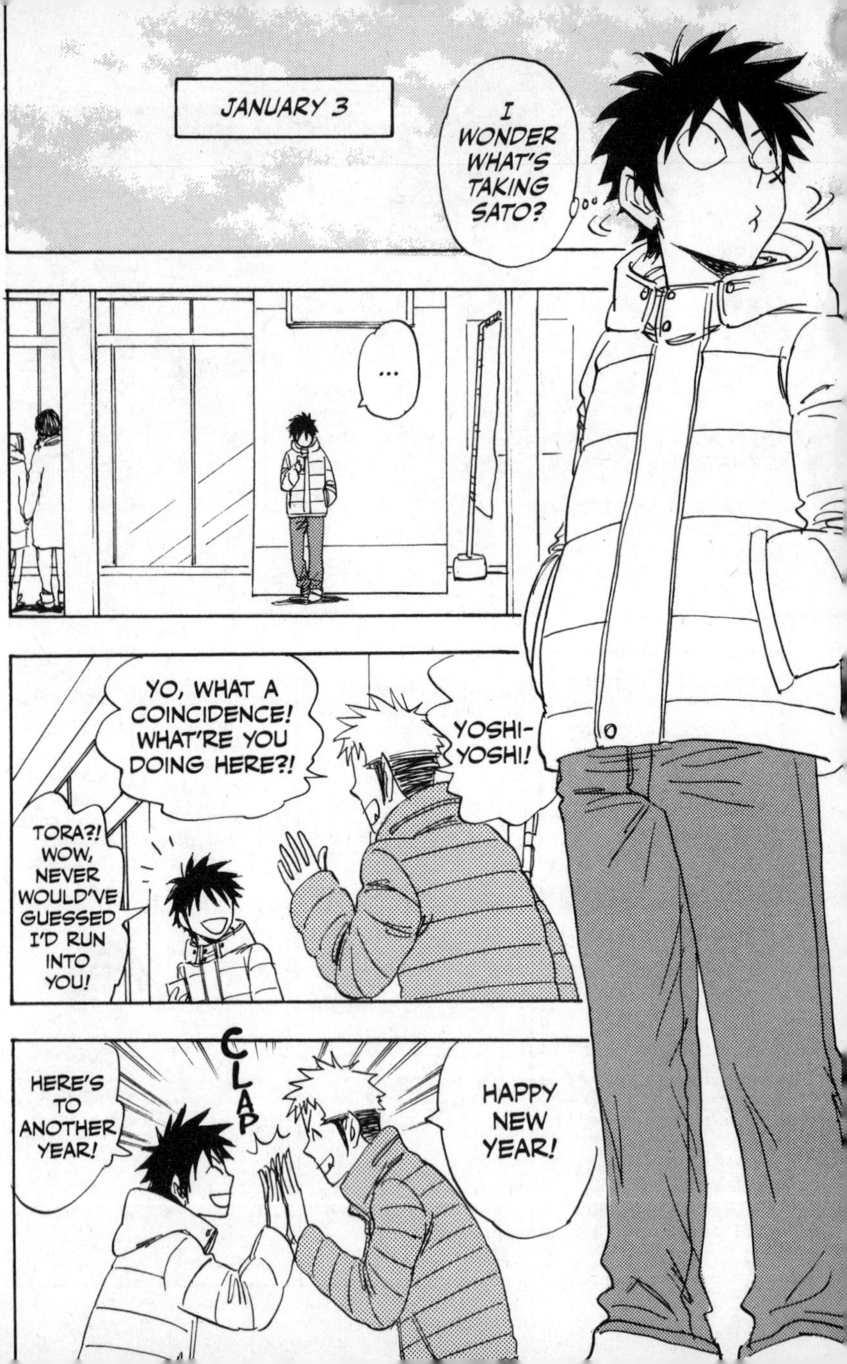
I WONDER WHAT'S TAKING SATO?
JANUARY 3
...
YOSHI-YOSHI!
YO, WHAT A COINCIDENCE! WHAT'RE YOU DOING HERE?!
TORA?! WOW, NEVER WOULD'VE GUESSED I'D RUN INTO YOU!
HAPPY NEW YEAR!
CLAP
HERE'S TO ANOTHER YEAR!

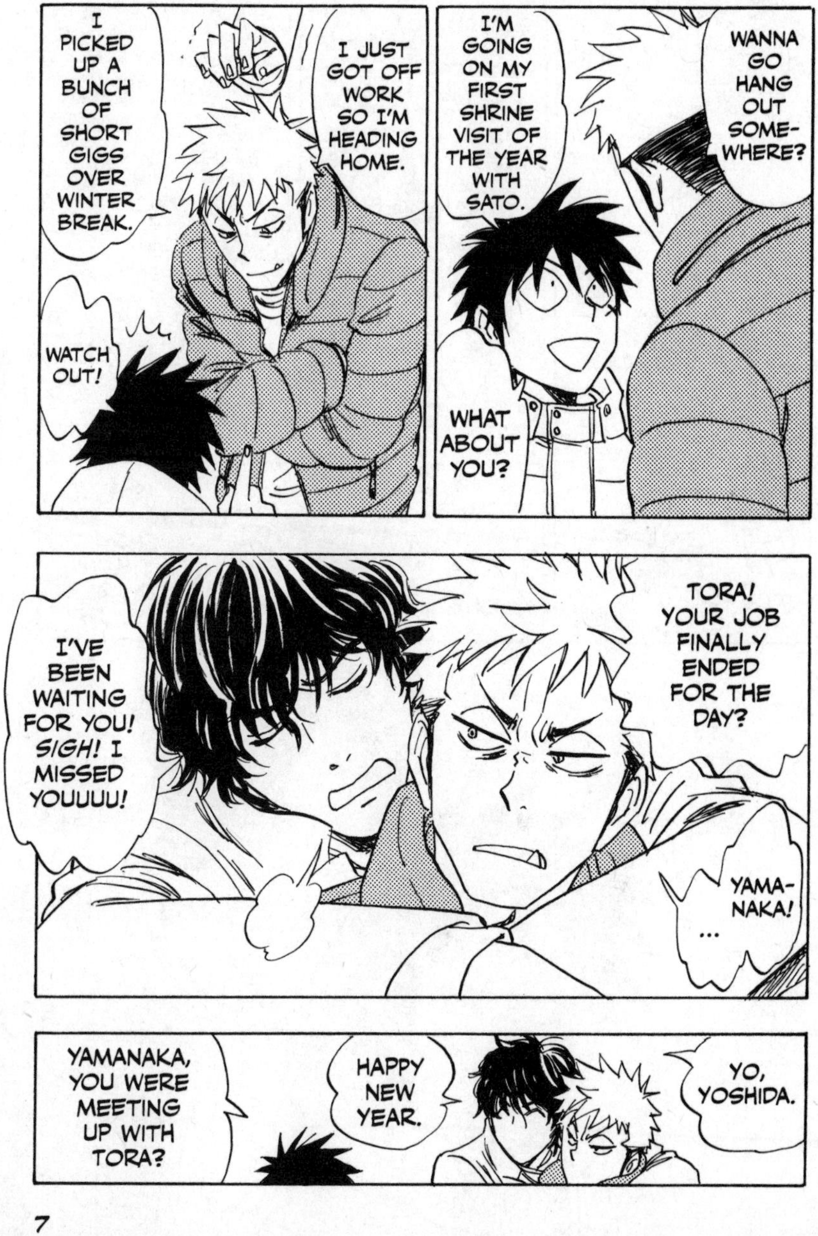
WANNA GO HANG OUT SOMEWHERE?
I'M GOING ON MY FIRST SHRINE VISIT OF THE YEAR WITH SATO.
WHAT ABOUT YOU?
I JUST GOT OFF WORK SO I'M HEADING HOME.
I PICKED UP A BUNCH OF SHORT GIGS OVER WINTER BREAK.
WATCH OUT!
TORA! YOUR JOB FINALLY ENDED FOR THE DAY?
YAMANAKA! ...
I'VE BEEN WAITING FOR YOU! *SIGH!* I MISSED YOUUUUU!
YO, YOSHIDA.
HAPPY NEW YEAR.
YAMANAKA, YOU WERE MEETING UP WITH TORA?

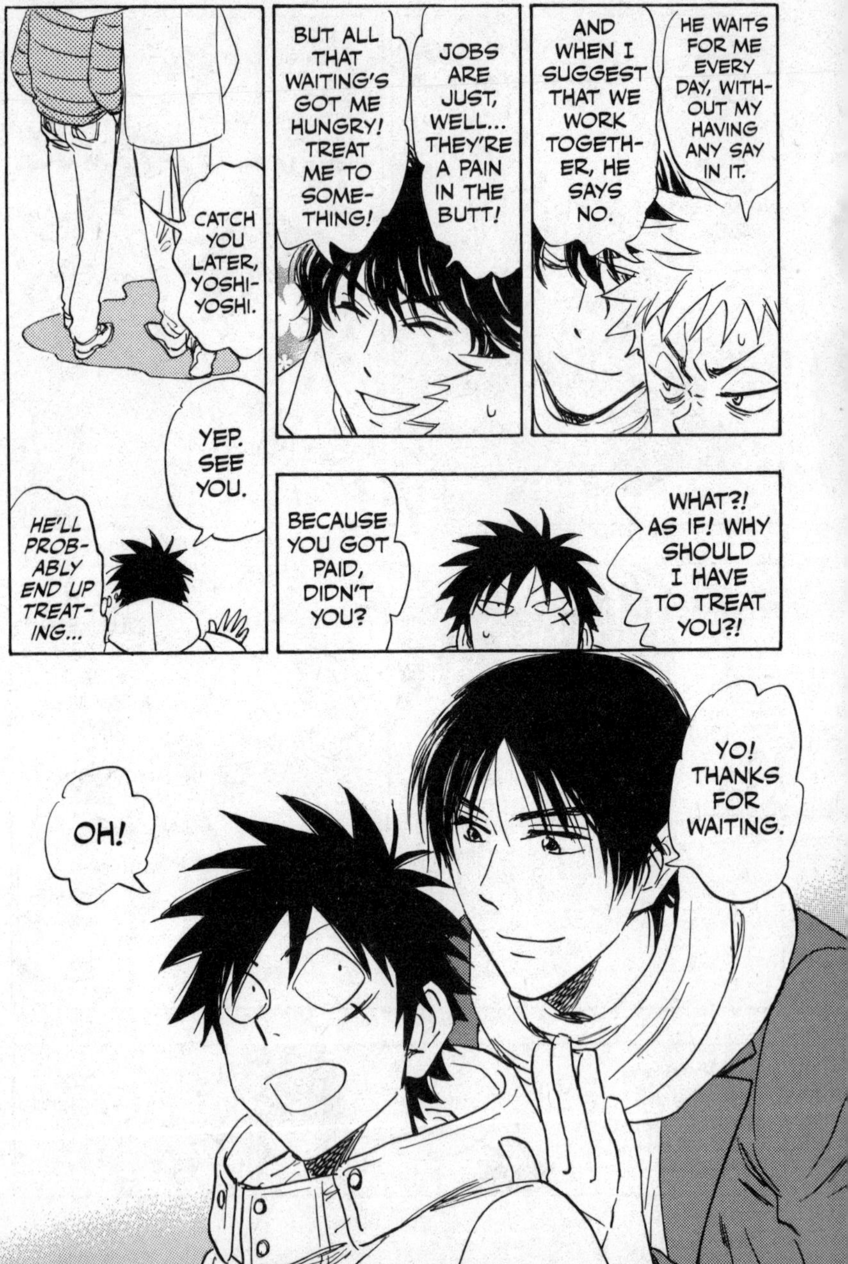
HE WAITS FOR ME EVERY DAY, WITHOUT MY HAVING ANY SAY IN IT.
AND WHEN I SUGGEST THAT WE WORK TOGETHER, HE SAYS NO.
JOBS ARE JUST, WELL... THEY'RE A PAIN IN THE BUTT!
BUT ALL THAT WAITING'S GOT ME HUNGRY! TREAT ME TO SOMETHING!
WHAT?! AS IF! WHY SHOULD I HAVE TO TREAT YOU?!
BECAUSE YOU GOT PAID, DIDN'T YOU?
CATCH YOU LATER, YOSHI-YOSHI.
YEP. SEE YOU.
HE'LL PROBABLY END UP TREATING...
YO! THANKS FOR WAITING.
OH!

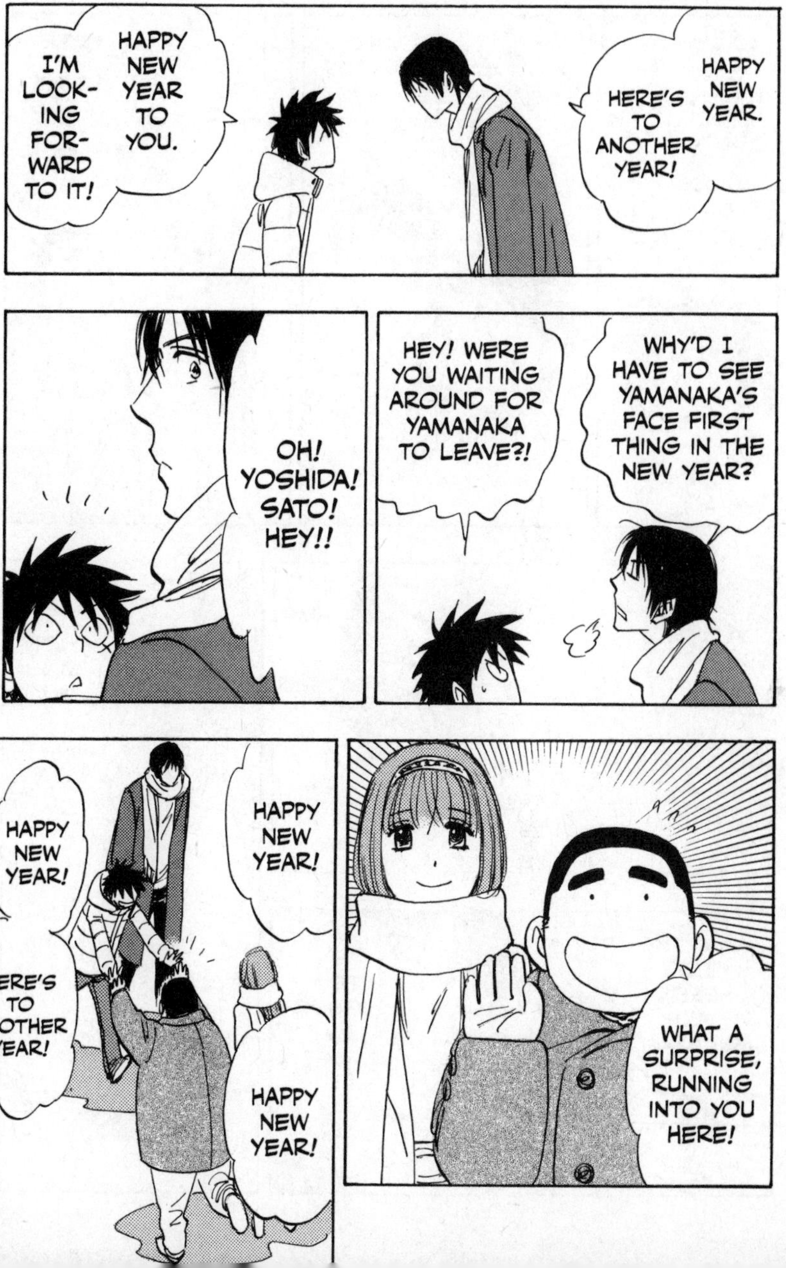
HAPPY NEW YEAR.
HERE'S TO ANOTHER YEAR!
HAPPY NEW YEAR TO YOU.
I'M LOOKING FORWARD TO IT!
WHY'D I HAVE TO SEE YAMANAKA'S FACE FIRST THING IN THE NEW YEAR?
HEY! WERE YOU WAITING AROUND FOR YAMANAKA TO LEAVE?!
OH! YOSHIDA! SATO! HEY!!
WHAT A SURPRISE, RUNNING INTO YOU HERE!
HAPPY NEW YEAR!
HAPPY NEW YEAR!
HERE'S TO ANOTHER YEAR!
HAPPY NEW YEAR!

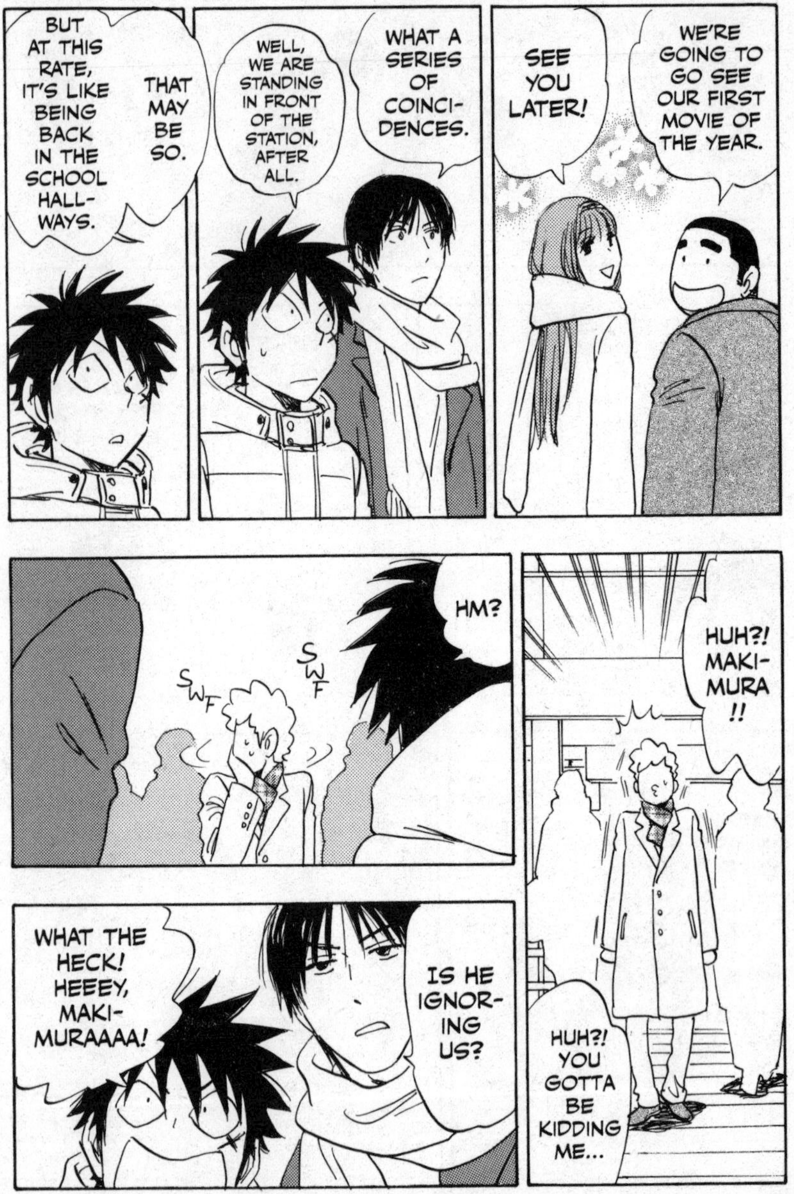
WE'RE GOING TO GO SEE OUR FIRST MOVIE OF THE YEAR.
SEE YOU LATER!
WHAT A SERIES OF COINCIDENCES.
WELL, WE ARE STANDING IN FRONT OF THE STATION, AFTER ALL.
THAT MAY BE SO.
BUT AT THIS RATE, IT'S LIKE BEING BACK IN THE SCHOOL HALLWAYS.
HUH?! MAKIMURA!!
HUH?! YOU GOTTA BE KIDDING ME...
HM?
SWF
SWF
IS HE IGNORING US?
WHAT THE HECK! HEEEY, MAKIMURAAAA!

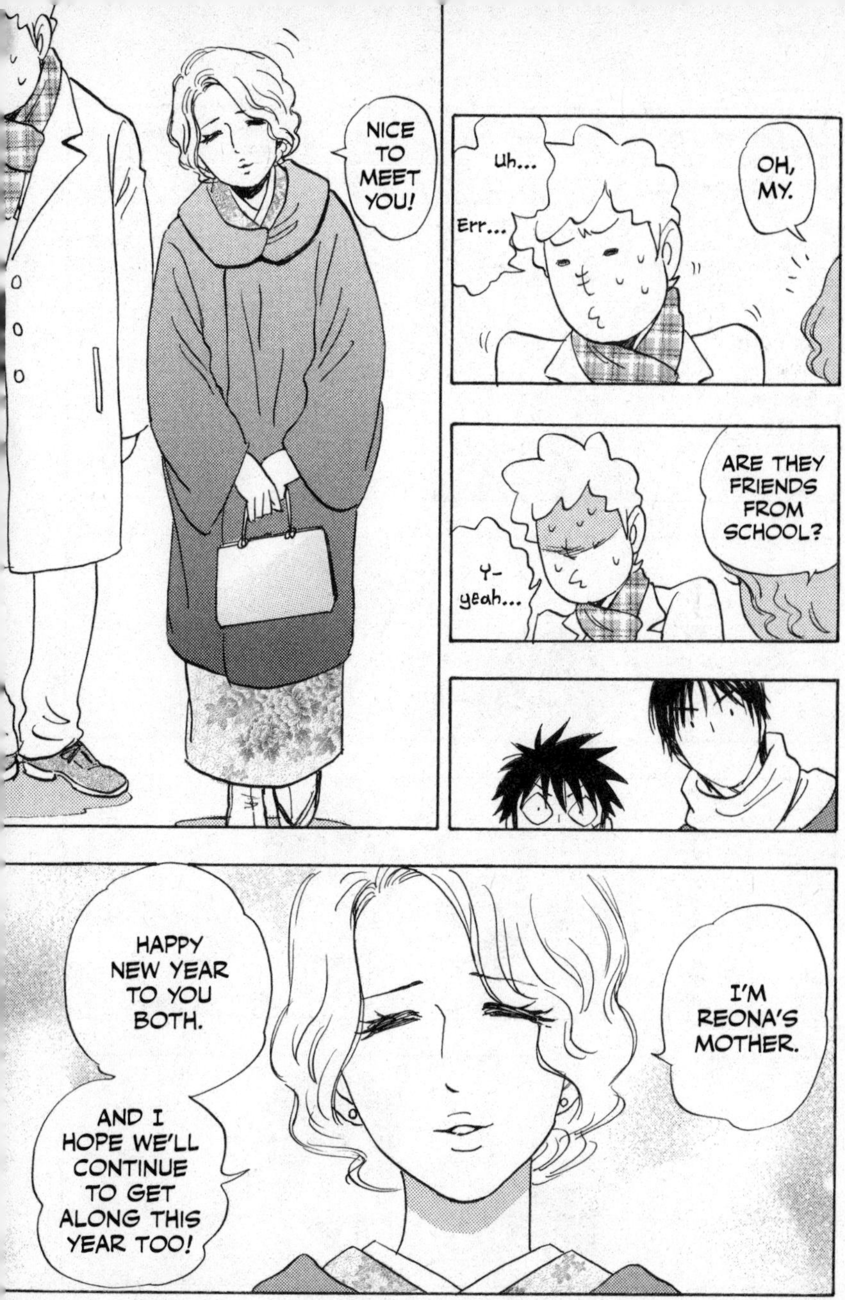
OH, MY.
Uh...
Err...
ARE THEY FRIENDS FROM SCHOOL?
Y-yeah...
NICE TO MEET YOU!
I'M REONA'S MOTHER.
HAPPY NEW YEAR TO YOU BOTH.
AND I HOPE WE'LL CONTINUE TO GET ALONG THIS YEAR TOO!

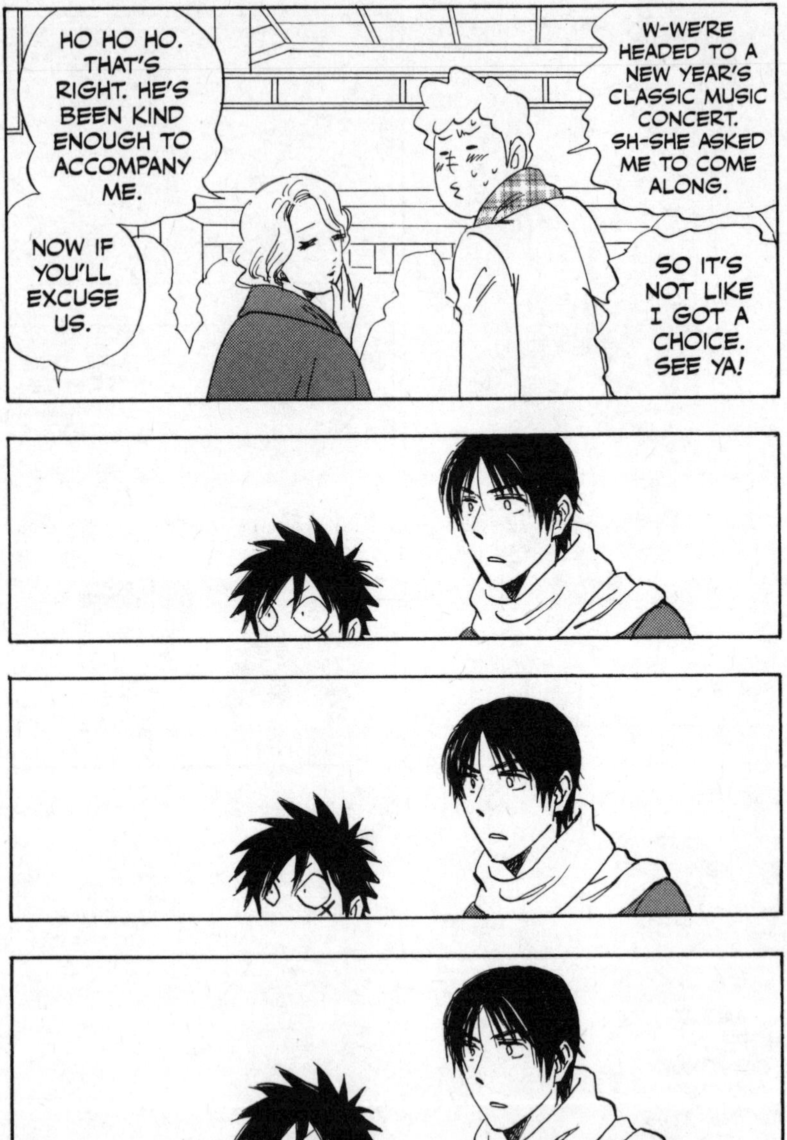
W-WE'RE HEADED TO A NEW YEAR'S CLASSIC MUSIC CONCERT. SH-SHE ASKED ME TO COME ALONG.
HO HO HO. THAT'S RIGHT. HE'S BEEN KIND ENOUGH TO ACCOMPANY ME.
SO IT'S NOT LIKE I GOT A CHOICE. SEE YA!
NOW IF YOU'LL EXCUSE US.

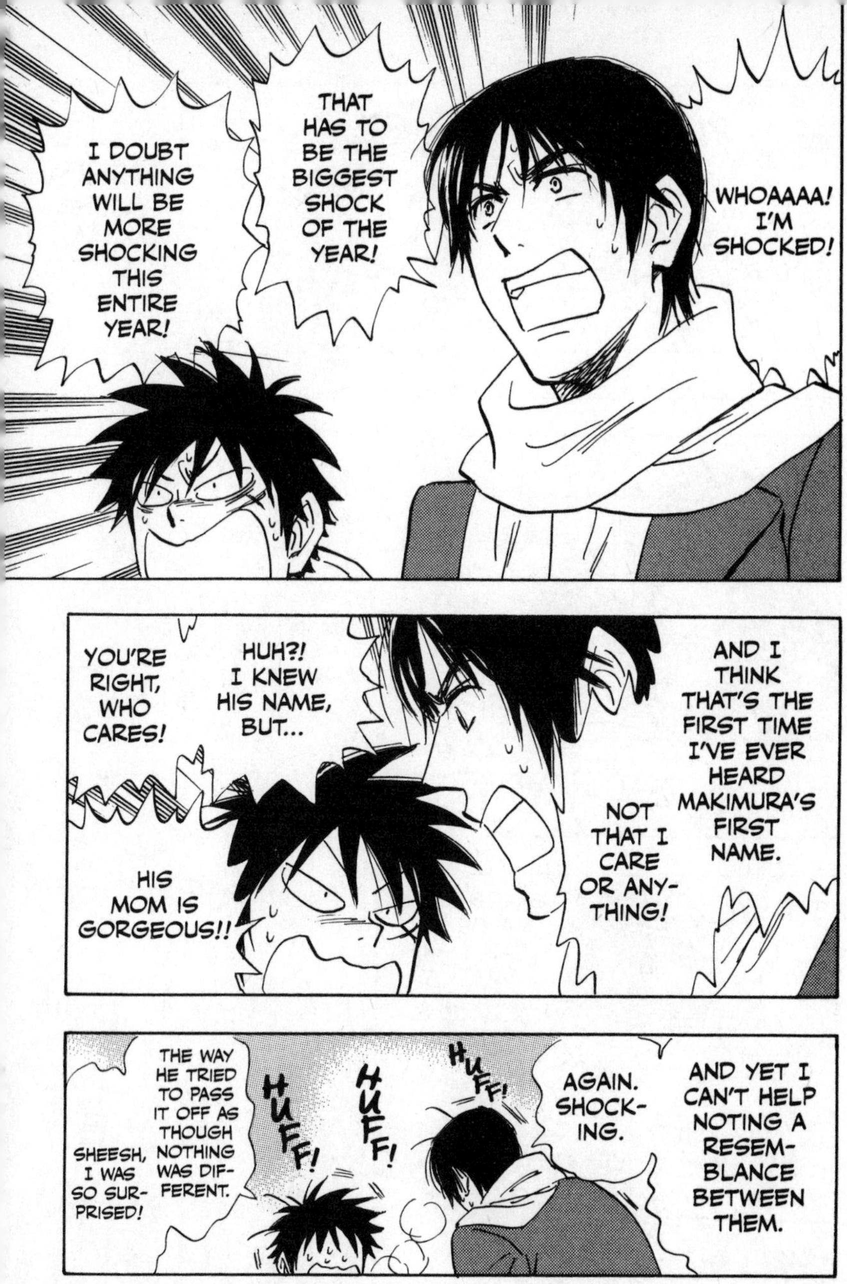
WHOAAAA! I'M SHOCKED!
THAT HAS TO BE THE BIGGEST SHOCK OF THE YEAR!
I DOUBT ANYTHING WILL BE MORE SHOCKING THIS ENTIRE YEAR!
AND I THINK THAT'S THE FIRST TIME I'VE EVER HEARD MAKIMURA'S FIRST NAME.
NOT THAT I CARE OR ANYTHING!
HUH?! I KNEW HIS NAME, BUT...
YOU'RE RIGHT, WHO CARES!
HIS MOM IS GORGEOUS!!
AND YET I CAN'T HELP NOTING A RESEMBLANCE BETWEEN THEM.
AGAIN. SHOCKING.
HUFF!
HUFF!
HUFF!
THE WAY HE TRIED TO PASS IT OFF AS THOUGH NOTHING WAS DIFFERENT.
SHEESH, I WAS SO SURPRISED!

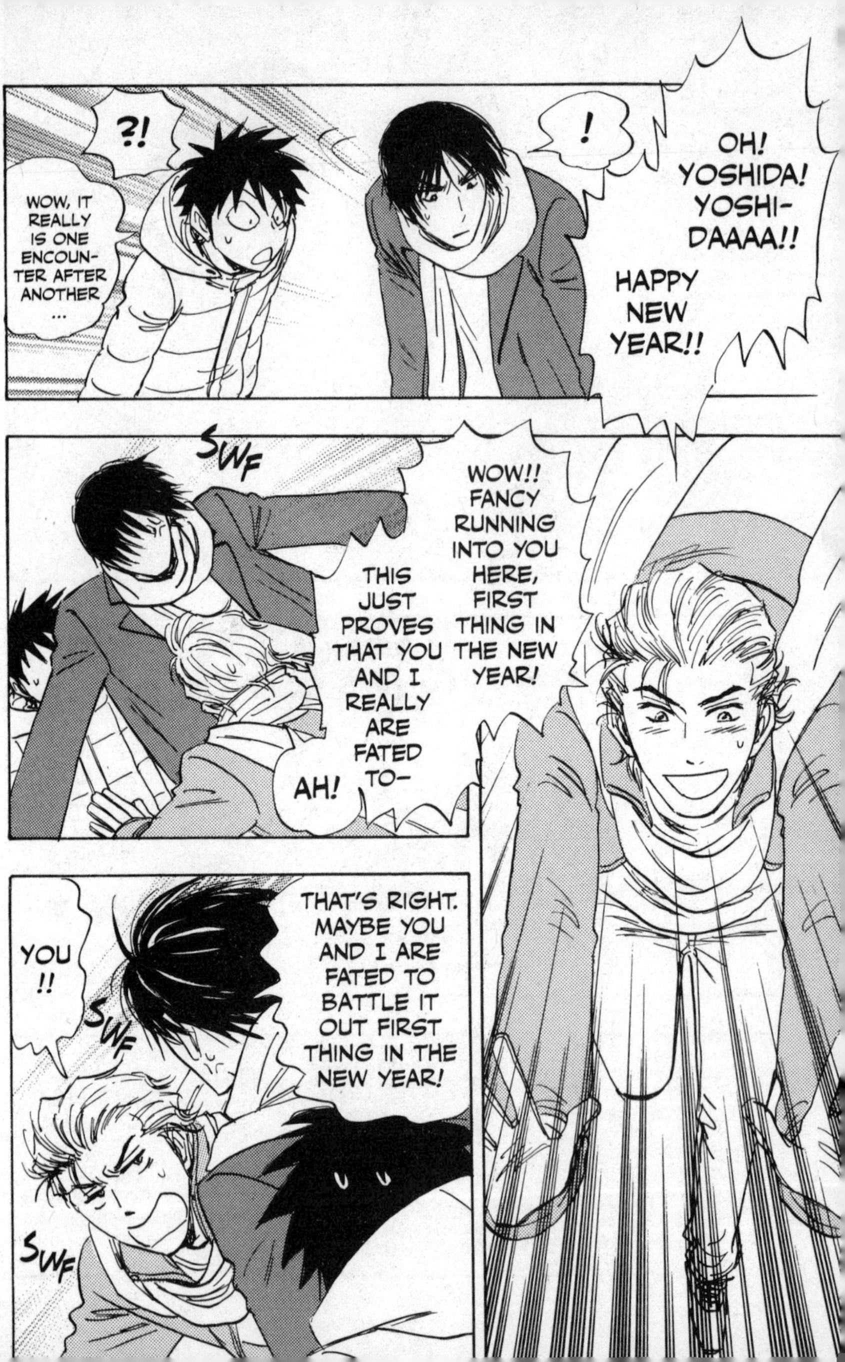
OH! YOSHIDA! YOSHI-DAAAA!!
HAPPY NEW YEAR!!
!
?!
WOW, IT REALLY IS ONE ENCOUN-TER AFTER ANOTHER ...
WOW!! FANCY RUNNING INTO YOU HERE, FIRST THING IN THE NEW YEAR!
THIS JUST PROVES THAT YOU AND I REALLY ARE FATED TO-
SWF
AH!
THAT'S RIGHT. MAYBE YOU AND I ARE FATED TO BATTLE IT OUT FIRST THING IN THE NEW YEAR!
YOU !!
SWF
SWF

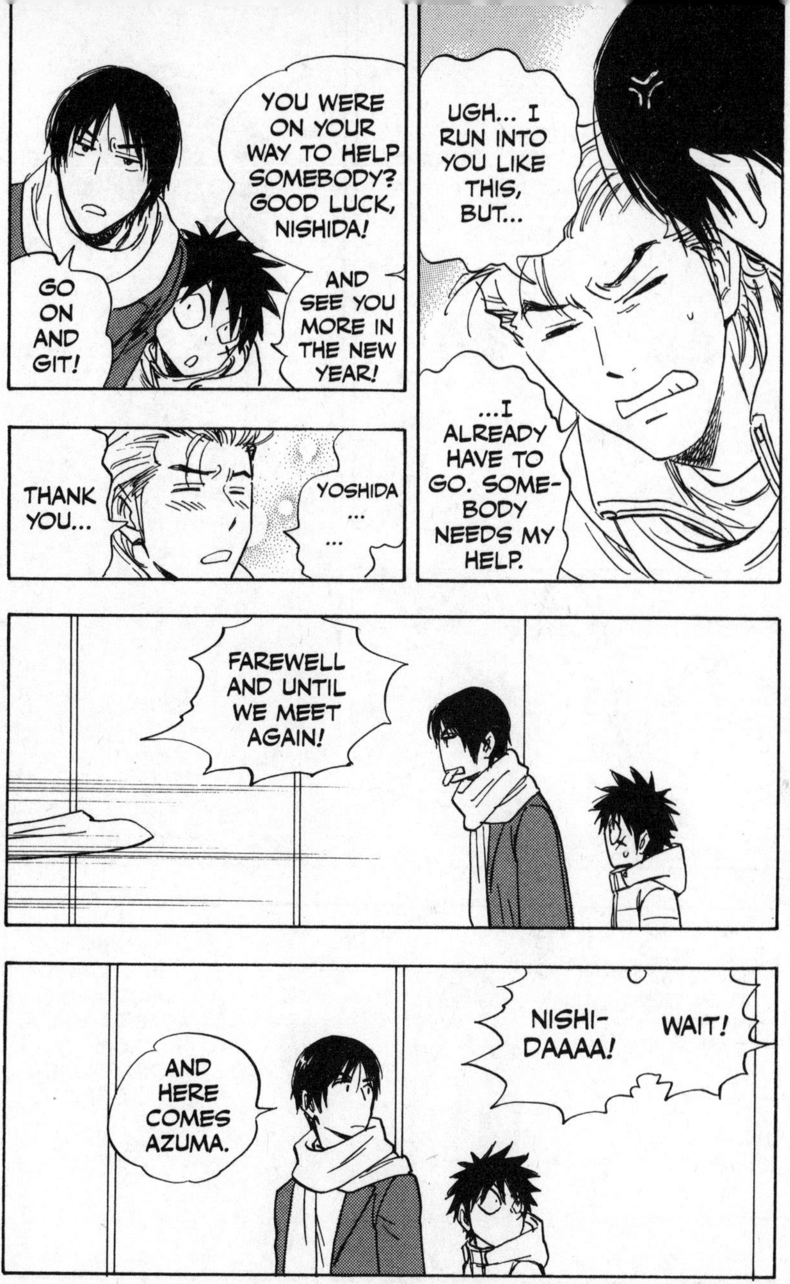
UGH... I RUN INTO YOU LIKE THIS, BUT...
...I ALREADY HAVE TO GO. SOMEBODY NEEDS MY HELP.
YOU WERE ON YOUR WAY TO HELP SOMEBODY? GOOD LUCK, NISHIDA!
AND SEE YOU MORE IN THE NEW YEAR!
GO ON AND GIT!
YOSHIDA... ...
THANK YOU...
FAREWELL AND UNTIL WE MEET AGAIN!
NISHIDAAAA! WAIT!
AND HERE COMES AZUMA.

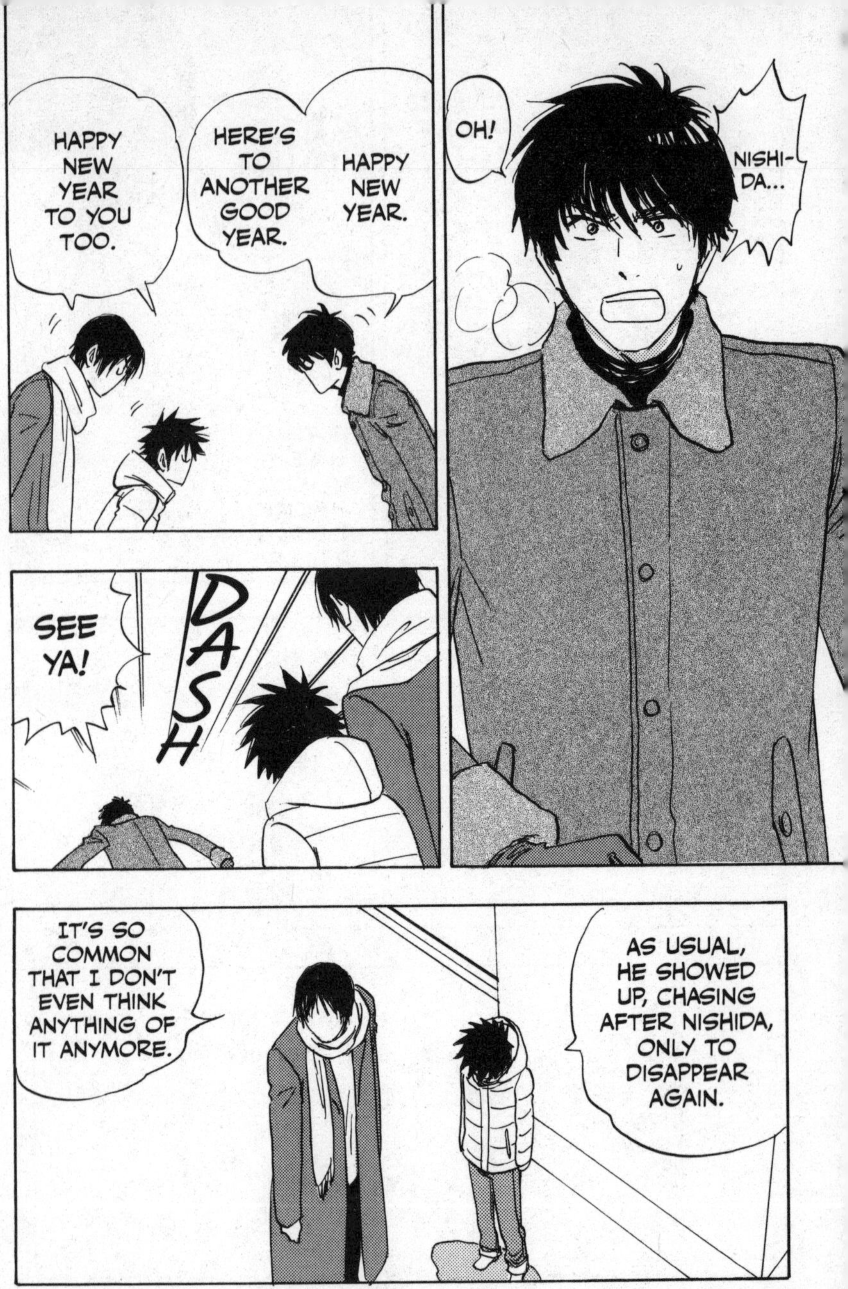
NISHI-DA...
OH!
HAPPY NEW YEAR.
HERE'S TO ANOTHER GOOD YEAR.
HAPPY NEW YEAR TO YOU TOO.
DASH
SEE YA!
AS USUAL, HE SHOWED UP, CHASING AFTER NISHIDA, ONLY TO DISAPPEAR AGAIN.
IT'S SO COMMON THAT I DON'T EVEN THINK ANYTHING OF IT ANYMORE.

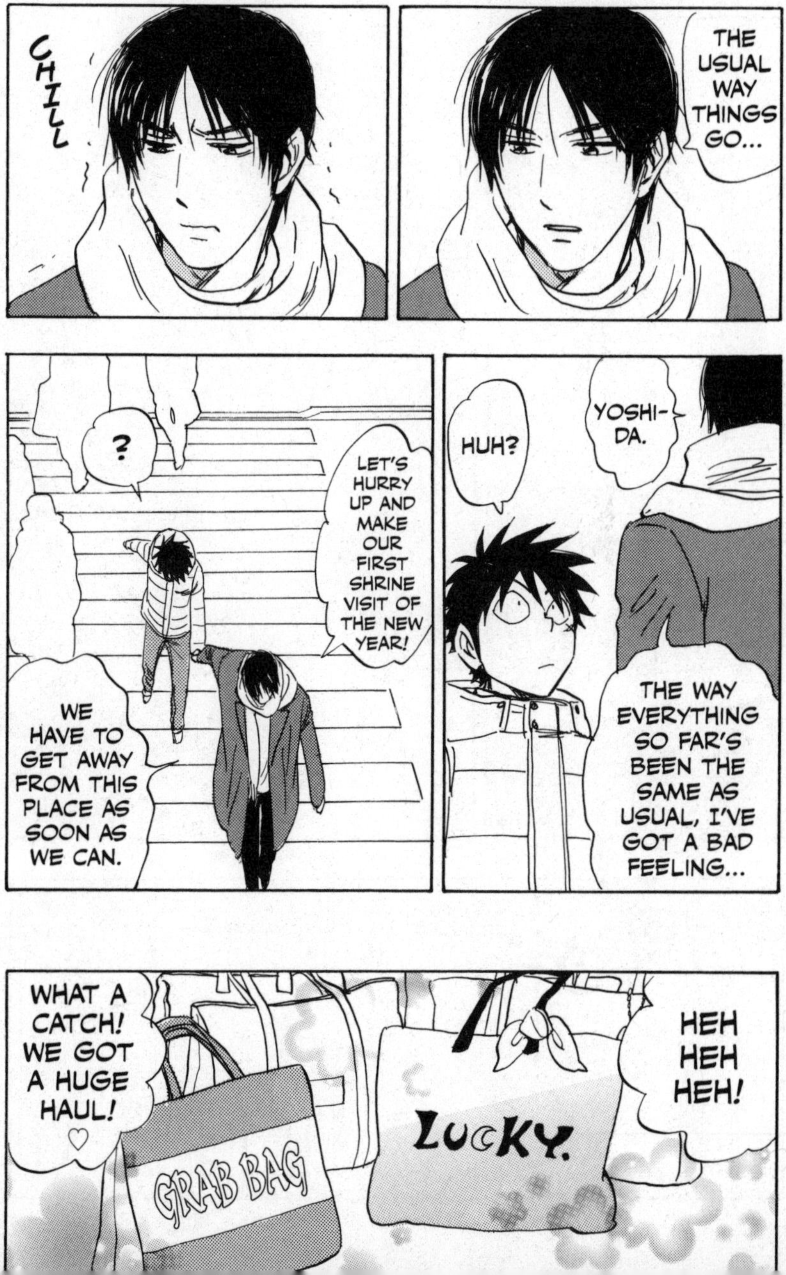
THE USUAL WAY THINGS GO...
CHILL
YOSHI-DA.
HUH?
THE WAY EVERYTHING SO FAR'S BEEN THE SAME AS USUAL, I'VE GOT A BAD FEELING...
LET'S HURRY UP AND MAKE OUR FIRST SHRINE VISIT OF THE NEW YEAR!
?
WE HAVE TO GET AWAY FROM THIS PLACE AS SOON AS WE CAN.
HEH HEH HEH!
WHAT A CATCH! WE GOT A HUGE HAUL! ♡
LUCKY.
GRAB BAG

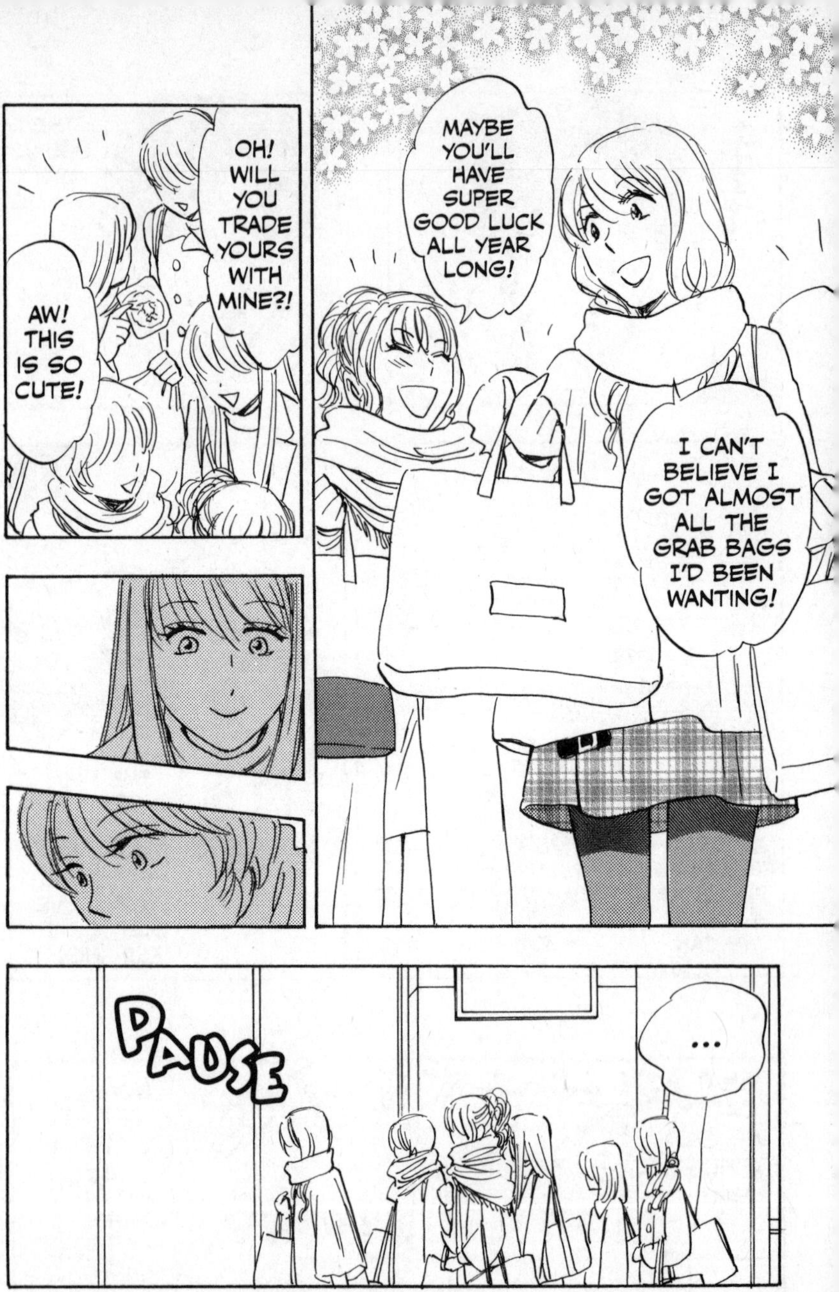
I CAN'T BELIEVE I GOT ALMOST ALL THE GRAB BAGS I'D BEEN WANTING!
MAYBE YOU'LL HAVE SUPER GOOD LUCK ALL YEAR LONG!
OH! WILL YOU TRADE YOURS WITH MINE?!
AW! THIS IS SO CUTE!
...
PAUSE

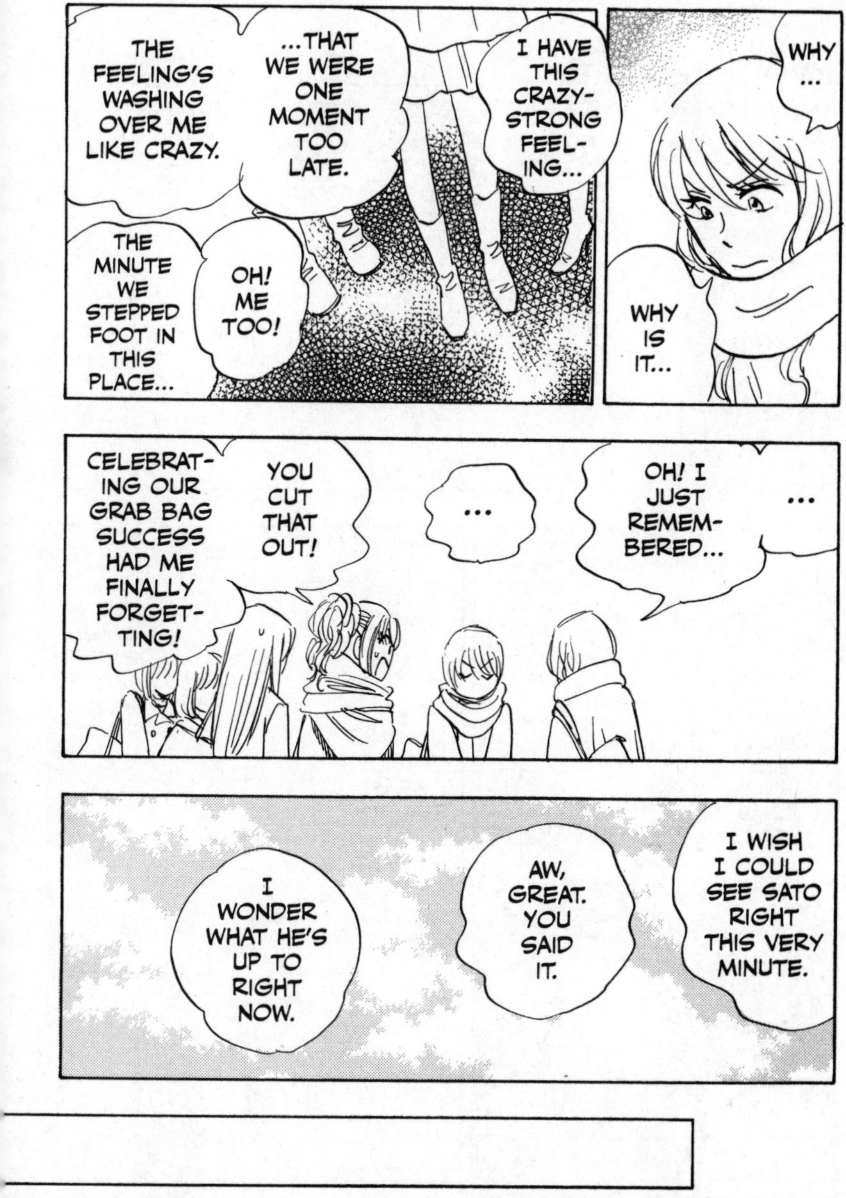
WHY...
WHY IS IT...
I HAVE THIS CRAZY-STRONG FEELING...
...THAT WE WERE ONE MOMENT TOO LATE.
THE FEELING'S WASHING OVER ME LIKE CRAZY.
OH! ME TOO!
THE MINUTE WE STEPPED FOOT IN THIS PLACE...
...
OH! I JUST REMEMBERED...
...
YOU CUT THAT OUT!
CELEBRATING OUR GRAB BAG SUCCESS HAD ME FINALLY FORGETTING!
I WISH I COULD SEE SATO RIGHT THIS VERY MINUTE.
AW, GREAT. YOU SAID IT.
I WONDER WHAT HE'S UP TO RIGHT NOW.

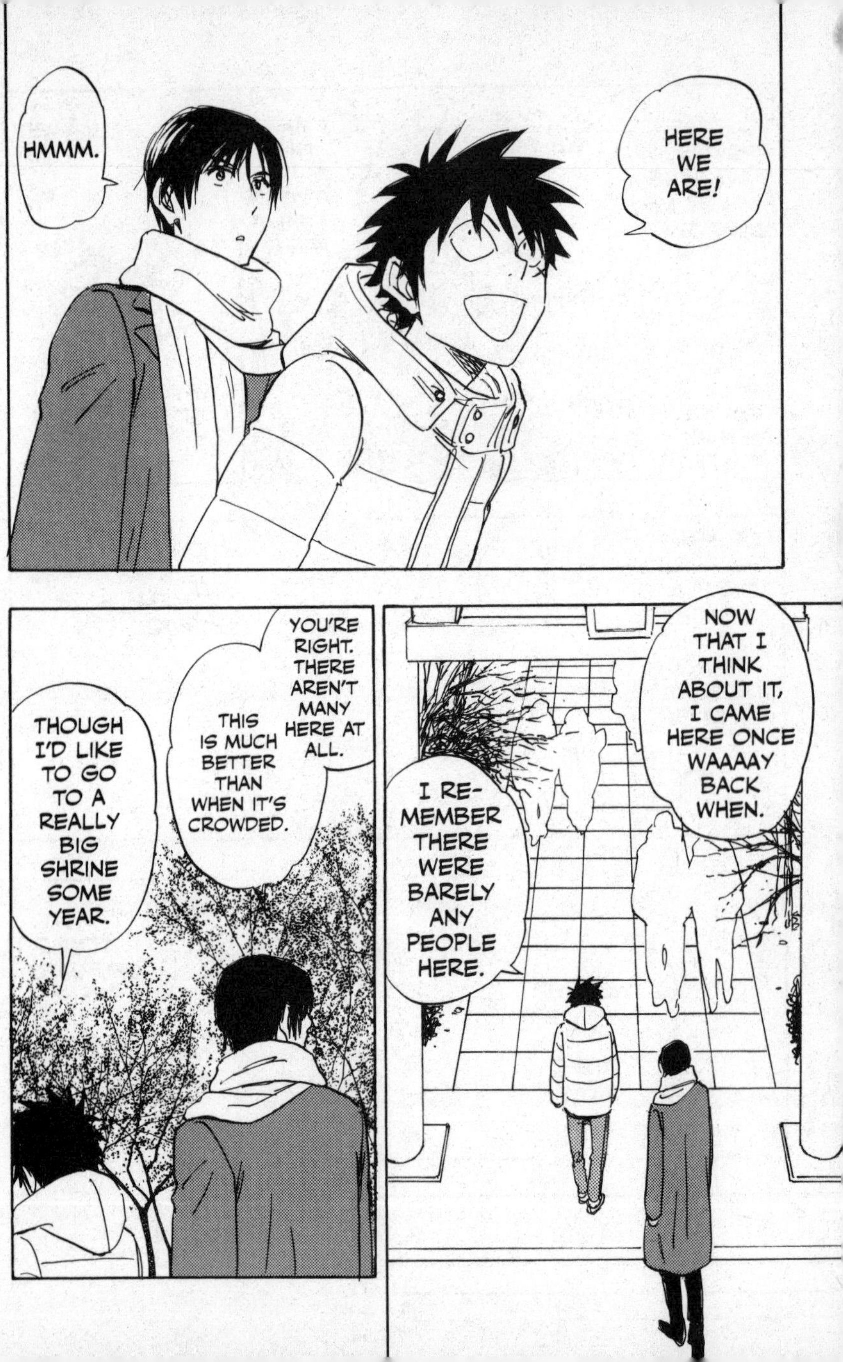
HERE WE ARE!
HMMM.
NOW THAT I THINK ABOUT IT, I CAME HERE ONCE WAAAAY BACK WHEN.
I RE-MEMBER THERE WERE BARELY ANY PEOPLE HERE.
YOU'RE RIGHT. THERE AREN'T MANY HERE AT ALL.
THIS IS MUCH BETTER THAN WHEN IT'S CROWDED.
THOUGH I'D LIKE TO GO TO A REALLY BIG SHRINE SOME YEAR.

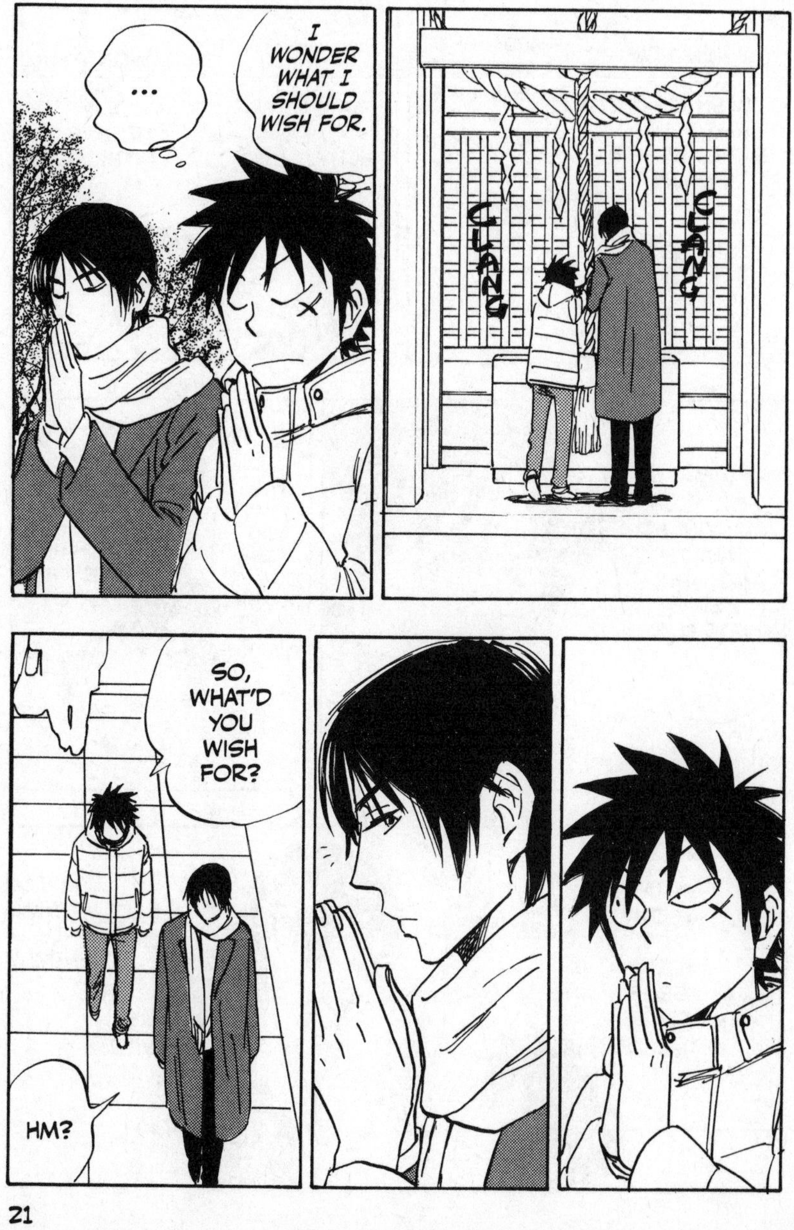
CLANG
CLANG
I WONDER WHAT I SHOULD WISH FOR.
...
SO, WHAT'D YOU WISH FOR?
HM?

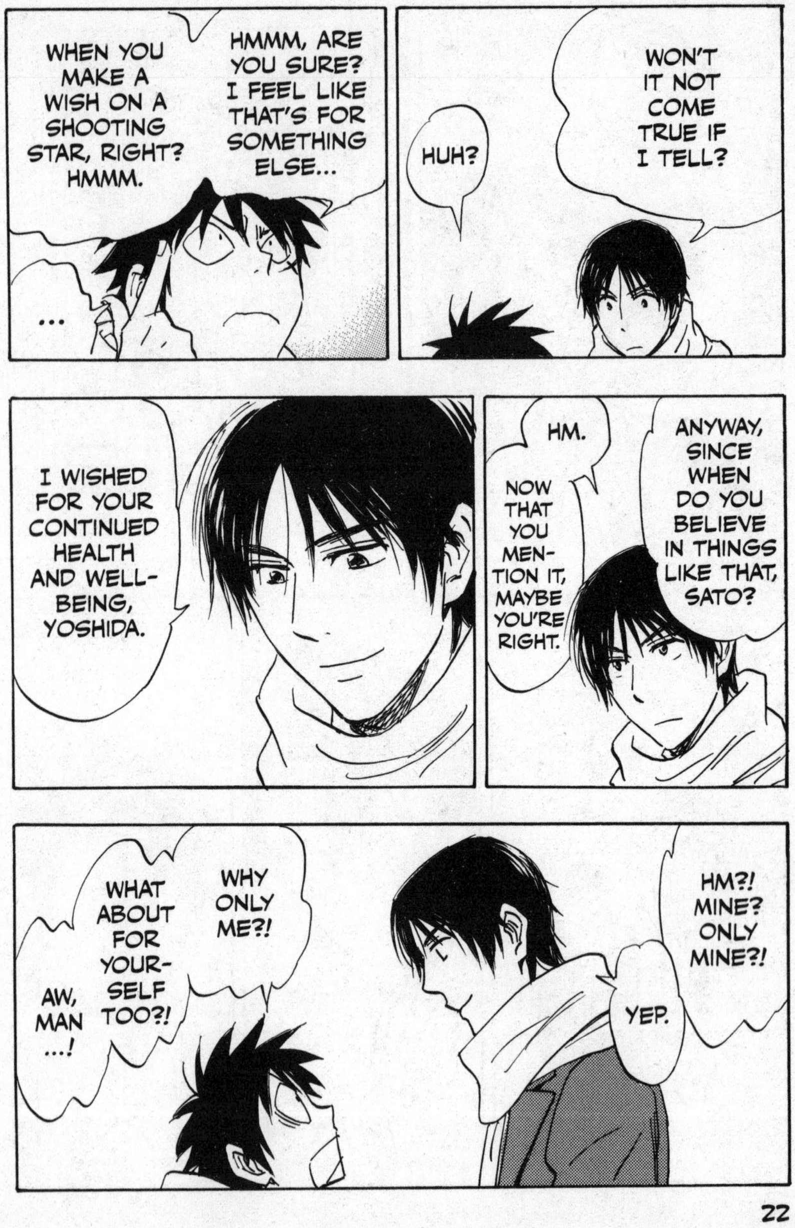
WON'T IT NOT COME TRUE IF I TELL?
HUH?
HMMM, ARE YOU SURE? I FEEL LIKE THAT'S FOR SOMETHING ELSE...
WHEN YOU MAKE A WISH ON A SHOOTING STAR, RIGHT? HMMM.
...
ANYWAY, SINCE WHEN DO YOU BELIEVE IN THINGS LIKE THAT, SATO?
HM.
NOW THAT YOU MEN-TION IT, MAYBE YOU'RE RIGHT.
I WISHED FOR YOUR CONTINUED HEALTH AND WELL-BEING, YOSHIDA.
HM?! MINE? ONLY MINE?!
YEP.
WHY ONLY ME?!
WHAT ABOUT FOR YOUR-SELF TOO?!
AW, MAN ...!

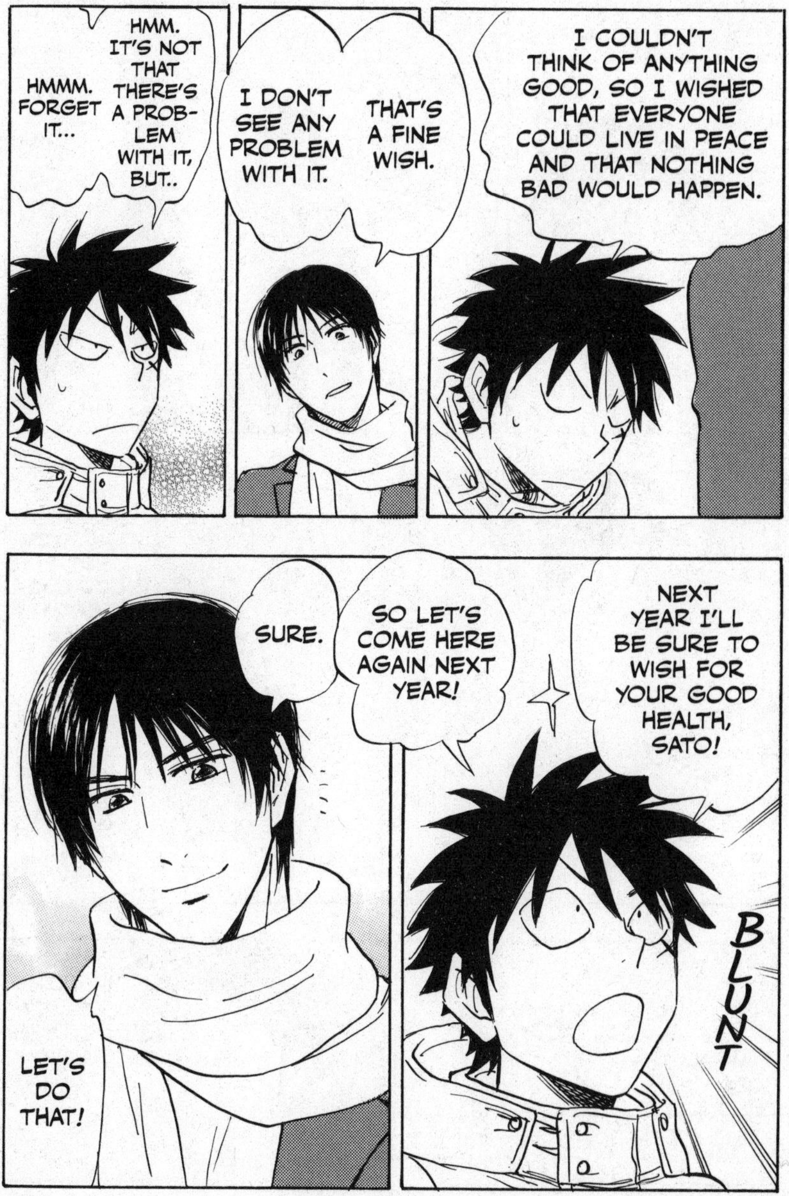
I COULDN'T THINK OF ANYTHING GOOD, SO I WISHED THAT EVERYONE COULD LIVE IN PEACE AND THAT NOTHING BAD WOULD HAPPEN.
THAT'S A FINE WISH.
I DON'T SEE ANY PROBLEM WITH IT.
HMM. IT'S NOT THAT THERE'S A PROB-LEM WITH IT, BUT..
HMMM. FORGET IT...
NEXT YEAR I'LL BE SURE TO WISH FOR YOUR GOOD HEALTH, SATO!
BLUNT
SO LET'S COME HERE AGAIN NEXT YEAR!
SURE.
LET'S DO THAT!

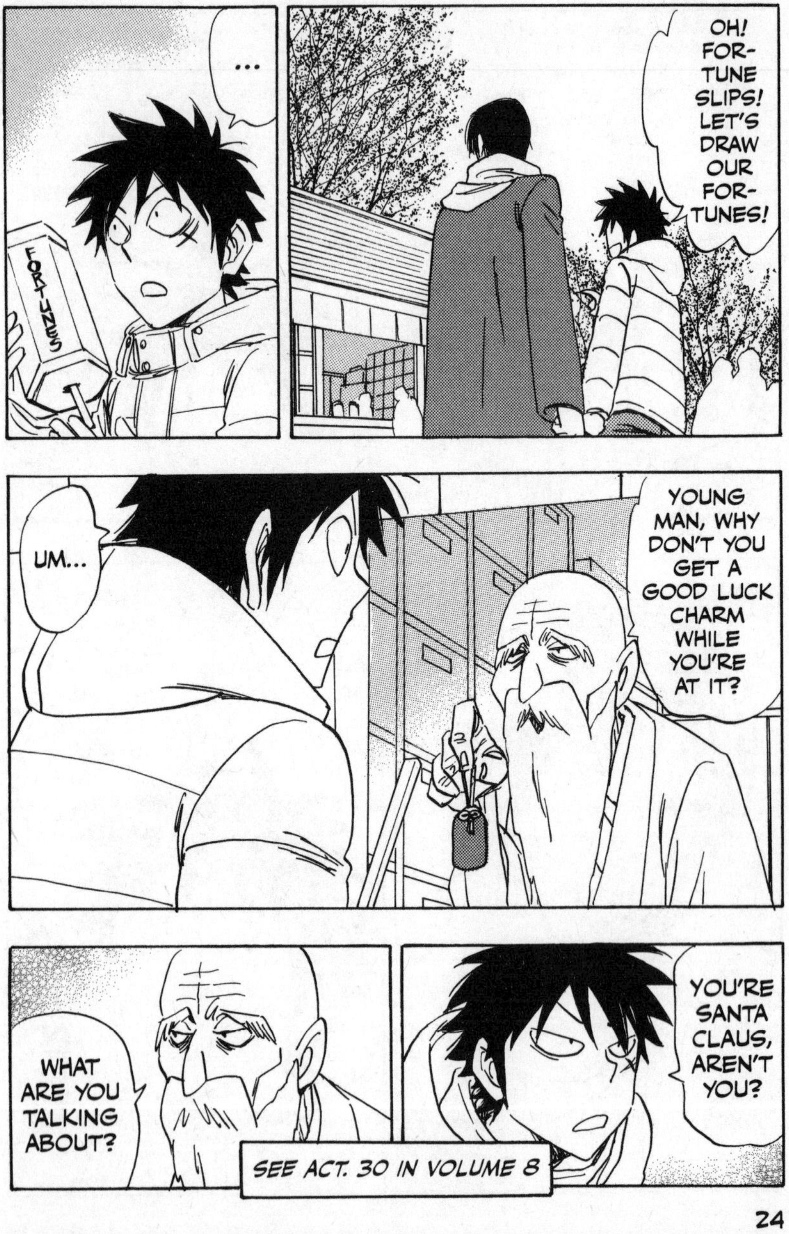
OH! FOR-TUNE SLIPS! LET'S DRAW OUR FOR-TUNES!
...
FORTUNES
YOUNG MAN, WHY DON'T YOU GET A GOOD LUCK CHARM WHILE YOU'RE AT IT?
UM...
YOU'RE SANTA CLAUS, AREN'T YOU?
WHAT ARE YOU TALKING ABOUT?
SEE ACT. 30 IN VOLUME 8

OH, NO YOU DON'T! YOU'RE SANTA! WHAT'RE YOU DOING HERE?!
I DON'T KNOW WHAT YOU COULD MEAN...
THE WAY YOU'D LAMBASTE YOUR ELDER FIRST THING IN THE NEW YEAR IS MOST DISTRESSING.
JUST LEAVE HIM BE, YOSHIDA!
I GET THE FEELING NOTHING YOU SAY WILL WORK ON THAT OLD MAN.
I CAN'T HELP IT! KNOWING THESE FOR-TUNE SLIPS ARE BEING SOLD BY THAT SANTA SUDDENLY MAKES ME NOT BELIEVE IN THEM!
WELL, WHEN YOU PUT IT THAT WAY...
I GOT MEDIUM LUCK!
HOW ABOUT YOU, YOSHI-DA?
THAT'S PRETTY GOOD, ALL THINGS CONSIDERED, RIGHT?
I WON'T BELIEVE ANYTHING I GET...
UHHH ...

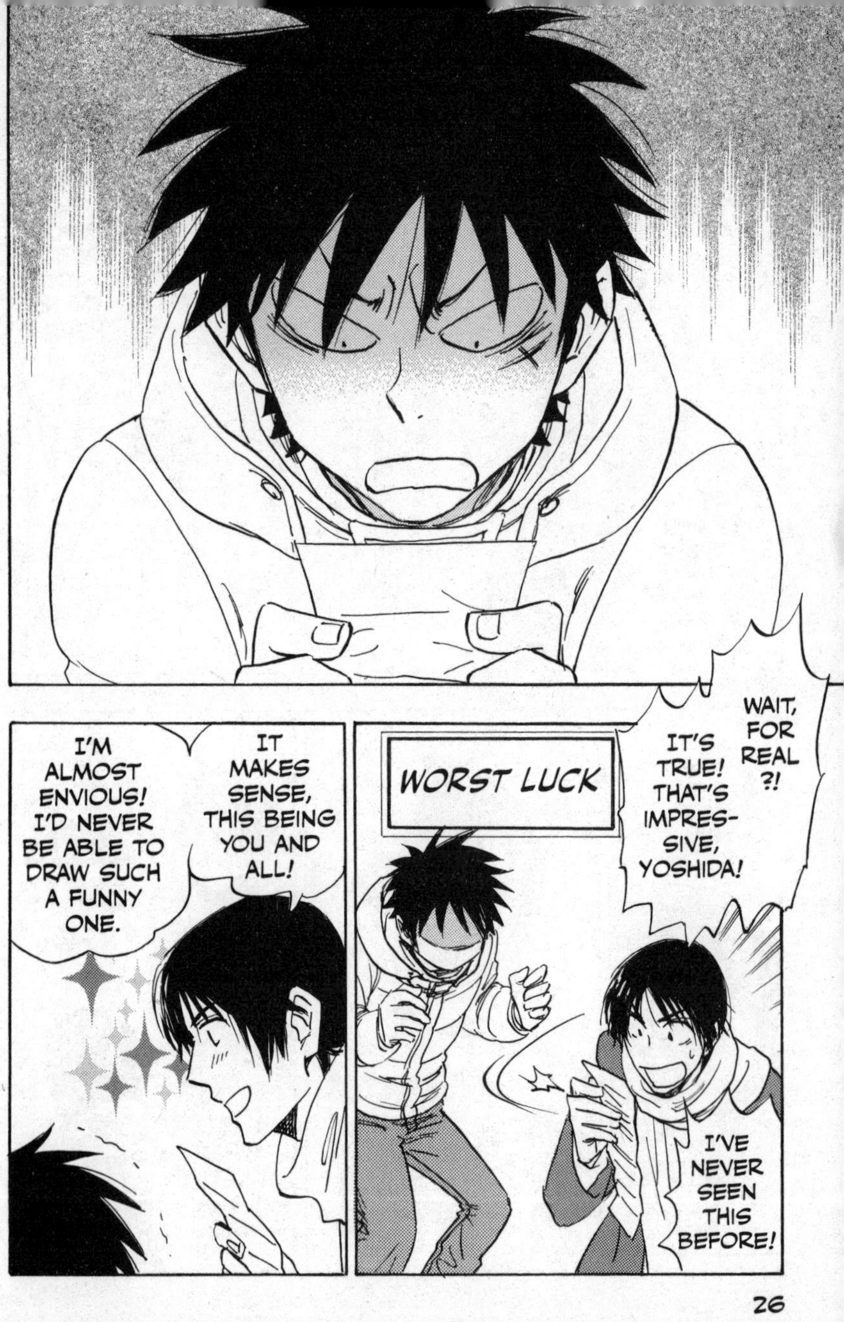
WAIT, FOR REAL?!
IT'S TRUE! THAT'S IMPRES-SIVE, YOSHIDA!
WORST LUCK
I'VE NEVER SEEN THIS BEFORE!
IT MAKES SENSE, THIS BEING YOU AND ALL!
I'M ALMOST ENVIOUS! I'D NEVER BE ABLE TO DRAW SUCH A FUNNY ONE.

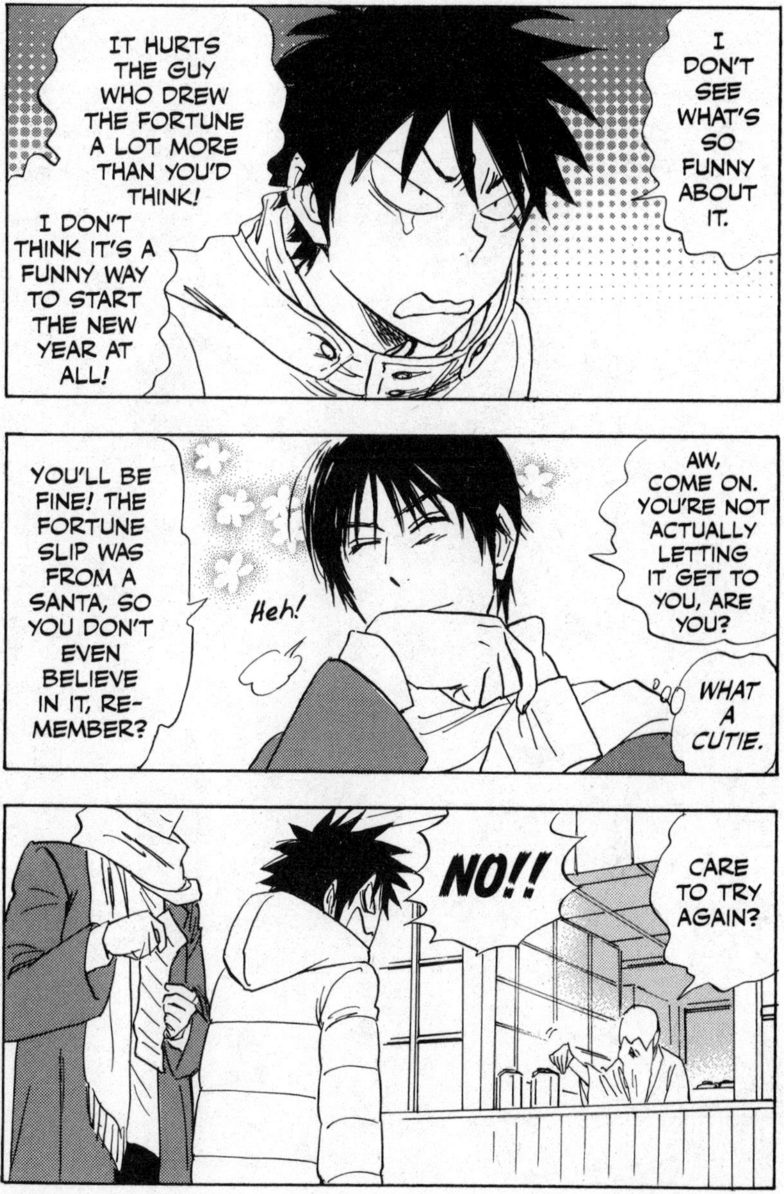
I DON'T SEE WHAT'S SO FUNNY ABOUT IT.
IT HURTS THE GUY WHO DREW THE FORTUNE A LOT MORE THAN YOU'D THINK!
I DON'T THINK IT'S A FUNNY WAY TO START THE NEW YEAR AT ALL!
AW, COME ON. YOU'RE NOT ACTUALLY LETTING IT GET TO YOU, ARE YOU?
WHAT A CUTIE.
Heh!
YOU'LL BE FINE! THE FORTUNE SLIP WAS FROM A SANTA, SO YOU DON'T EVEN BELIEVE IN IT, RE-MEMBER?
CARE TO TRY AGAIN?
NO!!

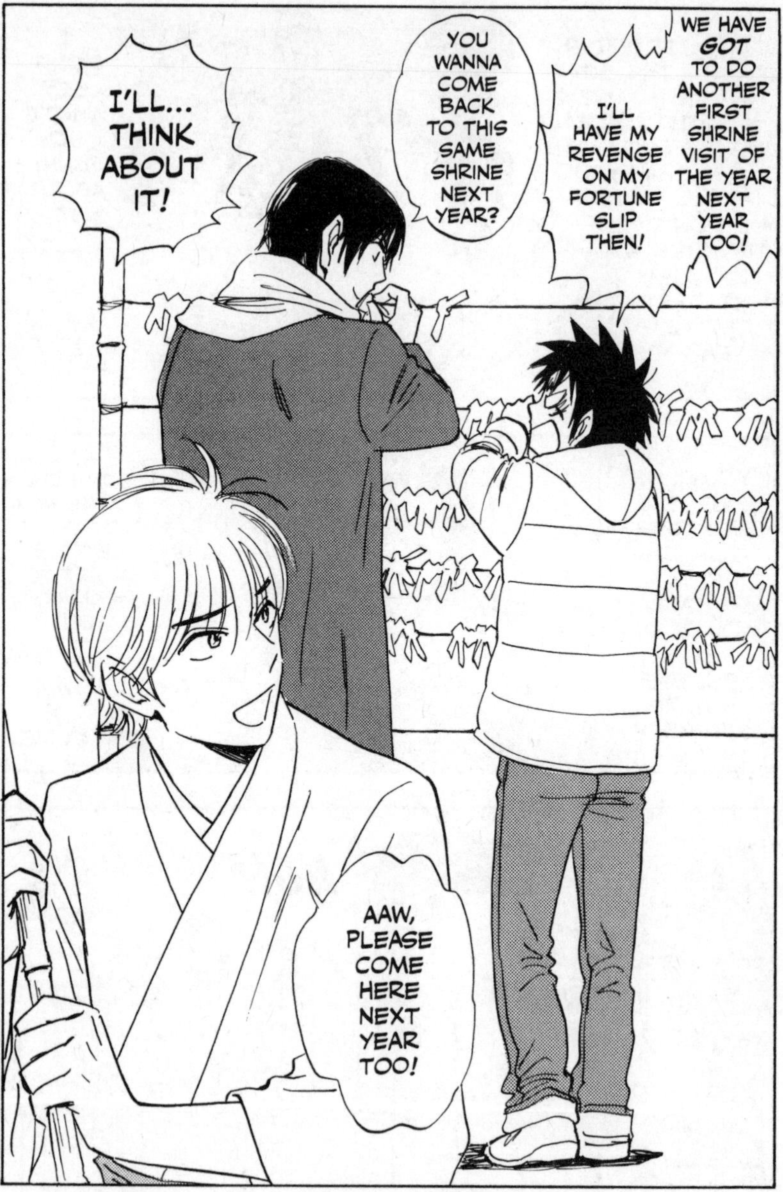
WE HAVE *GOT* TO DO ANOTHER FIRST SHRINE VISIT OF THE YEAR NEXT YEAR TOO!
I'LL HAVE MY REVENGE ON MY FORTUNE SLIP THEN!
YOU WANNA COME BACK TO THIS SAME SHRINE NEXT YEAR?
I'LL... THINK ABOUT IT!
AAW, PLEASE COME HERE NEXT YEAR TOO!

ACT. 49 / END

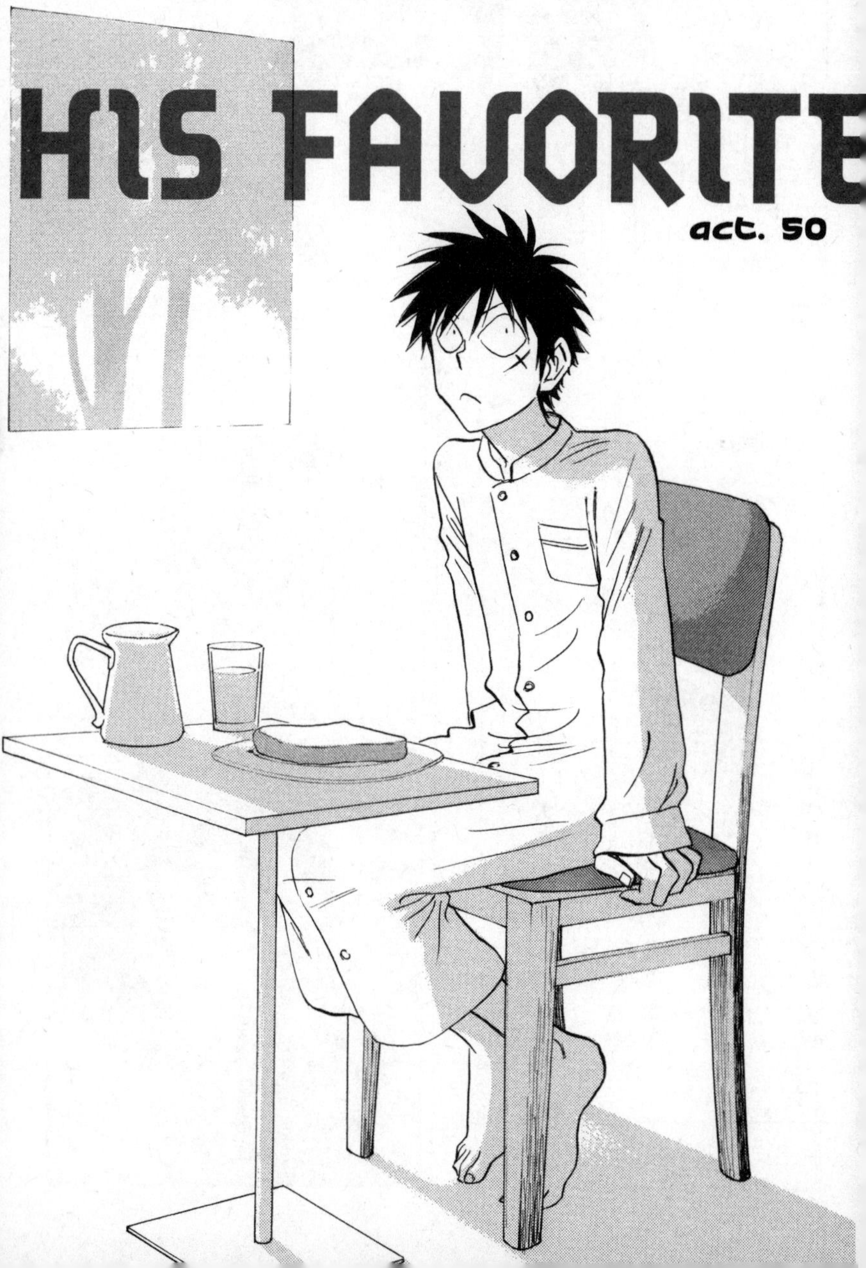
HIS FAVORITE
act. 50

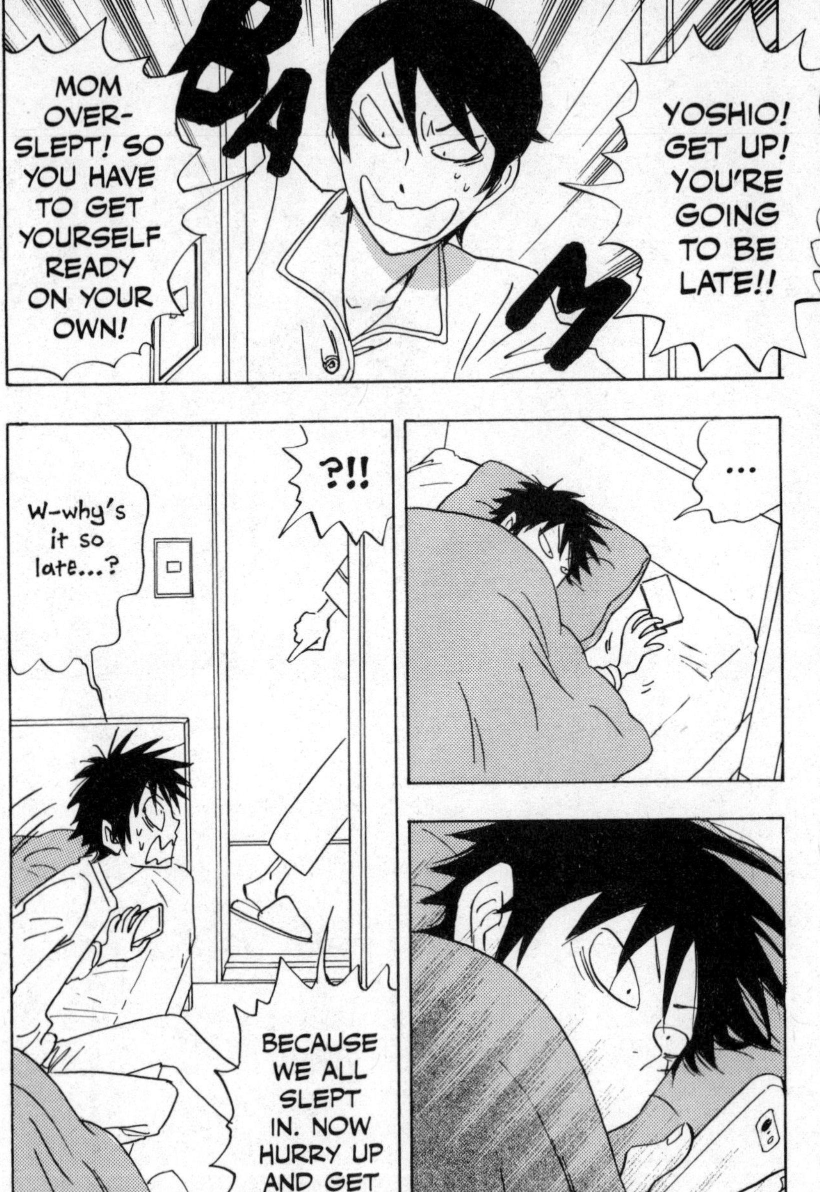
YOSHIO! GET UP! YOU'RE GOING TO BE LATE!!
BAM
MOM OVER-SLEPT! SO YOU HAVE TO GET YOURSELF READY ON YOUR OWN!
...
?!!
W-why's it so late...?
BECAUSE WE ALL SLEPT IN. NOW HURRY UP AND GET READY!

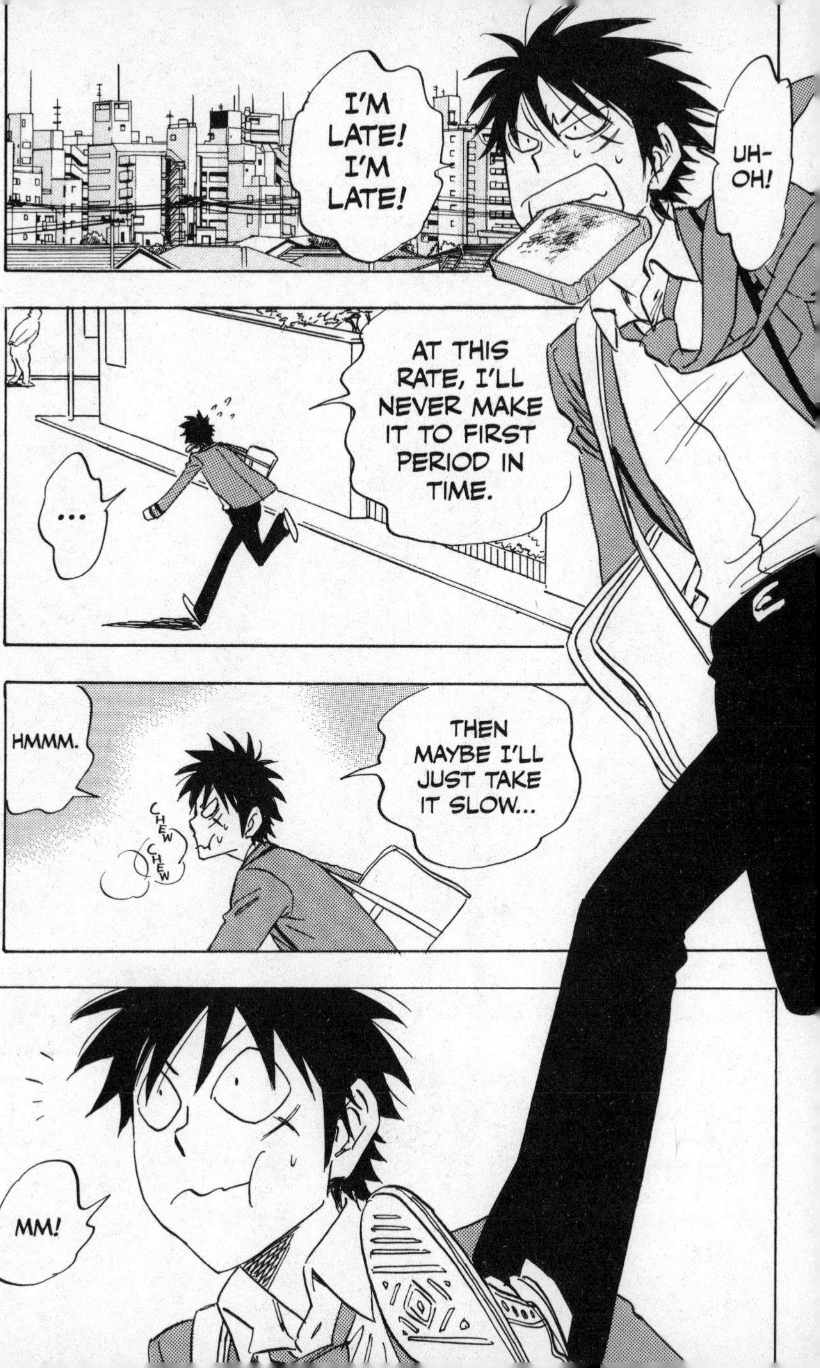
UH-OH!
I'M LATE! I'M LATE!
AT THIS RATE, I'LL NEVER MAKE IT TO FIRST PERIOD IN TIME.
...
THEN MAYBE I'LL JUST TAKE IT SLOW...
HMMM.
CHEW CHEW
MM!

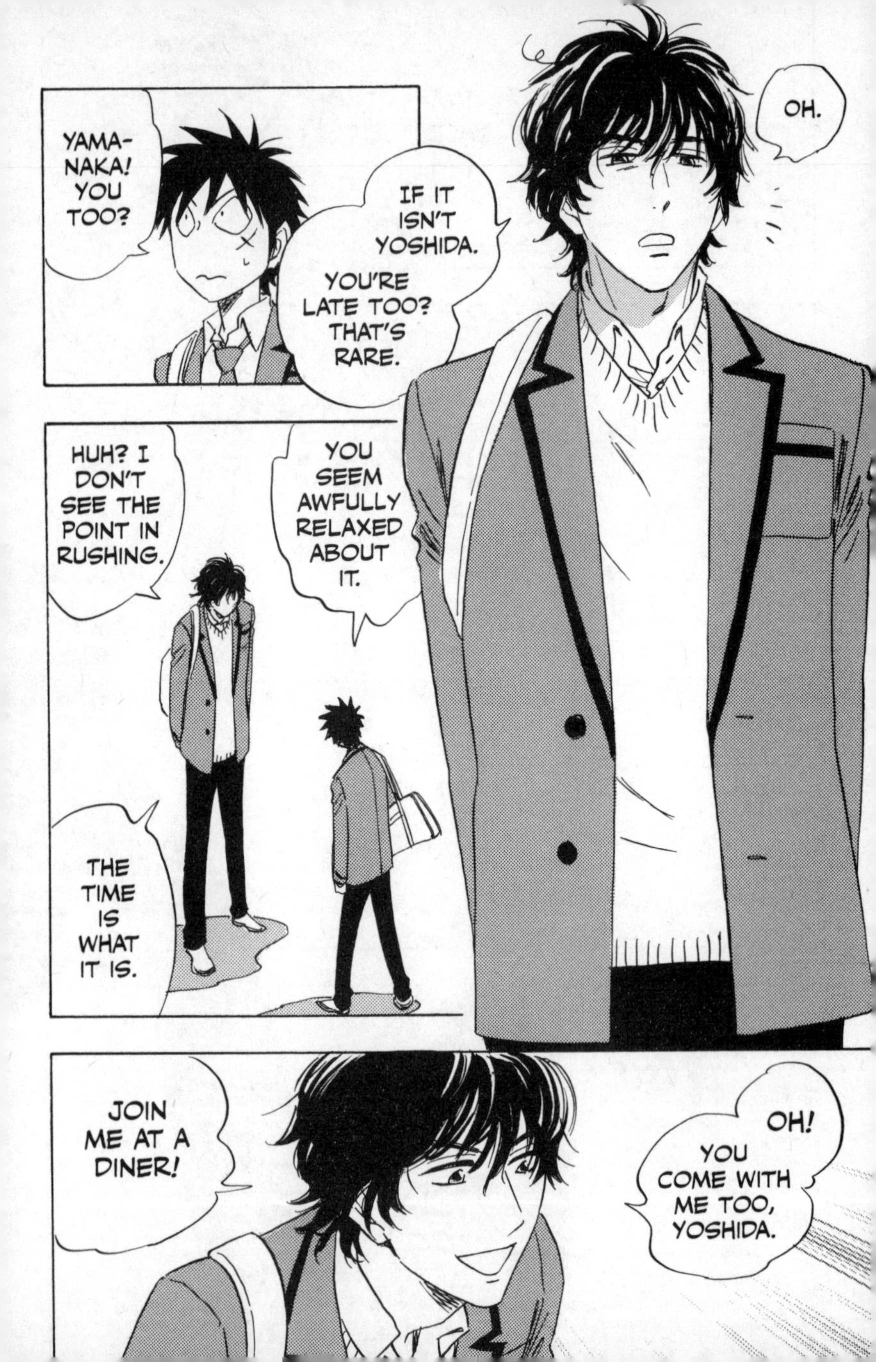
OH.
IF IT ISN'T YOSHIDA. YOU'RE LATE TOO? THAT'S RARE.
YAMA-NAKA! YOU TOO?
YOU SEEM AWFULLY RELAXED ABOUT IT.
HUH? I DON'T SEE THE POINT IN RUSHING.
THE TIME IS WHAT IT IS.
OH! YOU COME WITH ME TOO, YOSHIDA.
JOIN ME AT A DINER!

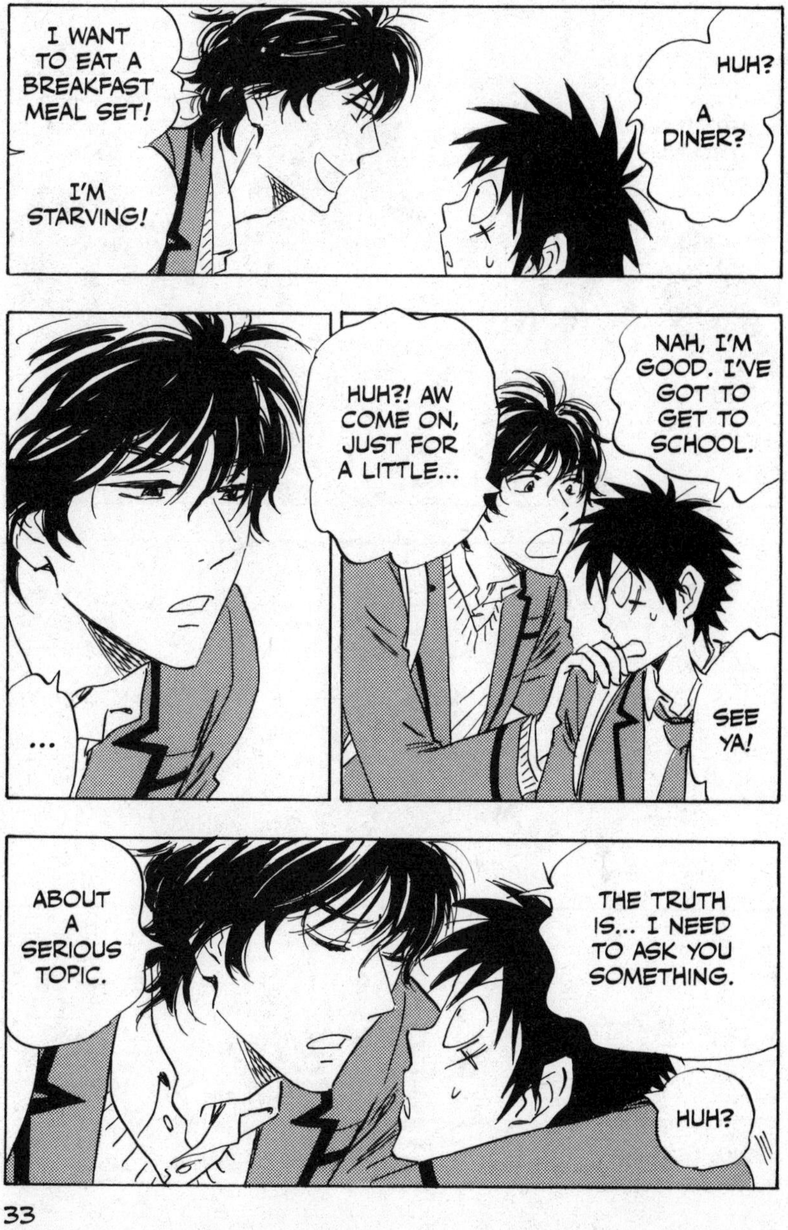
HUH? A DINER?
I WANT TO EAT A BREAKFAST MEAL SET!
I'M STARVING!
NAH, I'M GOOD. I'VE GOT TO GET TO SCHOOL.
HUH?! AW COME ON, JUST FOR A LITTLE...
SEE YA!
...
THE TRUTH IS... I NEED TO ASK YOU SOMETHING.
ABOUT A SERIOUS TOPIC.
HUH?

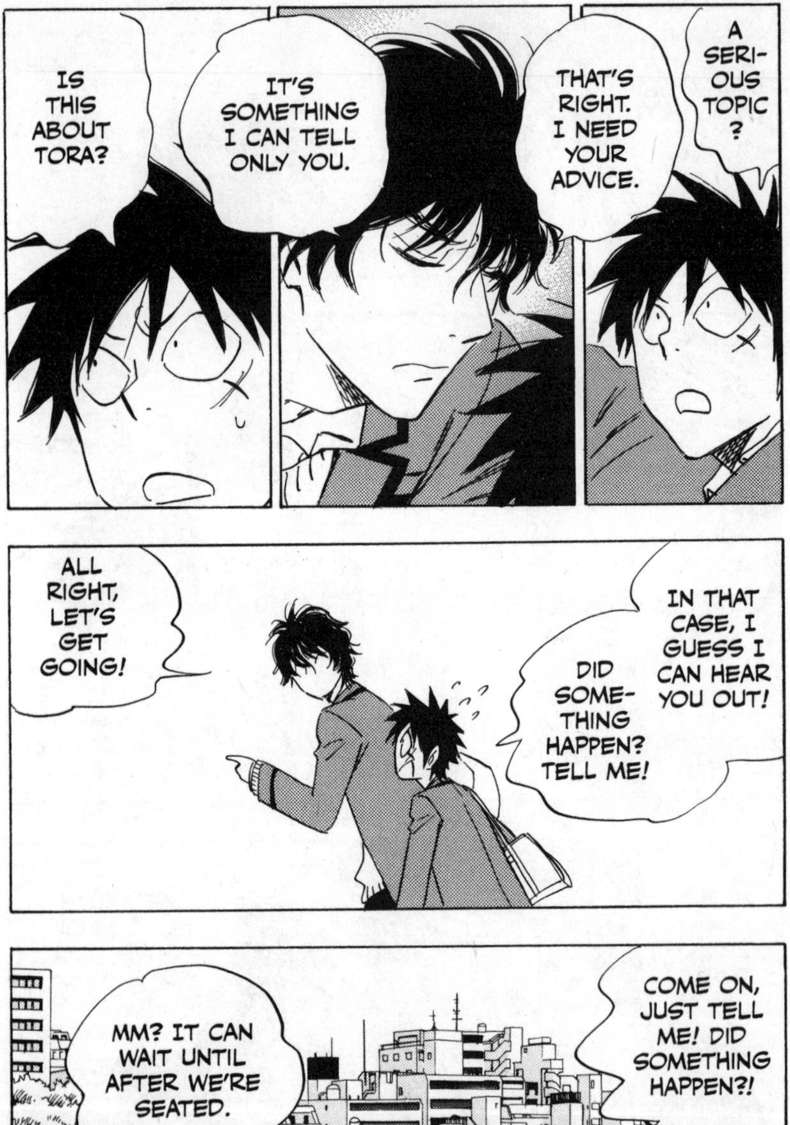
A SERIOUS TOPIC?
THAT'S RIGHT. I NEED YOUR ADVICE.
IT'S SOMETHING I CAN TELL ONLY YOU.
IS THIS ABOUT TORA?
IN THAT CASE, I GUESS I CAN HEAR YOU OUT!
DID SOMETHING HAPPEN? TELL ME!
ALL RIGHT, LET'S GET GOING!
COME ON, JUST TELL ME! DID SOMETHING HAPPEN?!
MM? IT CAN WAIT UNTIL AFTER WE'RE SEATED.

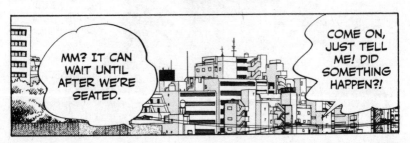

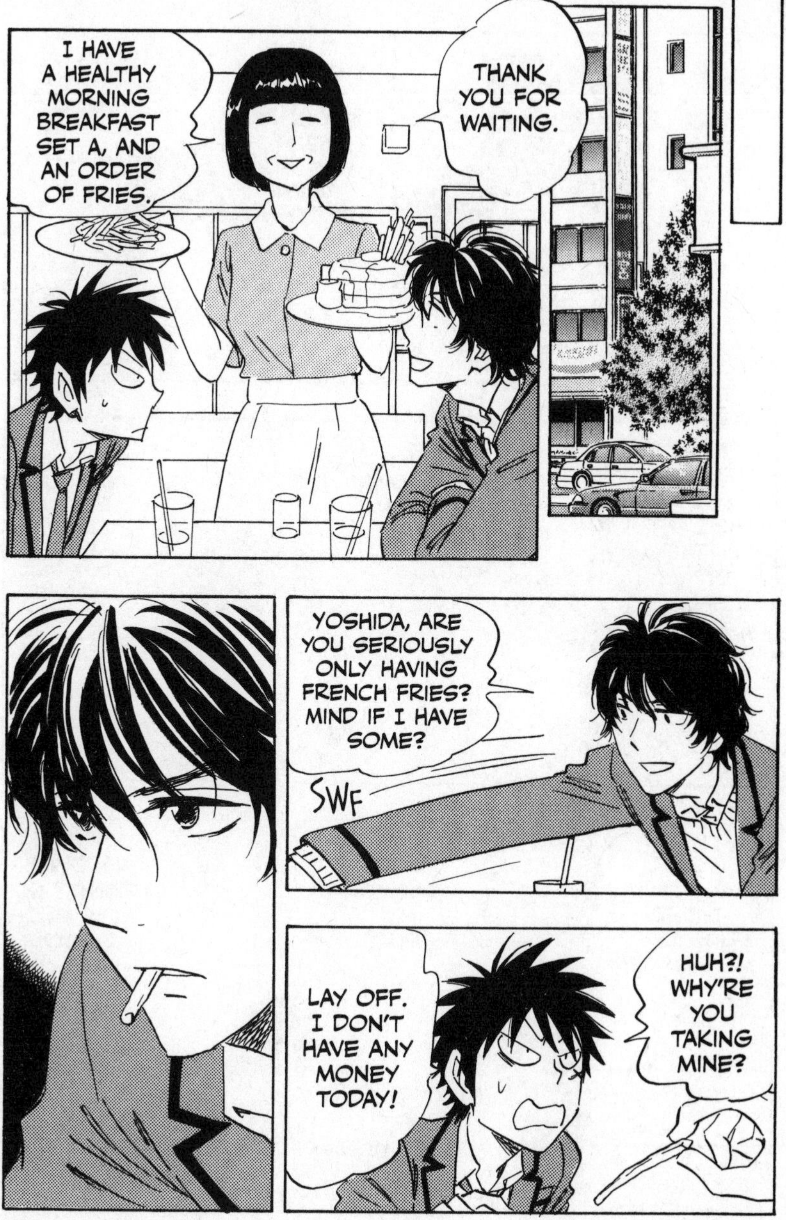
THANK YOU FOR WAITING.
I HAVE A HEALTHY MORNING BREAKFAST SET A, AND AN ORDER OF FRIES.
YOSHIDA, ARE YOU SERIOUSLY ONLY HAVING FRENCH FRIES? MIND IF I HAVE SOME?
SWF
HUH?! WHY'RE YOU TAKING MINE?
LAY OFF. I DON'T HAVE ANY MONEY TODAY!

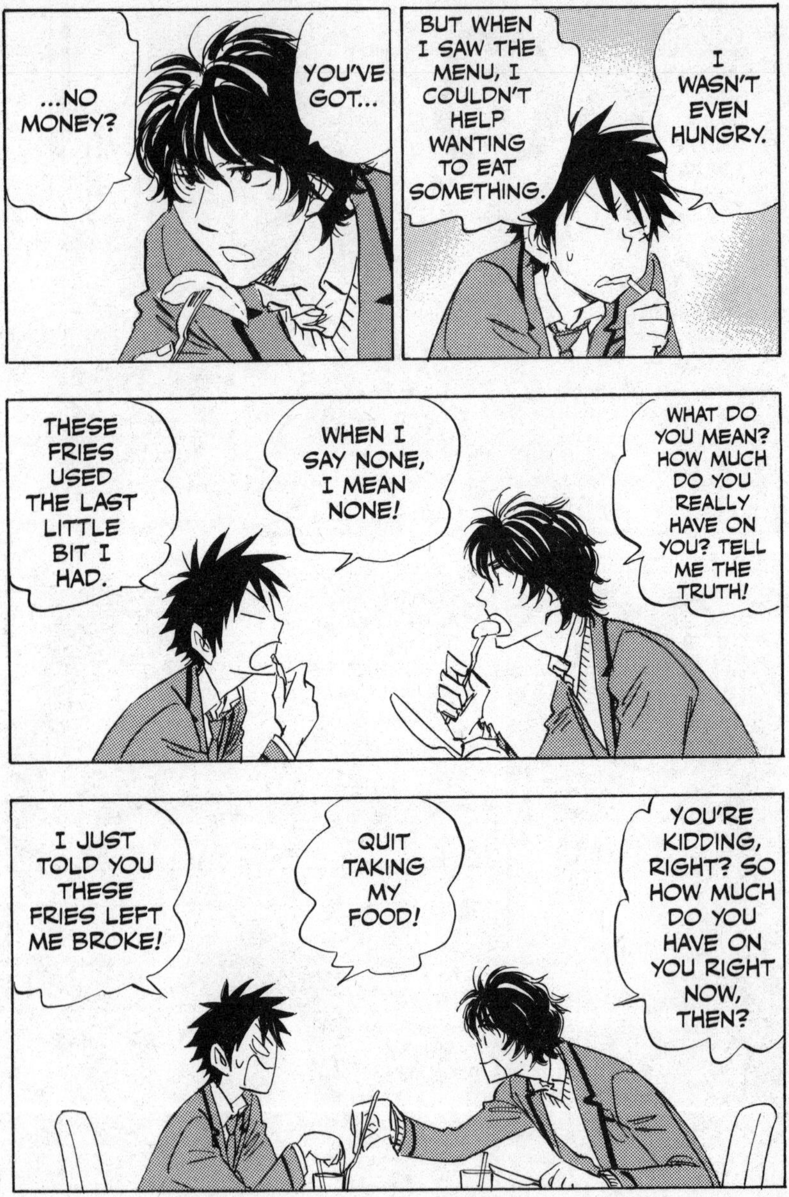
I WASN'T EVEN HUNGRY.
BUT WHEN I SAW THE MENU, I COULDN'T HELP WANTING TO EAT SOMETHING.
YOU'VE GOT...
...NO MONEY?
WHAT DO YOU MEAN? HOW MUCH DO YOU REALLY HAVE ON YOU? TELL ME THE TRUTH!
WHEN I SAY NONE, I MEAN NONE!
THESE FRIES USED THE LAST LITTLE BIT I HAD.
YOU'RE KIDDING, RIGHT? SO HOW MUCH DO YOU HAVE ON YOU RIGHT NOW, THEN?
QUIT TAKING MY FOOD!
I JUST TOLD YOU THESE FRIES LEFT ME BROKE!

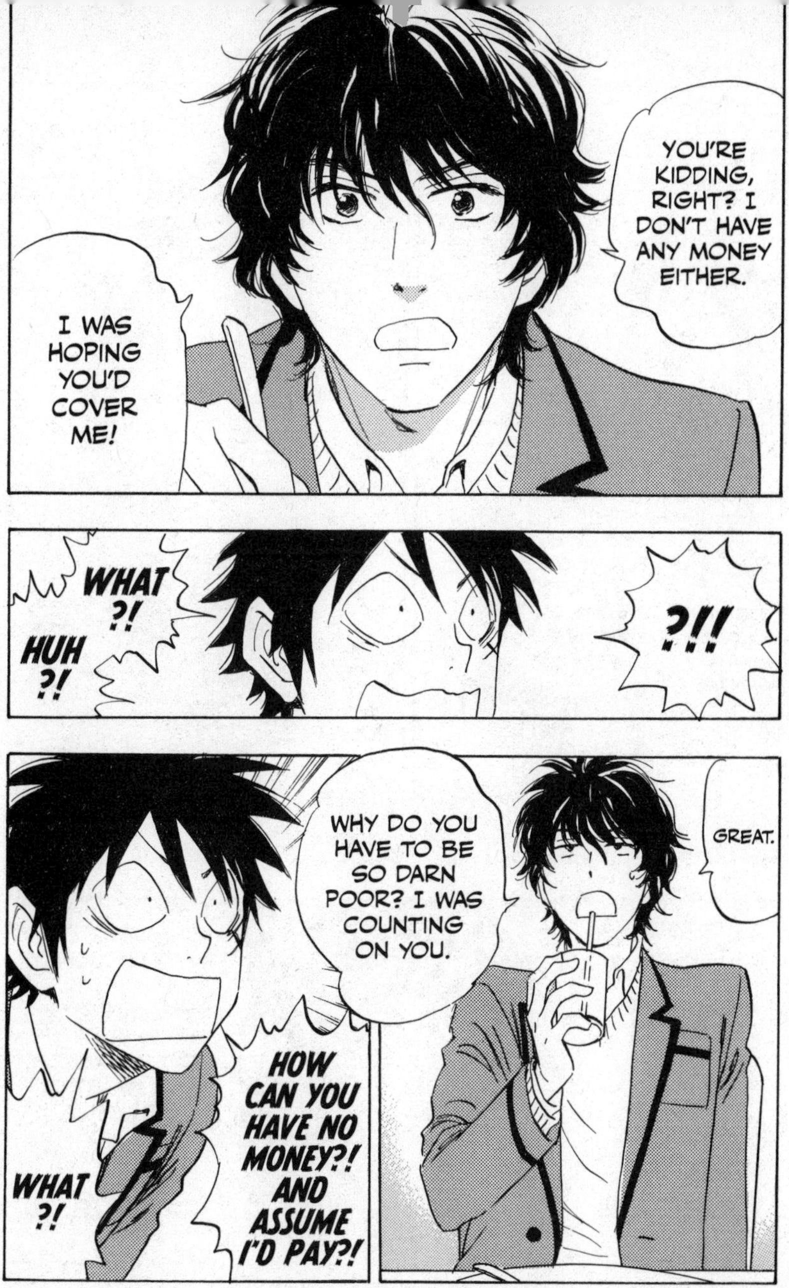

YOU'RE KIDDING, RIGHT? I DON'T HAVE ANY MONEY EITHER.
I WAS HOPING YOU'D COVER ME!
?!!
WHAT ?!
HUH ?!
GREAT.
WHY DO YOU HAVE TO BE SO DARN POOR? I WAS COUNTING ON YOU.
HOW CAN YOU HAVE NO MONEY?! AND ASSUME I'D PAY?!
WHAT ?!

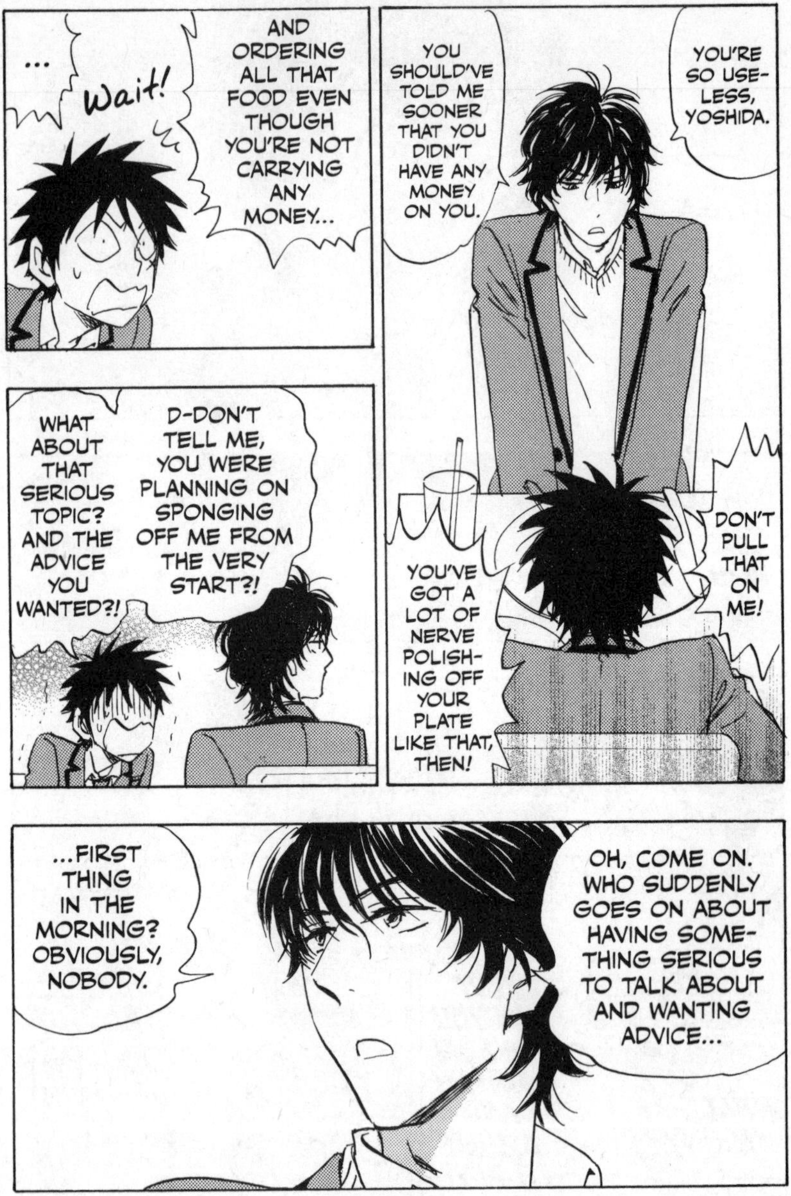
YOU'RE SO USELESS, YOSHIDA.
YOU SHOULD'VE TOLD ME SOONER THAT YOU DIDN'T HAVE ANY MONEY ON YOU.
DON'T PULL THAT ON ME!
YOU'VE GOT A LOT OF NERVE POLISHING OFF YOUR PLATE LIKE THAT, THEN!
AND ORDERING ALL THAT FOOD EVEN THOUGH YOU'RE NOT CARRYING ANY MONEY...
Wait!
...
D-DON'T TELL ME, YOU WERE PLANNING ON SPONGING OFF ME FROM THE VERY START?!
WHAT ABOUT THAT SERIOUS TOPIC? AND THE ADVICE YOU WANTED?!
OH, COME ON. WHO SUDDENLY GOES ON ABOUT HAVING SOMETHING SERIOUS TO TALK ABOUT AND WANTING ADVICE...
...FIRST THING IN THE MORNING? OBVIOUSLY, NOBODY.

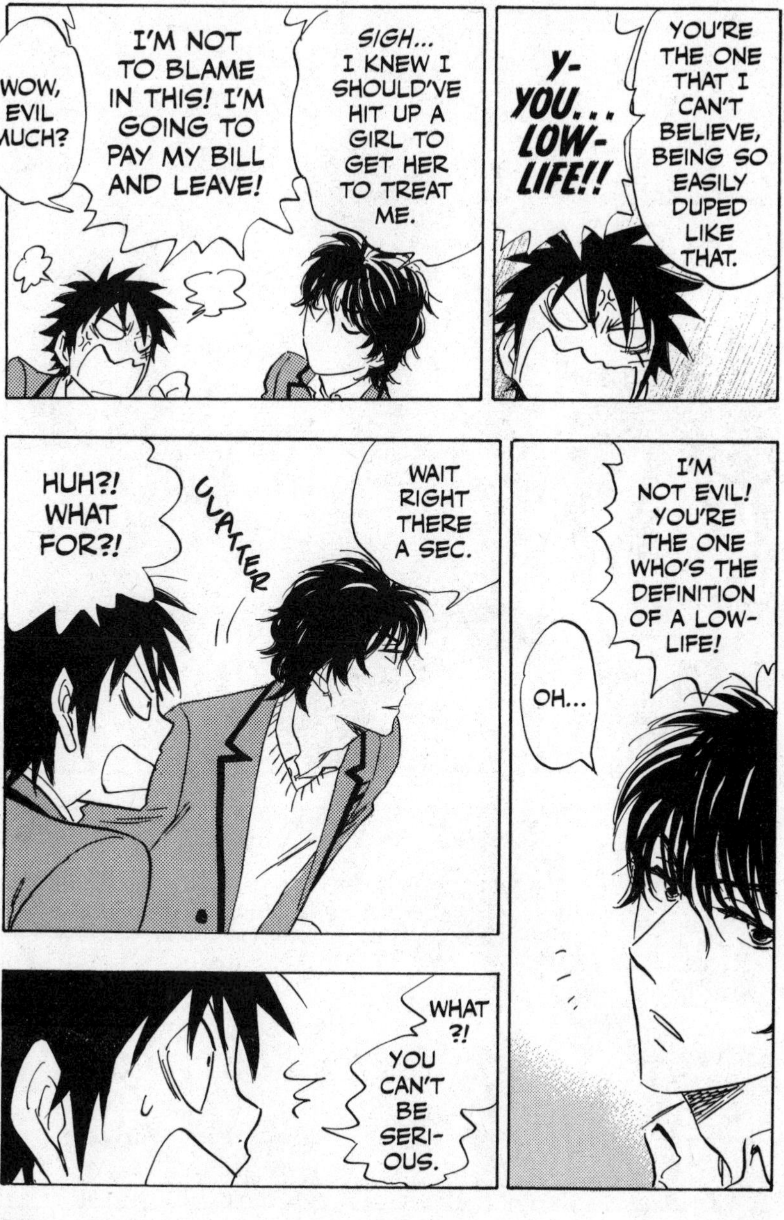
YOU'RE THE ONE THAT I CAN'T BELIEVE, BEING SO EASILY DUPED LIKE THAT.
Y-YOU... LOW-LIFE!!
SIGH... I KNEW I SHOULD'VE HIT UP A GIRL TO GET HER TO TREAT ME.
I'M NOT TO BLAME IN THIS! I'M GOING TO PAY MY BILL AND LEAVE!
WOW, EVIL MUCH?
I'M NOT EVIL! YOU'RE THE ONE WHO'S THE DEFINITION OF A LOW-LIFE!
OH...
WAIT RIGHT THERE A SEC.
CLATTER
HUH?! WHAT FOR?!
WHAT?! YOU CAN'T BE SERI-OUS.

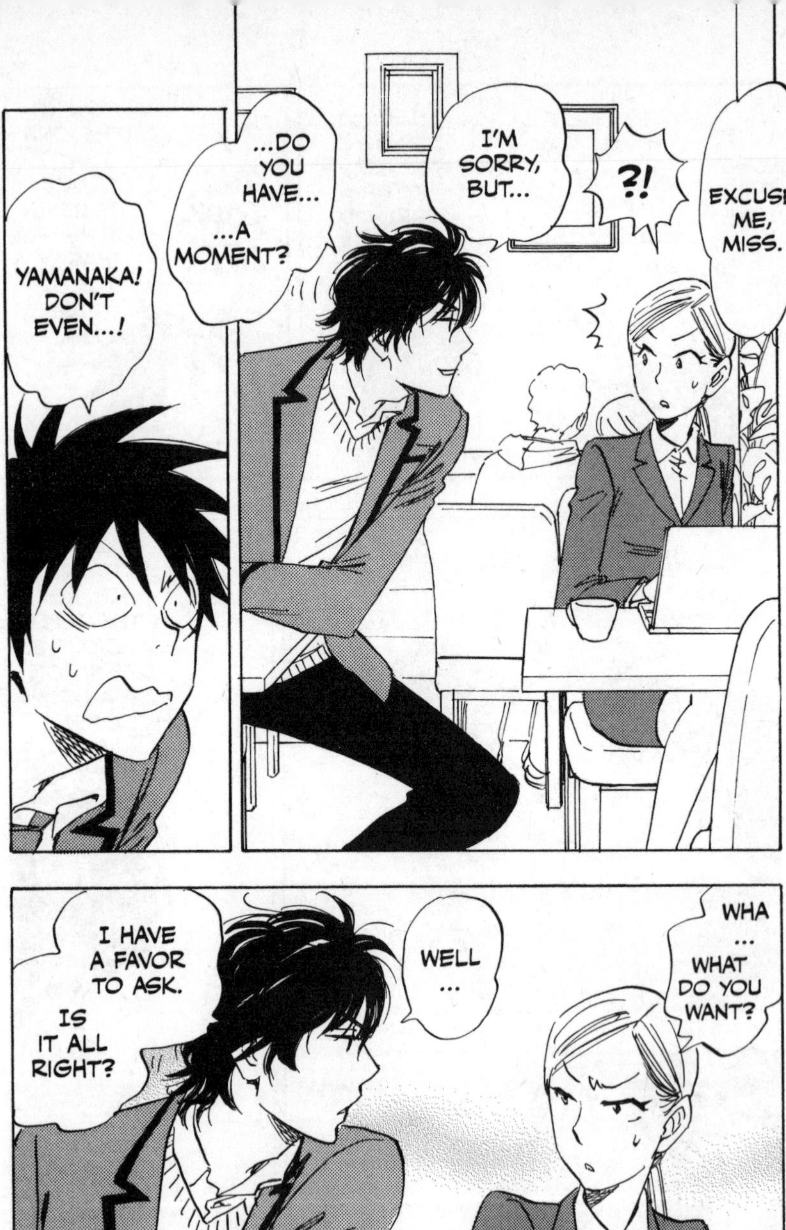
EXCUSE ME, MISS.
?!
I'M SORRY, BUT...
...DO YOU HAVE... ...A MOMENT?
YAMANAKA! DON'T EVEN...!
WHA ... WHAT DO YOU WANT?
WELL ...
I HAVE A FAVOR TO ASK. IS IT ALL RIGHT?

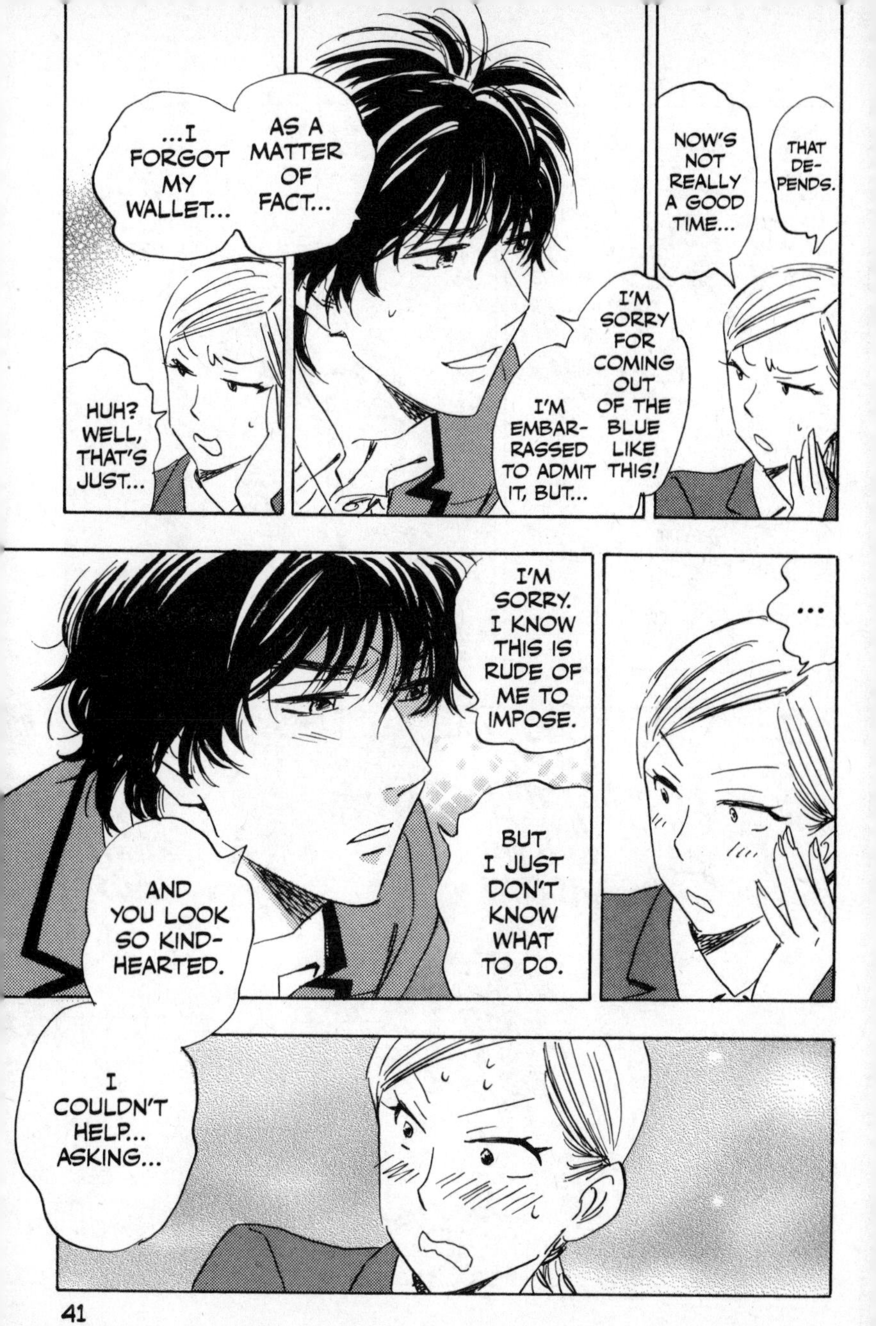
THAT DE-PENDS.
NOW'S NOT REALLY A GOOD TIME...
I'M SORRY FOR COMING OUT OF THE BLUE LIKE THIS!
I'M EMBARRASSED TO ADMIT IT, BUT...
AS A MATTER OF FACT...
...I FORGOT MY WALLET...
HUH? WELL, THAT'S JUST...
...
I'M SORRY. I KNOW THIS IS RUDE OF ME TO IMPOSE.
BUT I JUST DON'T KNOW WHAT TO DO.
AND YOU LOOK SO KIND-HEARTED.
I COULDN'T HELP... ASKING...

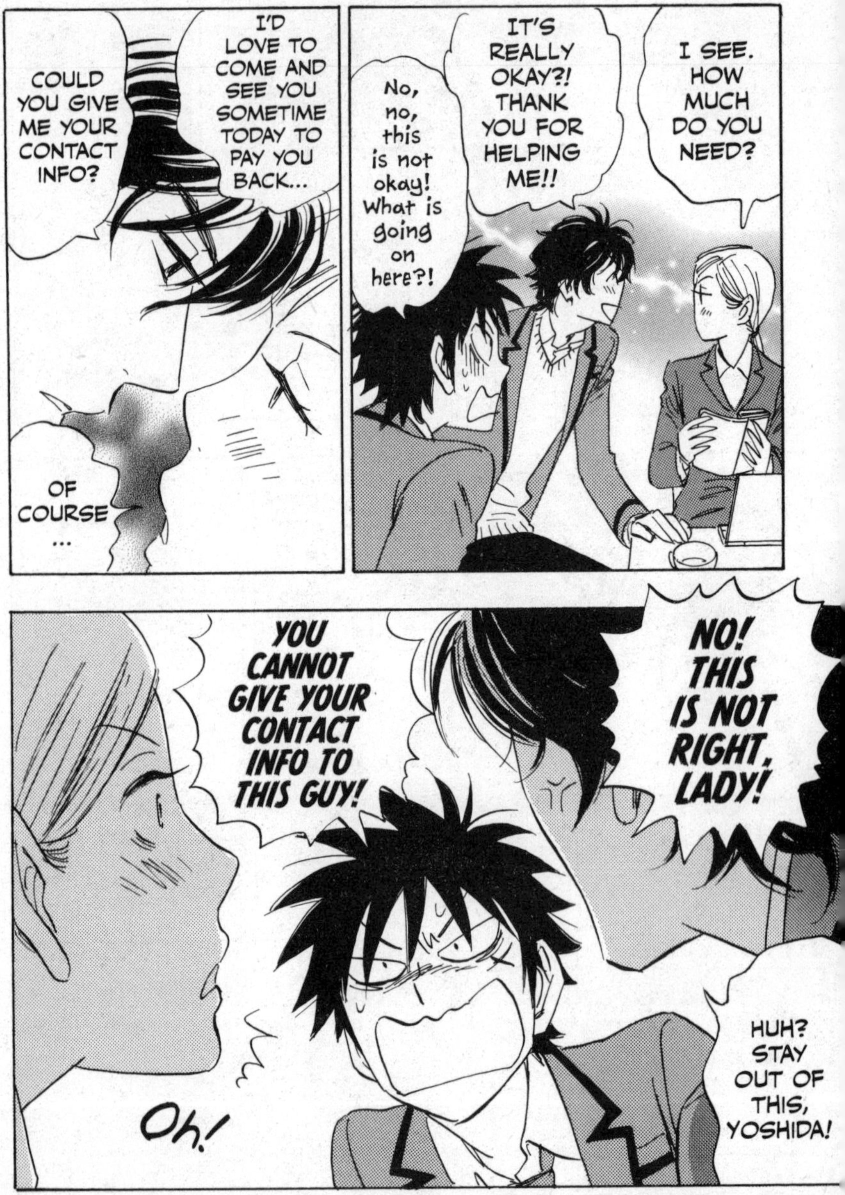
I SEE. HOW MUCH DO YOU NEED?
IT'S REALLY OKAY?! THANK YOU FOR HELPING ME!!
No, no, this is not okay! What is going on here?!
I'D LOVE TO COME AND SEE YOU SOMETIME TODAY TO PAY YOU BACK...
COULD YOU GIVE ME YOUR CONTACT INFO?
OF COURSE ...
NO! THIS IS NOT RIGHT, LADY!
YOU CANNOT GIVE YOUR CONTACT INFO TO THIS GUY!
HUH? STAY OUT OF THIS, YOSHIDA!
Oh!

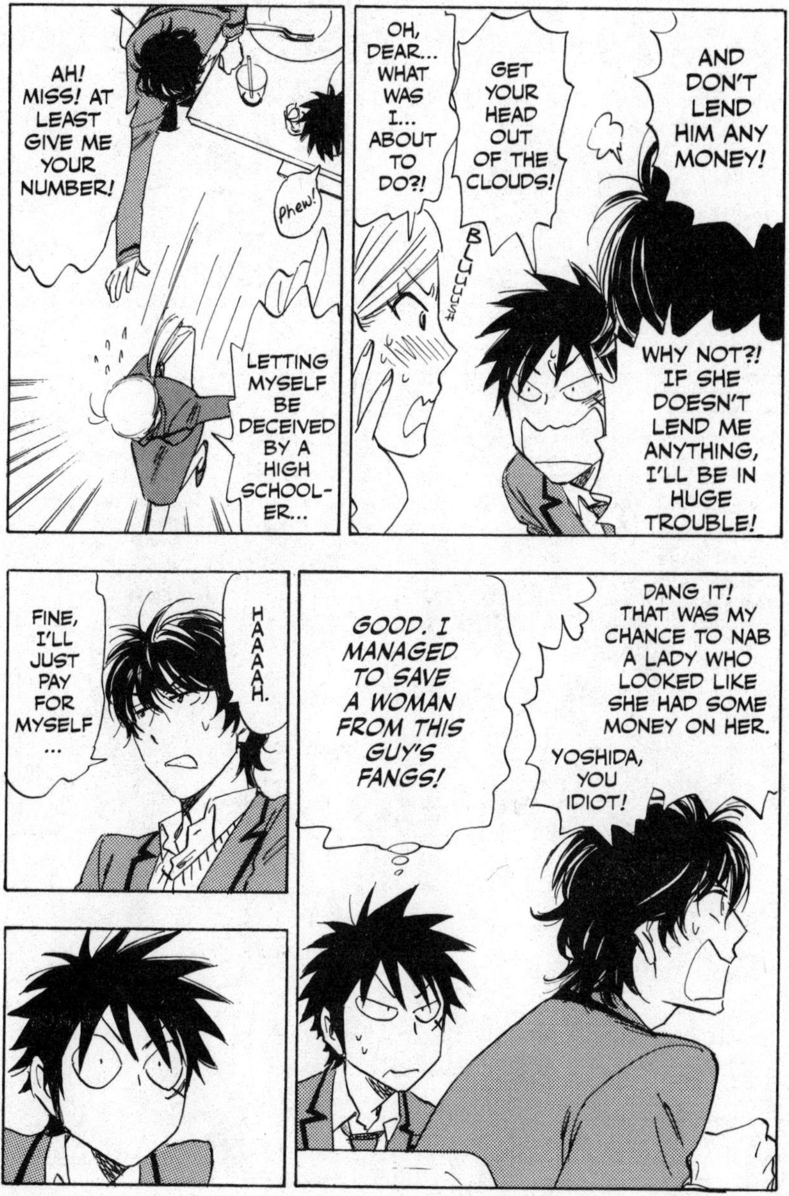
AND DON'T LEND HIM ANY MONEY!
GET YOUR HEAD OUT OF THE CLOUDS!
OH, DEAR... WHAT WAS I... ABOUT TO DO?!
BLUUUUSH
WHY NOT?! IF SHE DOESN'T LEND ME ANYTHING, I'LL BE IN HUGE TROUBLE!
AH! MISS! AT LEAST GIVE ME YOUR NUMBER!
Phew!
LETTING MYSELF BE DECEIVED BY A HIGH SCHOOL-ER...
DANG IT! THAT WAS MY CHANCE TO NAB A LADY WHO LOOKED LIKE SHE HAD SOME MONEY ON HER.
YOSHIDA, YOU IDIOT!
GOOD. I MANAGED TO SAVE A WOMAN FROM THIS GUY'S FANGS!
HAAAAH.
FINE, I'LL JUST PAY FOR MYSELF...

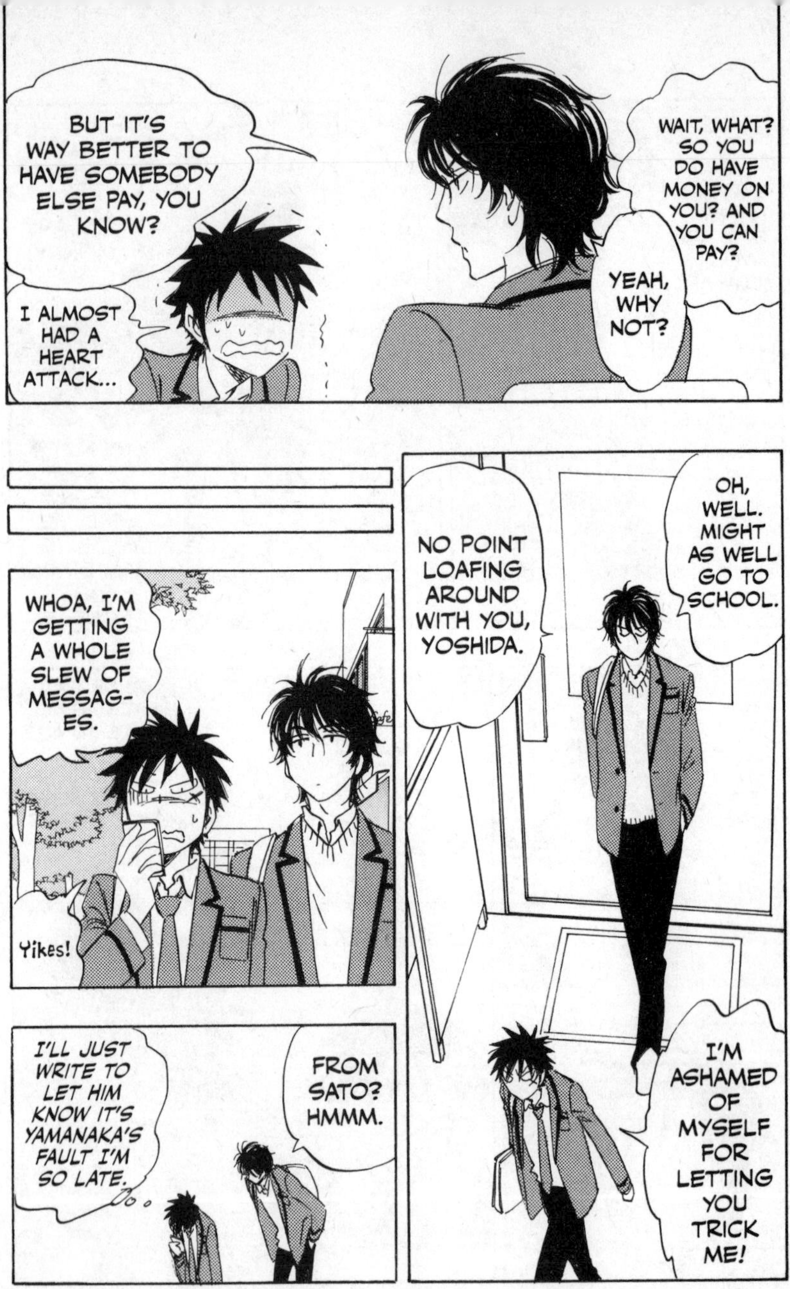
WAIT, WHAT? SO YOU DO HAVE MONEY ON YOU? AND YOU CAN PAY?
YEAH, WHY NOT?
BUT IT'S WAY BETTER TO HAVE SOMEBODY ELSE PAY, YOU KNOW?
I ALMOST HAD A HEART ATTACK...
OH, WELL. MIGHT AS WELL GO TO SCHOOL.
NO POINT LOAFING AROUND WITH YOU, YOSHIDA.
I'M ASHAMED OF MYSELF FOR LETTING YOU TRICK ME!
WHOA, I'M GETTING A WHOLE SLEW OF MESSAG-ES.
Yikes!
FROM SATO? HMMM.
I'LL JUST WRITE TO LET HIM KNOW IT'S YAMANAKA'S FAULT I'M SO LATE.

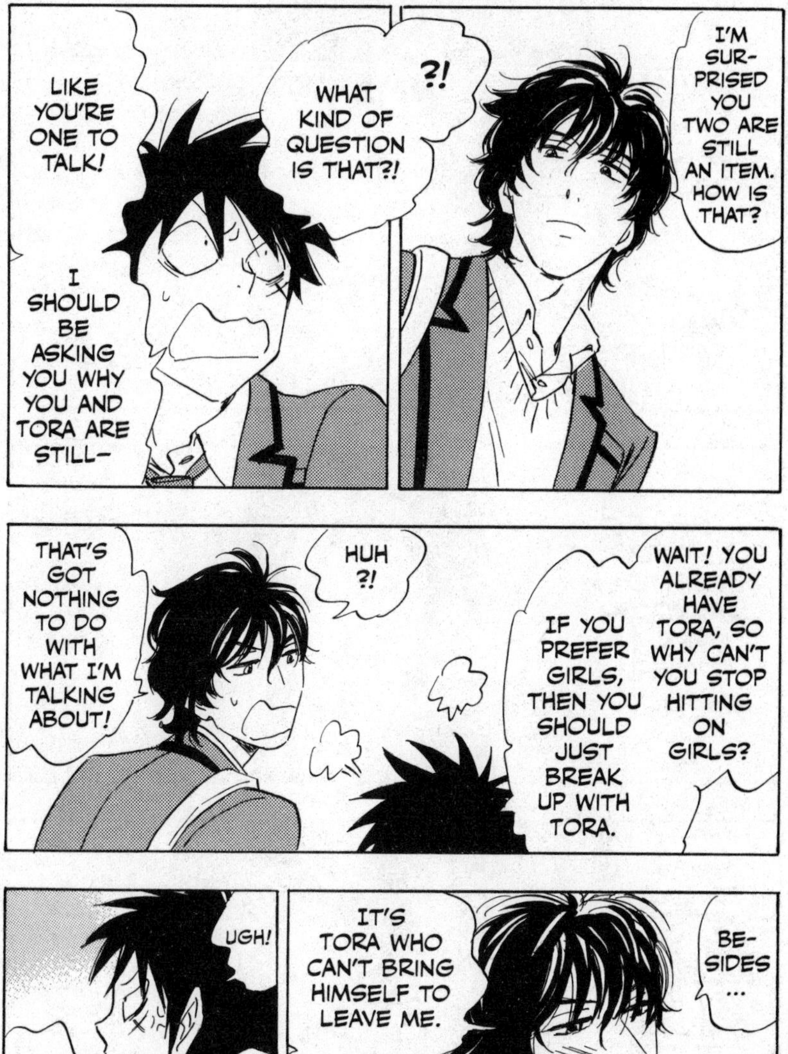
I'M SUR-PRISED YOU TWO ARE STILL AN ITEM. HOW IS THAT?
?!
WHAT KIND OF QUESTION IS THAT?!
LIKE YOU'RE ONE TO TALK!
I SHOULD BE ASKING YOU WHY YOU AND TORA ARE STILL–
WAIT! YOU ALREADY HAVE TORA, SO WHY CAN'T YOU STOP HITTING ON GIRLS?
IF YOU PREFER GIRLS, THEN YOU SHOULD JUST BREAK UP WITH TORA.
HUH ?!
THAT'S GOT NOTHING TO DO WITH WHAT I'M TALKING ABOUT!
BE-SIDES ...
IT'S TORA WHO CAN'T BRING HIMSELF TO LEAVE ME.
HE'LL ALWAYS STAY BY MY SIDE!
UGH!
THAT'S ...
... TRUE, BUT STILL ...

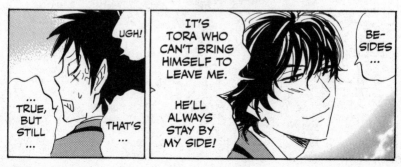

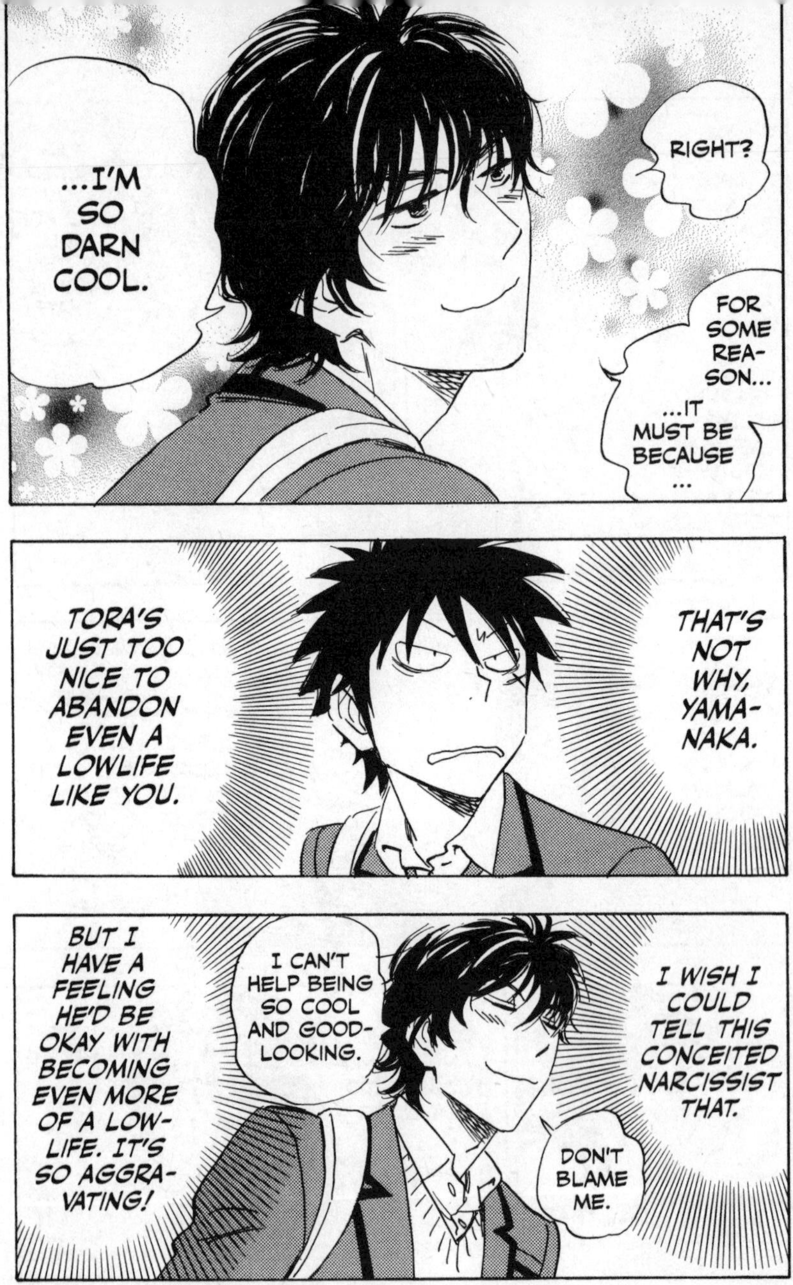
RIGHT?
FOR SOME REASON...
...IT MUST BE BECAUSE ...
...I'M SO DARN COOL.
THAT'S NOT WHY, YAMANAKA.
TORA'S JUST TOO NICE TO ABANDON EVEN A LOWLIFE LIKE YOU.
I WISH I COULD TELL THIS CONCEITED NARCISSIST THAT.
I CAN'T HELP BEING SO COOL AND GOOD-LOOKING.
DON'T BLAME ME.
BUT I HAVE A FEELING HE'D BE OKAY WITH BECOMING EVEN MORE OF A LOW-LIFE. IT'S SO AGGRAVATING!

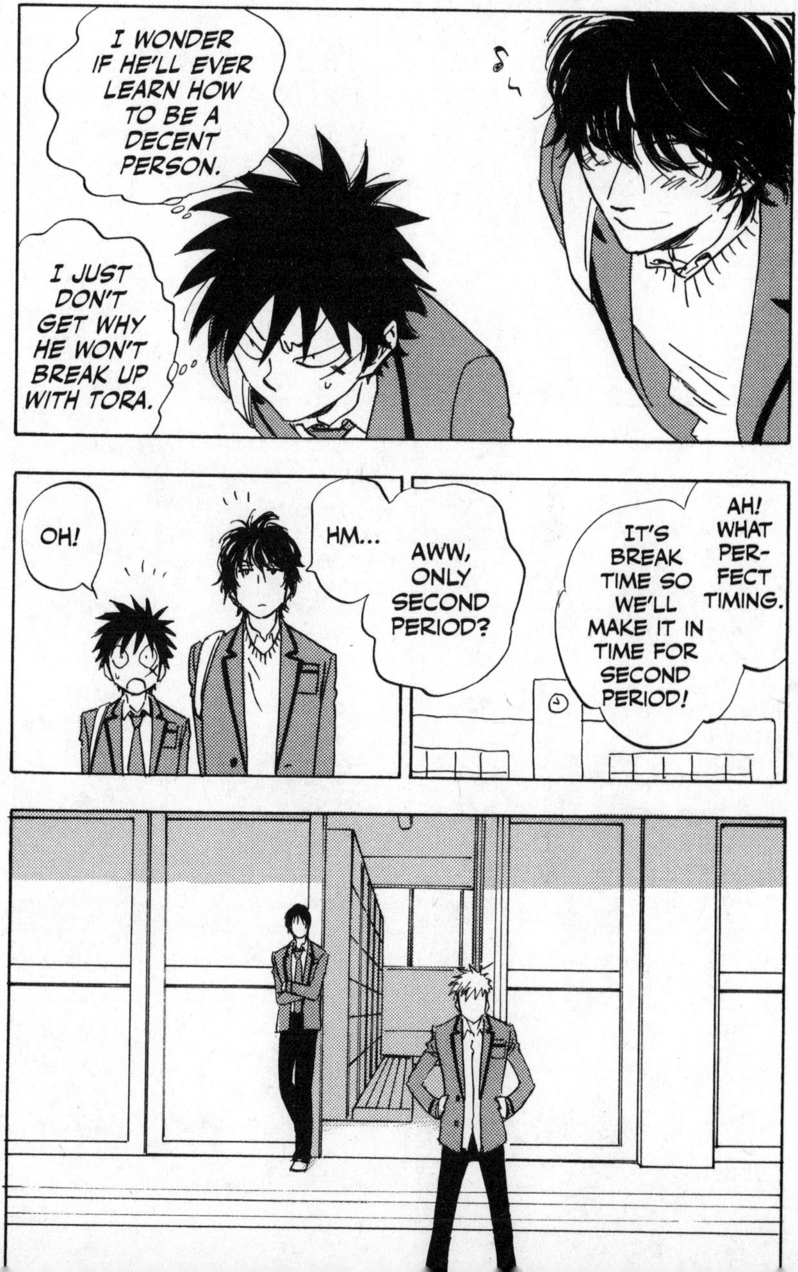
I WONDER IF HE'LL EVER LEARN HOW TO BE A DECENT PERSON.
I JUST DON'T GET WHY HE WON'T BREAK UP WITH TORA.
AH! WHAT PER-FECT TIMING.
IT'S BREAK TIME SO WE'LL MAKE IT IN TIME FOR SECOND PERIOD!
HM...
AWW, ONLY SECOND PERIOD?
OH!

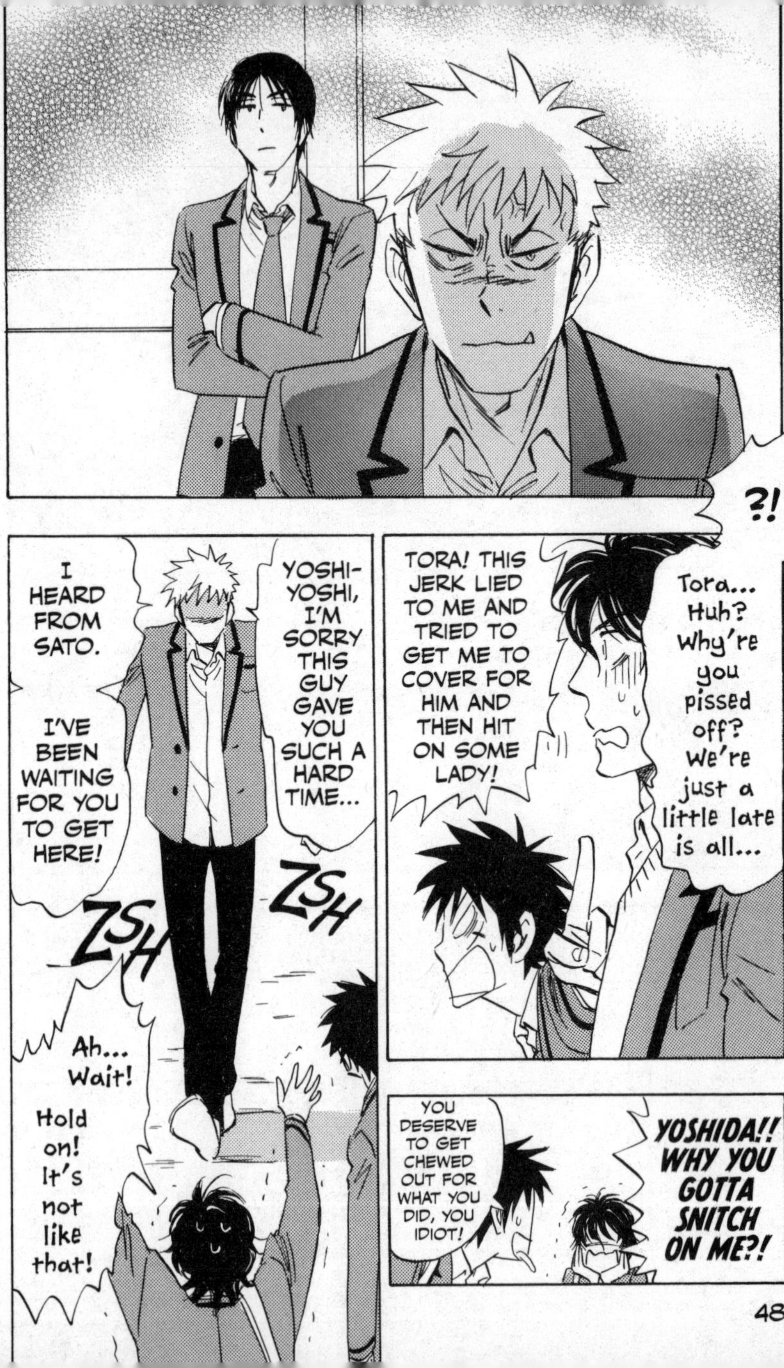
?!
Tora... Huh? Why're you pissed off? We're just a little late is all...
TORA! THIS JERK LIED TO ME AND TRIED TO GET ME TO COVER FOR HIM AND THEN HIT ON SOME LADY!
YOSHIDA!! WHY YOU GOTTA SNITCH ON ME?!
YOU DESERVE TO GET CHEWED OUT FOR WHAT YOU DID, YOU IDIOT!
YOSHI-YOSHI, I'M SORRY THIS GUY GAVE YOU SUCH A HARD TIME...
I HEARD FROM SATO.
I'VE BEEN WAITING FOR YOU TO GET HERE!
ZSH
ZSH
Ah... Wait!
Hold on! It's not like that!

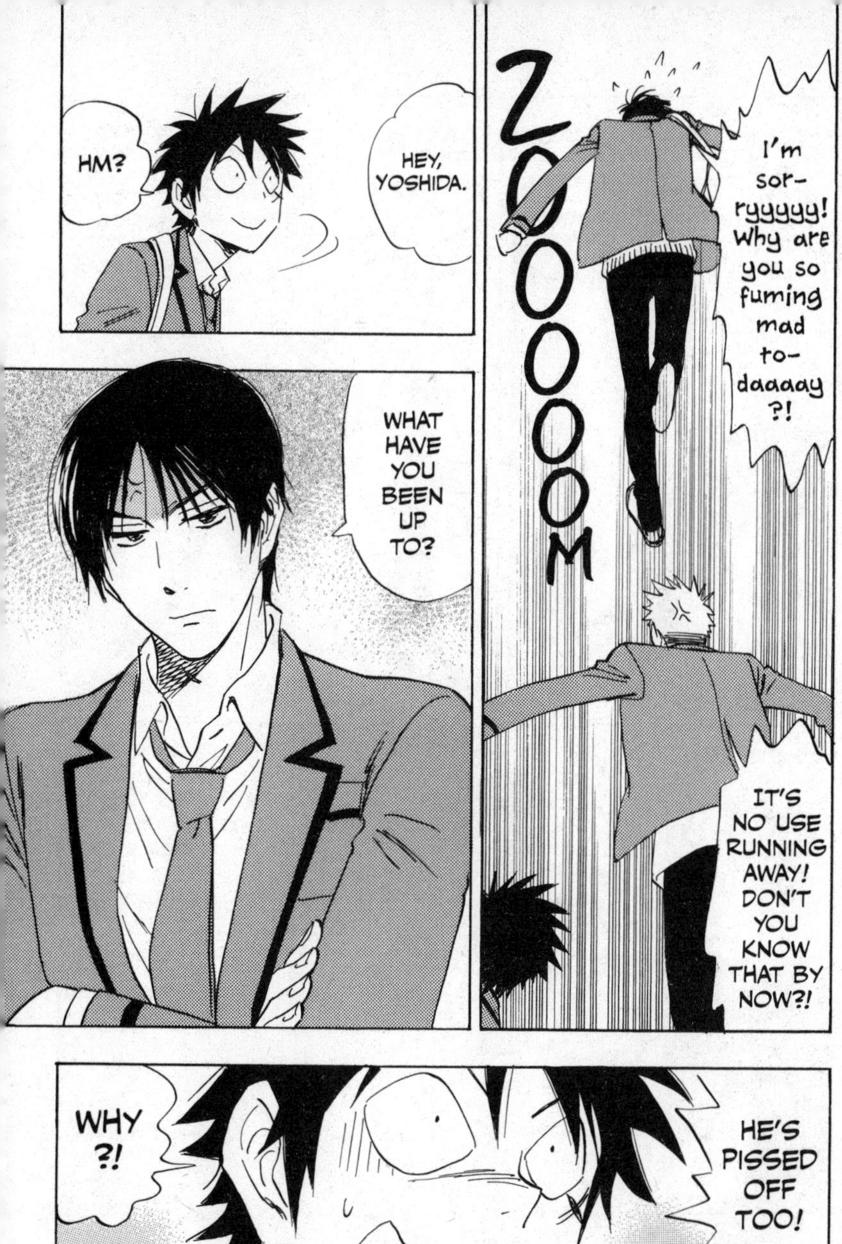
I'm sor-ryyyyy! Why are you so fuming mad to-daaaay?!
ZOOOOOOM
IT'S NO USE RUNNING AWAY! DON'T YOU KNOW THAT BY NOW?!
HEY, YOSHIDA.
HM?
WHAT HAVE YOU BEEN UP TO?
HE'S PISSED OFF TOO!
WHY?!

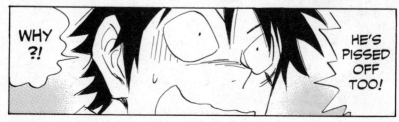

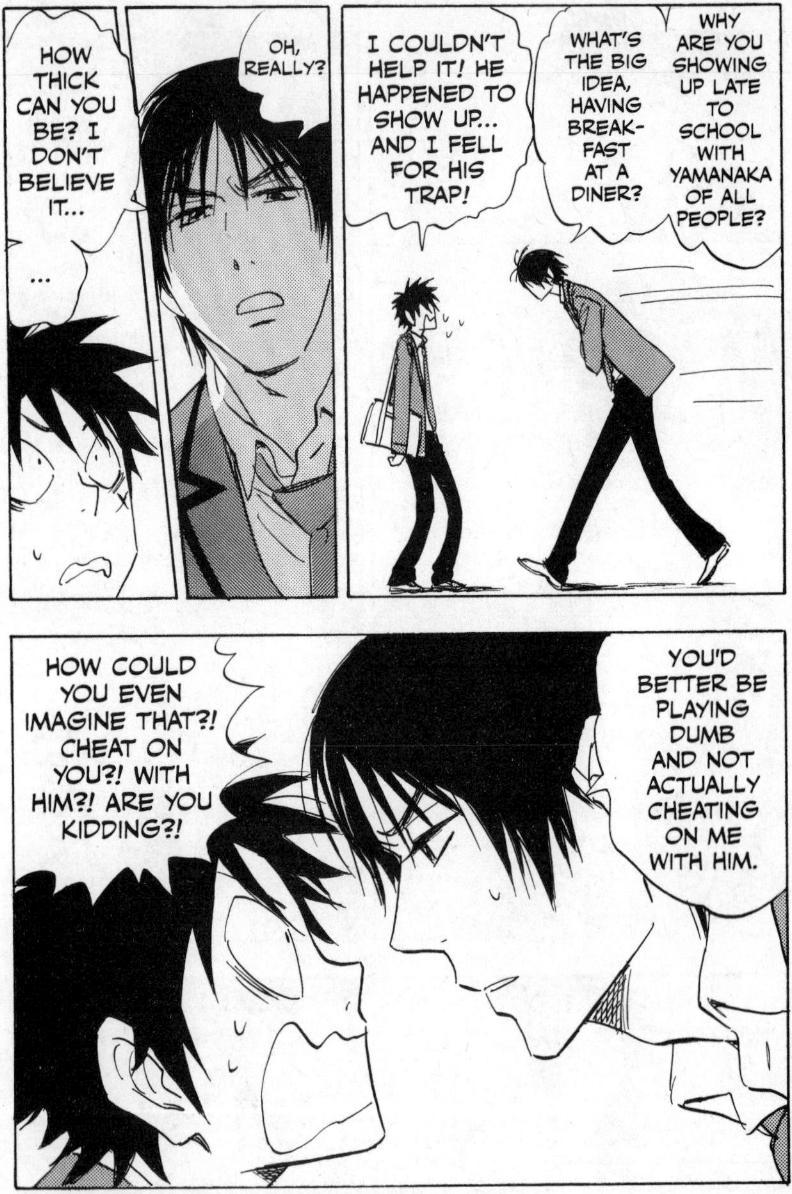
WHY ARE YOU SHOWING UP LATE TO SCHOOL WITH YAMANAKA OF ALL PEOPLE?
WHAT'S THE BIG IDEA, HAVING BREAK-FAST AT A DINER?
I COULDN'T HELP IT! HE HAPPENED TO SHOW UP... AND I FELL FOR HIS TRAP!
OH, REALLY?
HOW THICK CAN YOU BE? I DON'T BELIEVE IT...
...
YOU'D BETTER BE PLAYING DUMB AND NOT ACTUALLY CHEATING ON ME WITH HIM.
HOW COULD YOU EVEN IMAGINE THAT?! CHEAT ON YOU?! WITH HIM?! ARE YOU KIDDING?!

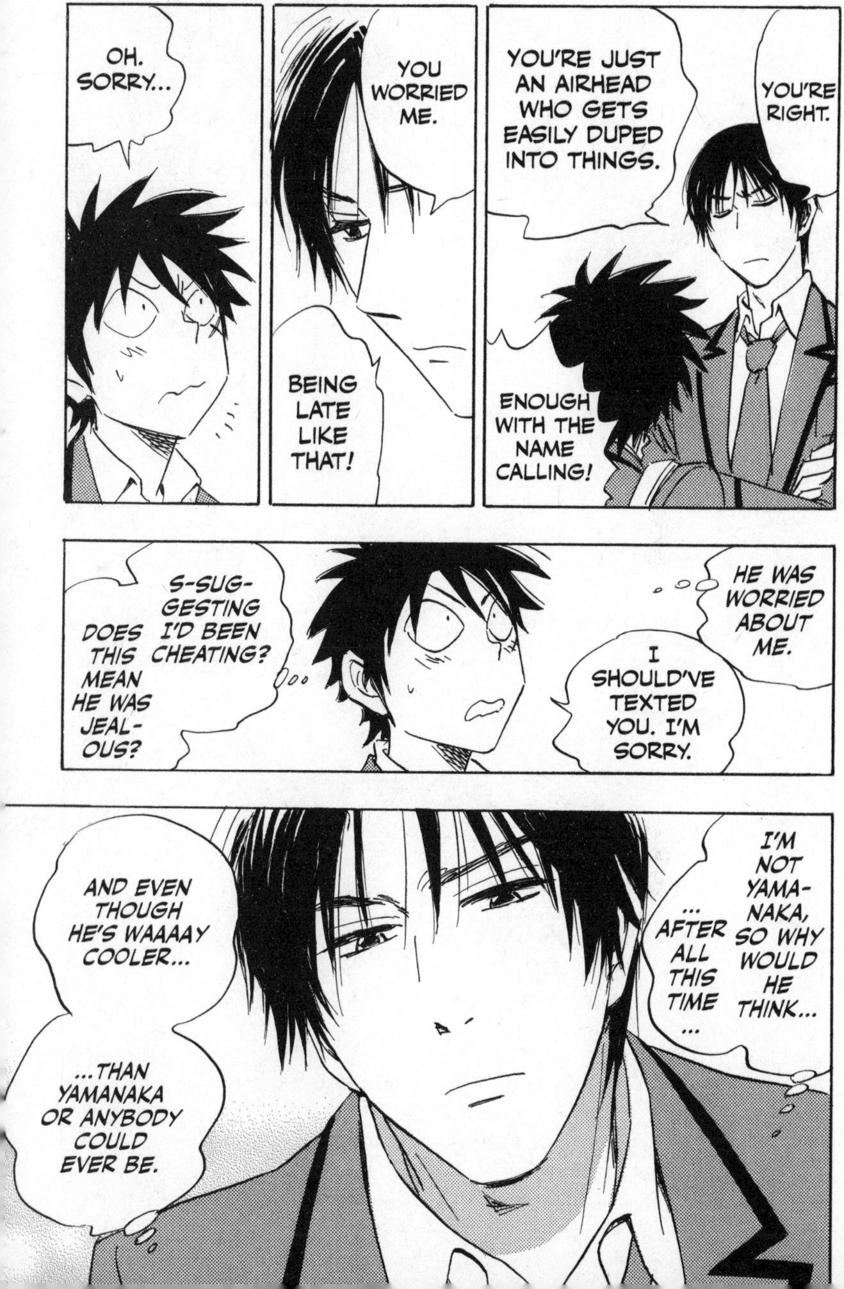
YOU'RE RIGHT.
YOU'RE JUST AN AIRHEAD WHO GETS EASILY DUPED INTO THINGS.
ENOUGH WITH THE NAME CALLING!
YOU WORRIED ME.
BEING LATE LIKE THAT!
OH. SORRY...
HE WAS WORRIED ABOUT ME.
I SHOULD'VE TEXTED YOU. I'M SORRY.
S-SUG-GESTING I'D BEEN CHEATING?
DOES THIS MEAN HE WAS JEAL-OUS?
I'M NOT YAMA-NAKA, SO WHY WOULD HE THINK...
...AFTER ALL THIS TIME...
AND EVEN THOUGH HE'S WAAAAY COOLER...
...THAN YAMANAKA OR ANYBODY COULD EVER BE.

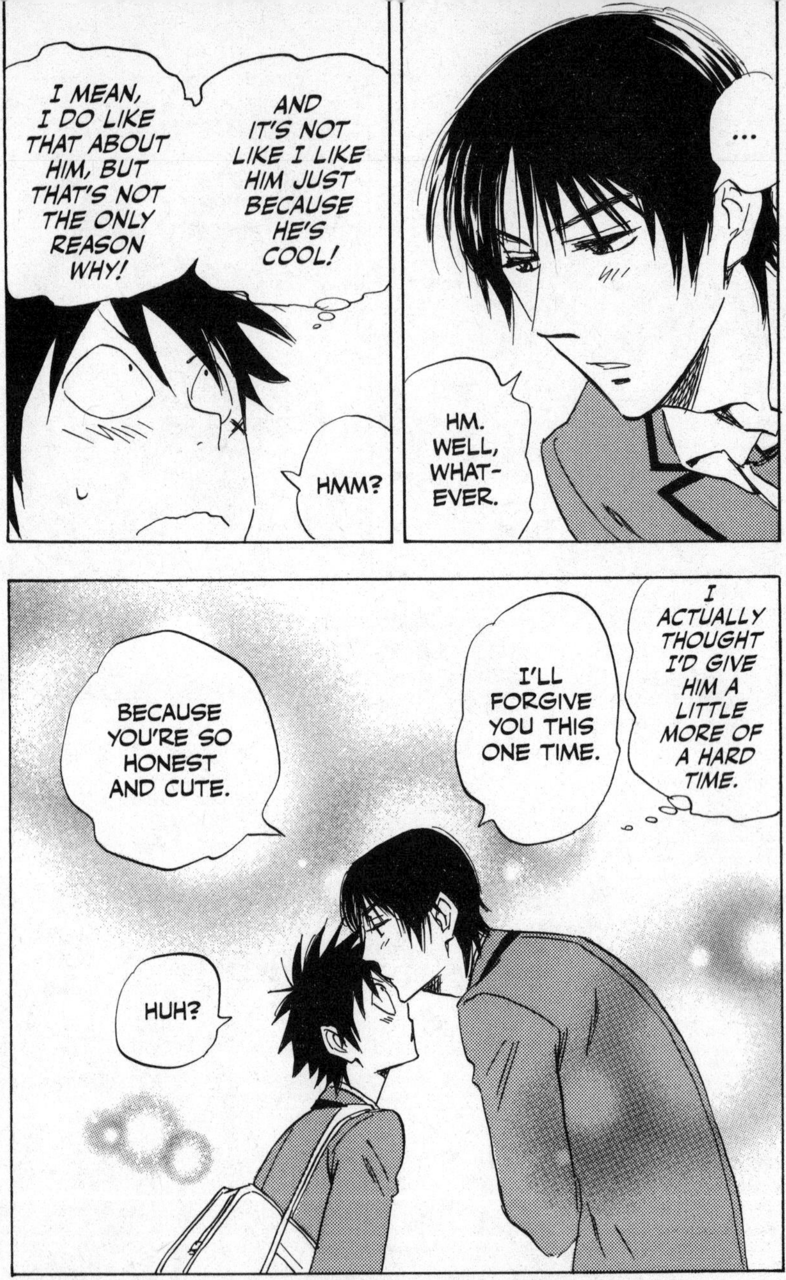
...
HM. WELL, WHAT-EVER.
AND IT'S NOT LIKE I LIKE HIM JUST BECAUSE HE'S COOL!
I MEAN, I DO LIKE THAT ABOUT HIM, BUT THAT'S NOT THE ONLY REASON WHY!
HMM?
I ACTUALLY THOUGHT I'D GIVE HIM A LITTLE MORE OF A HARD TIME.
I'LL FORGIVE YOU THIS ONE TIME.
BECAUSE YOU'RE SO HONEST AND CUTE.
HUH?

ACT. 50 / END

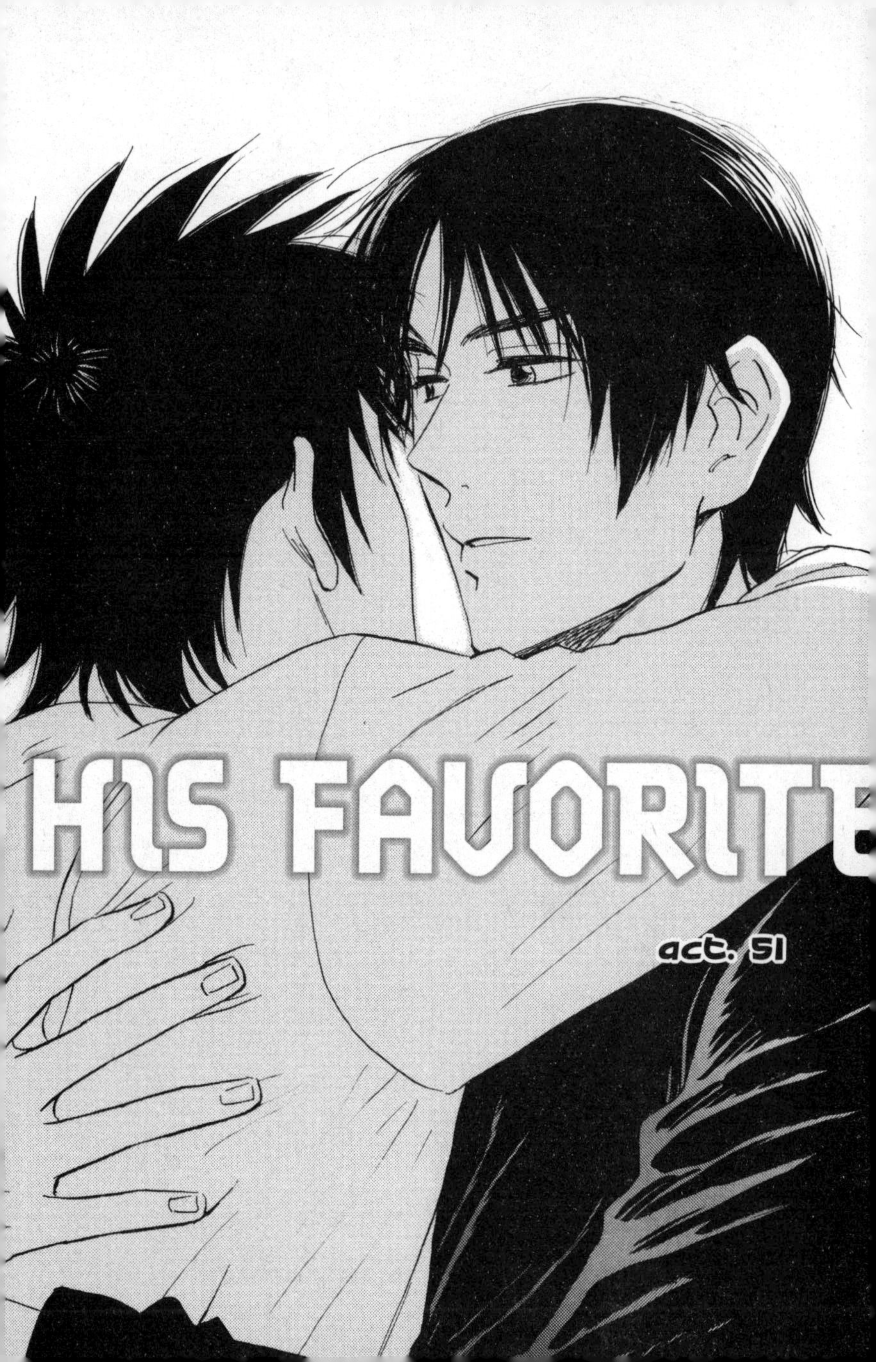
HIS FAVORITE
act. 51

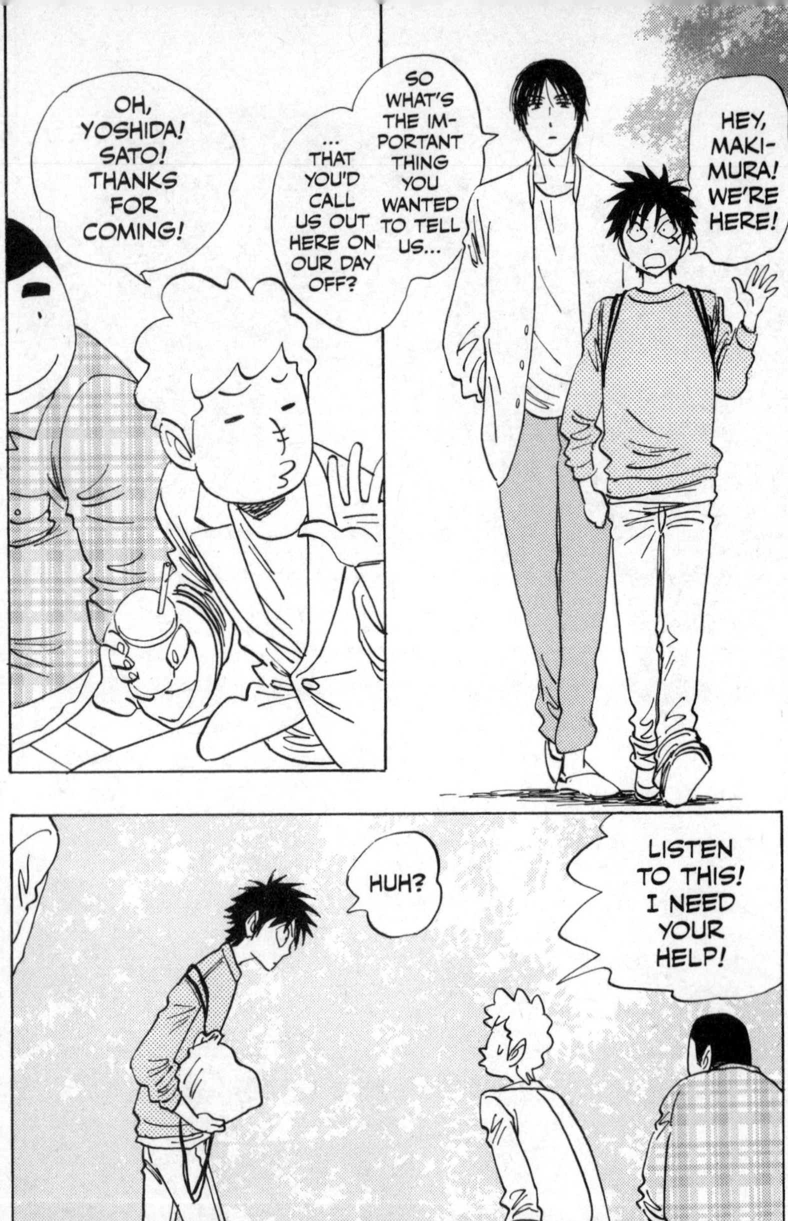
HEY, MAKI-MURA! WE'RE HERE!
SO WHAT'S THE IM-PORTANT THING YOU WANTED TO TELL US...
... THAT YOU'D CALL US OUT HERE ON OUR DAY OFF?
OH, YOSHIDA! SATO! THANKS FOR COMING!
LISTEN TO THIS! I NEED YOUR HELP!
HUH?

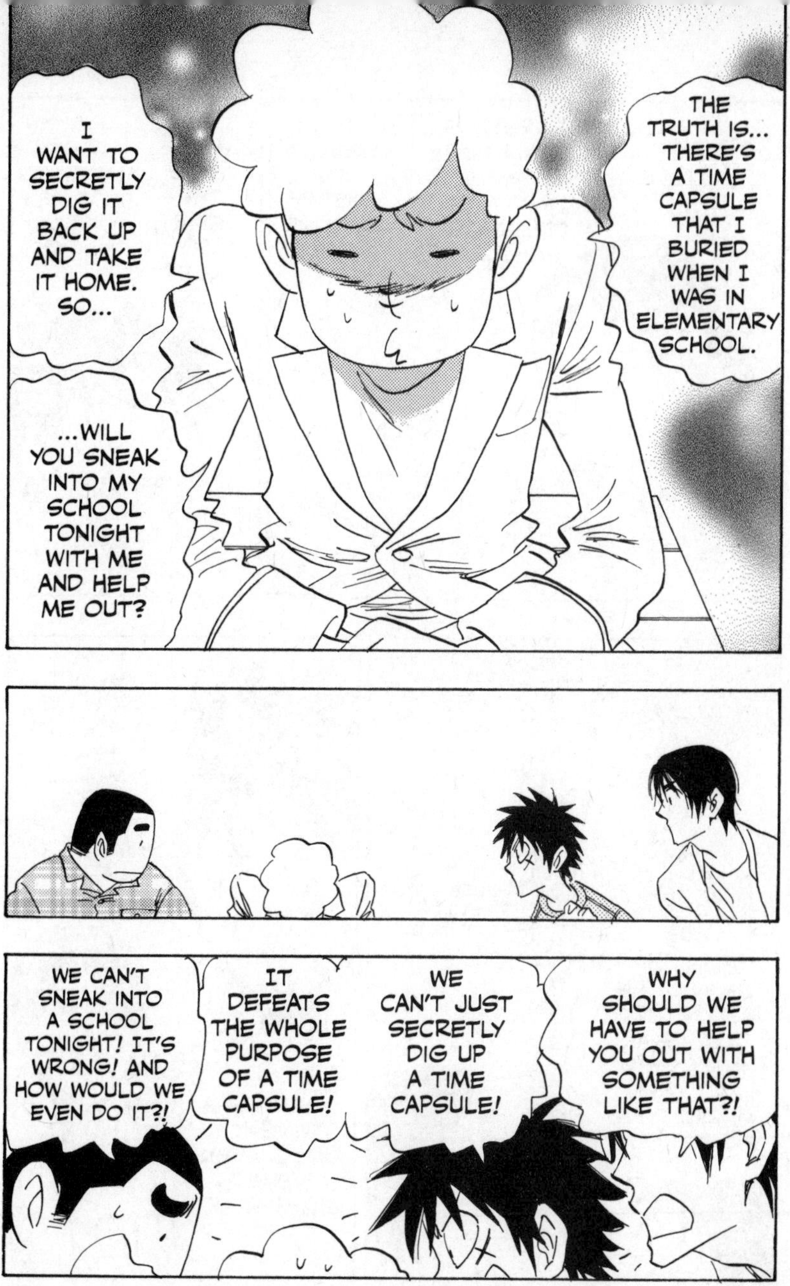
THE TRUTH IS... THERE'S A TIME CAPSULE THAT I BURIED WHEN I WAS IN ELEMENTARY SCHOOL.
I WANT TO SECRETLY DIG IT BACK UP AND TAKE IT HOME. SO...
...WILL YOU SNEAK INTO MY SCHOOL TONIGHT WITH ME AND HELP ME OUT?
WHY SHOULD WE HAVE TO HELP YOU OUT WITH SOMETHING LIKE THAT?!
WE CAN'T JUST SECRETLY DIG UP A TIME CAPSULE!
IT DEFEATS THE WHOLE PURPOSE OF A TIME CAPSULE!
WE CAN'T SNEAK INTO A SCHOOL TONIGHT! IT'S WRONG! AND HOW WOULD WE EVEN DO IT?!

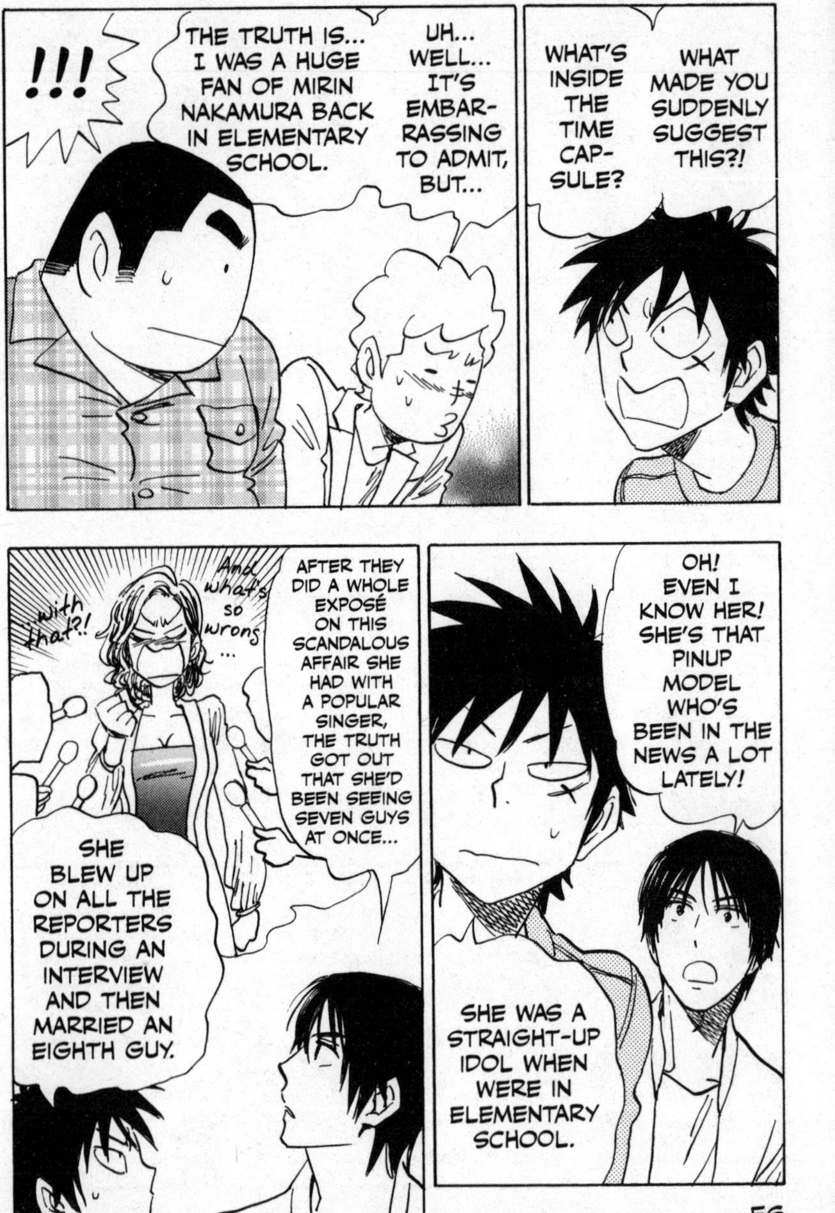
WHAT MADE YOU SUDDENLY SUGGEST THIS?!
WHAT'S INSIDE THE TIME CAPSULE?
UH... WELL... IT'S EMBARRASSING TO ADMIT, BUT...
THE TRUTH IS... I WAS A HUGE FAN OF MIRIN NAKAMURA BACK IN ELEMENTARY SCHOOL.
!!!
OH! EVEN I KNOW HER! SHE'S THAT PINUP MODEL WHO'S BEEN IN THE NEWS A LOT LATELY!
SHE WAS A STRAIGHT-UP IDOL WHEN WERE IN ELEMENTARY SCHOOL.
AFTER THEY DID A WHOLE EXPOSÉ ON THIS SCANDALOUS AFFAIR SHE HAD WITH A POPULAR SINGER, THE TRUTH GOT OUT THAT SHE'D BEEN SEEING SEVEN GUYS AT ONCE...
And what's so wrong...
...with that?!
SHE BLEW UP ON ALL THE REPORTERS DURING AN INTERVIEW AND THEN MARRIED AN EIGHTH GUY.

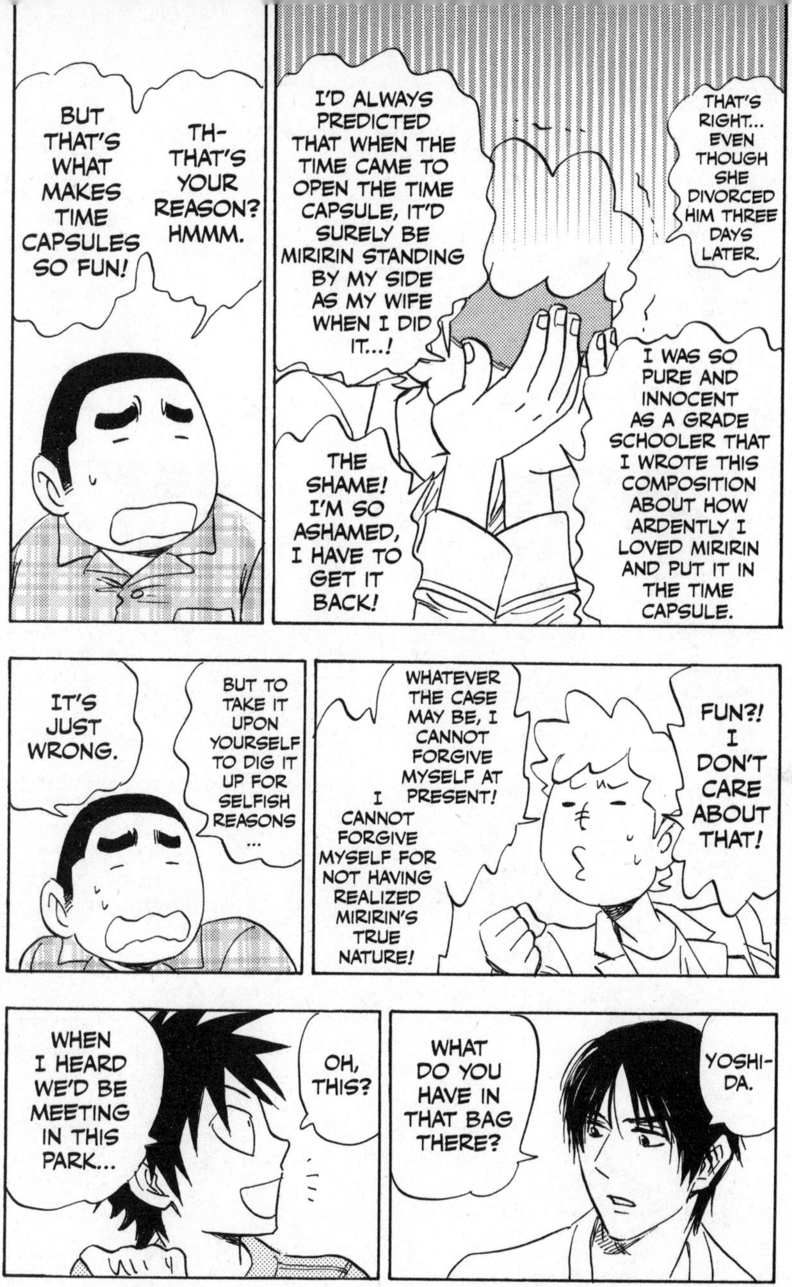
I'D ALWAYS PREDICTED THAT WHEN THE TIME CAME TO OPEN THE TIME CAPSULE, IT'D SURELY BE MIRIRIN STANDING BY MY SIDE AS MY WIFE WHEN I DID IT...!
THAT'S RIGHT... EVEN THOUGH SHE DIVORCED HIM THREE DAYS LATER.
I WAS SO PURE AND INNOCENT AS A GRADE SCHOOLER THAT I WROTE THIS COMPOSITION ABOUT HOW ARDENTLY I LOVED MIRIRIN AND PUT IT IN THE TIME CAPSULE.
THE SHAME! I'M SO ASHAMED, I HAVE TO GET IT BACK!
TH-THAT'S YOUR REASON? HMMM.
BUT THAT'S WHAT MAKES TIME CAPSULES SO FUN!
FUN?! I DON'T CARE ABOUT THAT!
WHATEVER THE CASE MAY BE, I CANNOT FORGIVE MYSELF AT PRESENT!
I CANNOT FORGIVE MYSELF FOR NOT HAVING REALIZED MIRIRIN'S TRUE NATURE!
BUT TO TAKE IT UPON YOURSELF TO DIG IT UP FOR SELFISH REASONS...
IT'S JUST WRONG.
YOSHI-DA.
WHAT DO YOU HAVE IN THAT BAG THERE?
OH, THIS?
WHEN I HEARD WE'D BE MEETING IN THIS PARK...

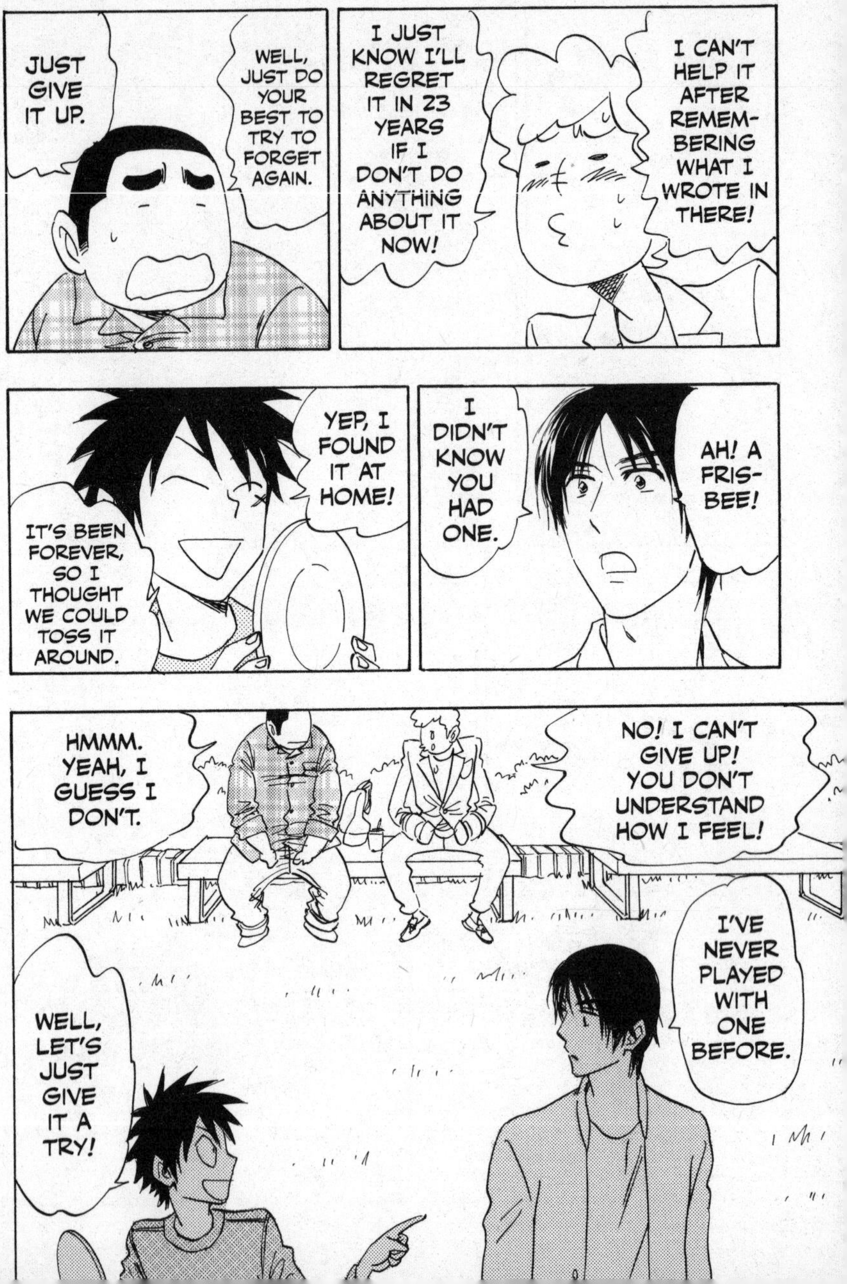
I CAN'T HELP IT AFTER REMEMBERING WHAT I WROTE IN THERE!
I JUST KNOW I'LL REGRET IT IN 23 YEARS IF I DON'T DO ANYTHING ABOUT IT NOW!
WELL, JUST DO YOUR BEST TO TRY TO FORGET AGAIN.
JUST GIVE IT UP.
AH! A FRISBEE!
I DIDN'T KNOW YOU HAD ONE.
YEP, I FOUND IT AT HOME!
IT'S BEEN FOREVER, SO I THOUGHT WE COULD TOSS IT AROUND.
NO! I CAN'T GIVE UP! YOU DON'T UNDERSTAND HOW I FEEL!
HMMM. YEAH, I GUESS I DON'T.
I'VE NEVER PLAYED WITH ONE BEFORE.
WELL, LET'S JUST GIVE IT A TRY!

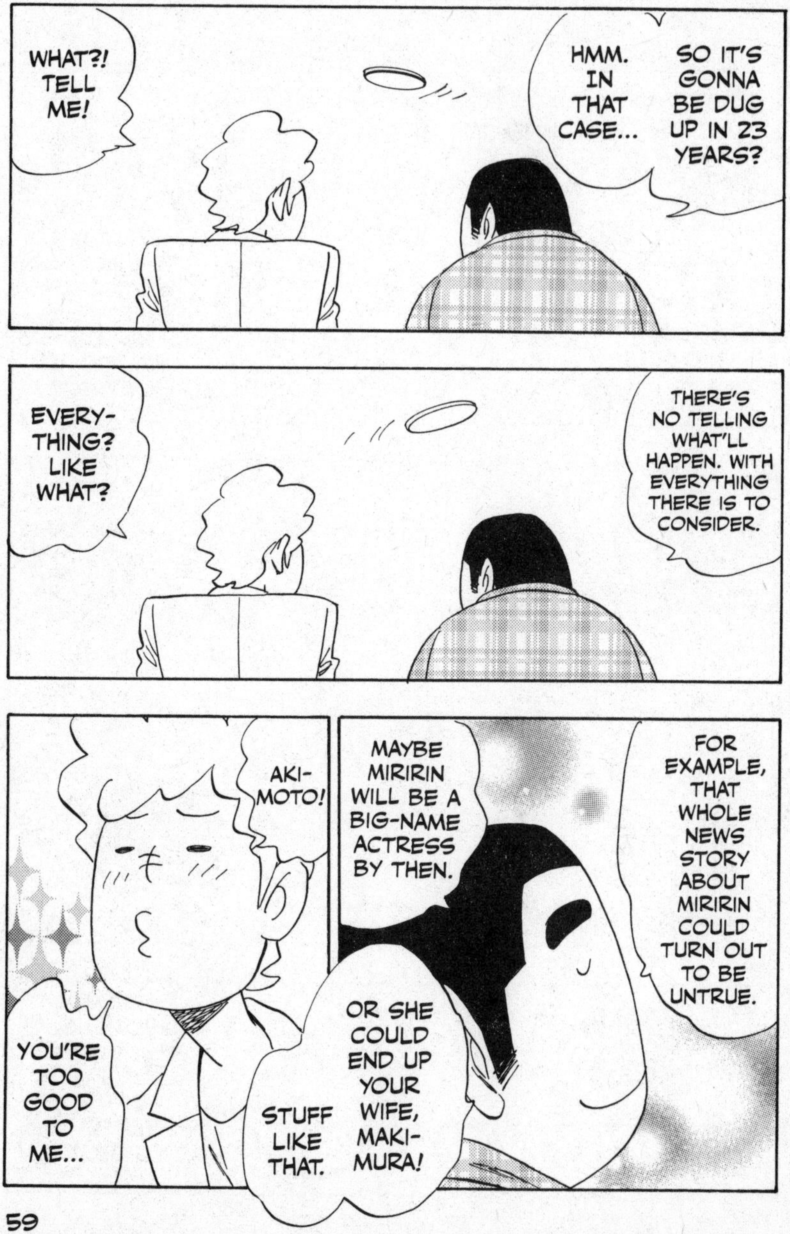
SO IT'S GONNA BE DUG UP IN 23 YEARS?
HMM. IN THAT CASE...
WHAT?! TELL ME!
THERE'S NO TELLING WHAT'LL HAPPEN. WITH EVERYTHING THERE IS TO CONSIDER.
EVERY-THING? LIKE WHAT?
FOR EXAMPLE, THAT WHOLE NEWS STORY ABOUT MIRIRIN COULD TURN OUT TO BE UNTRUE.
MAYBE MIRIRIN WILL BE A BIG-NAME ACTRESS BY THEN.
OR SHE COULD END UP YOUR WIFE, MAKI-MURA!
STUFF LIKE THAT.
AKI-MOTO!
YOU'RE TOO GOOD TO ME...

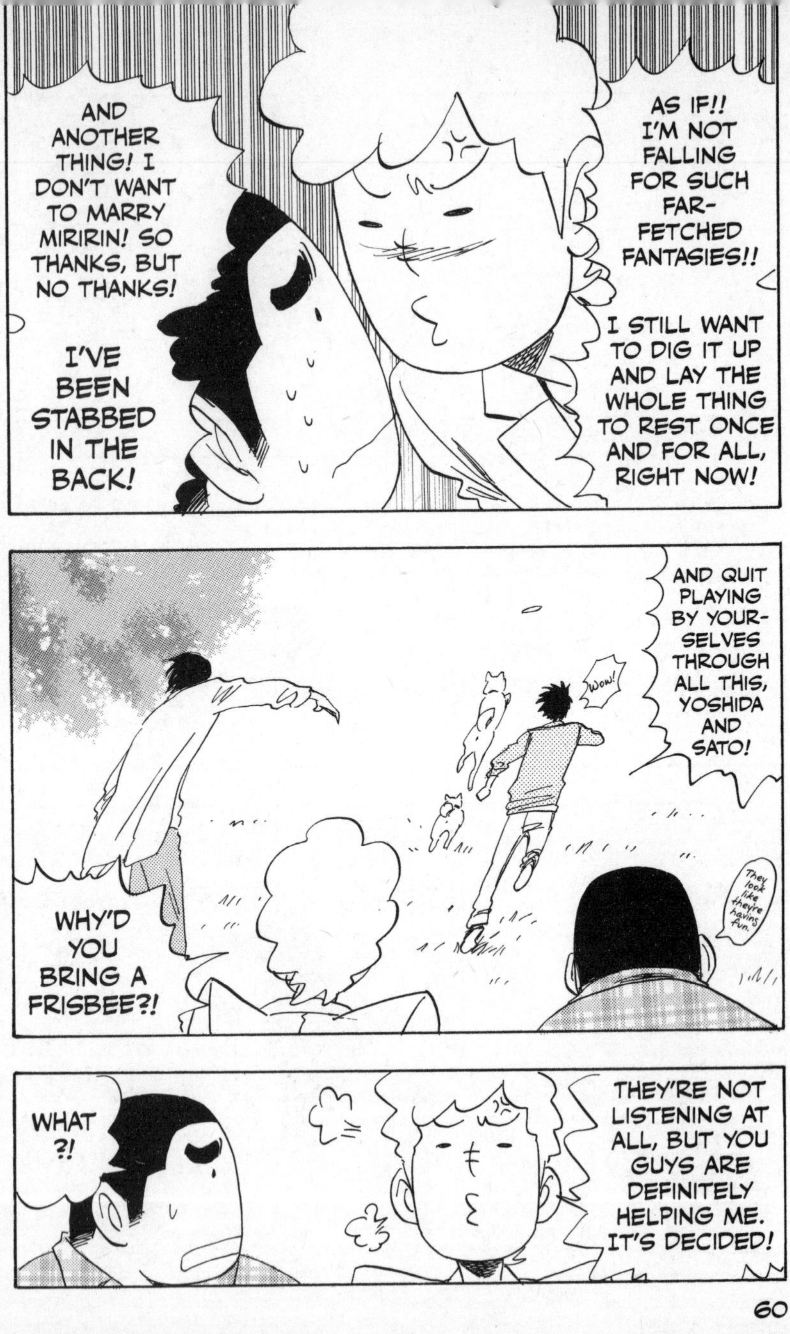
AS IF!! I'M NOT FALLING FOR SUCH FAR-FETCHED FANTASIES!!
I STILL WANT TO DIG IT UP AND LAY THE WHOLE THING TO REST ONCE AND FOR ALL, RIGHT NOW!
AND ANOTHER THING! I DON'T WANT TO MARRY MIRIRIN! SO THANKS, BUT NO THANKS!
I'VE BEEN STABBED IN THE BACK!
AND QUIT PLAYING BY YOUR-SELVES THROUGH ALL THIS, YOSHIDA AND SATO!
Wow!
They look like they're having fun.
WHY'D YOU BRING A FRISBEE?!
THEY'RE NOT LISTENING AT ALL, BUT YOU GUYS ARE DEFINITELY HELPING ME. IT'S DECIDED!
WHAT ?!

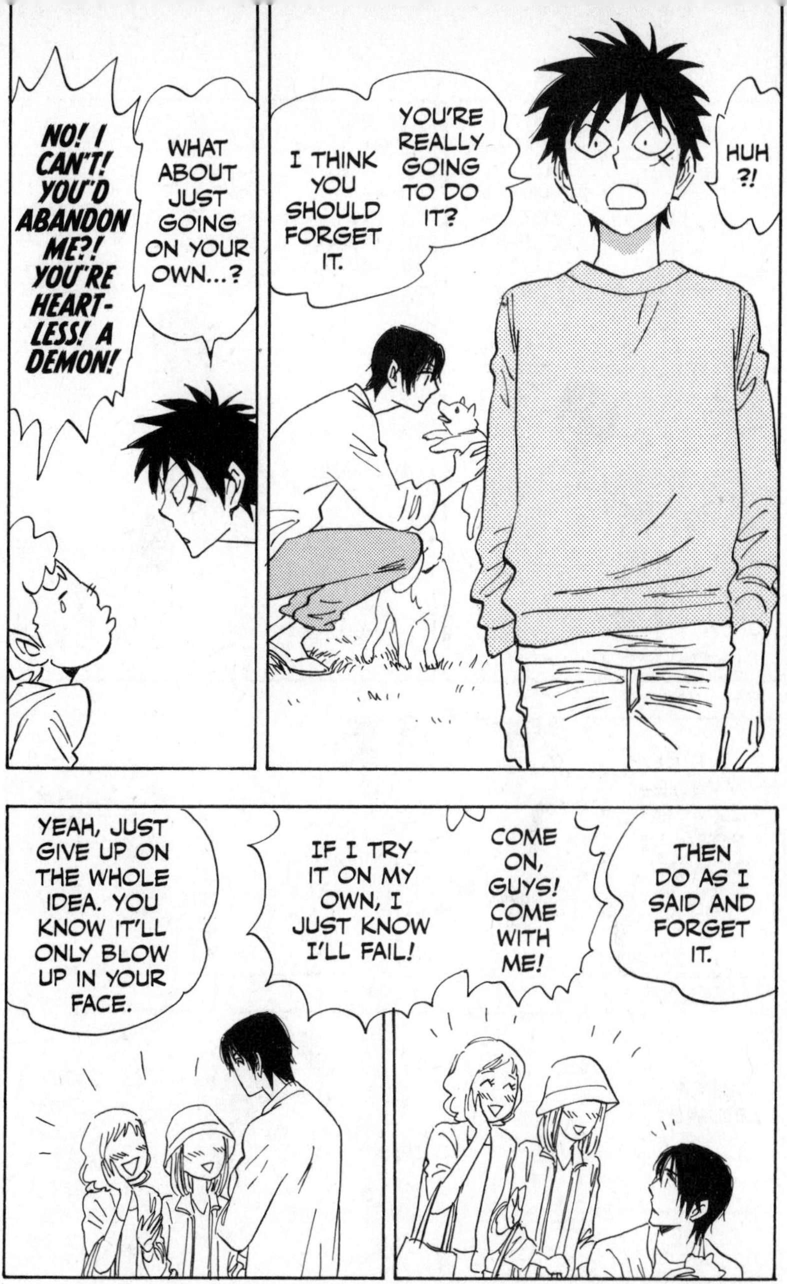
HUH ?!
YOU'RE REALLY GOING TO DO IT?
I THINK YOU SHOULD FORGET IT.
WHAT ABOUT JUST GOING ON YOUR OWN...?
NO! I CAN'T! YOU'D ABANDON ME?! YOU'RE HEART-LESS! A DEMON!
THEN DO AS I SAID AND FORGET IT.
COME ON, GUYS! COME WITH ME!
IF I TRY IT ON MY OWN, I JUST KNOW I'LL FAIL!
YEAH, JUST GIVE UP ON THE WHOLE IDEA. YOU KNOW IT'LL ONLY BLOW UP IN YOUR FACE.

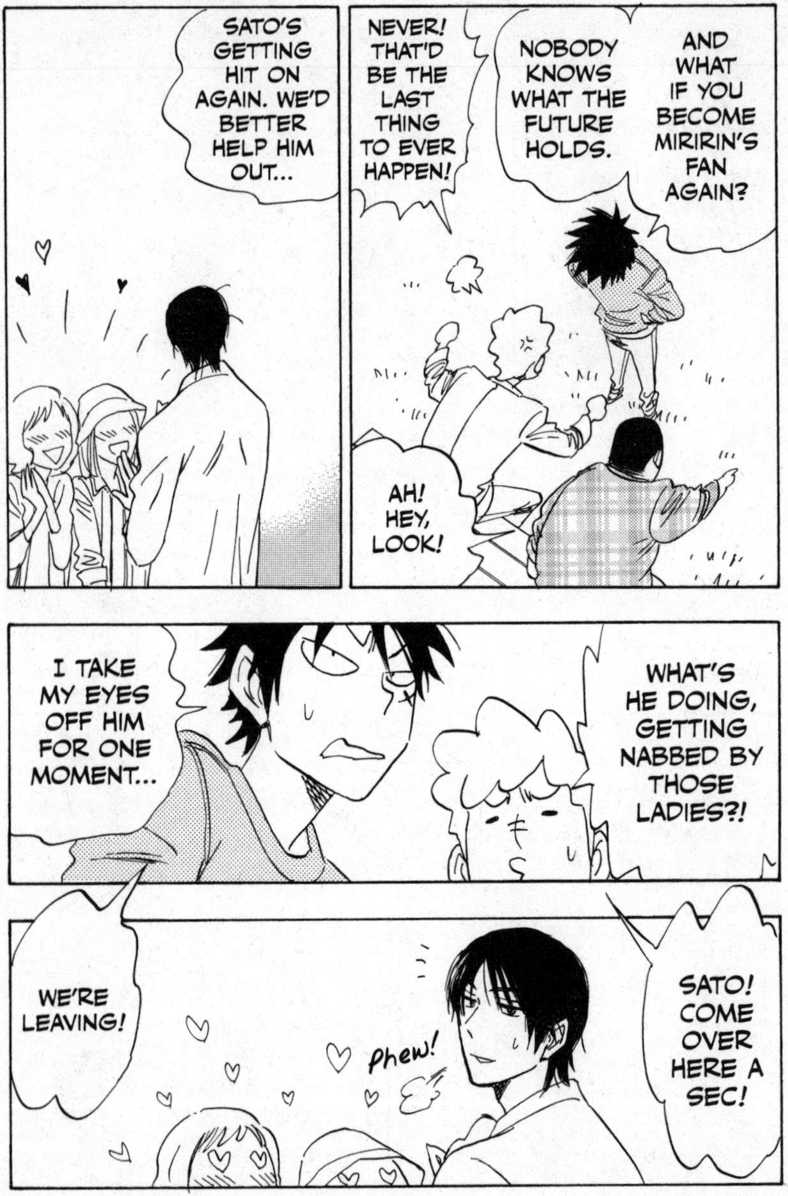
AND WHAT IF YOU BECOME MIRIRIN'S FAN AGAIN?
NOBODY KNOWS WHAT THE FUTURE HOLDS.
NEVER! THAT'D BE THE LAST THING TO EVER HAPPEN!
AH! HEY, LOOK!
SATO'S GETTING HIT ON AGAIN. WE'D BETTER HELP HIM OUT...
WHAT'S HE DOING, GETTING NABBED BY THOSE LADIES?!
I TAKE MY EYES OFF HIM FOR ONE MOMENT...
SATO! COME OVER HERE A SEC!
Phew!
WE'RE LEAVING!

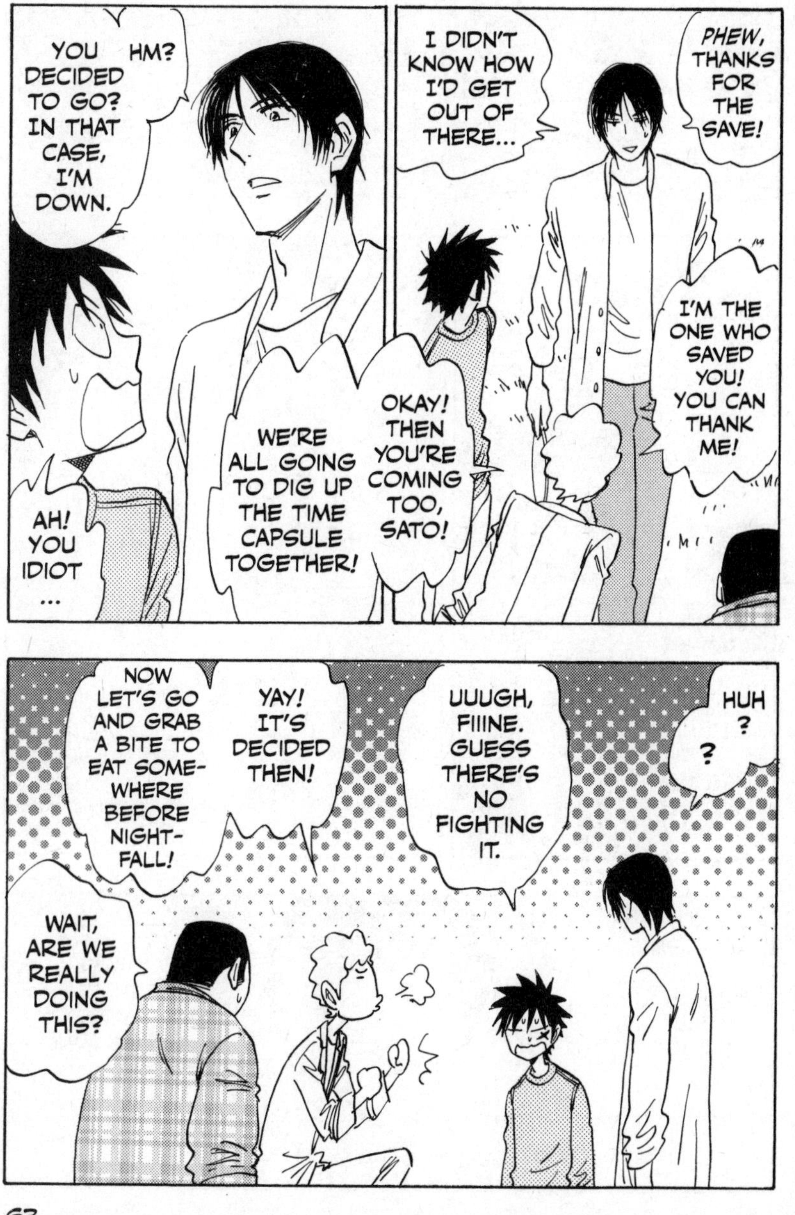
PHEW, THANKS FOR THE SAVE!
I DIDN'T KNOW HOW I'D GET OUT OF THERE...
I'M THE ONE WHO SAVED YOU! YOU CAN THANK ME!
OKAY! THEN YOU'RE COMING TOO, SATO!
HM?
YOU DECIDED TO GO? IN THAT CASE, I'M DOWN.
WE'RE ALL GOING TO DIG UP THE TIME CAPSULE TOGETHER!
AH! YOU IDIOT ...
HUH ? ?
UUUGH, FIIINE. GUESS THERE'S NO FIGHTING IT.
YAY! IT'S DECIDED THEN!
NOW LET'S GO AND GRAB A BITE TO EAT SOME-WHERE BEFORE NIGHT-FALL!
WAIT, ARE WE REALLY DOING THIS?

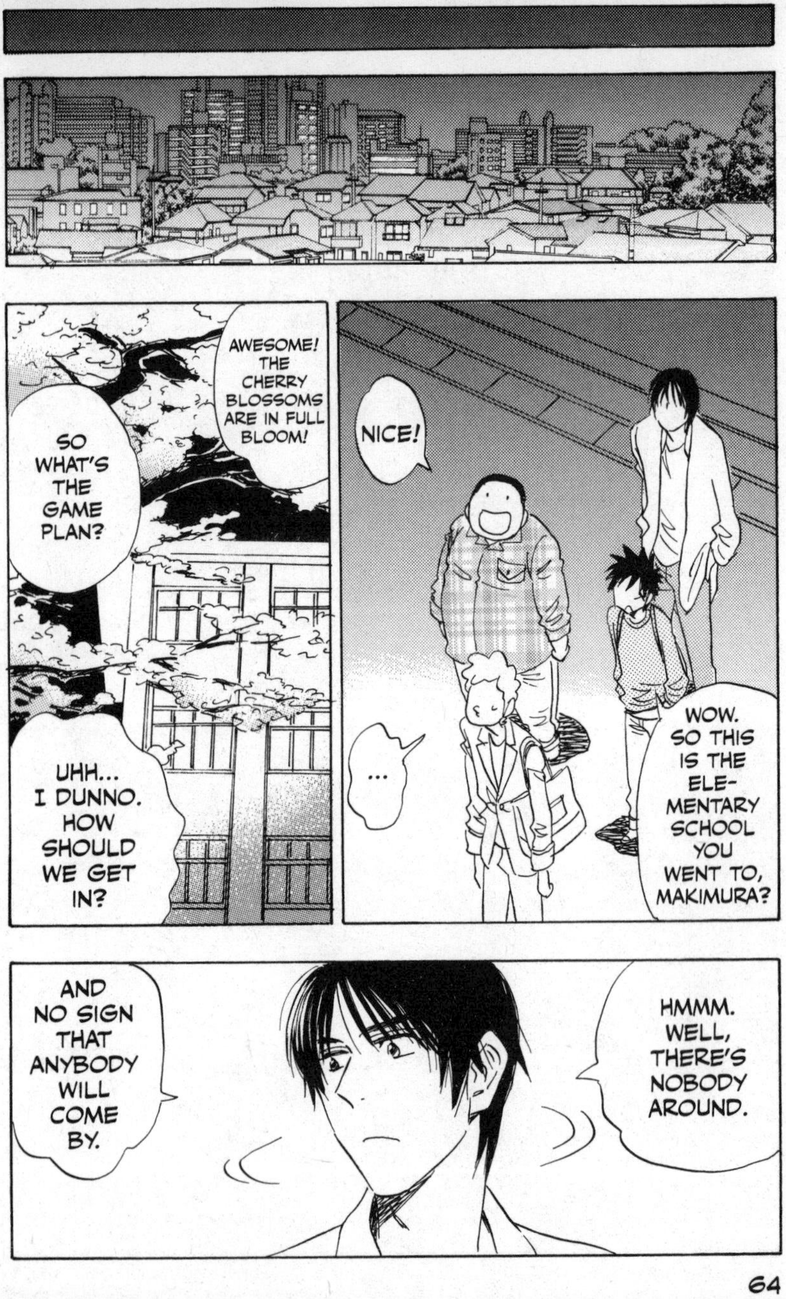
NICE!
WOW. SO THIS IS THE ELE-MENTARY SCHOOL YOU WENT TO, MAKIMURA?
...
AWESOME! THE CHERRY BLOSSOMS ARE IN FULL BLOOM!
SO WHAT'S THE GAME PLAN?
UHH... I DUNNO. HOW SHOULD WE GET IN?
HMMM. WELL, THERE'S NOBODY AROUND.
AND NO SIGN THAT ANYBODY WILL COME BY.

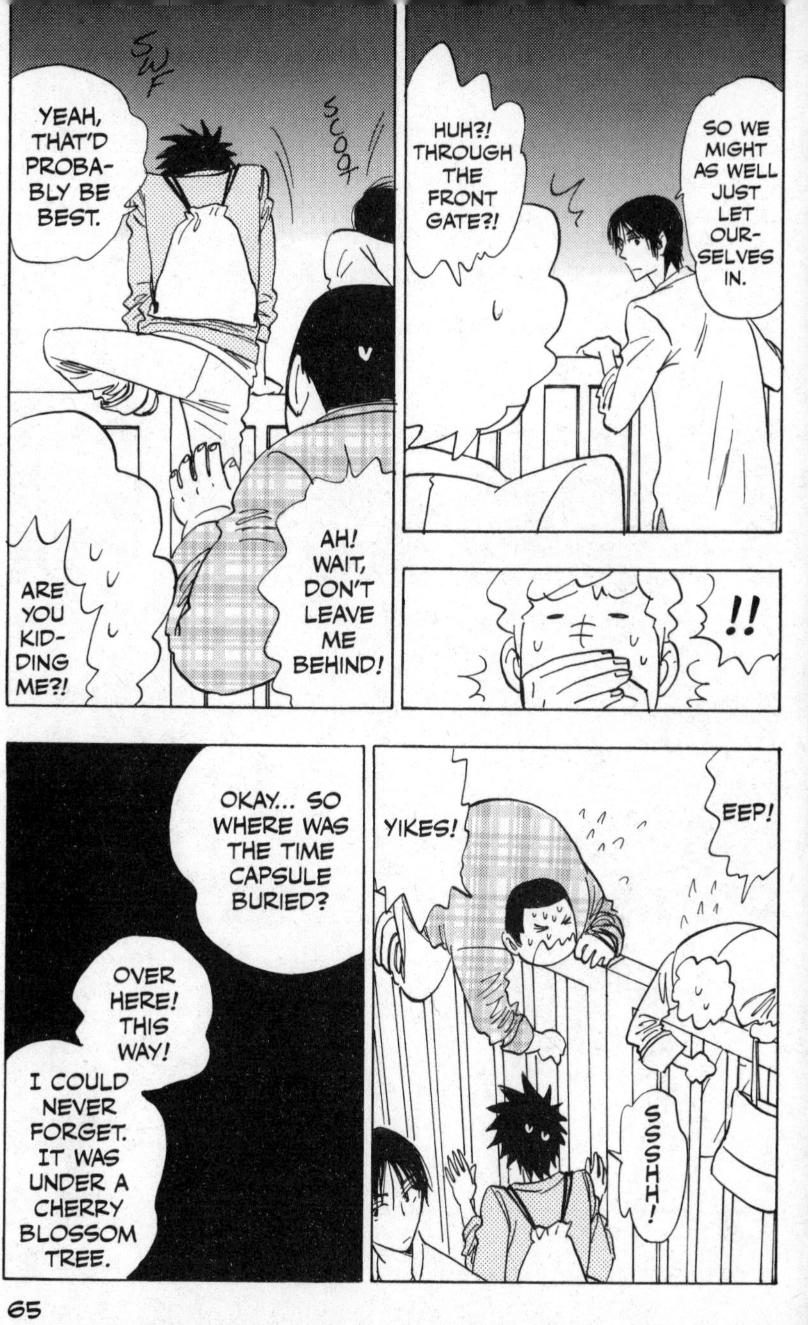
SO WE MIGHT AS WELL JUST LET OURSELVES IN.
HUH?! THROUGH THE FRONT GATE?!
!!
SWF
SCOOT
YEAH, THAT'D PROBABLY BE BEST.
AH! WAIT, DON'T LEAVE ME BEHIND!
ARE YOU KIDDING ME?!
EEP!
YIKES!
SSSHH!
OKAY... SO WHERE WAS THE TIME CAPSULE BURIED?
OVER HERE! THIS WAY!
I COULD NEVER FORGET. IT WAS UNDER A CHERRY BLOSSOM TREE.

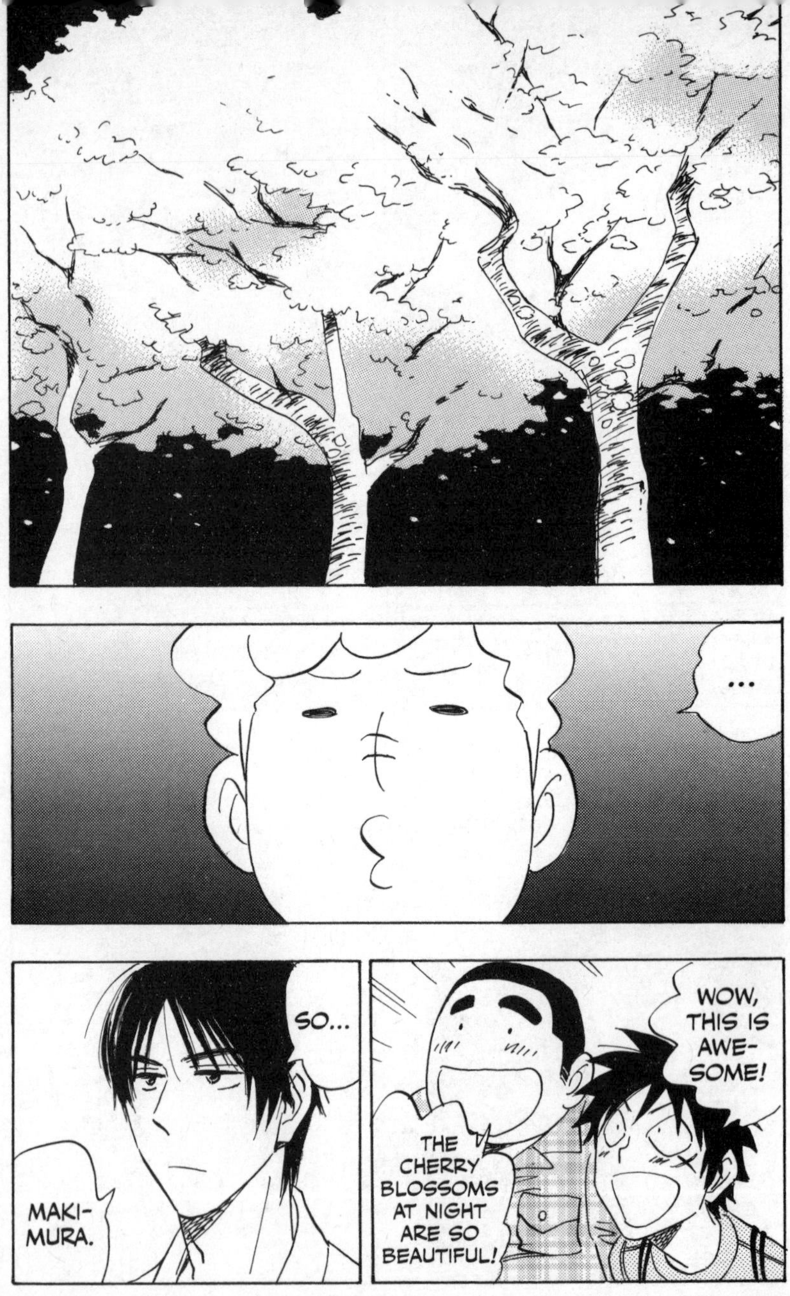
...
WOW, THIS IS AWE-SOME!
THE CHERRY BLOSSOMS AT NIGHT ARE SO BEAUTIFUL!
SO...
MAKI-MURA.

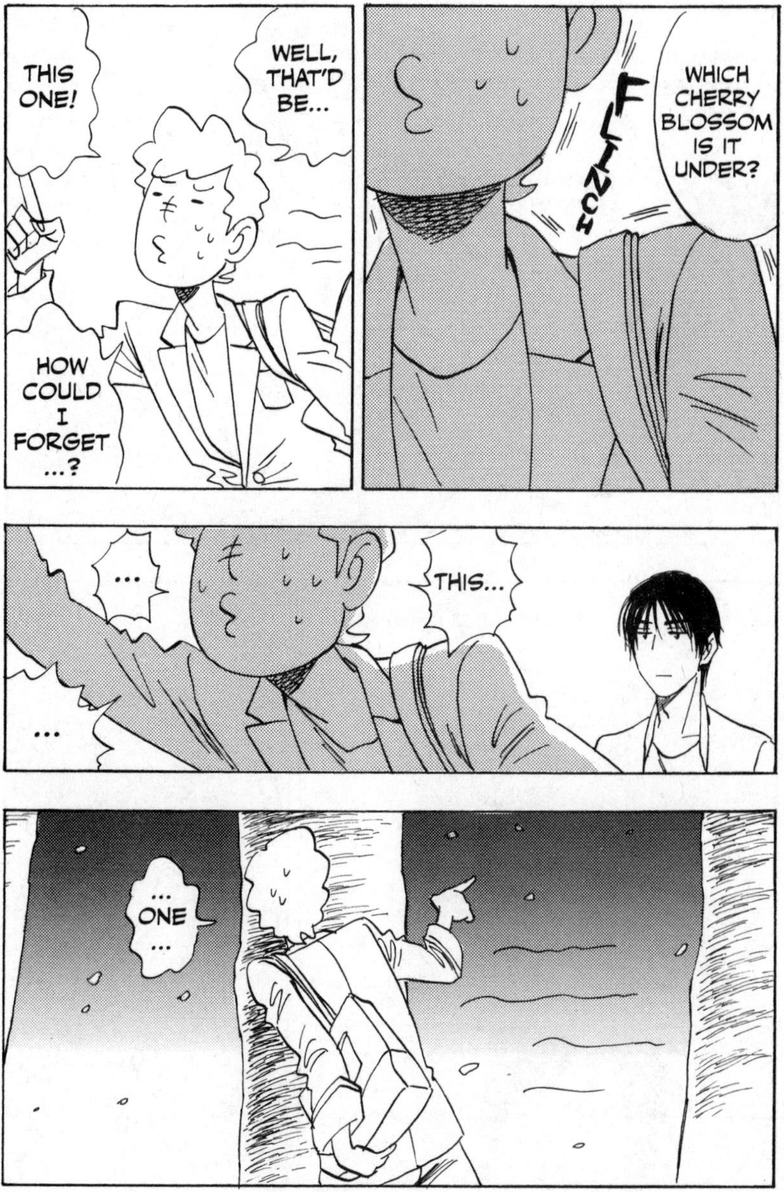
WHICH CHERRY BLOSSOM IS IT UNDER?
FLINCH
WELL, THAT'D BE...
THIS ONE!
HOW COULD I FORGET ...?
THIS...
...
...
... ONE ...

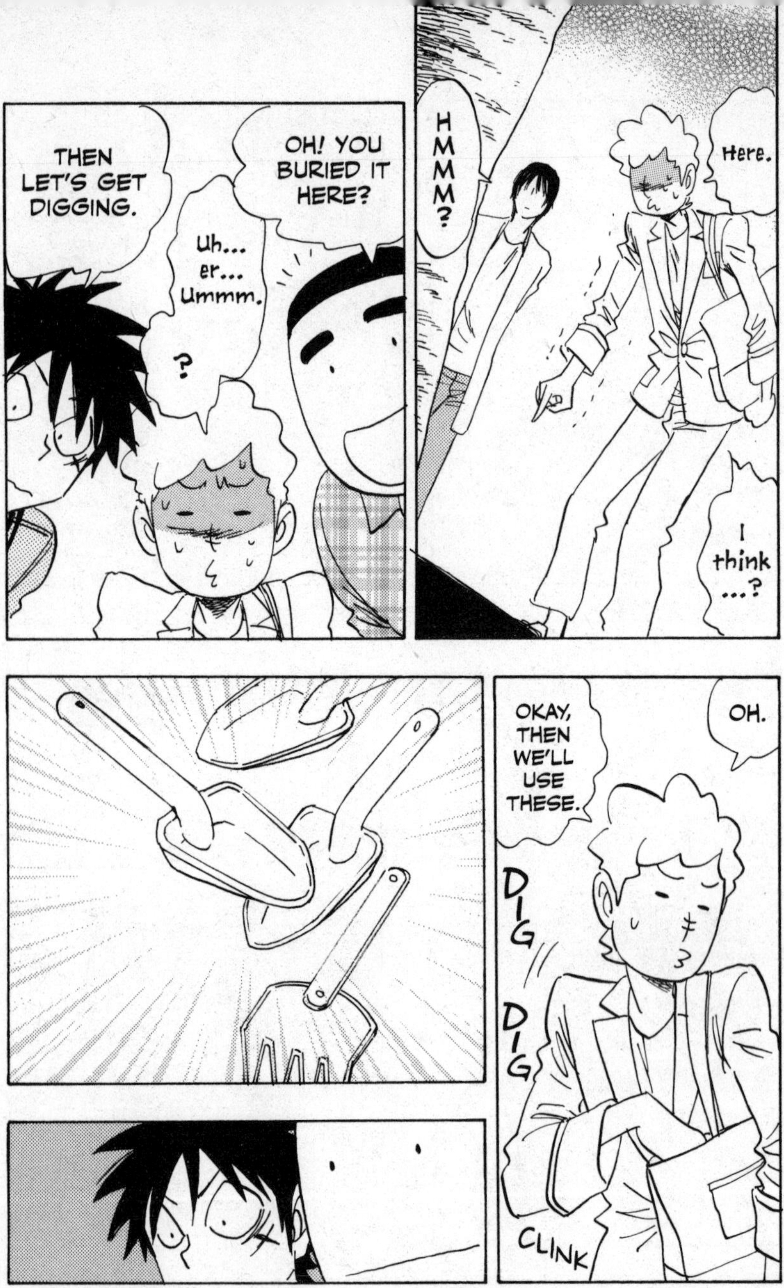
Here.
HMMMM?
I think...?
OH! YOU BURIED IT HERE?
THEN LET'S GET DIGGING.
Uh... er... Ummm.
?
OH.
OKAY, THEN WE'LL USE THESE.
DIG DIG
CLINK

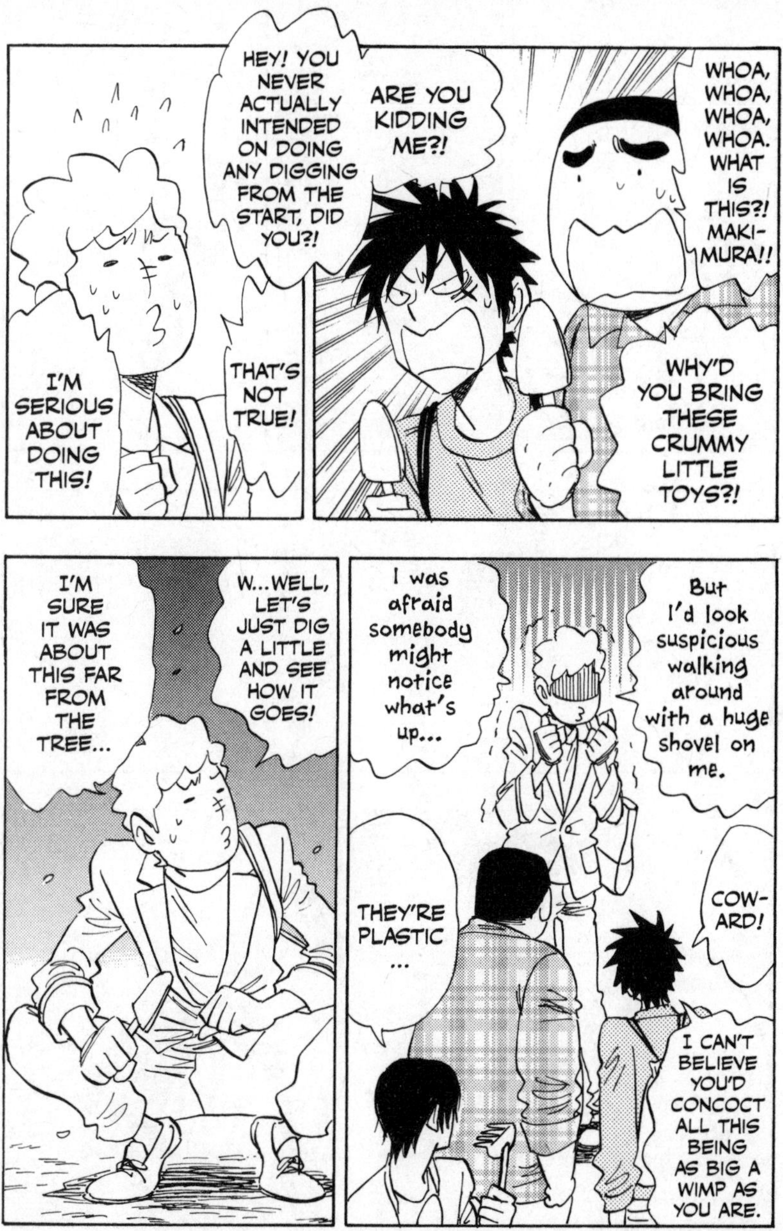
WHOA, WHOA, WHOA, WHOA. WHAT IS THIS?! MAKI-MURA!!
WHY'D YOU BRING THESE CRUMMY LITTLE TOYS?!
ARE YOU KIDDING ME?!
HEY! YOU NEVER ACTUALLY INTENDED ON DOING ANY DIGGING FROM THE START, DID YOU?!
THAT'S NOT TRUE!
I'M SERIOUS ABOUT DOING THIS!
I was afraid somebody might notice what's up...
But I'd look suspicious walking around with a huge shovel on me.
COW-ARD!
THEY'RE PLASTIC...
I CAN'T BELIEVE YOU'D CONCOCT ALL THIS BEING AS BIG A WIMP AS YOU ARE.
W...WELL, LET'S JUST DIG A LITTLE AND SEE HOW IT GOES!
I'M SURE IT WAS ABOUT THIS FAR FROM THE TREE...

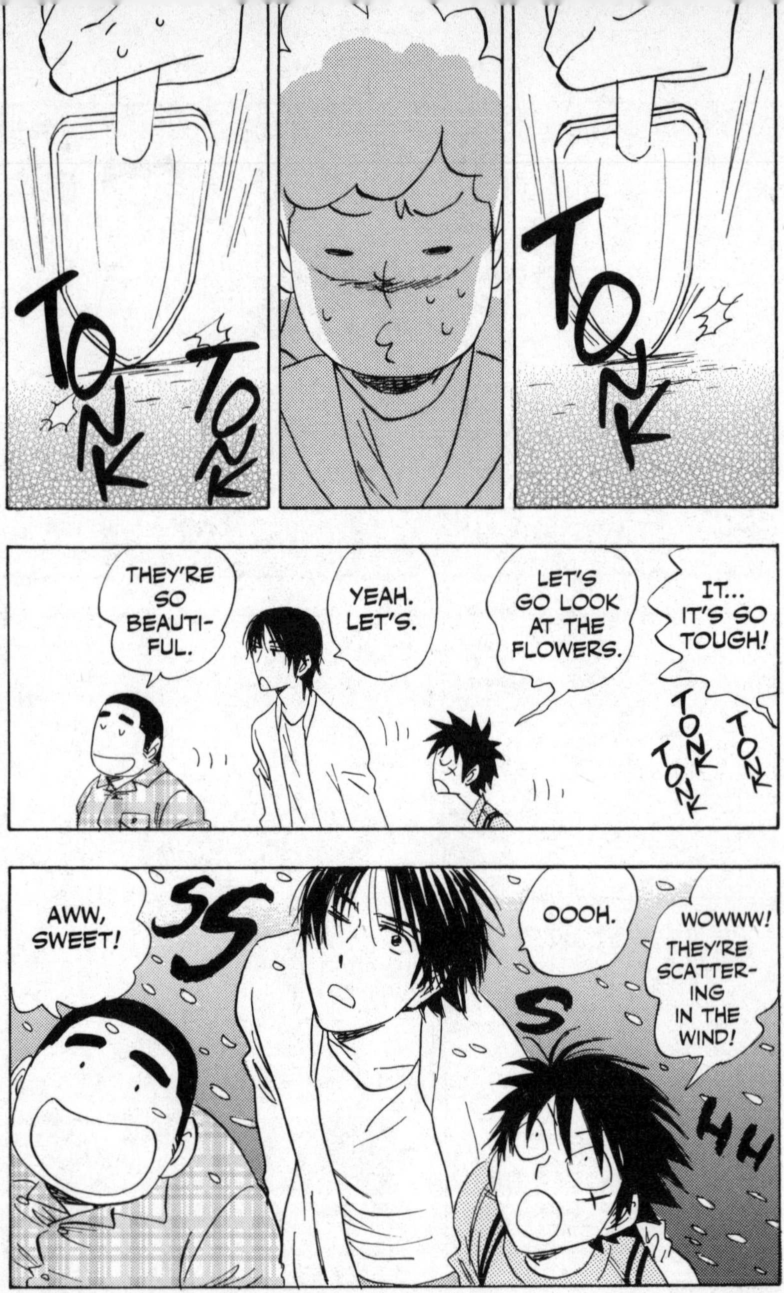
TONK
TONK
TONK
IT... IT'S SO TOUGH!
TONK
TONK
TONK
LET'S GO LOOK AT THE FLOWERS.
YEAH. LET'S.
THEY'RE SO BEAUTI-FUL.
WOWWW! THEY'RE SCATTER-ING IN THE WIND!
HH
S
OOOH.
SS
AWW, SWEET!

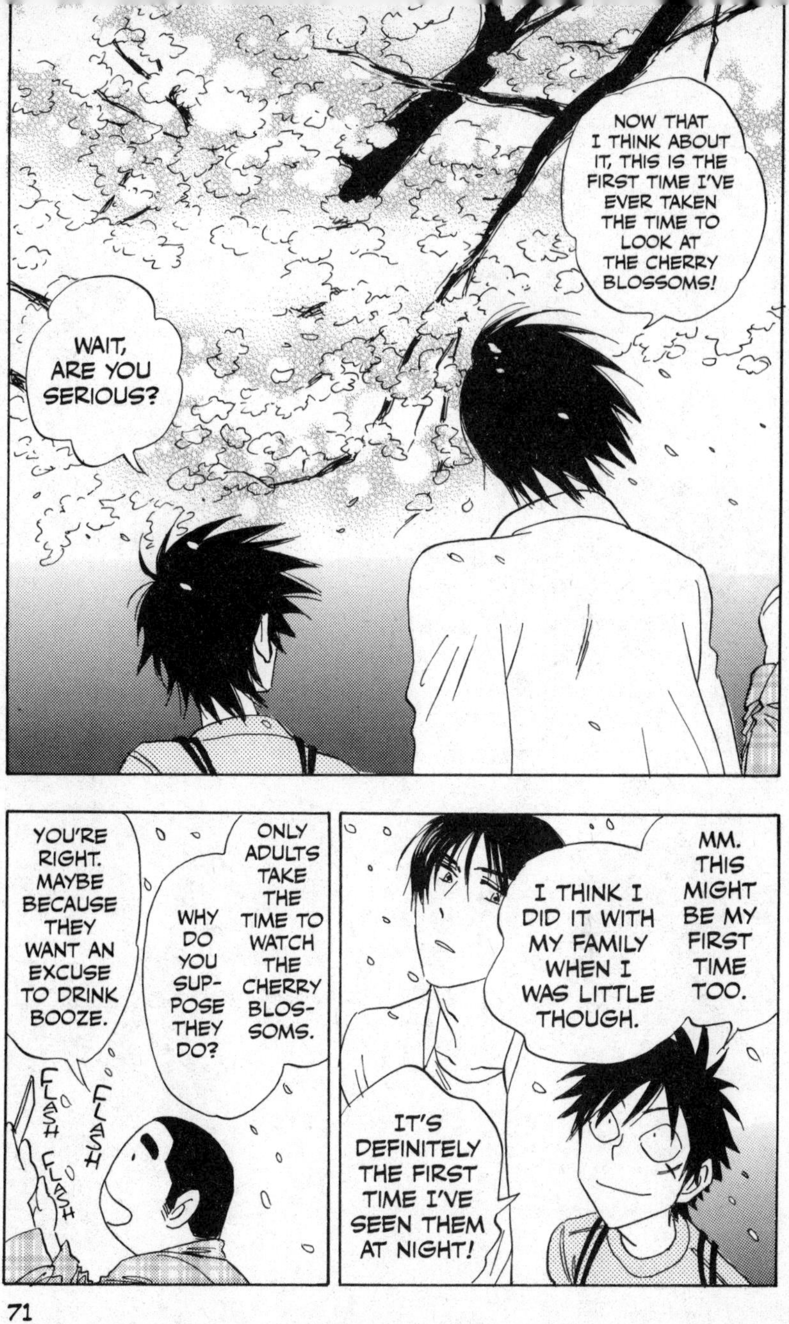
NOW THAT I THINK ABOUT IT, THIS IS THE FIRST TIME I'VE EVER TAKEN THE TIME TO LOOK AT THE CHERRY BLOSSOMS!
WAIT, ARE YOU SERIOUS?
MM. THIS MIGHT BE MY FIRST TIME TOO.
I THINK I DID IT WITH MY FAMILY WHEN I WAS LITTLE THOUGH.
IT'S DEFINITELY THE FIRST TIME I'VE SEEN THEM AT NIGHT!
ONLY ADULTS TAKE THE TIME TO WATCH THE CHERRY BLOSSOMS.
WHY DO YOU SUP-POSE THEY DO?
YOU'RE RIGHT. MAYBE BECAUSE THEY WANT AN EXCUSE TO DRINK BOOZE.
FLASH
FLASH FLASH

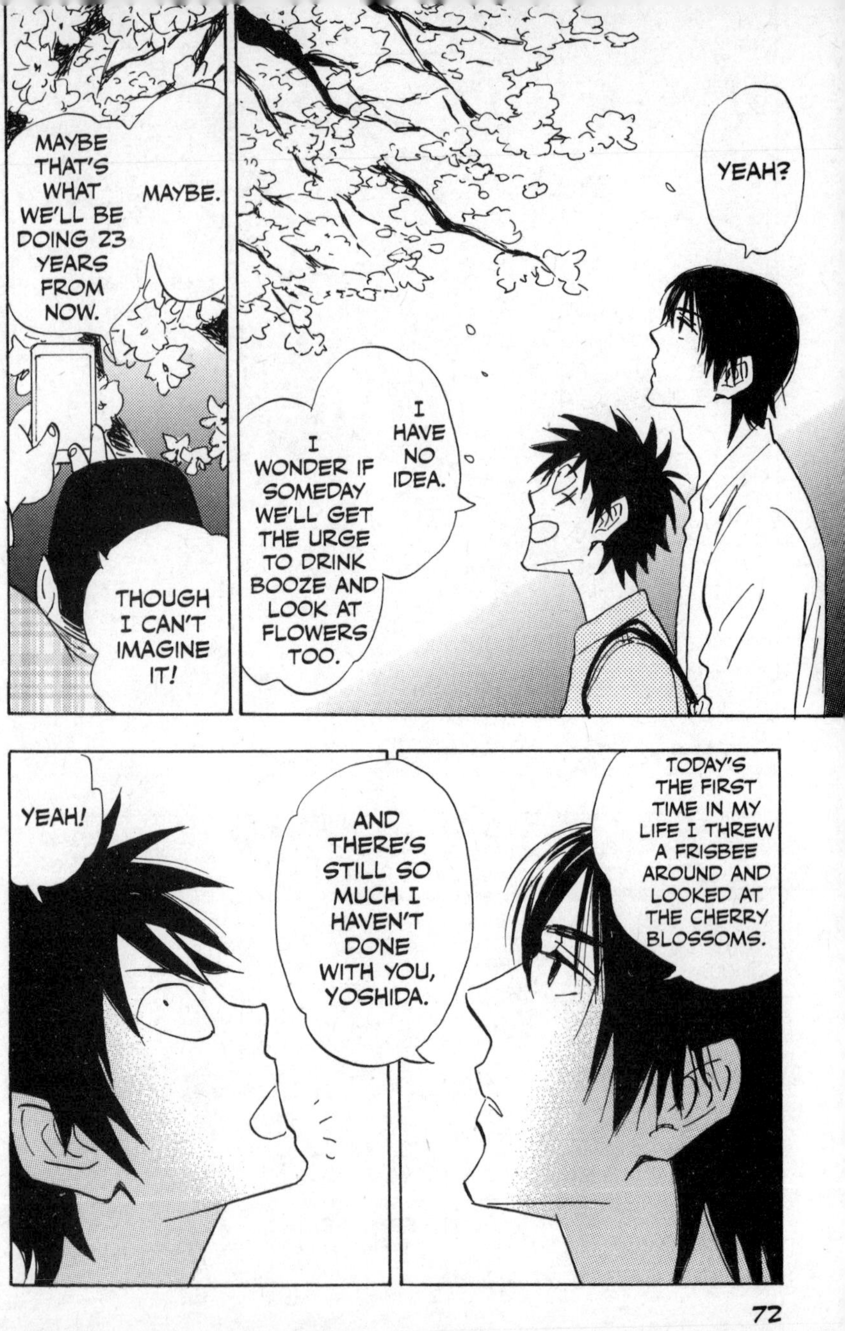
YEAH?
I HAVE NO IDEA.
I WONDER IF SOMEDAY WE'LL GET THE URGE TO DRINK BOOZE AND LOOK AT FLOWERS TOO.
MAYBE.
MAYBE THAT'S WHAT WE'LL BE DOING 23 YEARS FROM NOW.
THOUGH I CAN'T IMAGINE IT!
TODAY'S THE FIRST TIME IN MY LIFE I THREW A FRISBEE AROUND AND LOOKED AT THE CHERRY BLOSSOMS.
AND THERE'S STILL SO MUCH I HAVEN'T DONE WITH YOU, YOSHIDA.
YEAH!

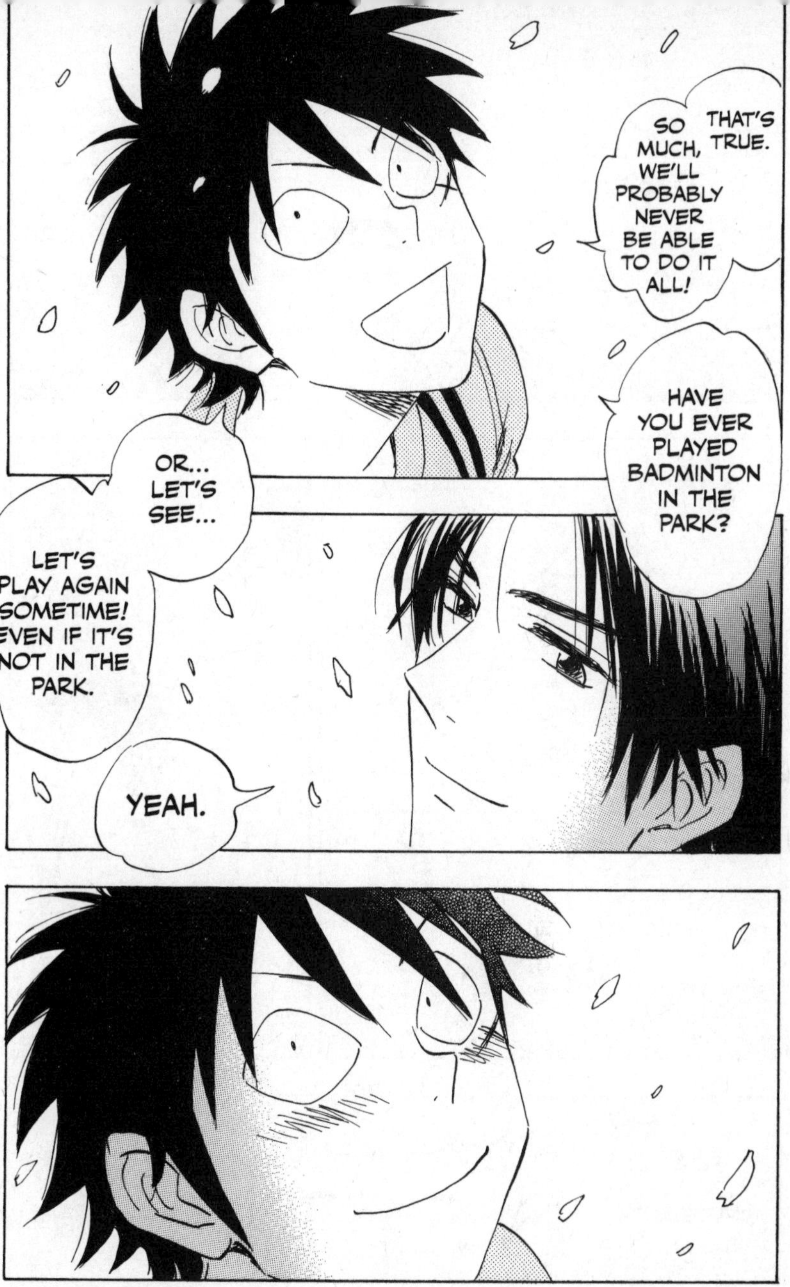
THAT'S TRUE.
SO MUCH, WE'LL PROBABLY NEVER BE ABLE TO DO IT ALL!
HAVE YOU EVER PLAYED BADMINTON IN THE PARK?
OR... LET'S SEE...
LET'S PLAY AGAIN SOMETIME! EVEN IF IT'S NOT IN THE PARK.
YEAH.

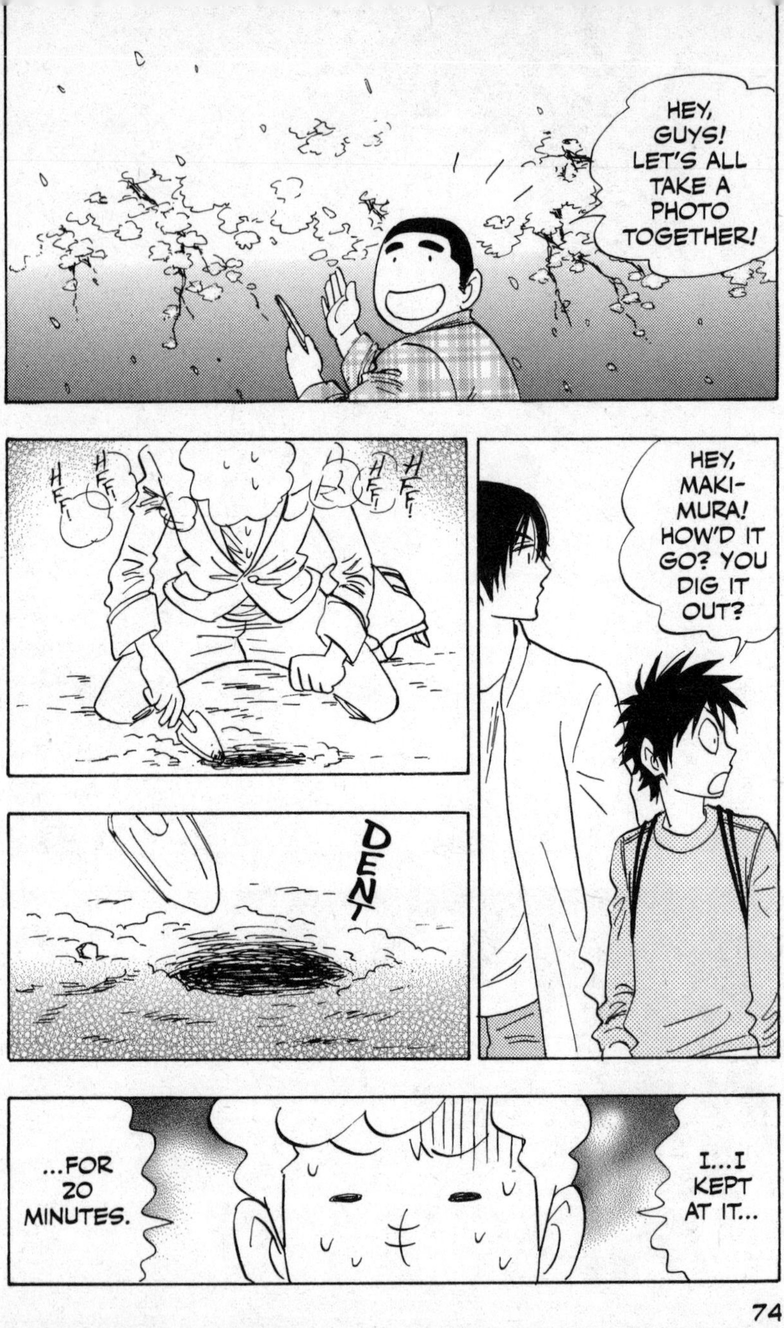
HEY, GUYS! LET'S ALL TAKE A PHOTO TOGETHER!
HEY, MAKI-MURA! HOW'D IT GO? YOU DIG IT OUT?
HFF! HFF!
HFF! HFF!
DENT
I...I KEPT AT IT...
...FOR 20 MINUTES.

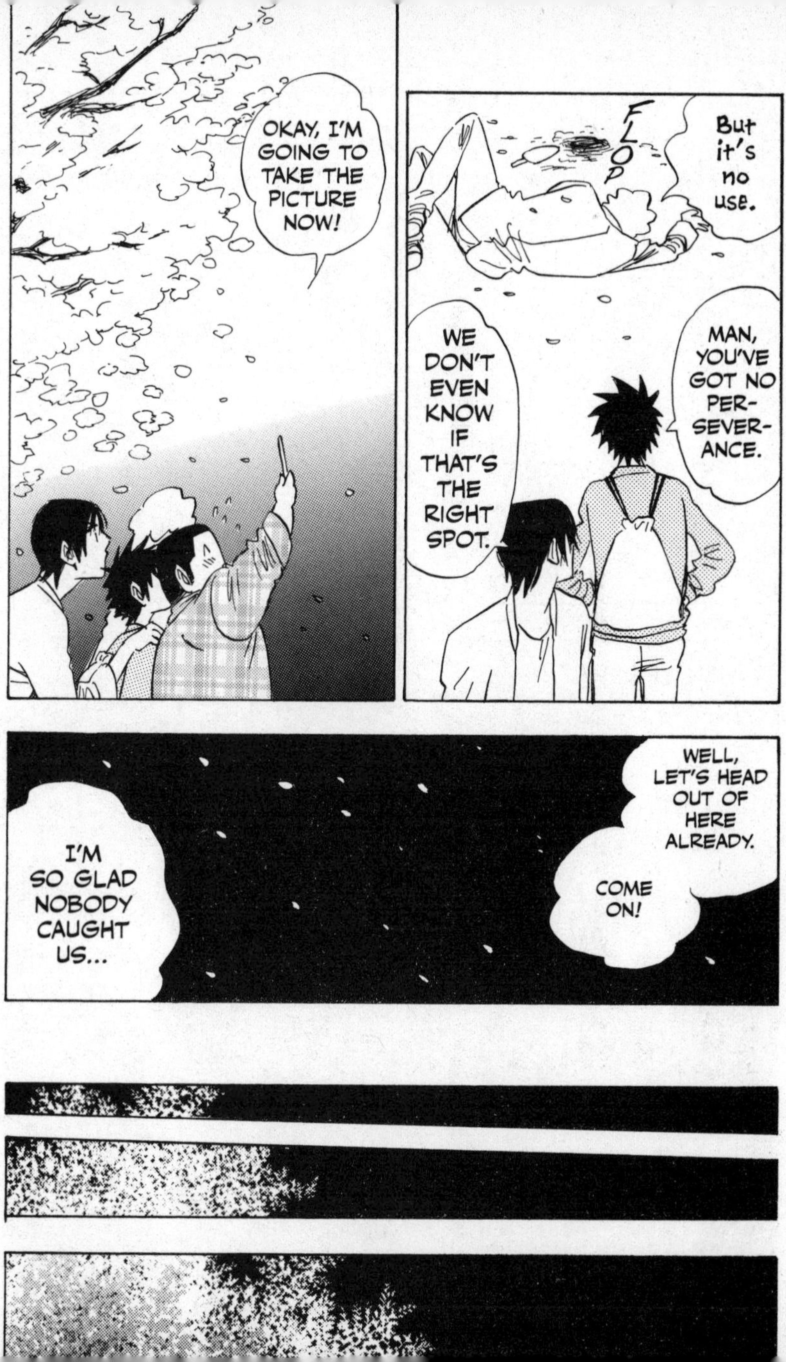
But it's no use.
FLOP
MAN, YOU'VE GOT NO PER-SEVERANCE.
WE DON'T EVEN KNOW IF THAT'S THE RIGHT SPOT.
OKAY, I'M GOING TO TAKE THE PICTURE NOW!
WELL, LET'S HEAD OUT OF HERE ALREADY.
COME ON!
I'M SO GLAD NOBODY CAUGHT US...

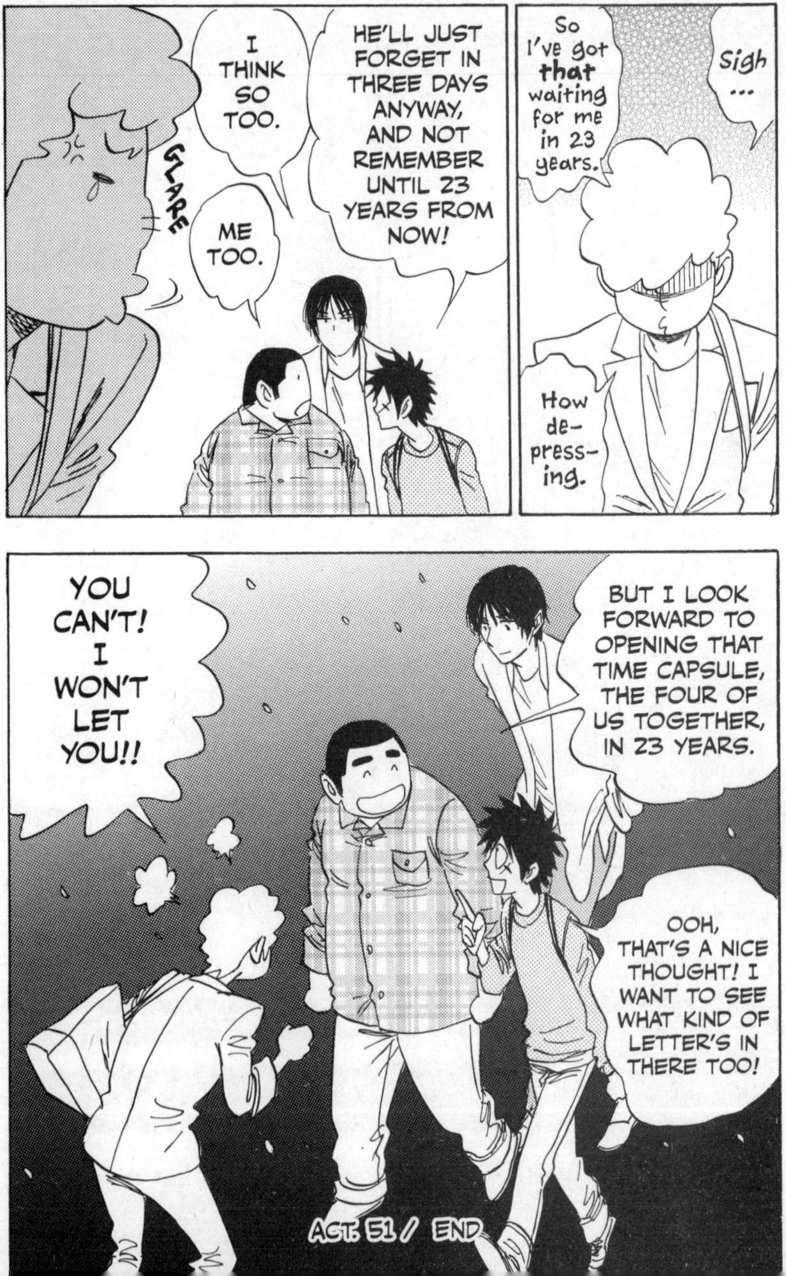
Sigh ...
So I've got **that** waiting for me in 23 years.
How de-press-ing.
HE'LL JUST FORGET IN THREE DAYS ANYWAY, AND NOT REMEMBER UNTIL 23 YEARS FROM NOW!
I THINK SO TOO.
ME TOO.
GLARE
BUT I LOOK FORWARD TO OPENING THAT TIME CAPSULE, THE FOUR OF US TOGETHER, IN 23 YEARS.
YOU CAN'T! I WON'T LET YOU!!
OOH, THAT'S A NICE THOUGHT! I WANT TO SEE WHAT KIND OF LETTER'S IN THERE TOO!
ACT. 51 / END

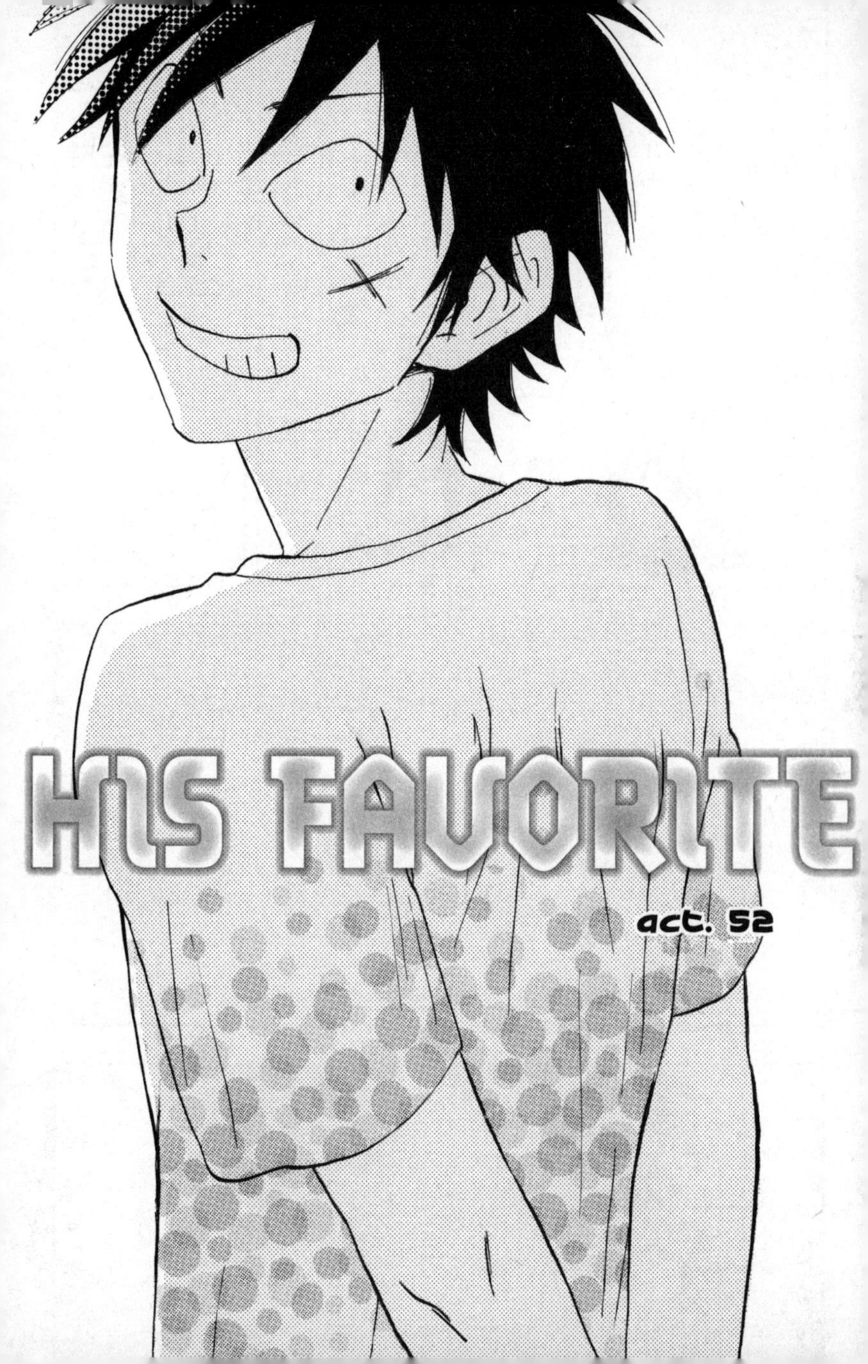
HIS FAVORITE
act. 52

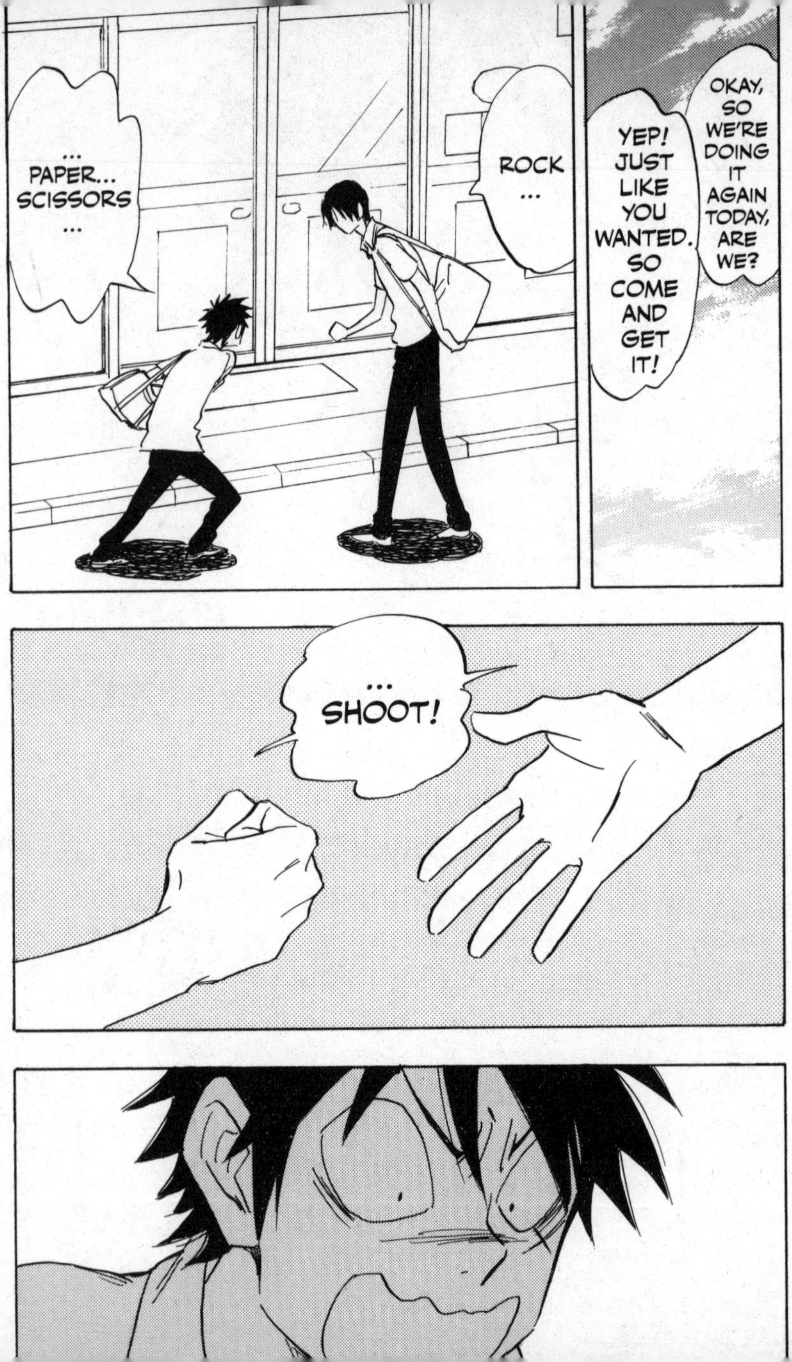
OKAY, SO WE'RE DOING IT AGAIN TODAY, ARE WE?
YEP! JUST LIKE YOU WANTED. SO COME AND GET IT!
ROCK ...
... PAPER... SCISSORS ...
... SHOOT!

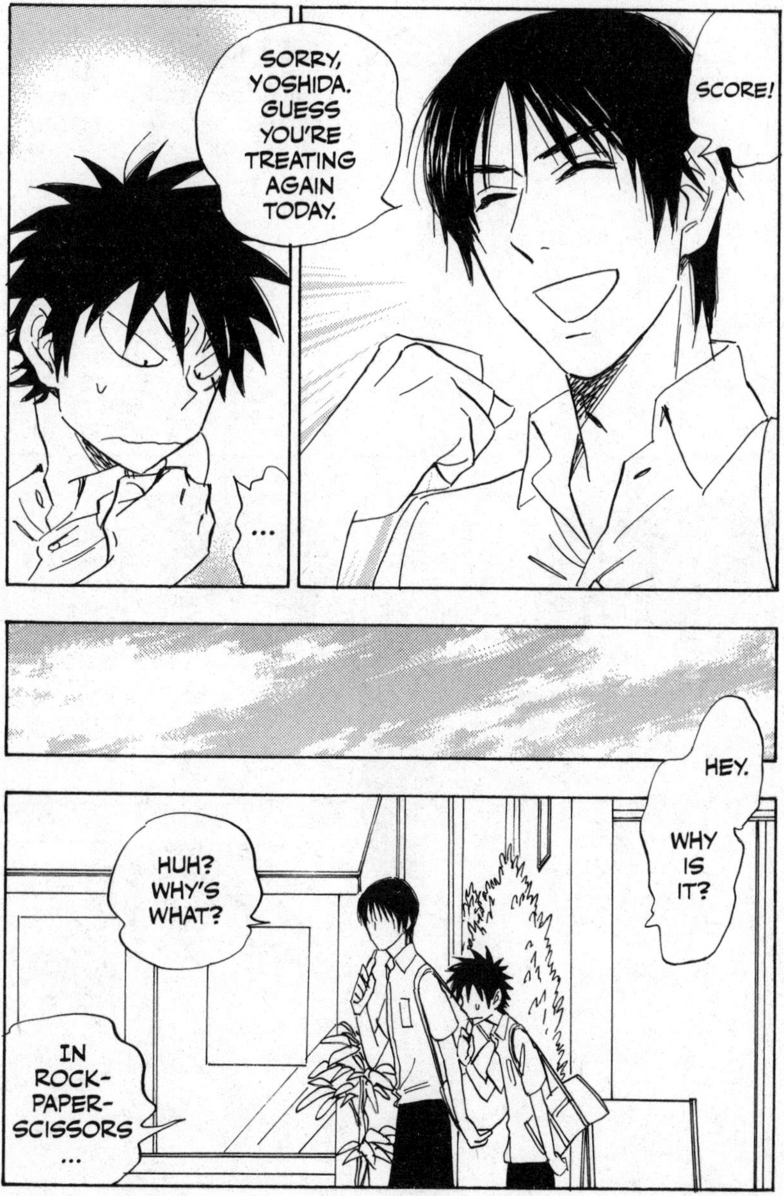
SCORE!
SORRY, YOSHIDA. GUESS YOU'RE TREATING AGAIN TODAY.
...
HEY.
WHY IS IT?
HUH? WHY'S WHAT?
IN ROCK-PAPER-SCISSORS...

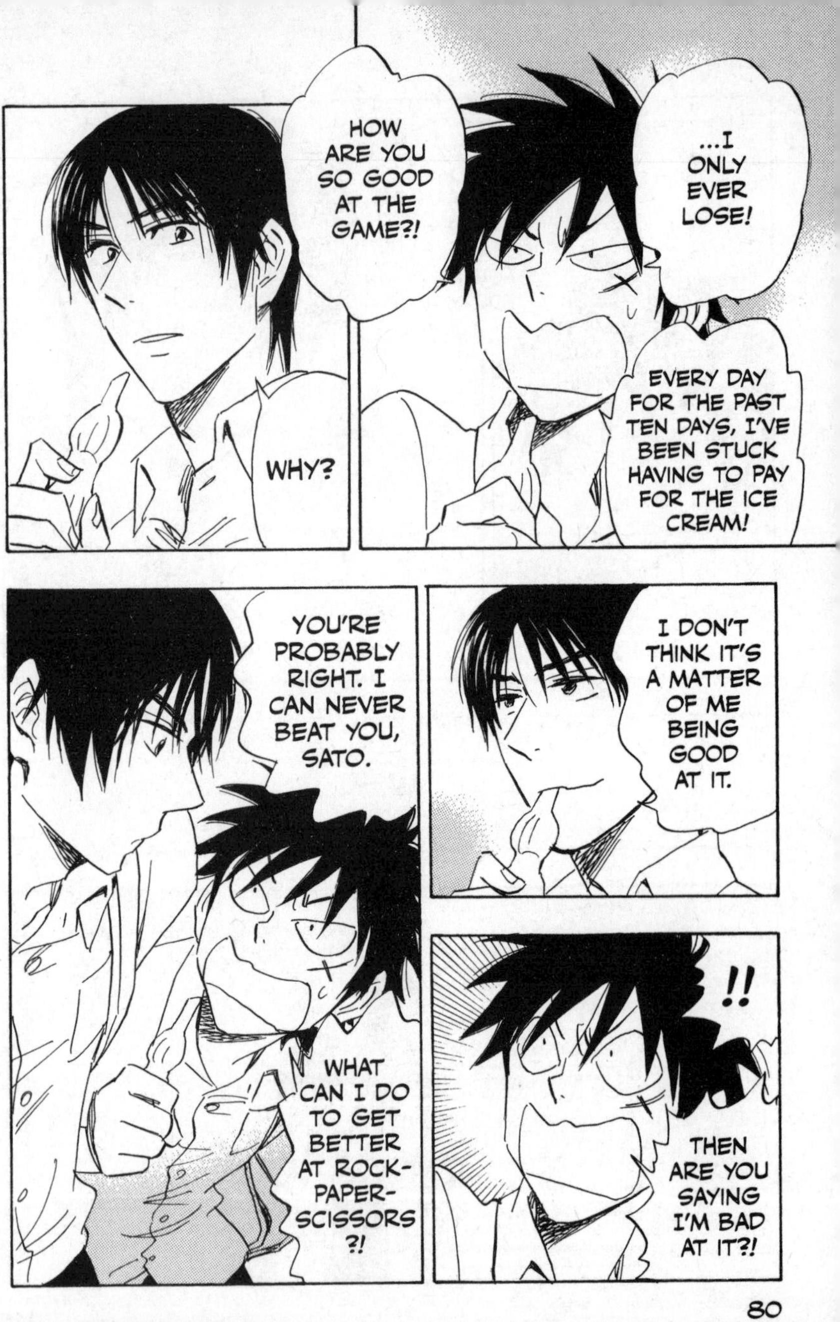
...I ONLY EVER LOSE!
EVERY DAY FOR THE PAST TEN DAYS, I'VE BEEN STUCK HAVING TO PAY FOR THE ICE CREAM!
HOW ARE YOU SO GOOD AT THE GAME?!
WHY?
I DON'T THINK IT'S A MATTER OF ME BEING GOOD AT IT.
!!
THEN ARE YOU SAYING I'M BAD AT IT?!
YOU'RE PROBABLY RIGHT. I CAN NEVER BEAT YOU, SATO.
WHAT CAN I DO TO GET BETTER AT ROCK-PAPER-SCISSORS?!

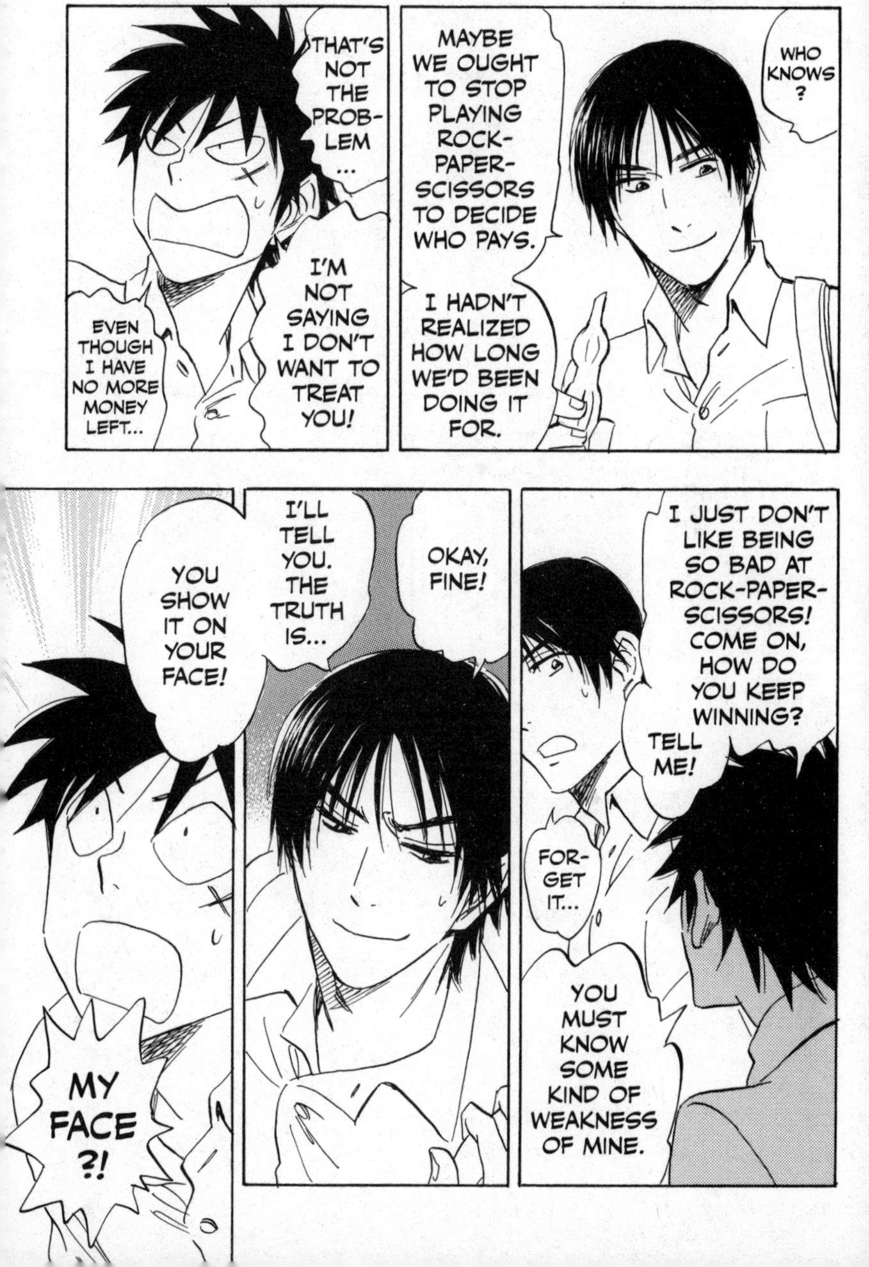
WHO KNOWS?
MAYBE WE OUGHT TO STOP PLAYING ROCK-PAPER-SCISSORS TO DECIDE WHO PAYS.
I HADN'T REALIZED HOW LONG WE'D BEEN DOING IT FOR.
THAT'S NOT THE PROBLEM...
I'M NOT SAYING I DON'T WANT TO TREAT YOU!
EVEN THOUGH I HAVE NO MORE MONEY LEFT...
I JUST DON'T LIKE BEING SO BAD AT ROCK-PAPER-SCISSORS! COME ON, HOW DO YOU KEEP WINNING?
TELL ME!
FORGET IT...
YOU MUST KNOW SOME KIND OF WEAKNESS OF MINE.
OKAY, FINE!
I'LL TELL YOU. THE TRUTH IS...
YOU SHOW IT ON YOUR FACE!
MY FACE?!

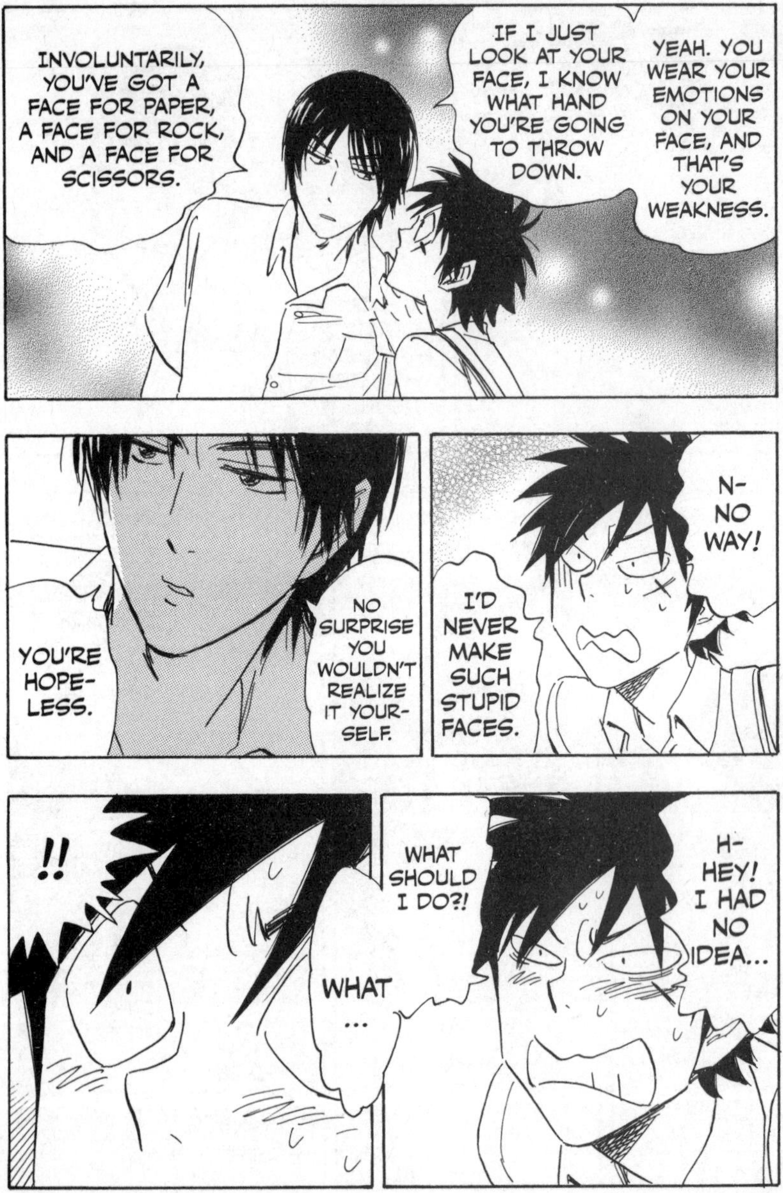
YEAH. YOU WEAR YOUR EMOTIONS ON YOUR FACE, AND THAT'S YOUR WEAKNESS.
IF I JUST LOOK AT YOUR FACE, I KNOW WHAT HAND YOU'RE GOING TO THROW DOWN.
INVOLUNTARILY, YOU'VE GOT A FACE FOR PAPER, A FACE FOR ROCK, AND A FACE FOR SCISSORS.
N- NO WAY!
I'D NEVER MAKE SUCH STUPID FACES.
NO SURPRISE YOU WOULDN'T REALIZE IT YOUR-SELF.
YOU'RE HOPE-LESS.
H- HEY! I HAD NO IDEA...
WHAT SHOULD I DO?!
WHAT ...
!!

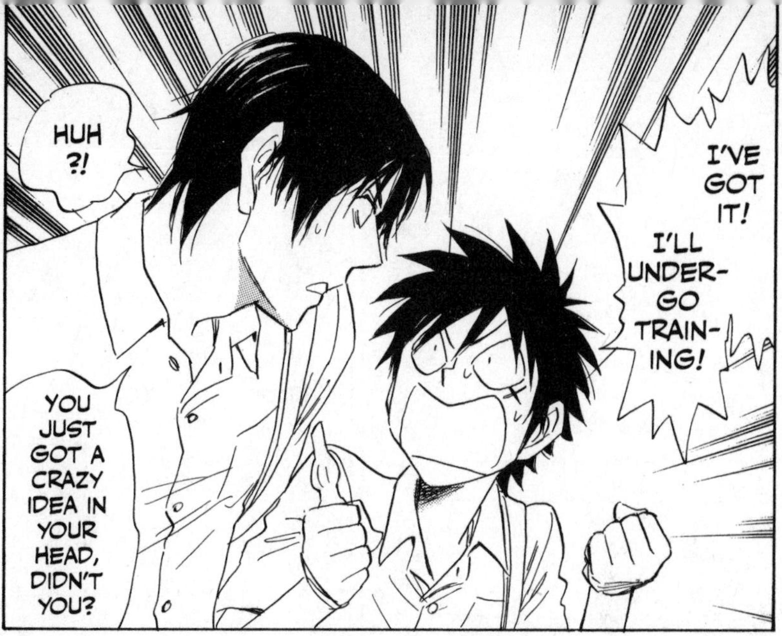
I'VE GOT IT!
I'LL UNDER-GO TRAIN-ING!
HUH ?!
YOU JUST GOT A CRAZY IDEA IN YOUR HEAD, DIDN'T YOU?

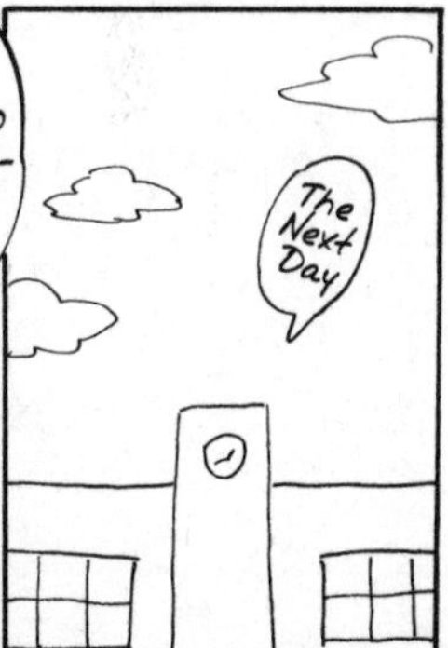
The Next Day

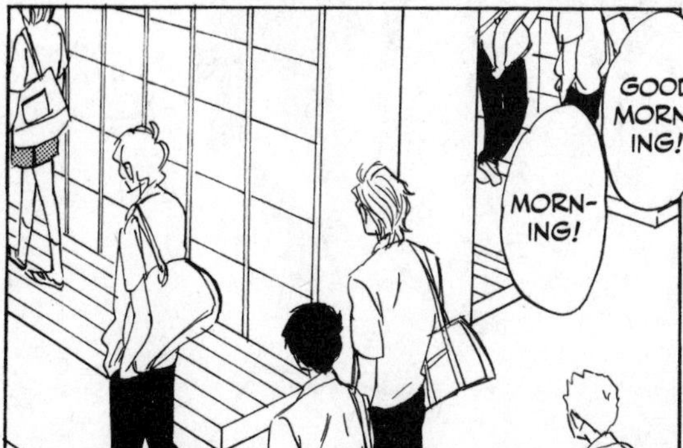
GOOD MORN-ING!
MORN-ING!

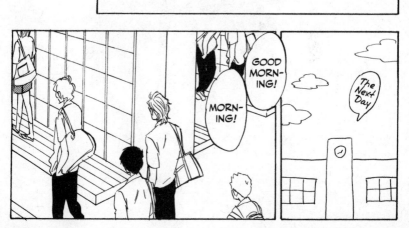

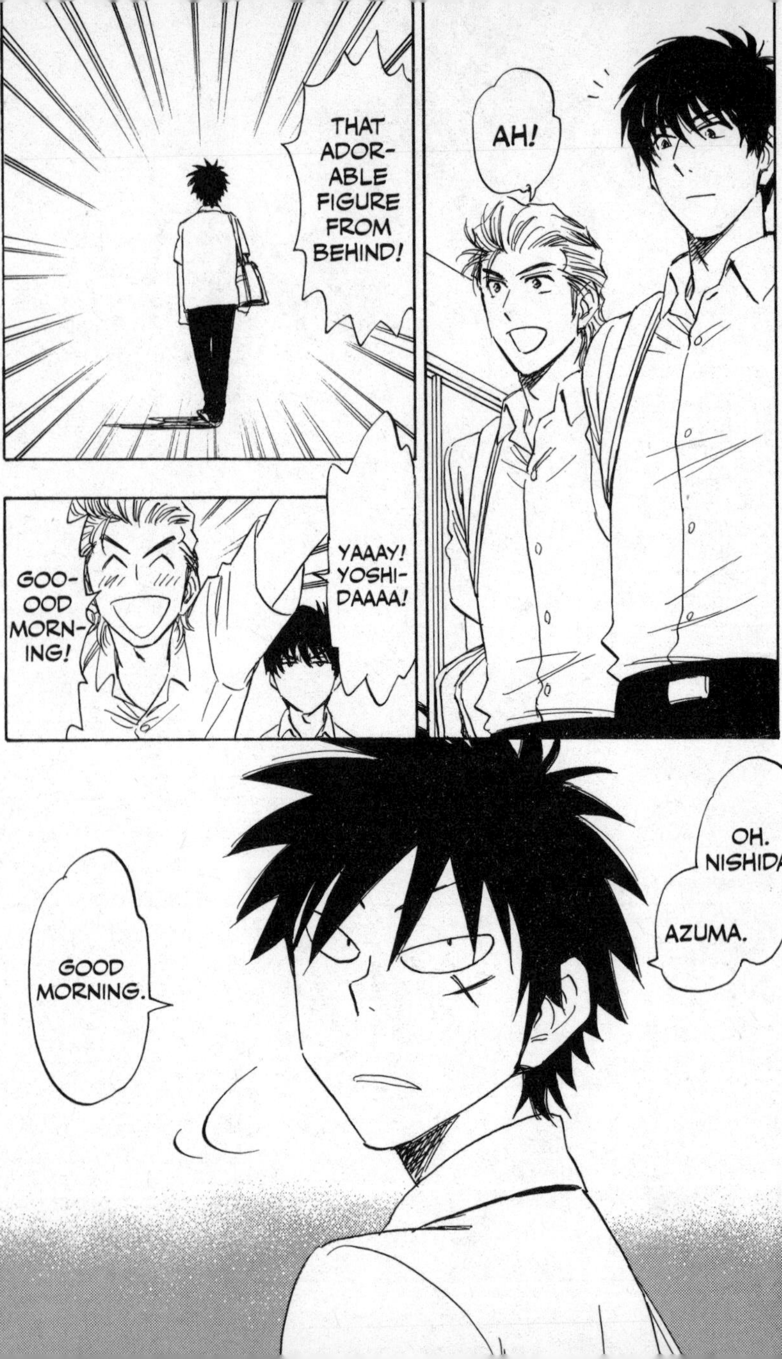
AH!
THAT ADORABLE FIGURE FROM BEHIND!
YAAAY! YOSHIDAAAA!
GOO-OOD MORNING!
OH. NISHIDA.
AZUMA.
GOOD MORNING.

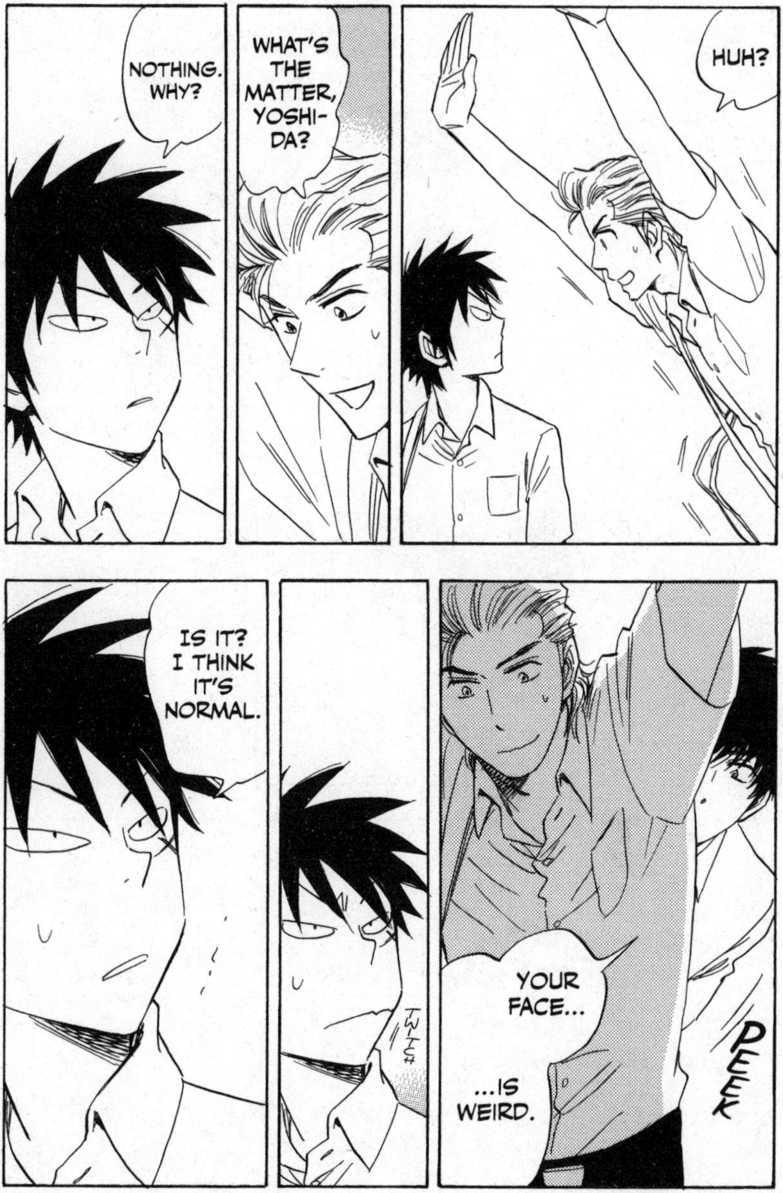
HUH?
WHAT'S THE MATTER, YOSHIDA?
NOTHING. WHY?
YOUR FACE...
...IS WEIRD.
PEEK
TWITCH
IS IT? I THINK IT'S NORMAL.

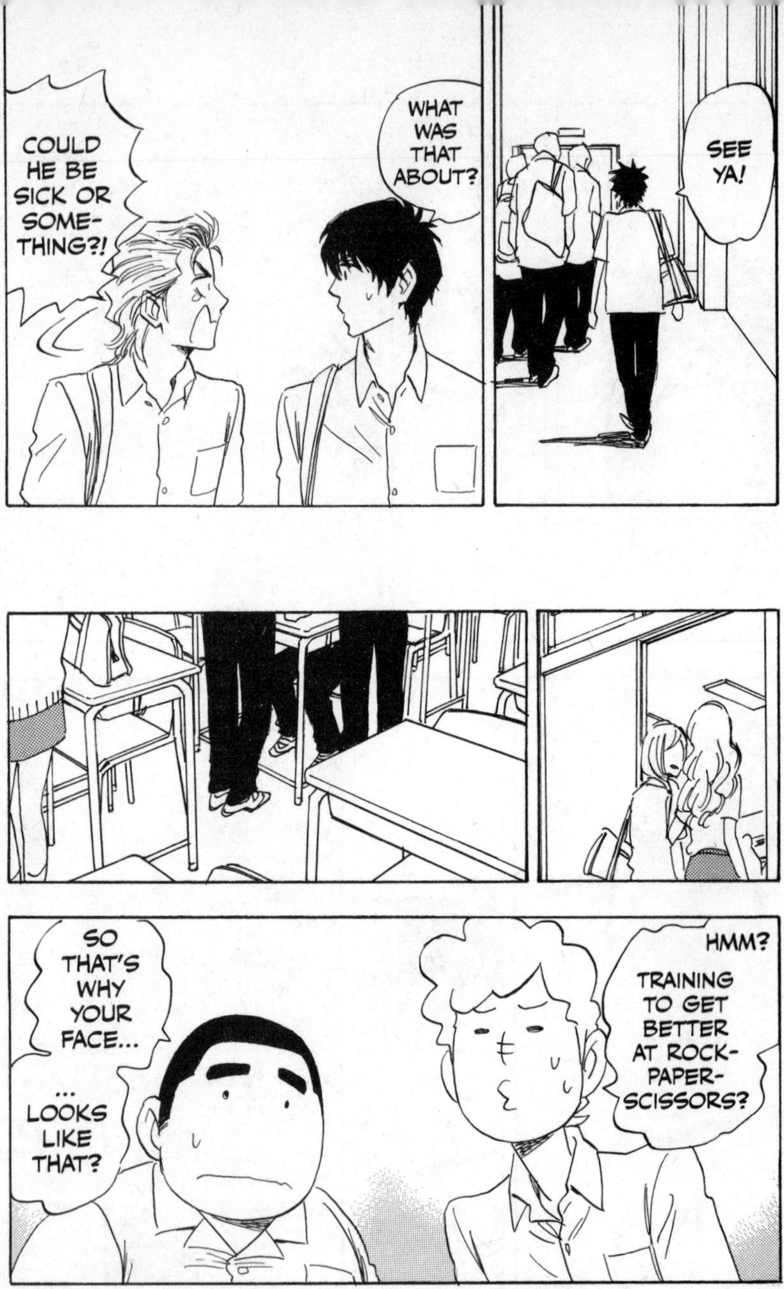
SEE YA!
WHAT WAS THAT ABOUT?
COULD HE BE SICK OR SOMETHING?!
HMM?
TRAINING TO GET BETTER AT ROCK-PAPER-SCISSORS?
SO THAT'S WHY YOUR FACE...
...LOOKS LIKE THAT?

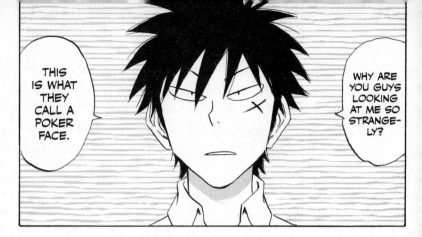

WHY ARE YOU GUYS LOOKING AT ME SO STRANGE-LY?
THIS IS WHAT THEY CALL A POKER FACE.
POKER ...
... FACE!
THAT'S RIGHT! TO GET BETTER AT ROCK-PAPER-SCISSORS, IT'S ALL ABOUT NOT LETTING IT SHOW ON MY FACE.
IN OTHER WORDS, I SHOULD ALWAYS KEEP MY FACE EXPRESSION-LESS!
HAH!
HEY, DON'T LAUGH!
OOPS.

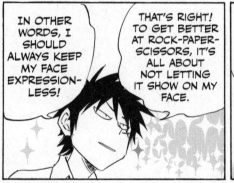

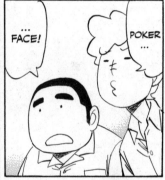

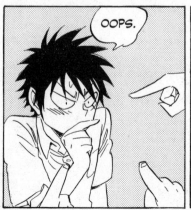

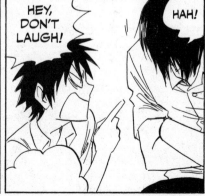

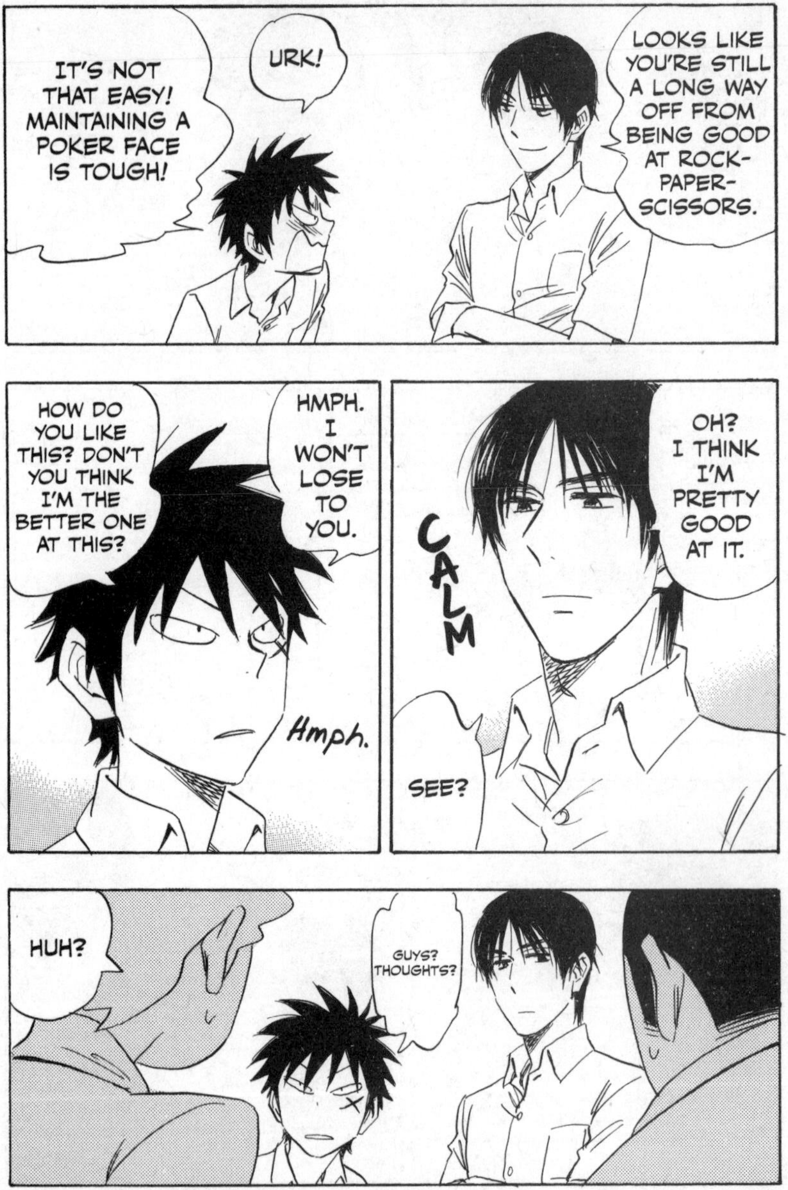
LOOKS LIKE YOU'RE STILL A LONG WAY OFF FROM BEING GOOD AT ROCK-PAPER-SCISSORS.
URK!
IT'S NOT THAT EASY! MAINTAINING A POKER FACE IS TOUGH!
OH? I THINK I'M PRETTY GOOD AT IT.
CALM
SEE?
HMPH. I WON'T LOSE TO YOU.
HOW DO YOU LIKE THIS? DON'T YOU THINK I'M THE BETTER ONE AT THIS?
Hmph.
GUYS? THOUGHTS?
HUH?

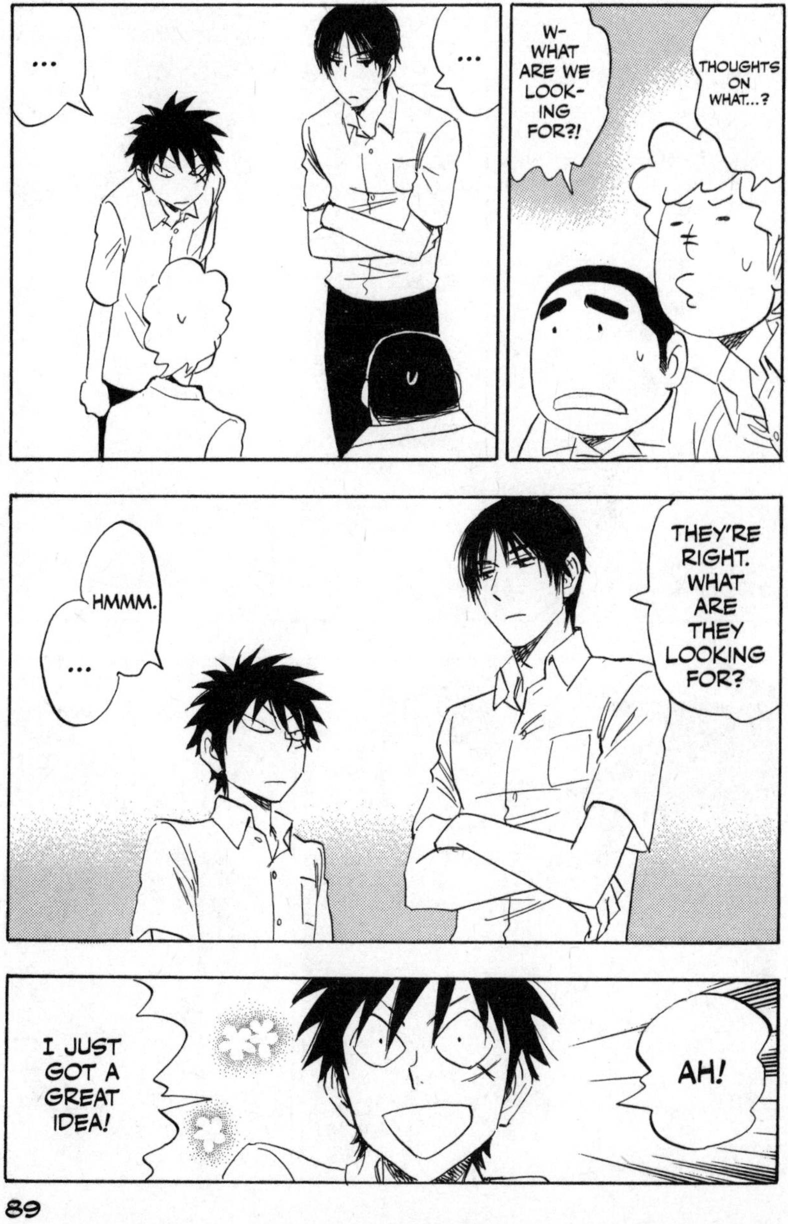
THOUGHTS ON WHAT...?
W- WHAT ARE WE LOOK-ING FOR?!
...
...
THEY'RE RIGHT. WHAT ARE THEY LOOKING FOR?
HMMM.
...
AH!
I JUST GOT A GREAT IDEA!

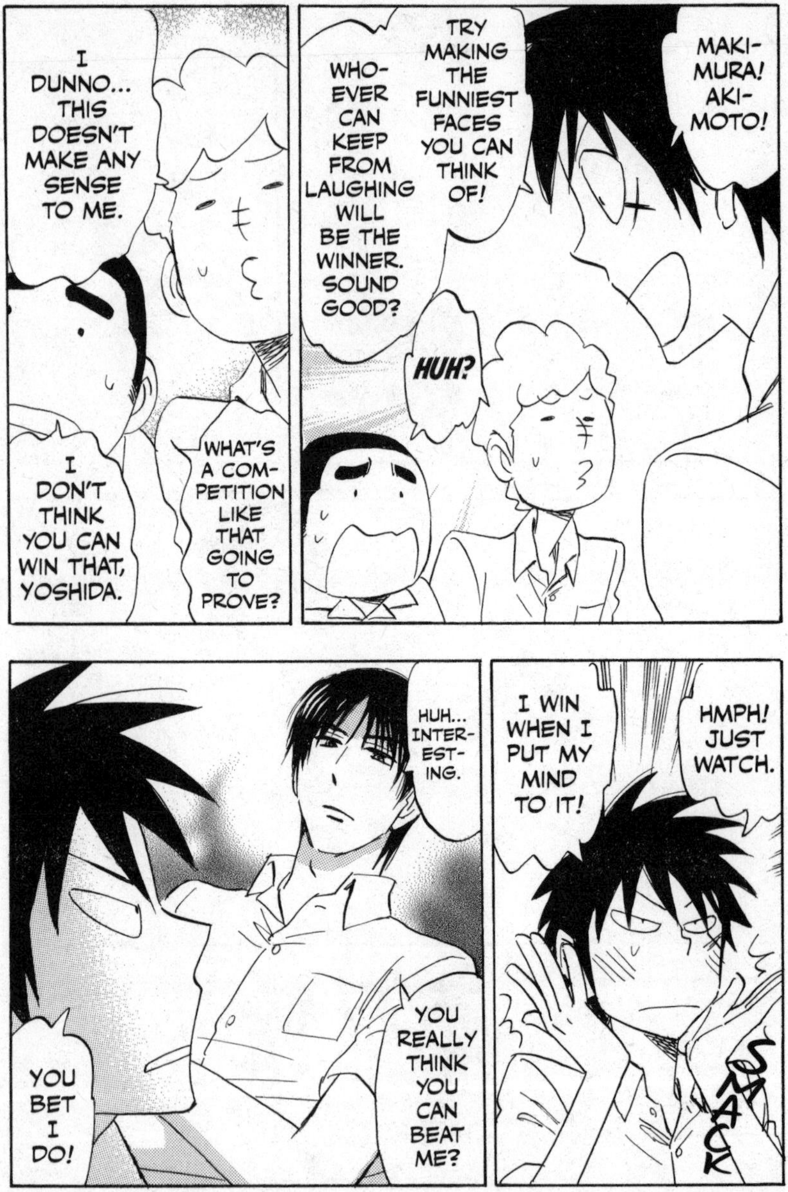
MAKI-MURA! AKI-MOTO!
TRY MAKING THE FUNNIEST FACES YOU CAN THINK OF!
WHO-EVER CAN KEEP FROM LAUGHING WILL BE THE WINNER. SOUND GOOD?
HUH?
I DUNNO... THIS DOESN'T MAKE ANY SENSE TO ME.
WHAT'S A COM-PETITION LIKE THAT GOING TO PROVE?
I DON'T THINK YOU CAN WIN THAT, YOSHIDA.
HMPH! JUST WATCH.
I WIN WHEN I PUT MY MIND TO IT!
SMACK
HUH... INTER-EST-ING.
YOU REALLY THINK YOU CAN BEAT ME?
YOU BET I DO!

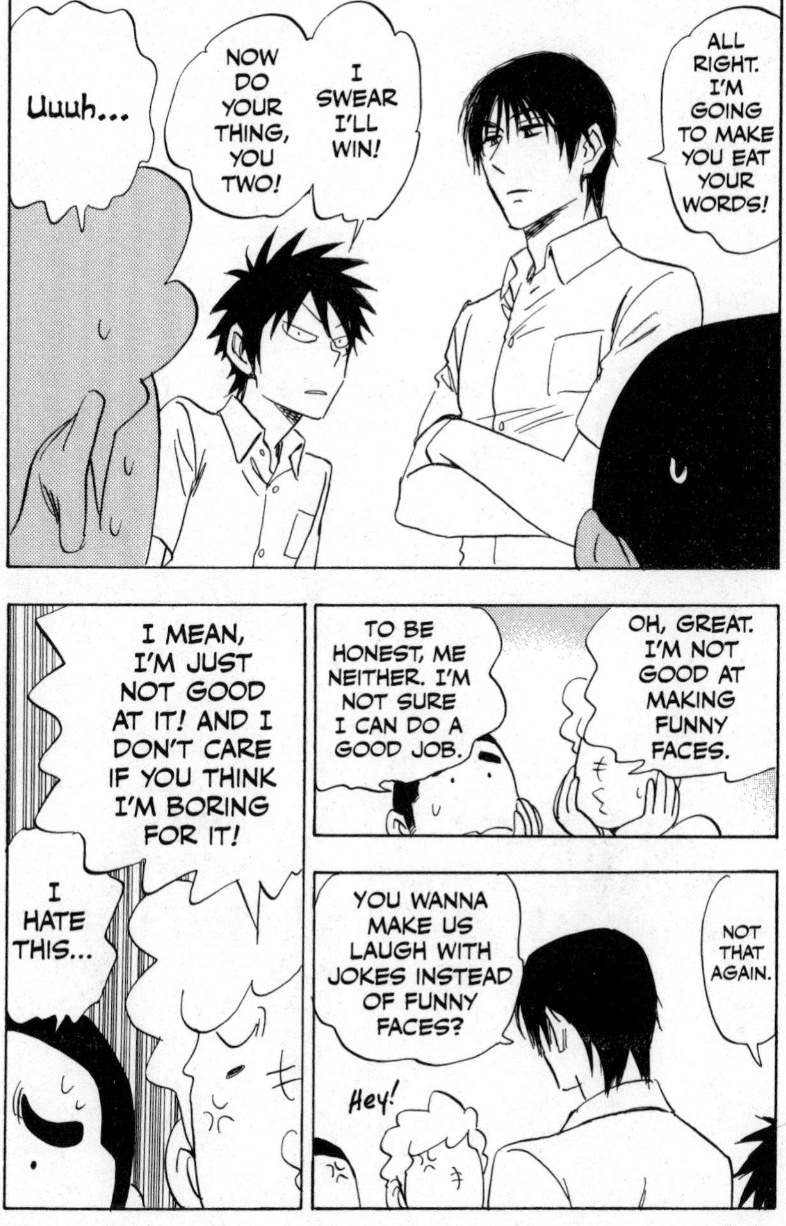
ALL RIGHT. I'M GOING TO MAKE YOU EAT YOUR WORDS!
I SWEAR I'LL WIN!
NOW DO YOUR THING, YOU TWO!
Uuuh...
OH, GREAT. I'M NOT GOOD AT MAKING FUNNY FACES.
TO BE HONEST, ME NEITHER. I'M NOT SURE I CAN DO A GOOD JOB.
NOT THAT AGAIN.
YOU WANNA MAKE US LAUGH WITH JOKES INSTEAD OF FUNNY FACES?
Hey!
I MEAN, I'M JUST NOT GOOD AT IT! AND I DON'T CARE IF YOU THINK I'M BORING FOR IT!
I HATE THIS...

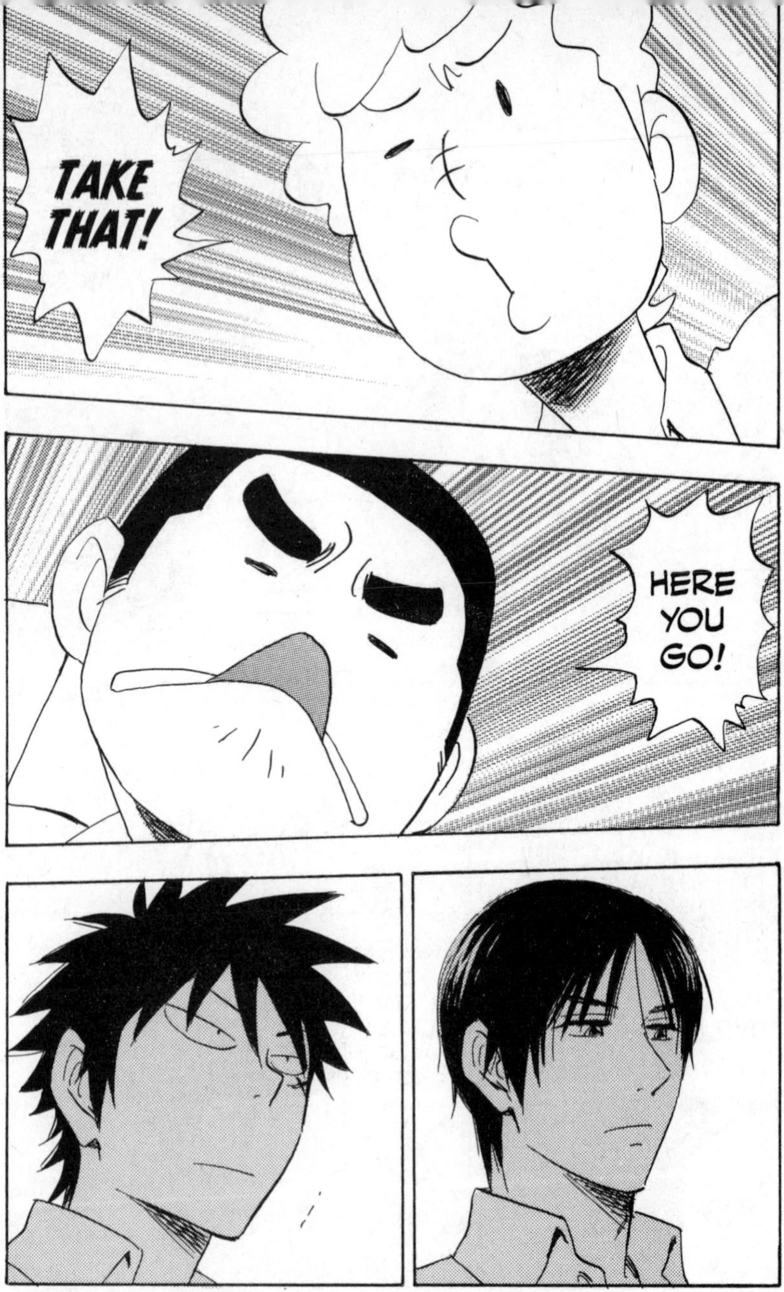
TAKE THAT!
HERE YOU GO!

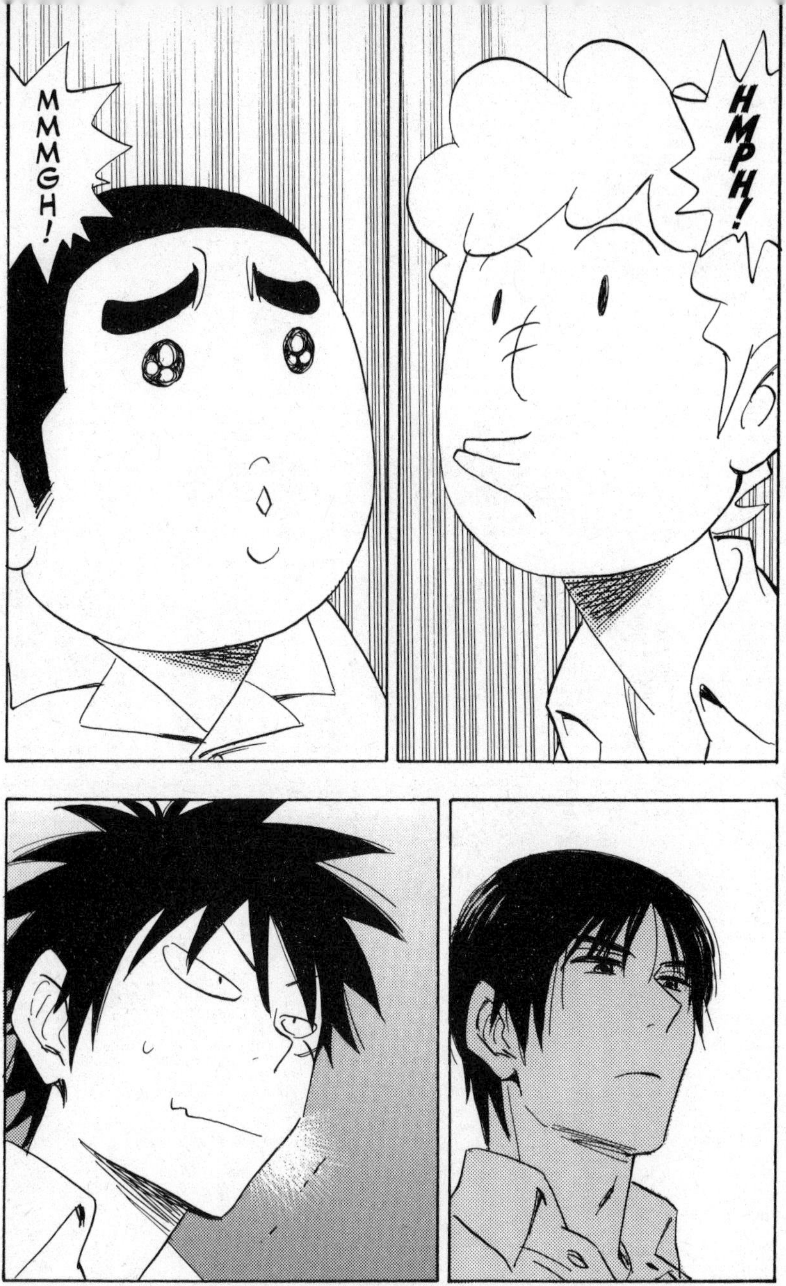
HMPH!
MMMGH!

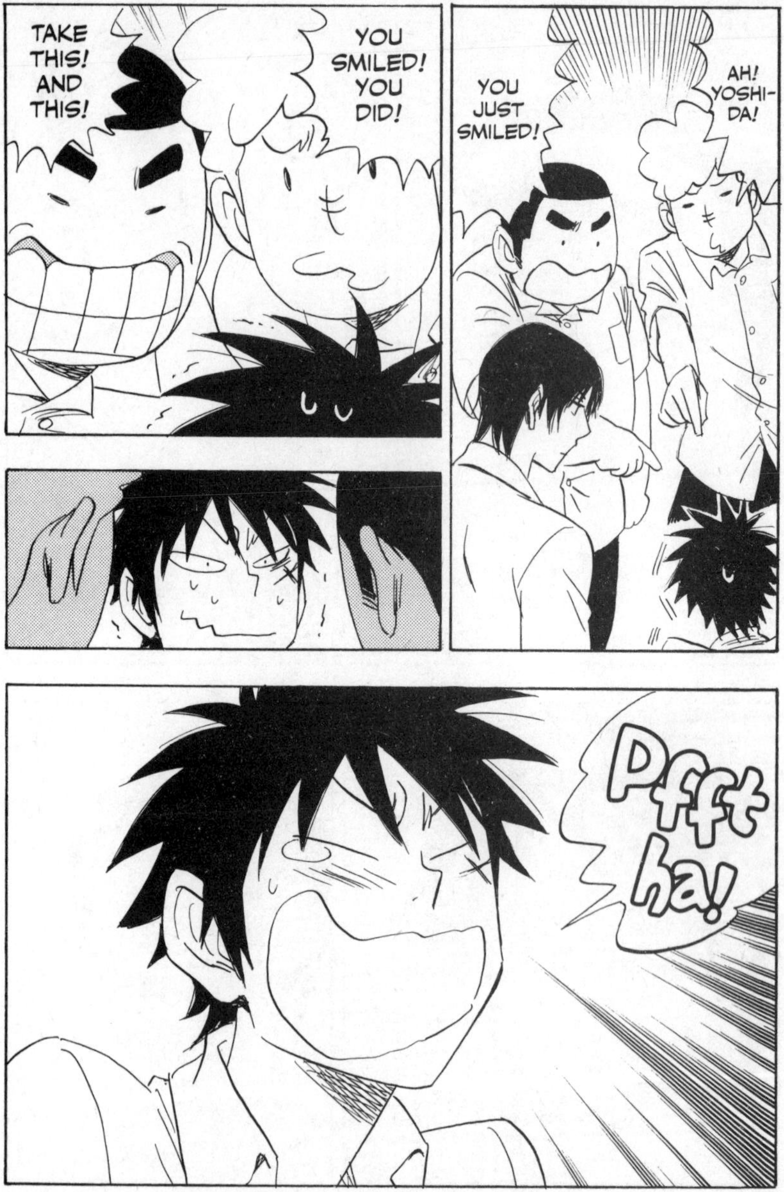
AH! YOSHI-DA!
YOU JUST SMILED!
YOU SMILED! YOU DID!
TAKE THIS! AND THIS!
Pfft ha!

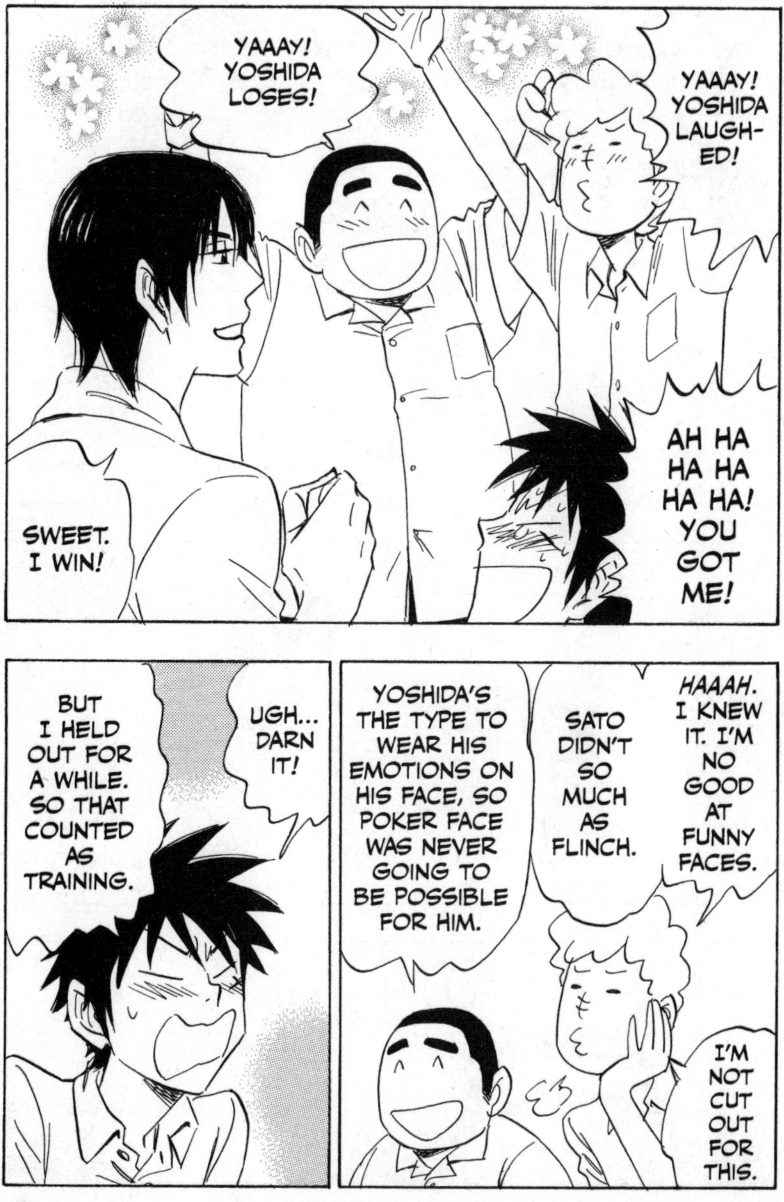
YAAAY! YOSHIDA LAUGHED!
YAAAY! YOSHIDA LOSES!
AH HA HA HA HA HA! YOU GOT ME!
SWEET. I WIN!
HAAAH. I KNEW IT. I'M NO GOOD AT FUNNY FACES.
SATO DIDN'T SO MUCH AS FLINCH.
YOSHIDA'S THE TYPE TO WEAR HIS EMOTIONS ON HIS FACE, SO POKER FACE WAS NEVER GOING TO BE POSSIBLE FOR HIM.
I'M NOT CUT OUT FOR THIS.
UGH... DARN IT!
BUT I HELD OUT FOR A WHILE. SO THAT COUNTED AS TRAINING.

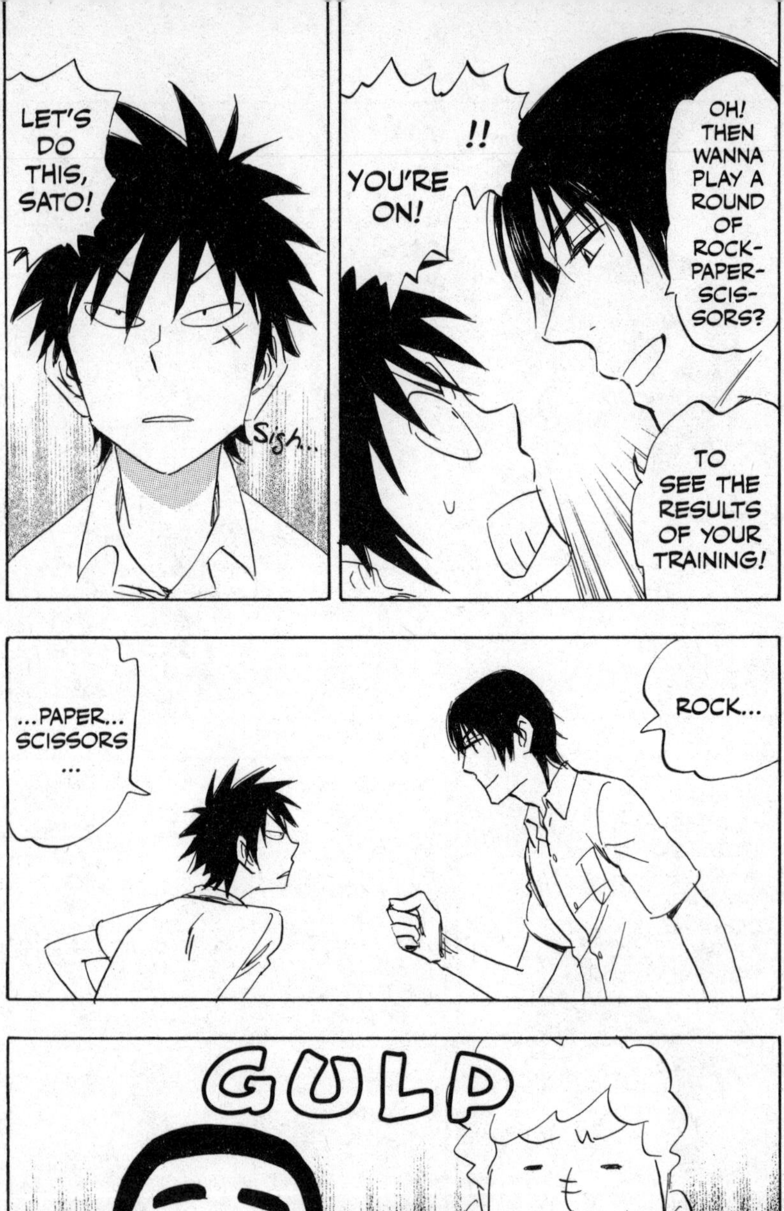
OH! THEN WANNA PLAY A ROUND OF ROCK-PAPER-SCISSORS?
TO SEE THE RESULTS OF YOUR TRAINING!
!!
YOU'RE ON!
LET'S DO THIS, SATO!
Sish...
ROCK...
...PAPER... SCISSORS ...
GULP

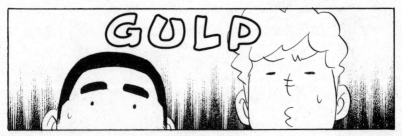

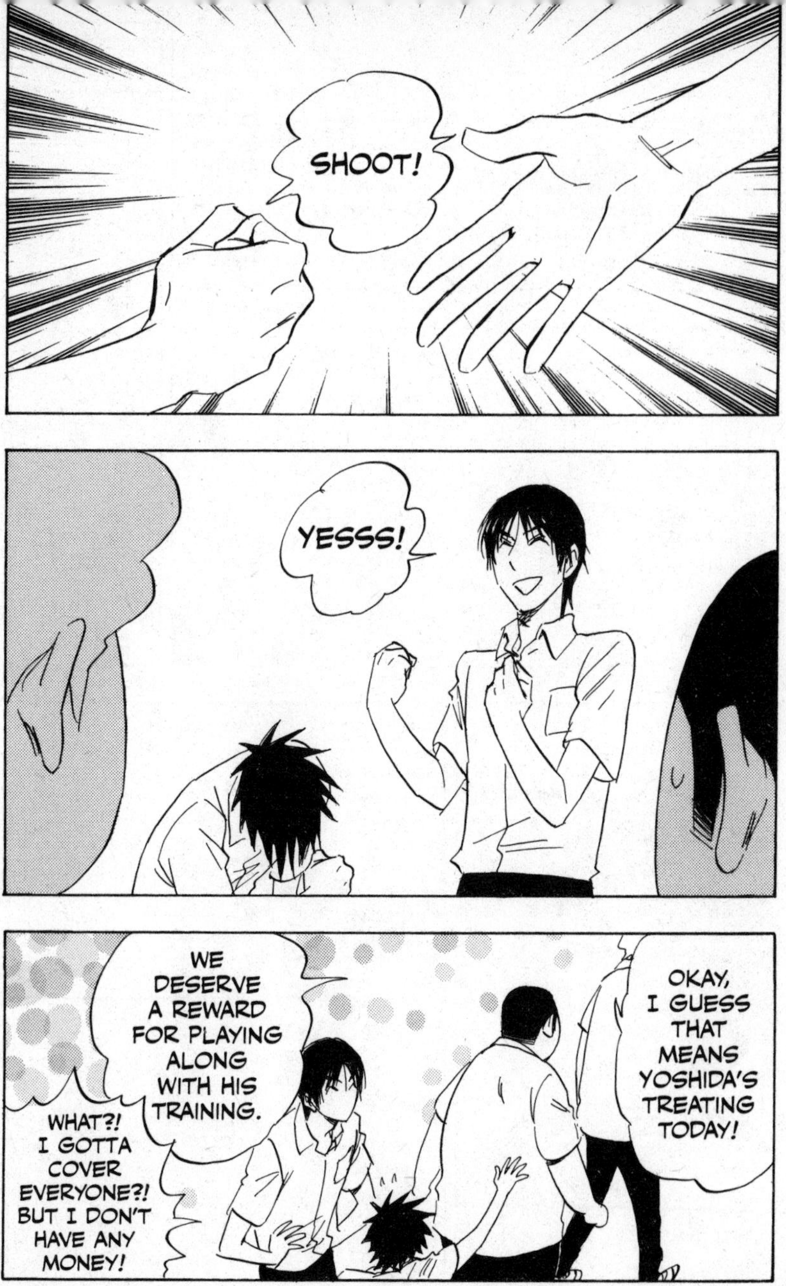
SHOOT!
YESSS!
OKAY, I GUESS THAT MEANS YOSHIDA'S TREATING TODAY!
WE DESERVE A REWARD FOR PLAYING ALONG WITH HIS TRAINING.
WHAT?! I GOTTA COVER EVERYONE?! BUT I DON'T HAVE ANY MONEY!

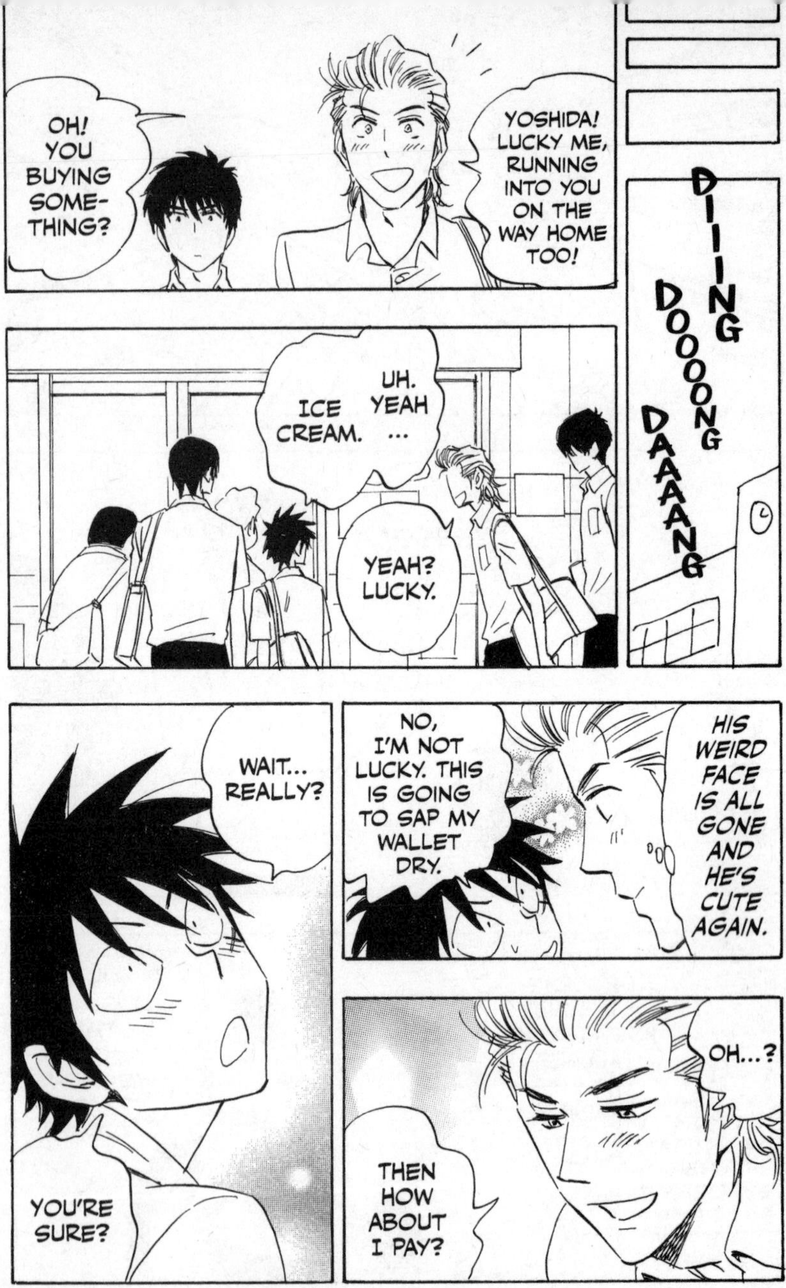
DIIING DOOOONG DAAAANG
YOSHIDA! LUCKY ME, RUNNING INTO YOU ON THE WAY HOME TOO!
OH! YOU BUYING SOME-THING?
UH. YEAH ...
ICE CREAM.
YEAH? LUCKY.
HIS WEIRD FACE IS ALL GONE AND HE'S CUTE AGAIN.
NO, I'M NOT LUCKY. THIS IS GOING TO SAP MY WALLET DRY.
OH...?
THEN HOW ABOUT I PAY?
WAIT... REALLY?
YOU'RE SURE?

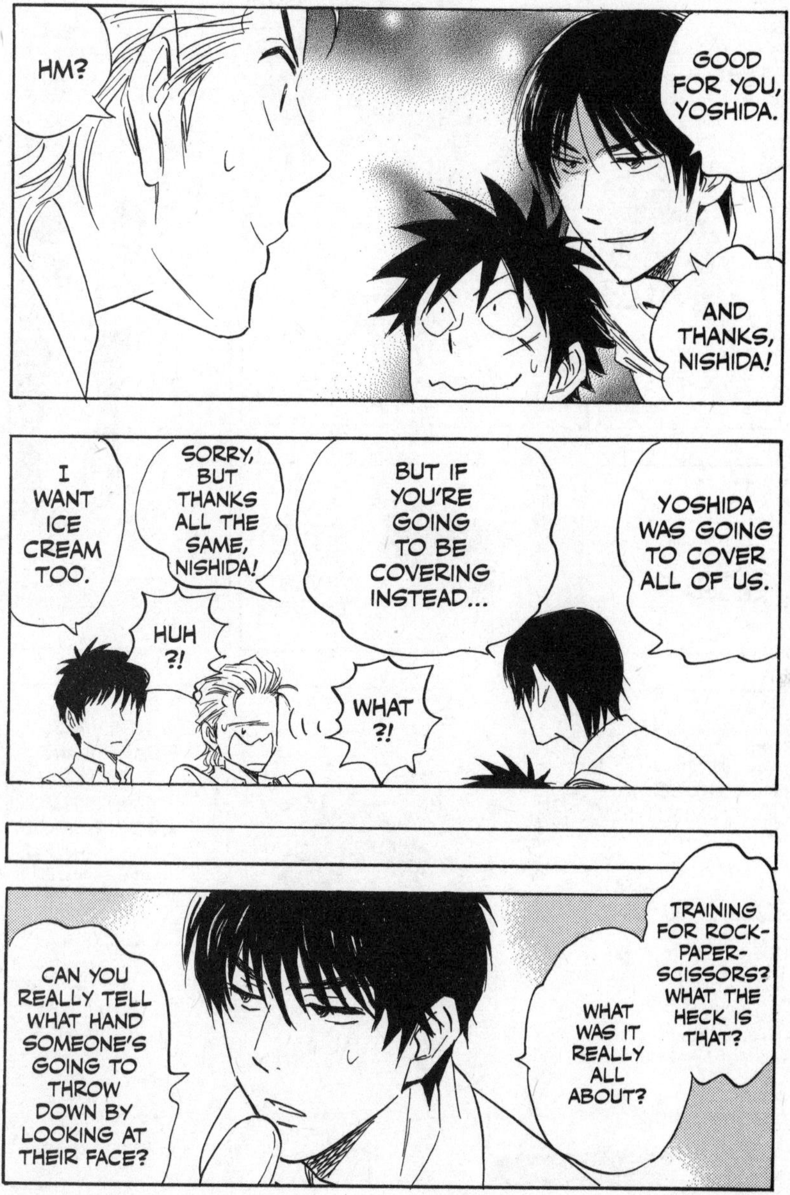
GOOD FOR YOU, YOSHIDA.
AND THANKS, NISHIDA!
HM?
YOSHIDA WAS GOING TO COVER ALL OF US.
BUT IF YOU'RE GOING TO BE COVERING INSTEAD...
WHAT ?!
SORRY, BUT THANKS ALL THE SAME, NISHIDA!
HUH ?!
I WANT ICE CREAM TOO.
TRAINING FOR ROCK-PAPER-SCISSORS? WHAT THE HECK IS THAT?
WHAT WAS IT REALLY ALL ABOUT?
CAN YOU REALLY TELL WHAT HAND SOMEONE'S GOING TO THROW DOWN BY LOOKING AT THEIR FACE?

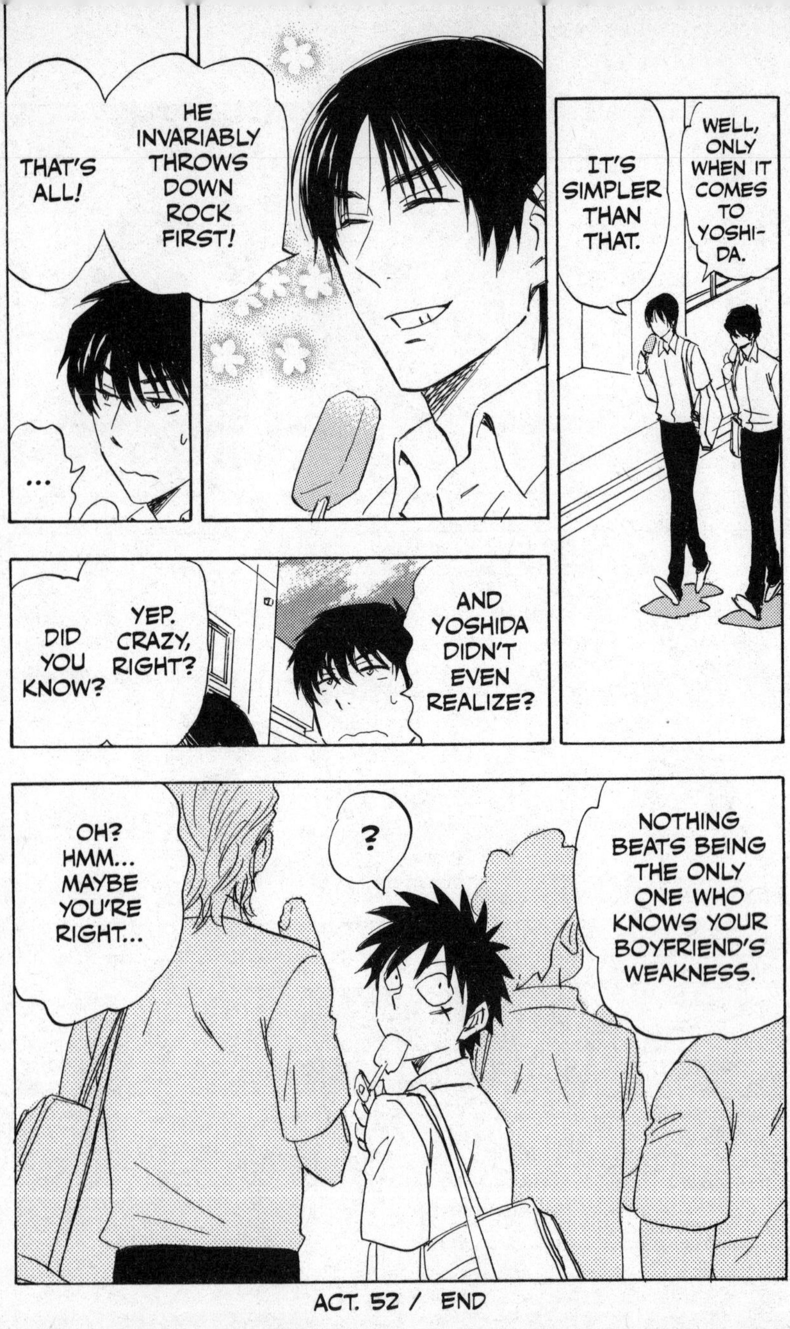
WELL, ONLY WHEN IT COMES TO YOSHIDA.
IT'S SIMPLER THAN THAT.
HE INVARIABLY THROWS DOWN ROCK FIRST!
THAT'S ALL!
...
AND YOSHIDA DIDN'T EVEN REALIZE?
YEP. CRAZY, RIGHT?
DID YOU KNOW?
NOTHING BEATS BEING THE ONLY ONE WHO KNOWS YOUR BOYFRIEND'S WEAKNESS.
?
OH? HMM... MAYBE YOU'RE RIGHT...

ACT. 52 / END

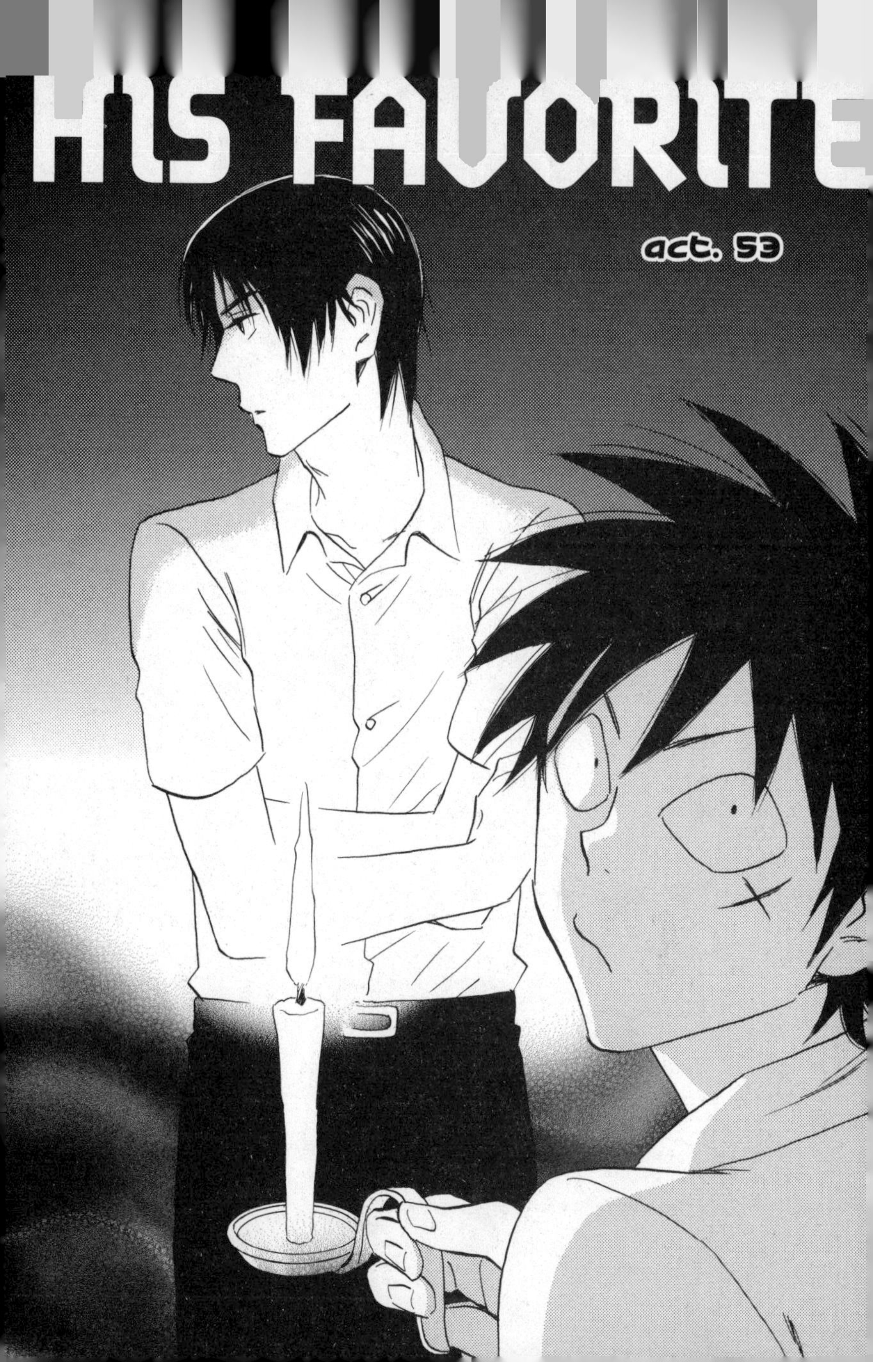
HIS FAVORITE
act. 53

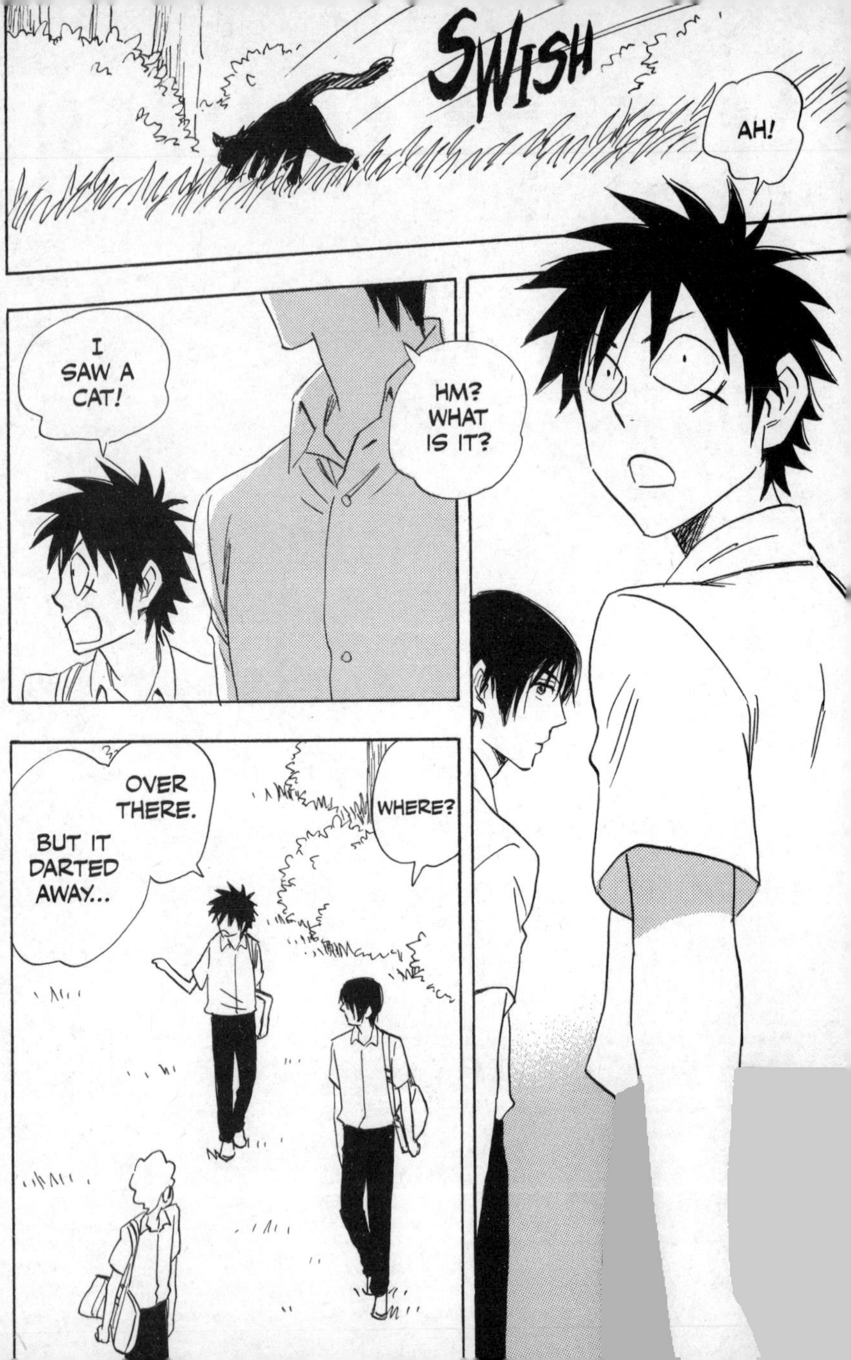
SWISH
AH!
HM? WHAT IS IT?
I SAW A CAT!
WHERE?
OVER THERE.
BUT IT DARTED AWAY...

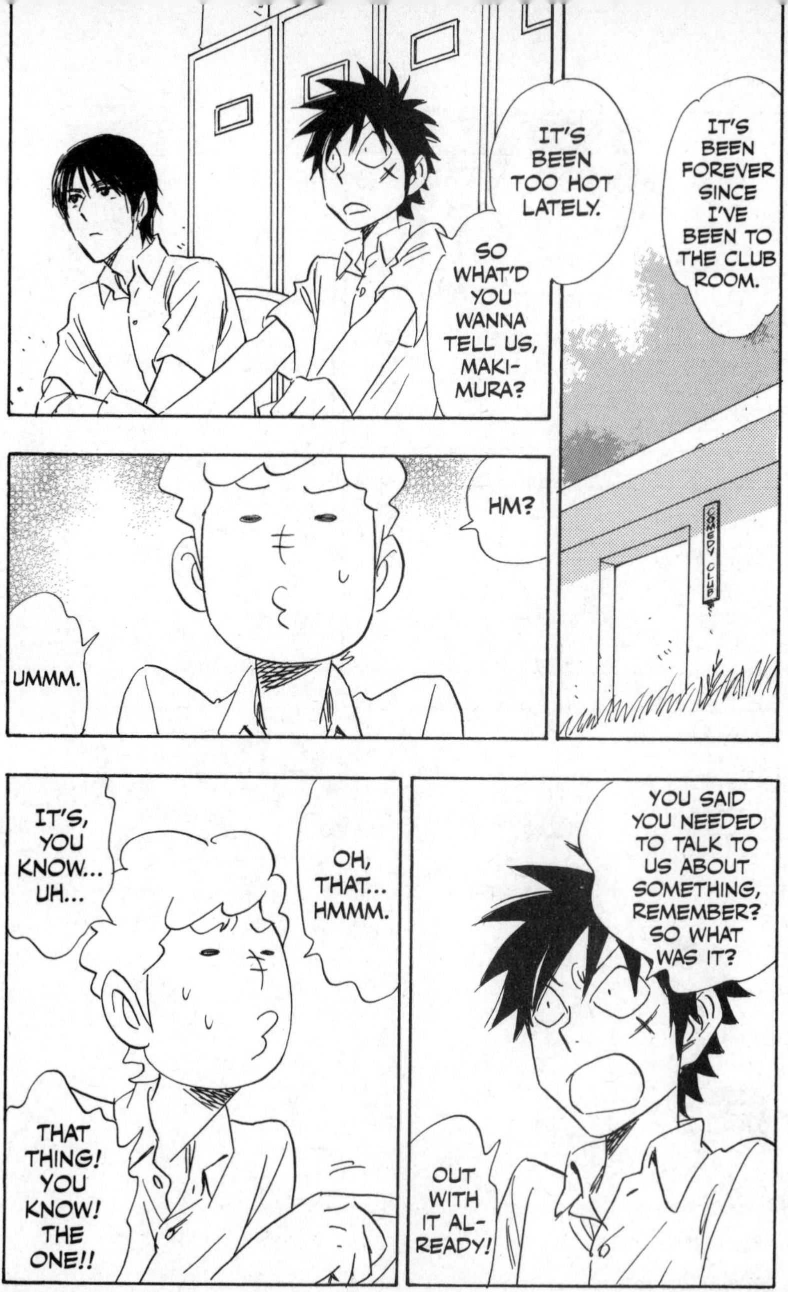
IT'S BEEN FOREVER SINCE I'VE BEEN TO THE CLUB ROOM.
COMEDY CLUB
IT'S BEEN TOO HOT LATELY.
SO WHAT'D YOU WANNA TELL US, MAKI-MURA?
HM?
UMMM.
YOU SAID YOU NEEDED TO TALK TO US ABOUT SOMETHING, REMEMBER? SO WHAT WAS IT?
OUT WITH IT AL-READY!
OH, THAT... HMMM.
IT'S, YOU KNOW... UH...
THAT THING! YOU KNOW! THE ONE!!

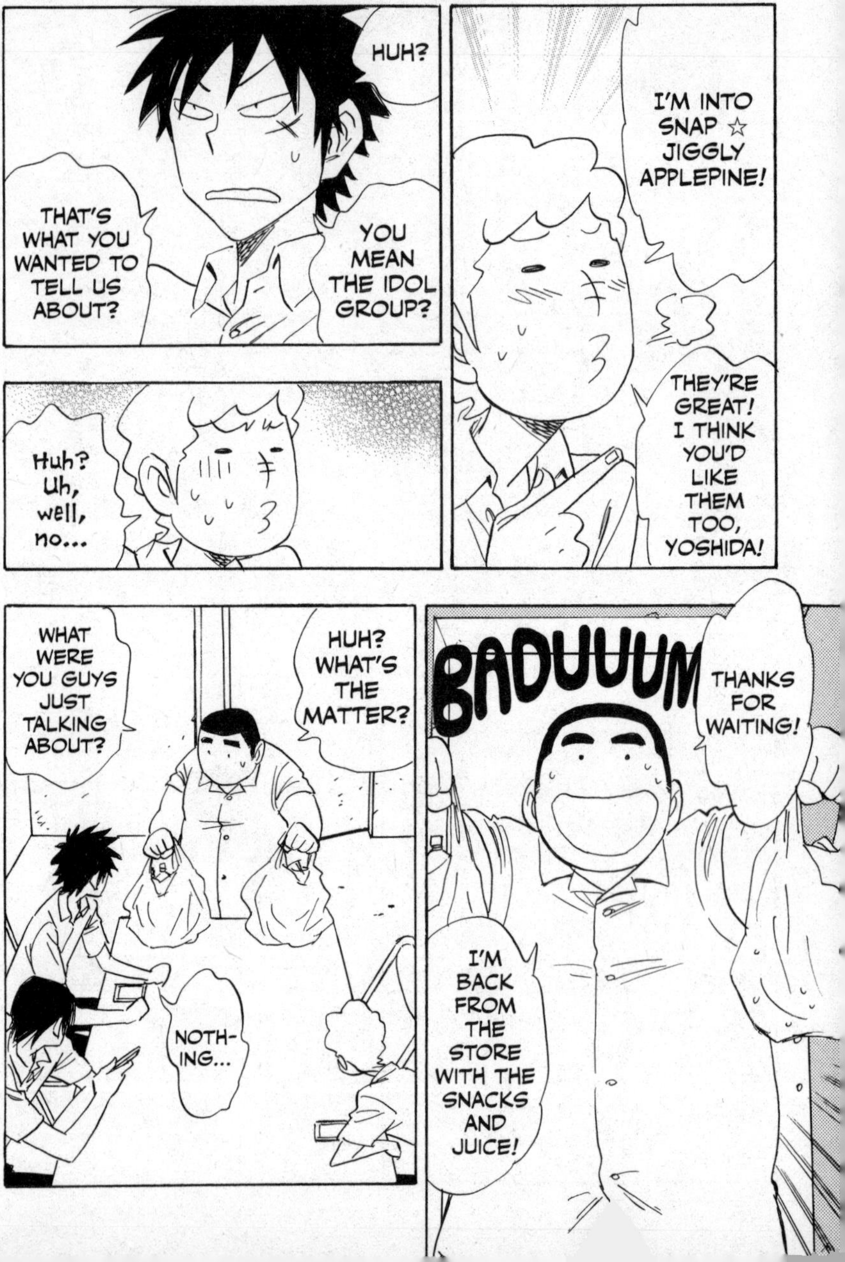
I'M INTO SNAP ☆ JIGGLY APPLEPINE!
THEY'RE GREAT! I THINK YOU'D LIKE THEM TOO, YOSHIDA!
HUH?
YOU MEAN THE IDOL GROUP?
THAT'S WHAT YOU WANTED TO TELL US ABOUT?
Huh? Uh, well, no...
BADUUUM
THANKS FOR WAITING!
I'M BACK FROM THE STORE WITH THE SNACKS AND JUICE!
HUH? WHAT'S THE MATTER?
WHAT WERE YOU GUYS JUST TALKING ABOUT?
NOTH-ING...

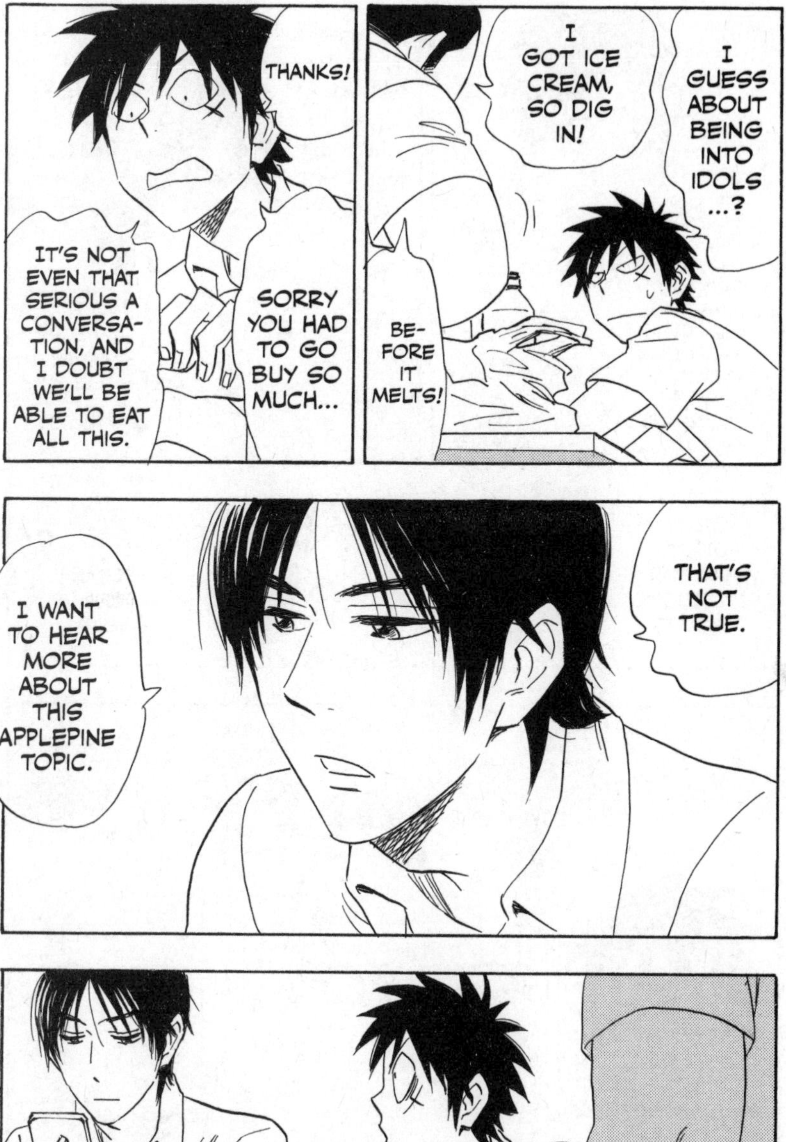
I GUESS ABOUT BEING INTO IDOLS ...?
I GOT ICE CREAM, SO DIG IN!
BE-FORE IT MELTS!
THANKS!
SORRY YOU HAD TO GO BUY SO MUCH...
IT'S NOT EVEN THAT SERIOUS A CONVERSA-TION, AND I DOUBT WE'LL BE ABLE TO EAT ALL THIS.
THAT'S NOT TRUE.
I WANT TO HEAR MORE ABOUT THIS APPLEPINE TOPIC.

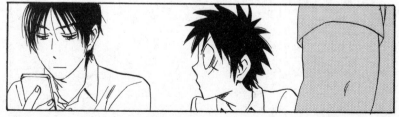

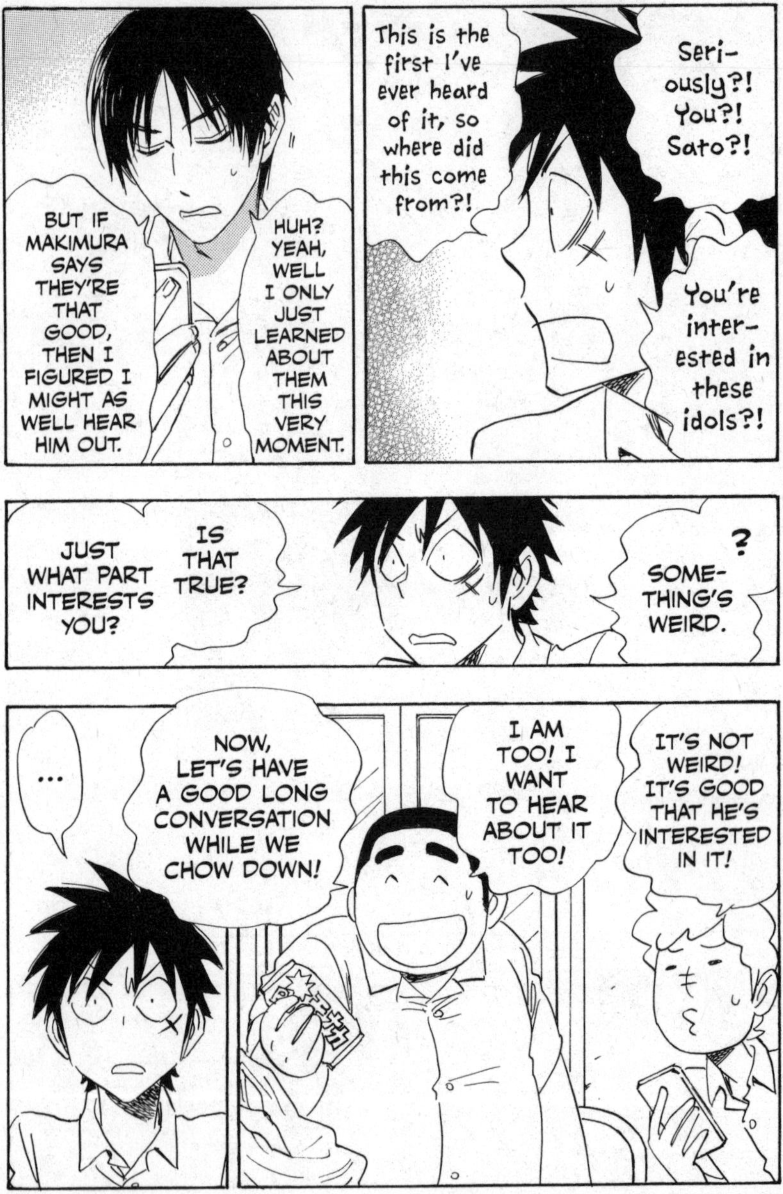
Seriously?! You?! Sato?!
You're interested in these idols?!
This is the first I've ever heard of it, so where did this come from?!
HUH? YEAH, WELL I ONLY JUST LEARNED ABOUT THEM THIS VERY MOMENT.
BUT IF MAKIMURA SAYS THEY'RE THAT GOOD, THEN I FIGURED I MIGHT AS WELL HEAR HIM OUT.
?
SOMETHING'S WEIRD.
IS THAT TRUE?
JUST WHAT PART INTERESTS YOU?
IT'S NOT WEIRD! IT'S GOOD THAT HE'S INTERESTED IN IT!
I AM TOO! I WANT TO HEAR ABOUT IT TOO!
NOW, LET'S HAVE A GOOD LONG CONVERSATION WHILE WE CHOW DOWN!
...

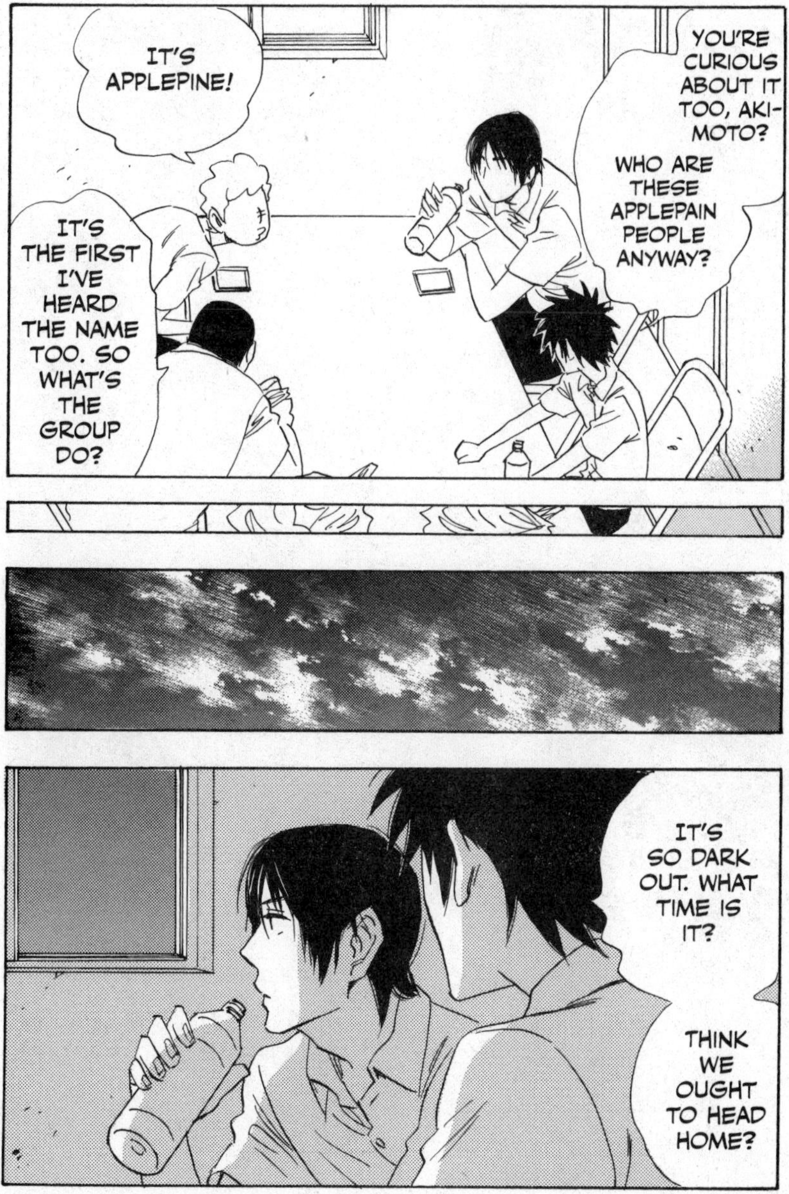
YOU'RE CURIOUS ABOUT IT TOO, AKI-MOTO?
WHO ARE THESE APPLEPAIN PEOPLE ANYWAY?
IT'S APPLEPINE!
IT'S THE FIRST I'VE HEARD THE NAME TOO. SO WHAT'S THE GROUP DO?
IT'S SO DARK OUT. WHAT TIME IS IT?
THINK WE OUGHT TO HEAD HOME?

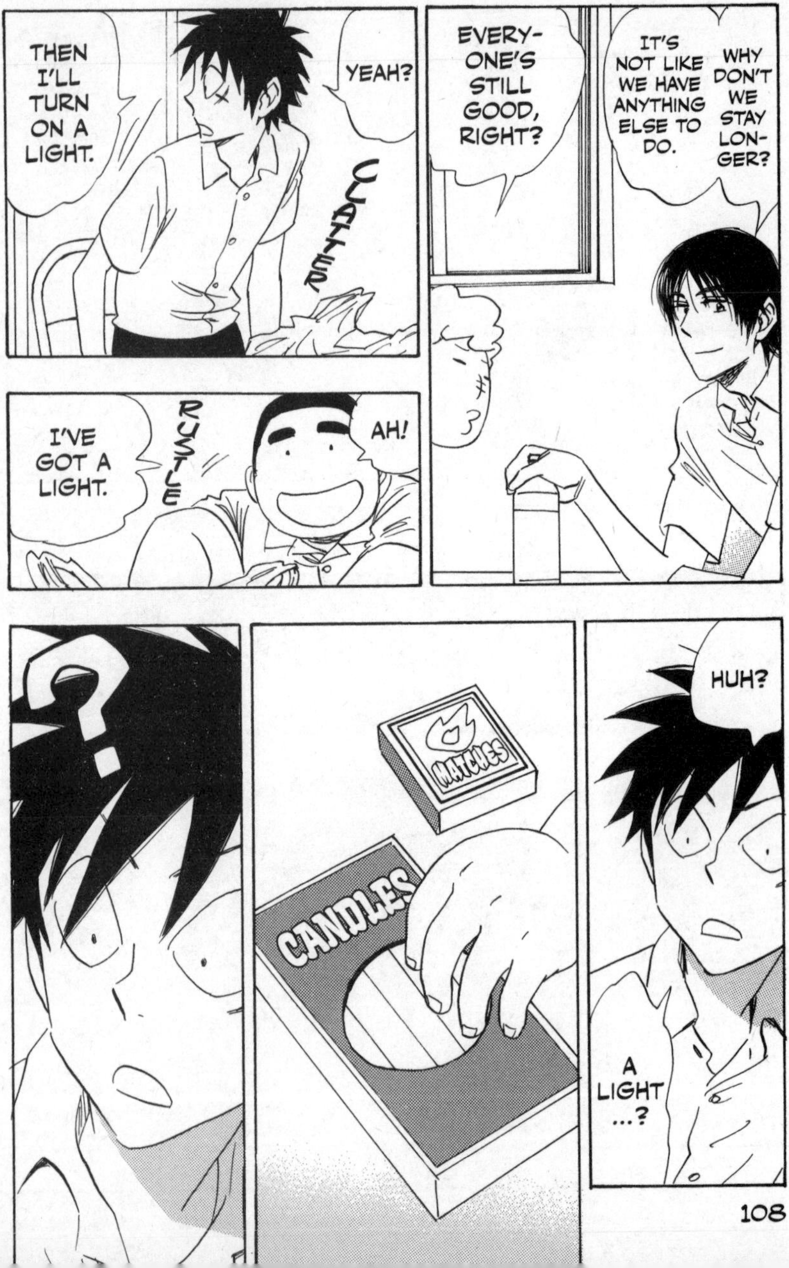
WHY DON'T WE STAY LONGER?
IT'S NOT LIKE WE HAVE ANYTHING ELSE TO DO.
EVERYONE'S STILL GOOD, RIGHT?
YEAH?
CLATTER
THEN I'LL TURN ON A LIGHT.
AH!
RUSTLE
I'VE GOT A LIGHT.
HUH?
A LIGHT ...?
MATCHES
CANDLES
?

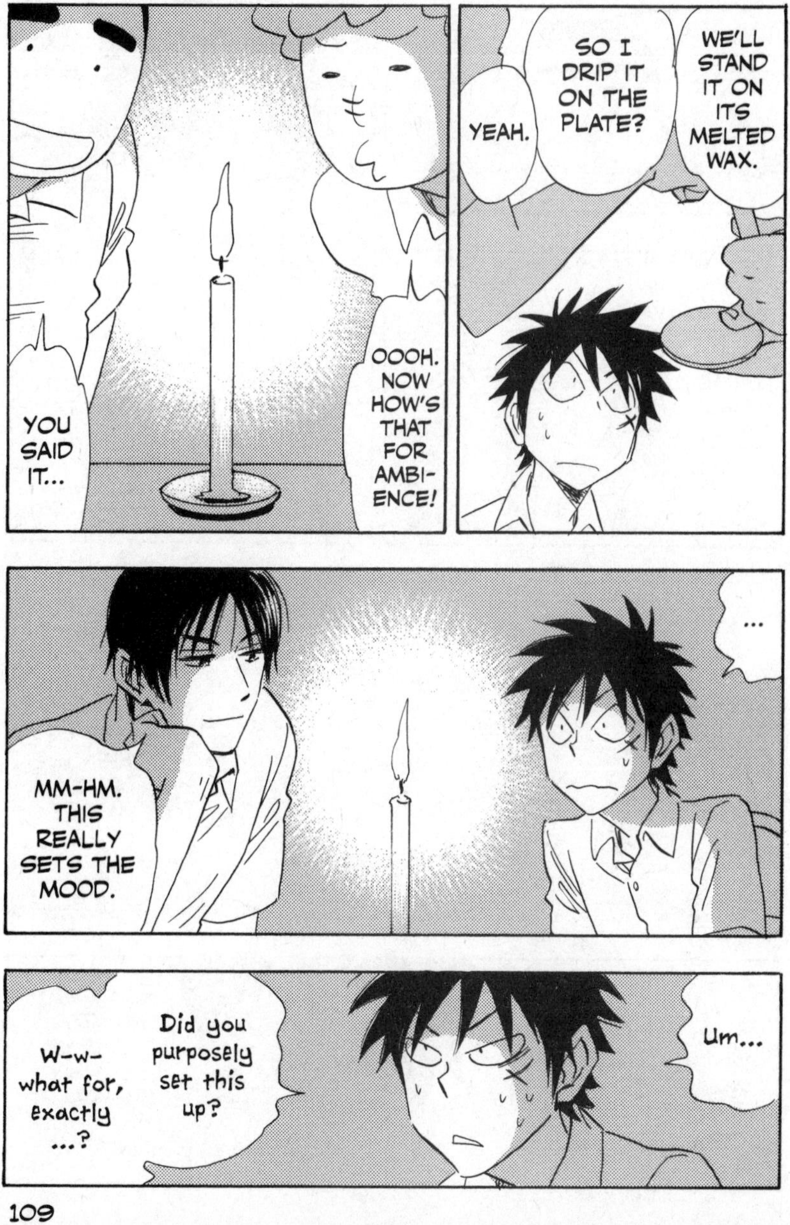
WE'LL STAND IT ON ITS MELTED WAX.
SO I DRIP IT ON THE PLATE?
YEAH.
OOOH. NOW HOW'S THAT FOR AMBIENCE!
YOU SAID IT...
...
MM-HM. THIS REALLY SETS THE MOOD.
Um...
Did you purposely set this up?
W-w- what for, exactly ...?

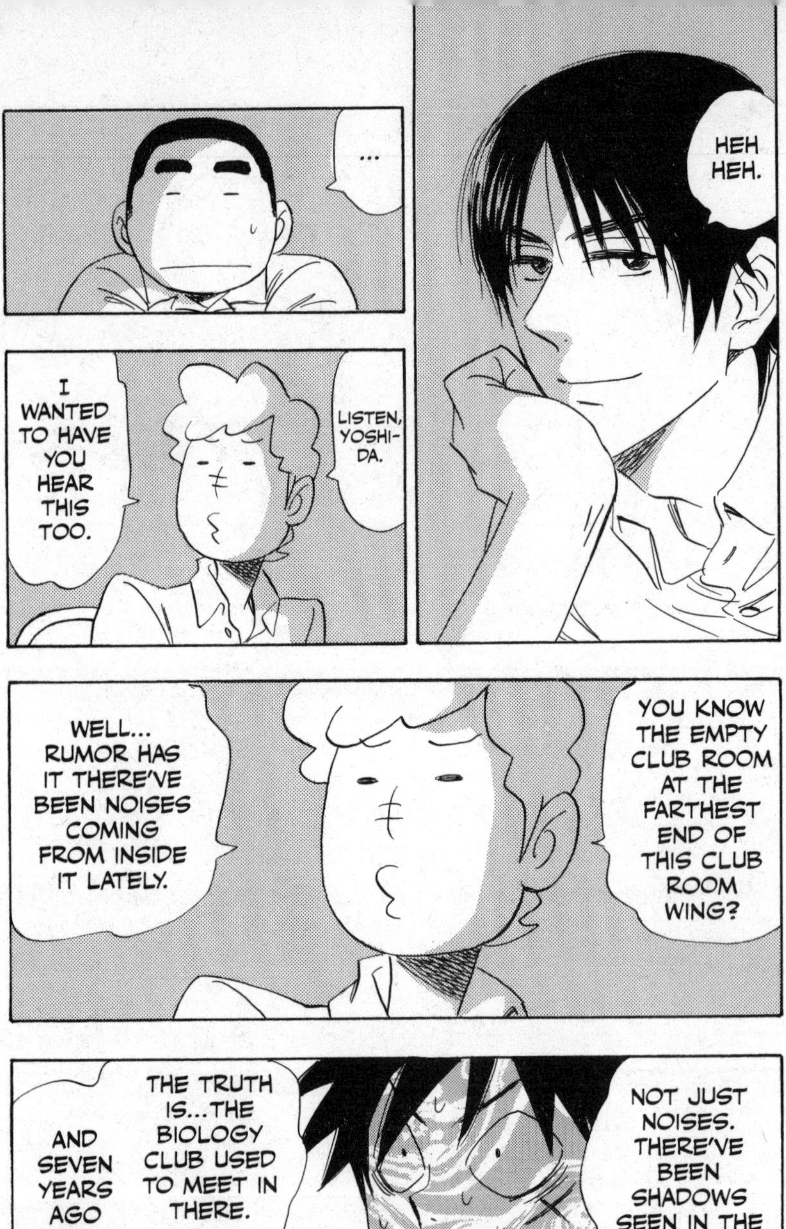
HEH HEH.
...
LISTEN, YOSHI-DA.
I WANTED TO HAVE YOU HEAR THIS TOO.
YOU KNOW THE EMPTY CLUB ROOM AT THE FARTHEST END OF THIS CLUB ROOM WING?
WELL... RUMOR HAS IT THERE'VE BEEN NOISES COMING FROM INSIDE IT LATELY.
NOT JUST NOISES. THERE'VE BEEN SHADOWS SEEN IN THE WINDOWS.
THE TRUTH IS...THE BIOLOGY CLUB USED TO MEET IN THERE.
AND SEVEN YEARS AGO TODAY...

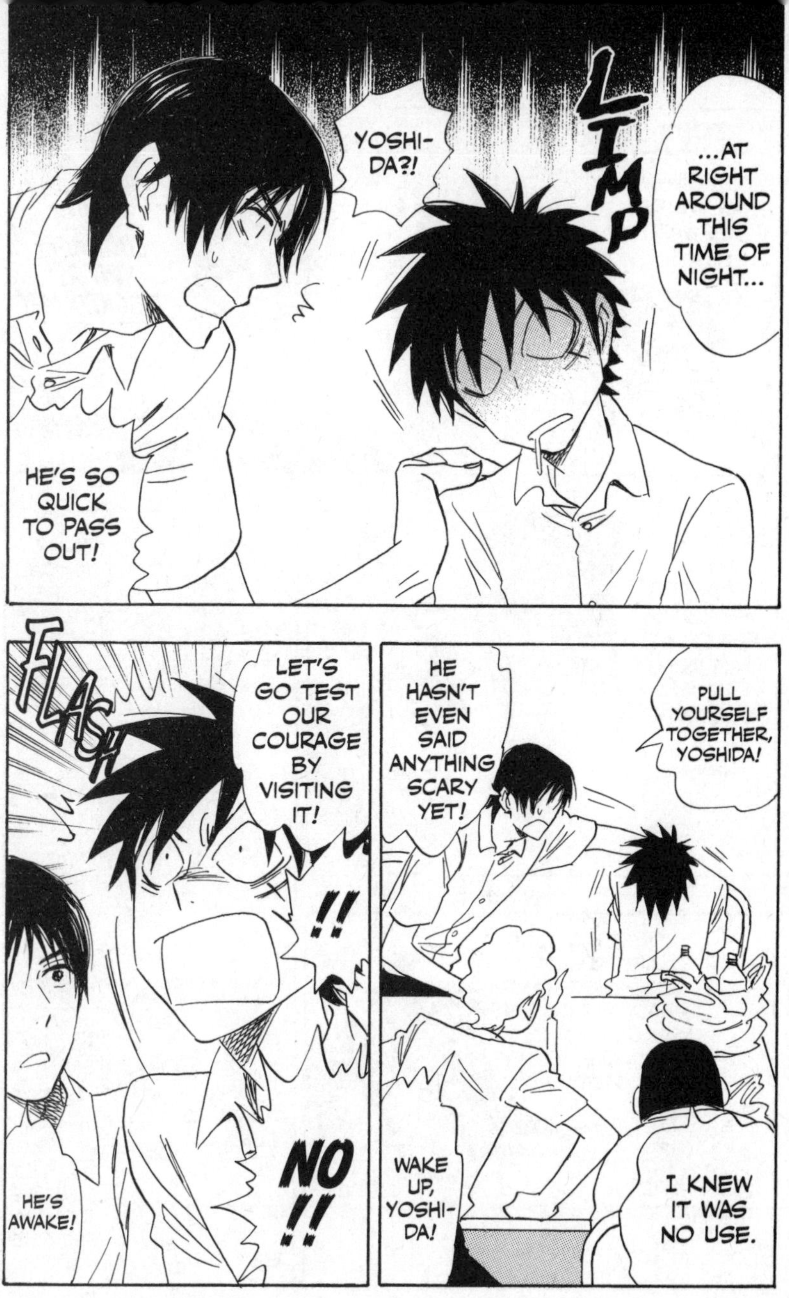
...AT RIGHT AROUND THIS TIME OF NIGHT...
LIMP
YOSHI-DA?!
HE'S SO QUICK TO PASS OUT!
PULL YOURSELF TOGETHER, YOSHIDA!
HE HASN'T EVEN SAID ANYTHING SCARY YET!
I KNEW IT WAS NO USE.
WAKE UP, YOSHI-DA!
LET'S GO TEST OUR COURAGE BY VISITING IT!
FLASH
!!
NO !!
HE'S AWAKE!

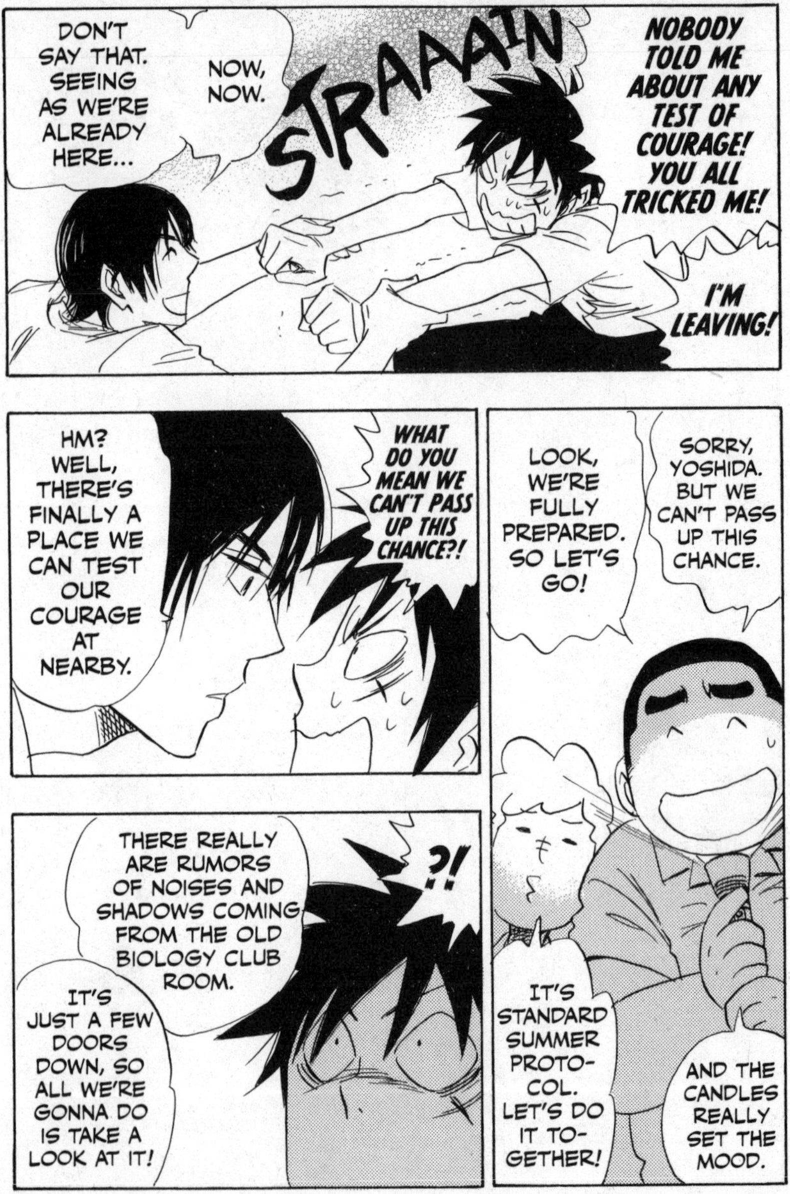
NOBODY TOLD ME ABOUT ANY TEST OF COURAGE! YOU ALL TRICKED ME!
I'M LEAVING!
STRAAAIN
NOW, NOW.
DON'T SAY THAT. SEEING AS WE'RE ALREADY HERE...
SORRY, YOSHIDA. BUT WE CAN'T PASS UP THIS CHANCE.
LOOK, WE'RE FULLY PREPARED. SO LET'S GO!
AND THE CANDLES REALLY SET THE MOOD.
IT'S STANDARD SUMMER PROTO-COL. LET'S DO IT TO-GETHER!
WHAT DO YOU MEAN WE CAN'T PASS UP THIS CHANCE?!
HM? WELL, THERE'S FINALLY A PLACE WE CAN TEST OUR COURAGE AT NEARBY.
?!
THERE REALLY ARE RUMORS OF NOISES AND SHADOWS COMING FROM THE OLD BIOLOGY CLUB ROOM.
IT'S JUST A FEW DOORS DOWN, SO ALL WE'RE GONNA DO IS TAKE A LOOK AT IT!

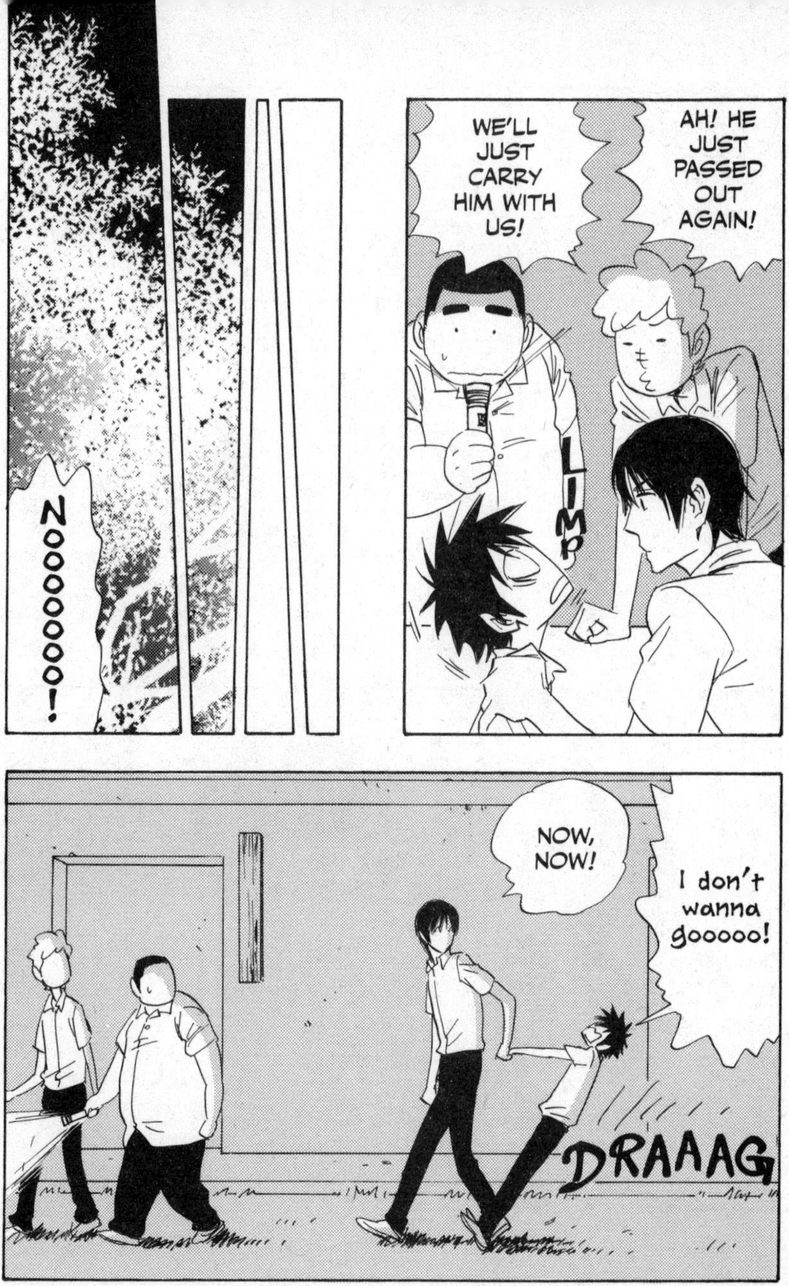
AH! HE JUST PASSED OUT AGAIN!
WE'LL JUST CARRY HIM WITH US!
LIMP
NOOOOOOOO!
I don't wanna gooooo!
NOW, NOW!
DRAAAG

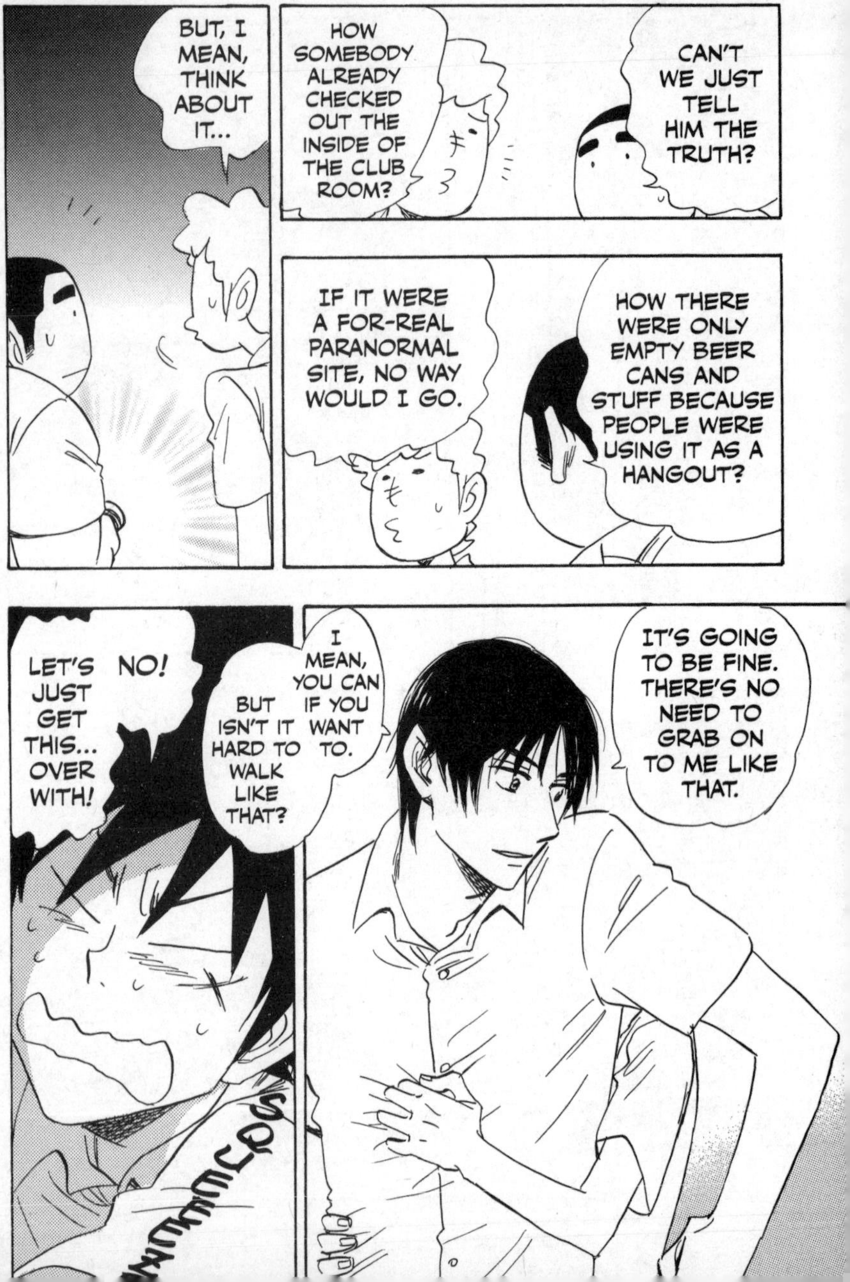
CAN'T WE JUST TELL HIM THE TRUTH?
HOW SOMEBODY ALREADY CHECKED OUT THE INSIDE OF THE CLUB ROOM?
HOW THERE WERE ONLY EMPTY BEER CANS AND STUFF BECAUSE PEOPLE WERE USING IT AS A HANGOUT?
IF IT WERE A FOR-REAL PARANORMAL SITE, NO WAY WOULD I GO.
BUT, I MEAN, THINK ABOUT IT...
IT'S GOING TO BE FINE. THERE'S NO NEED TO GRAB ON TO ME LIKE THAT.
I MEAN, YOU CAN IF YOU WANT TO.
BUT ISN'T IT HARD TO WALK LIKE THAT?
NO!
LET'S JUST GET THIS... OVER WITH!

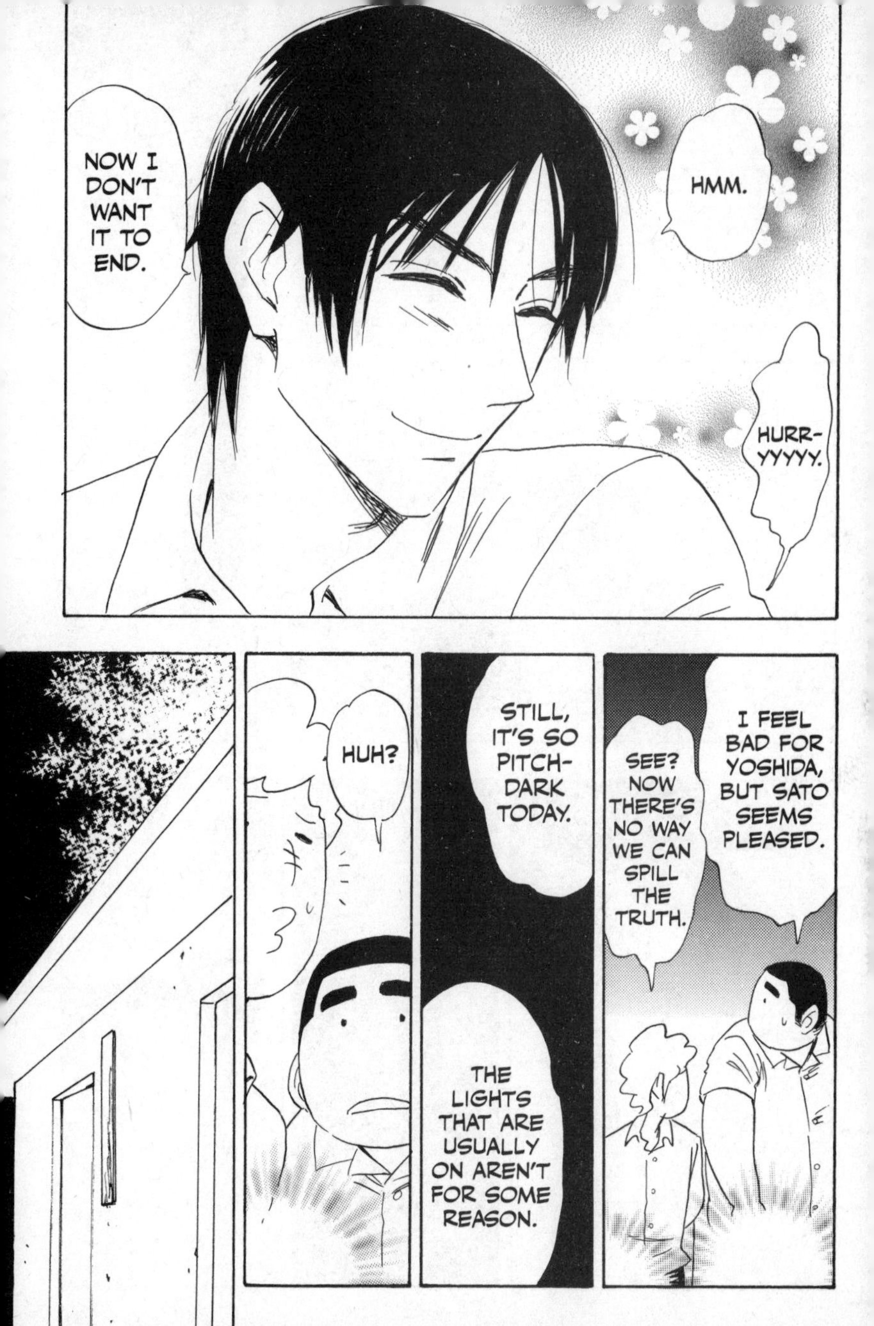
HMM.
HURR-YYYYY.
NOW I DON'T WANT IT TO END.
I FEEL BAD FOR YOSHIDA, BUT SATO SEEMS PLEASED.
SEE? NOW THERE'S NO WAY WE CAN SPILL THE TRUTH.
STILL, IT'S SO PITCH-DARK TODAY.
THE LIGHTS THAT ARE USUALLY ON AREN'T FOR SOME REASON.
HUH?

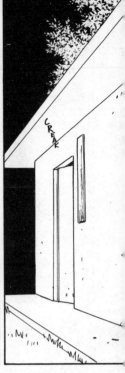

IT-IT-IT MOVED?!

IT-IT-IT'S OPEN?!

?!
?!
?!

BRUSH

Tell me ...

W-what is it? Did something happen?

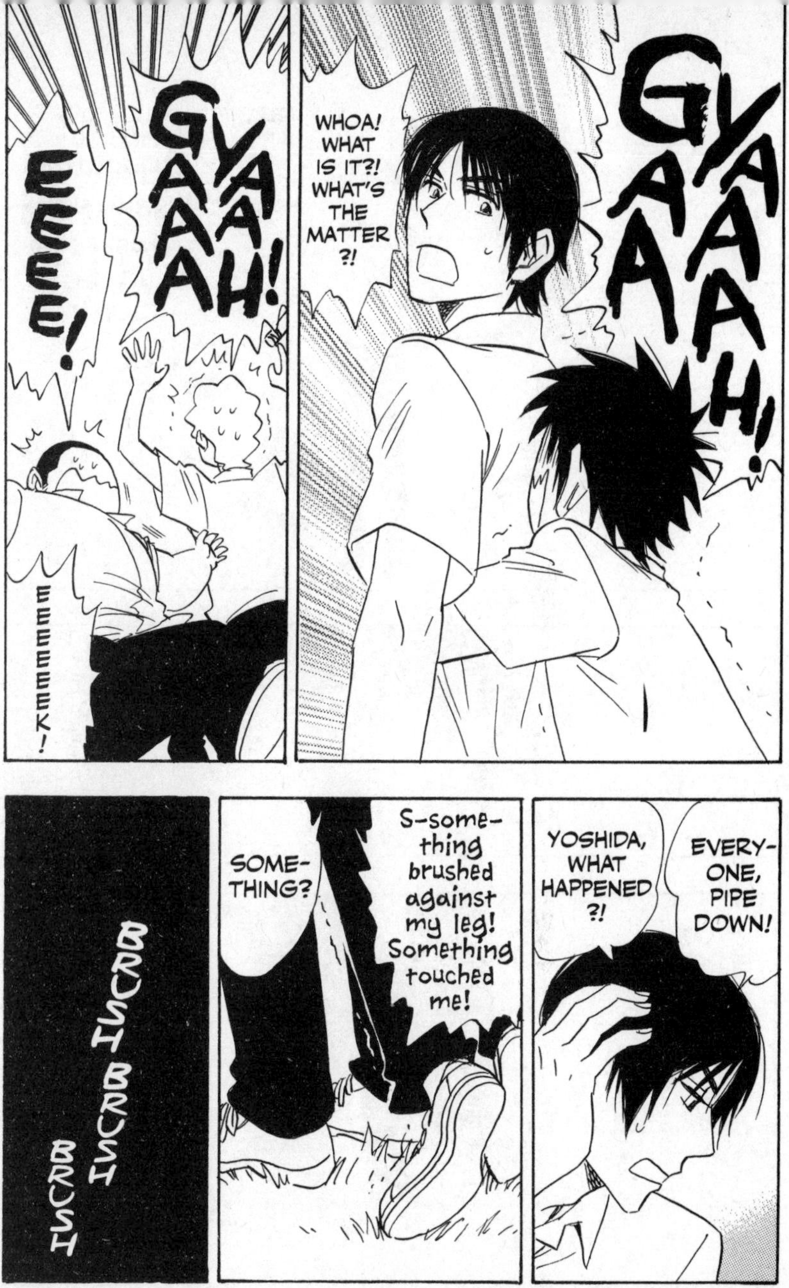
GYAAAAAH!
WHOA! WHAT IS IT?! WHAT'S THE MATTER ?!
GYAAAAH!
EEEEE!
EEEEEEEK!
EVERY-ONE, PIPE DOWN!
YOSHIDA, WHAT HAPPENED ?!
S-some-thing brushed against my leg! Something touched me!
SOME-THING?
BRUSH BRUSH BRUSH

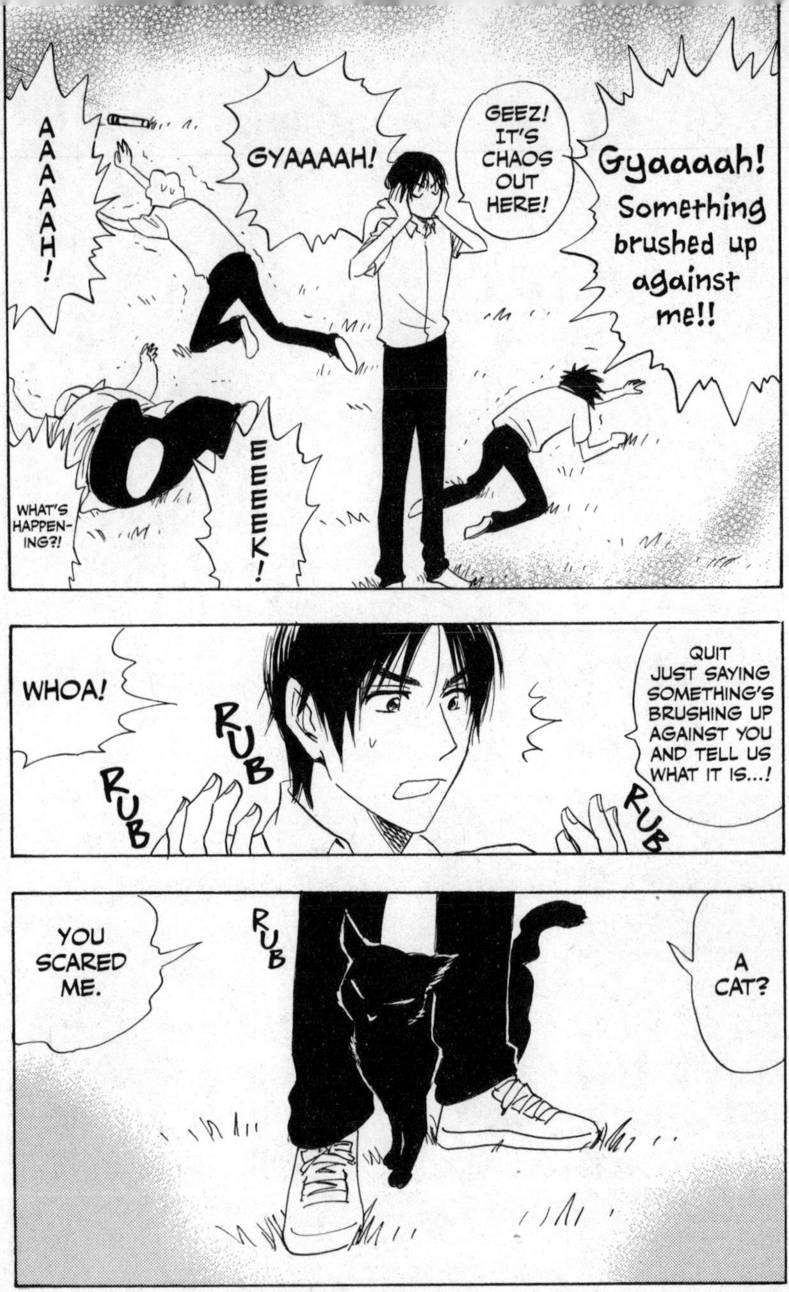
Gyaaaah! Something brushed up against me!!
GEEZ! IT'S CHAOS OUT HERE!
GYAAAAH!
AAAAAAH!
EEEEEK!
WHAT'S HAPPEN-ING?!
QUIT JUST SAYING SOMETHING'S BRUSHING UP AGAINST YOU AND TELL US WHAT IT IS...!
RUB
RUB
RUB
WHOA!
A CAT?
RUB
YOU SCARED ME.

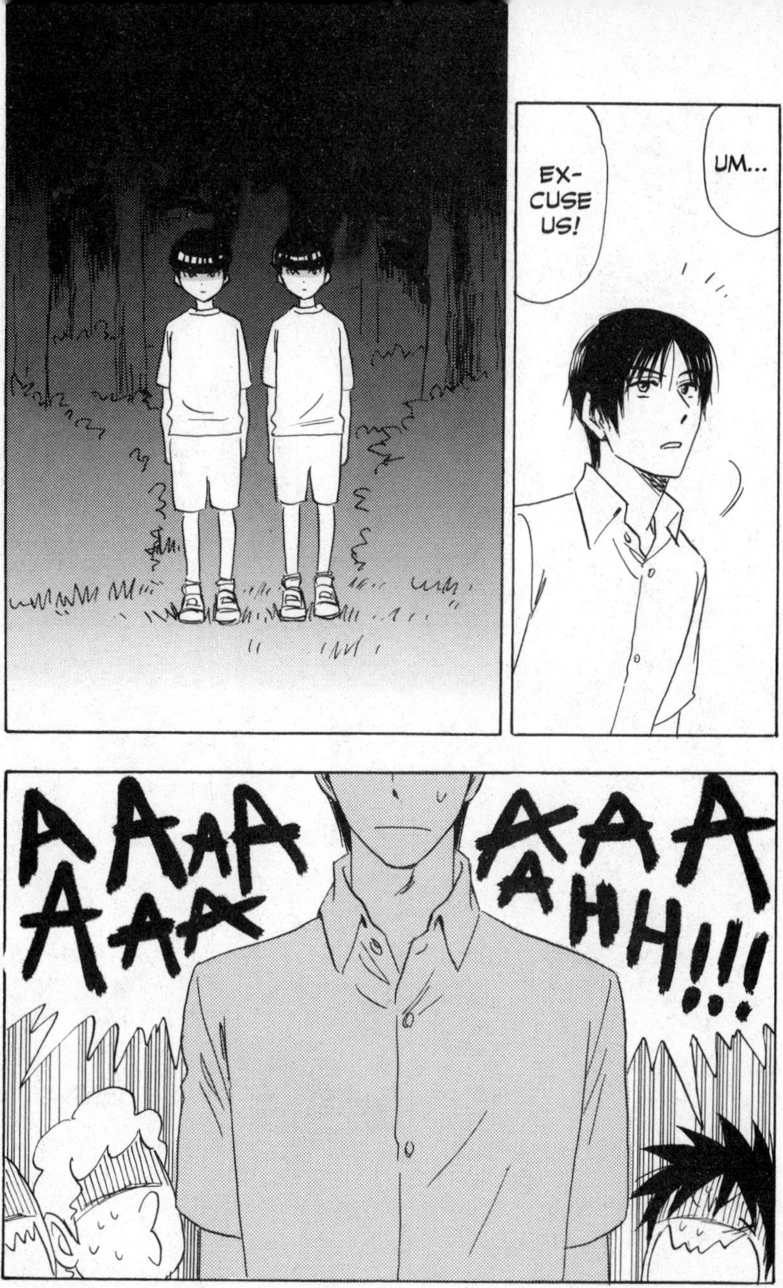
UM...
EX-CUSE US!
AAAAAA
AAAAAHH!!!

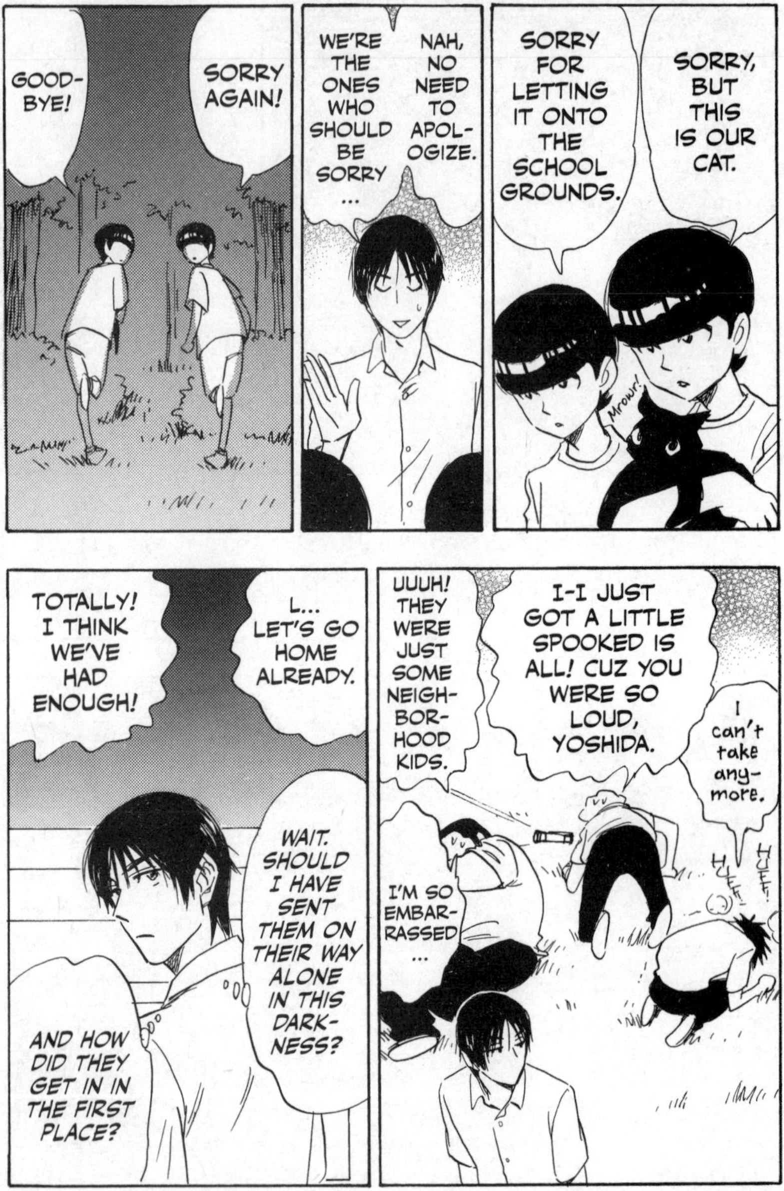
SORRY, BUT THIS IS OUR CAT.
SORRY FOR LETTING IT ONTO THE SCHOOL GROUNDS.
Mrowr!
NAH, NO NEED TO APOLOGIZE.
WE'RE THE ONES WHO SHOULD BE SORRY ...
SORRY AGAIN!
GOOD-BYE!
I can't take anymore.
HUFF HUFF!
I-I JUST GOT A LITTLE SPOOKED IS ALL! CUZ YOU WERE SO LOUD, YOSHIDA.
UUUH! THEY WERE JUST SOME NEIGHBORHOOD KIDS.
I'M SO EMBARRASSED ...
L... LET'S GO HOME ALREADY.
TOTALLY! I THINK WE'VE HAD ENOUGH!
WAIT. SHOULD I HAVE SENT THEM ON THEIR WAY ALONE IN THIS DARKNESS?
AND HOW DID THEY GET IN IN THE FIRST PLACE?

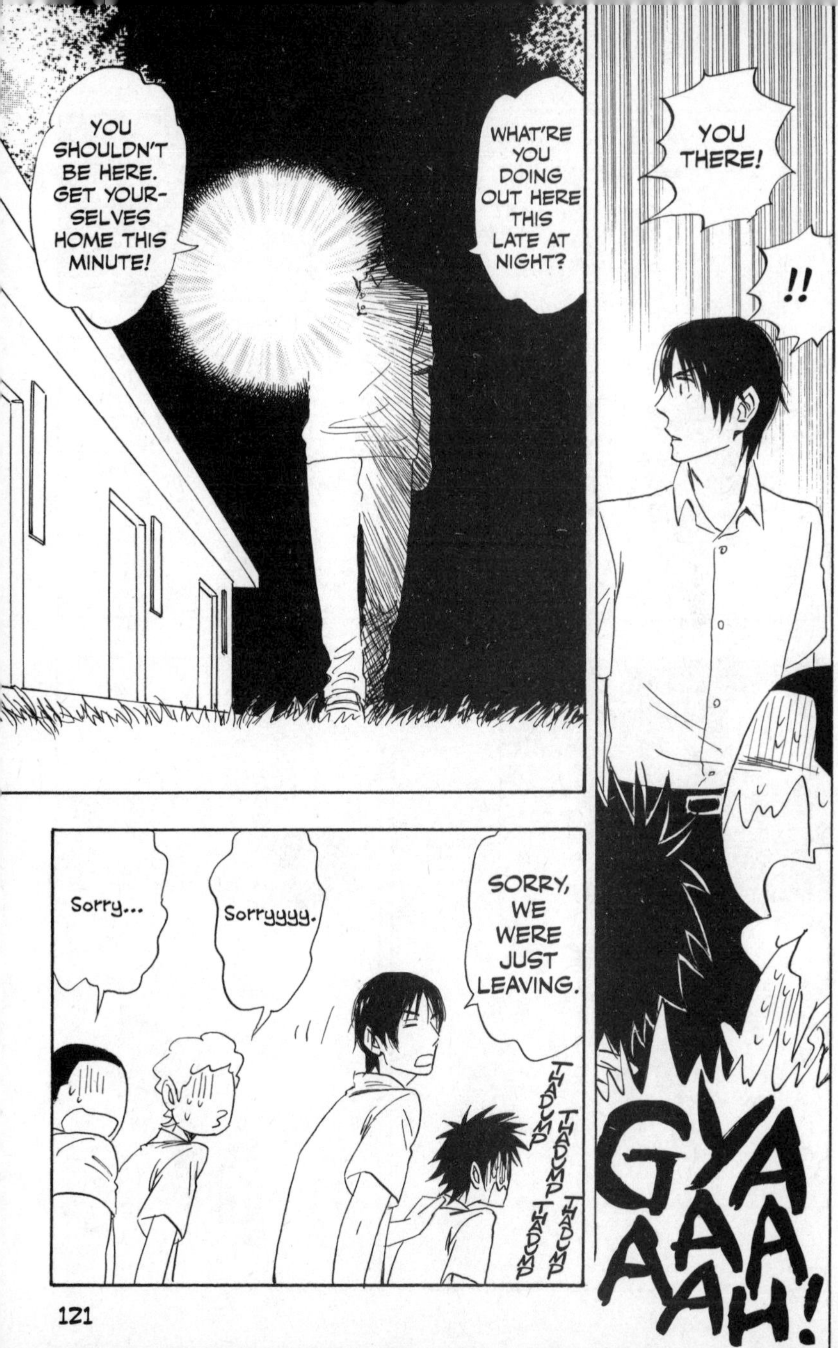
YOU THERE!
!!
GYAAAAAH!
WHAT'RE YOU DOING OUT HERE THIS LATE AT NIGHT?
YOU SHOULDN'T BE HERE. GET YOURSELVES HOME THIS MINUTE!
SORRY, WE WERE JUST LEAVING.
THADUMP THADUMP THADUMP THADUMP
Sorryyyy.
Sorry...

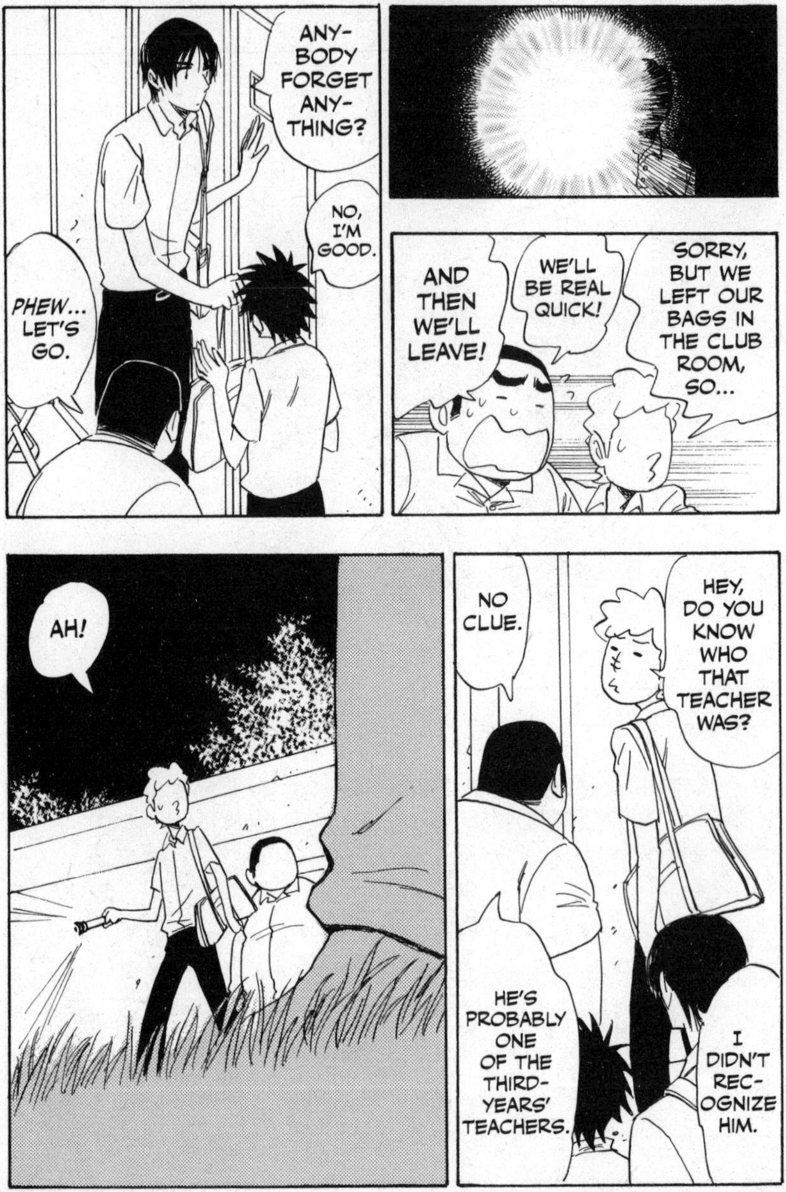
SORRY, BUT WE LEFT OUR BAGS IN THE CLUB ROOM, SO...
WE'LL BE REAL QUICK!
AND THEN WE'LL LEAVE!
ANYBODY FORGET ANYTHING?
NO, I'M GOOD.
PHEW... LET'S GO.
HEY, DO YOU KNOW WHO THAT TEACHER WAS?
NO CLUE.
I DIDN'T RECOGNIZE HIM.
HE'S PROBABLY ONE OF THE THIRD-YEARS' TEACHERS.
AH!

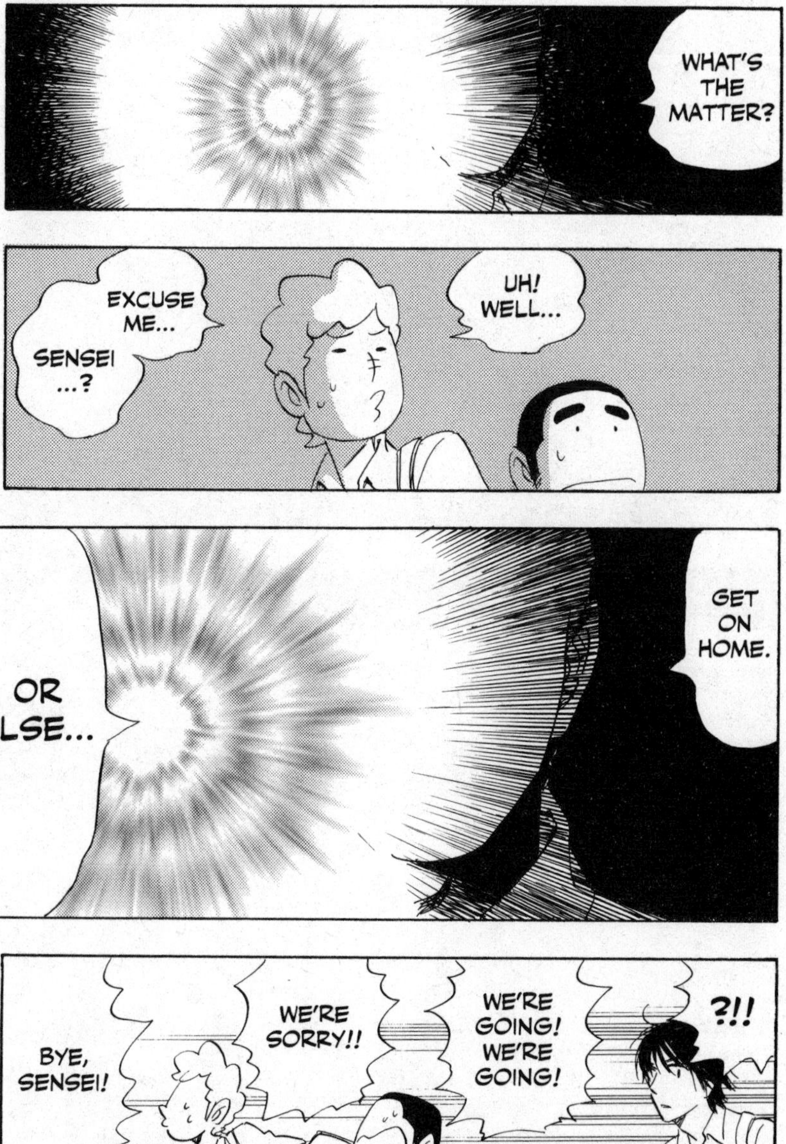
WHAT'S THE MATTER?
UH! WELL...
EXCUSE ME... SENSEI ...?
GET ON HOME.
OR ELSE...
?!!
WE'RE GOING! WE'RE GOING!
WE'RE SORRY!!
BYE, SENSEI!

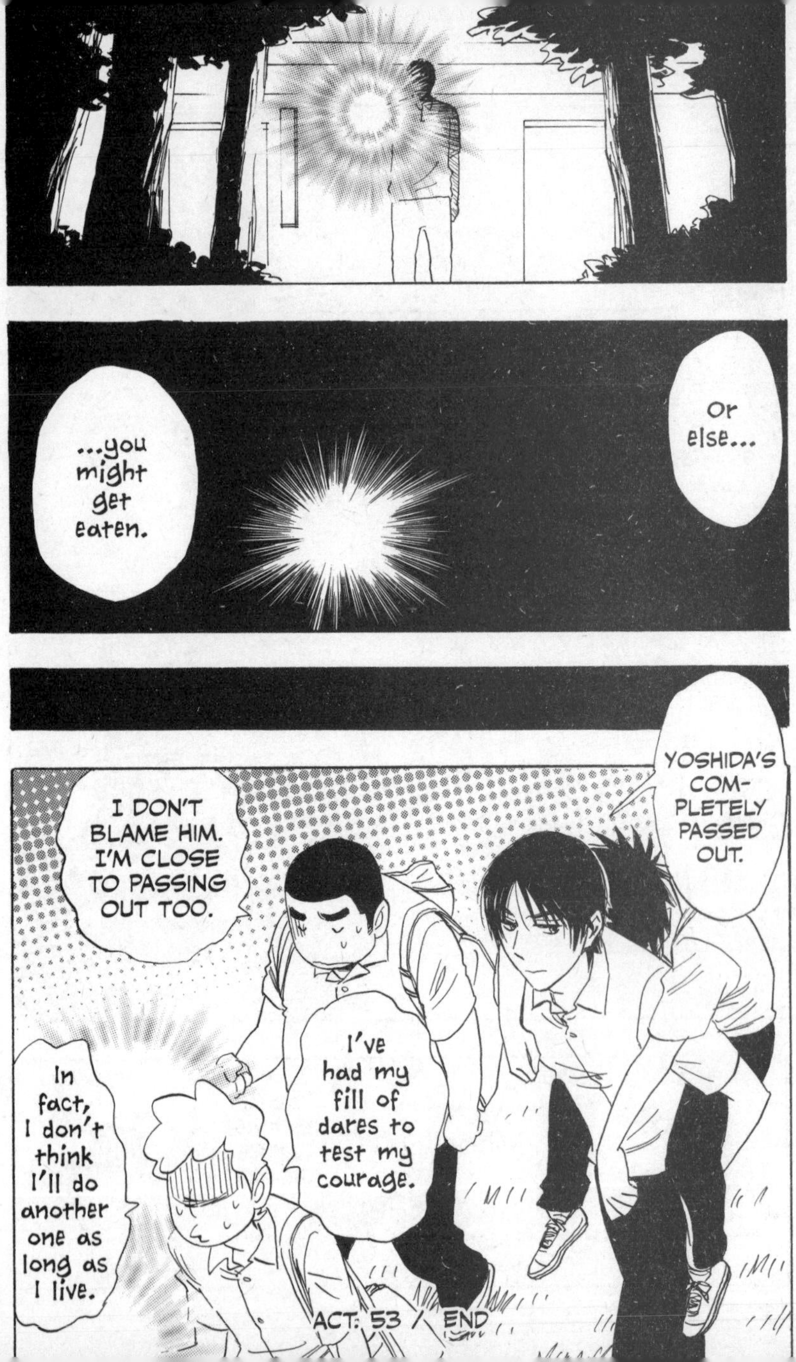
Or else...
...you might get eaten.
YOSHIDA'S COM-PLETELY PASSED OUT.
I DON'T BLAME HIM. I'M CLOSE TO PASSING OUT TOO.
I've had my fill of dares to test my courage.
In fact, I don't think I'll do another one as long as I live.
ACT: 53 / END

HIS FAVORITE

HIS
FAVORITE

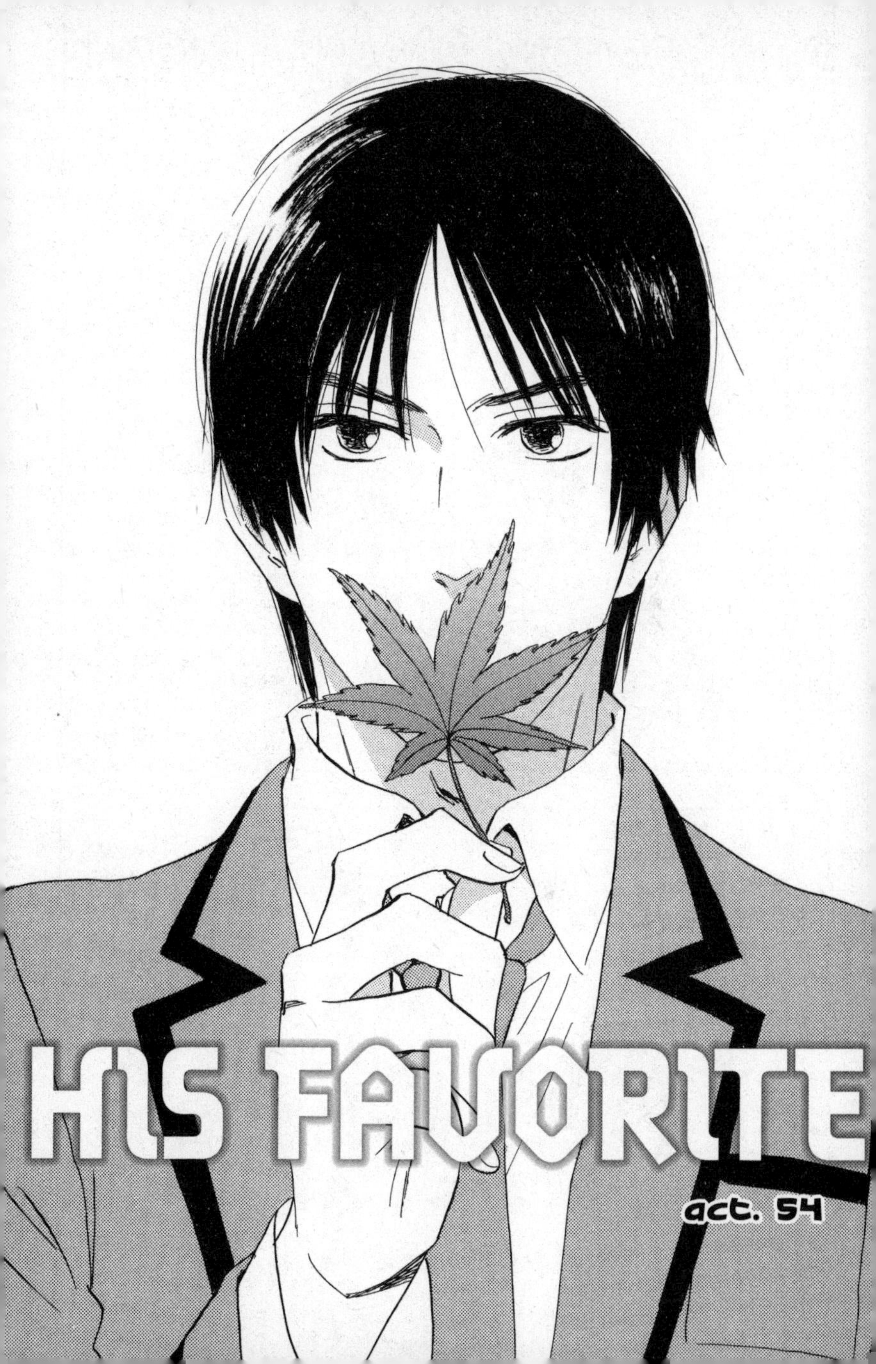
HIS FAVORITE
act. 54

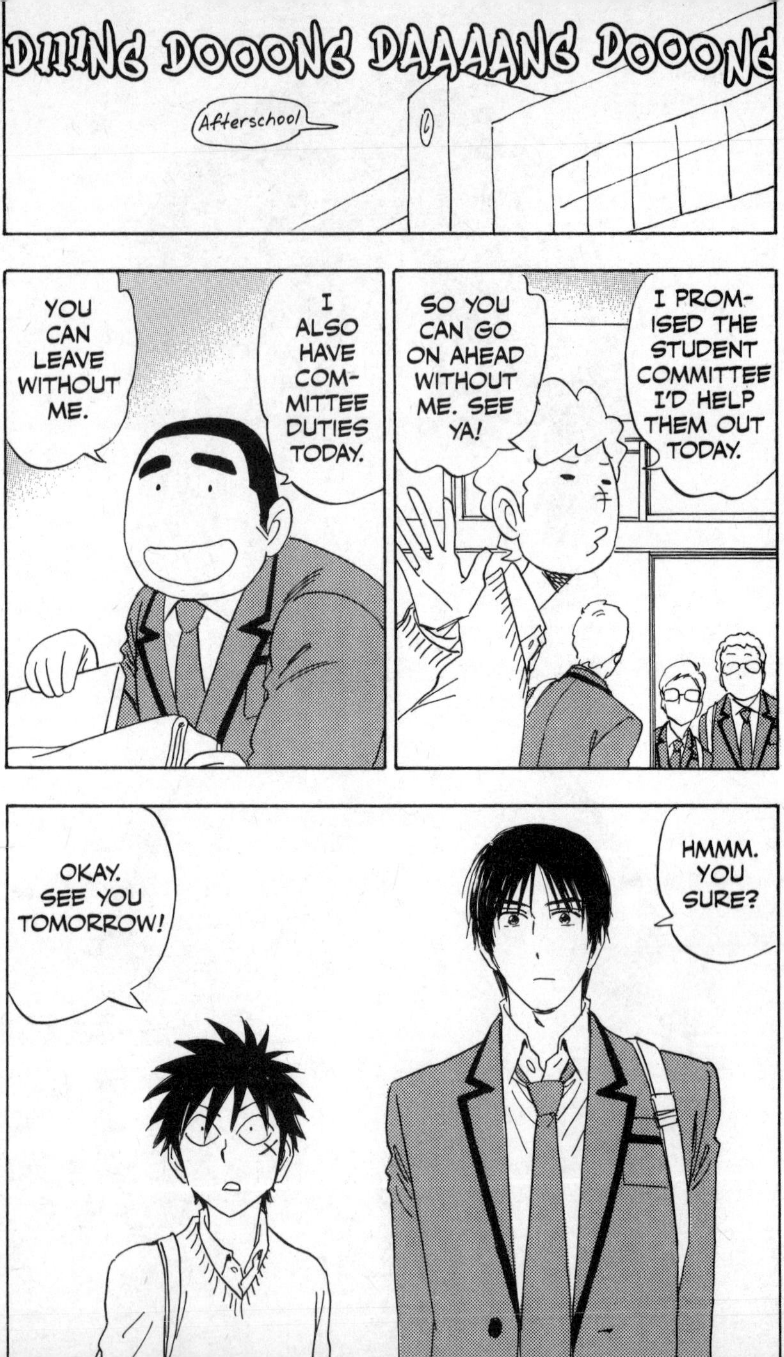
DIIING DOOONG DAAAANG DOOONG
Afterschool
I PROMISED THE STUDENT COMMITTEE I'D HELP THEM OUT TODAY.
SO YOU CAN GO ON AHEAD WITHOUT ME. SEE YA!
I ALSO HAVE COMMITTEE DUTIES TODAY.
YOU CAN LEAVE WITHOUT ME.
HMMM. YOU SURE?
OKAY. SEE YOU TOMORROW!

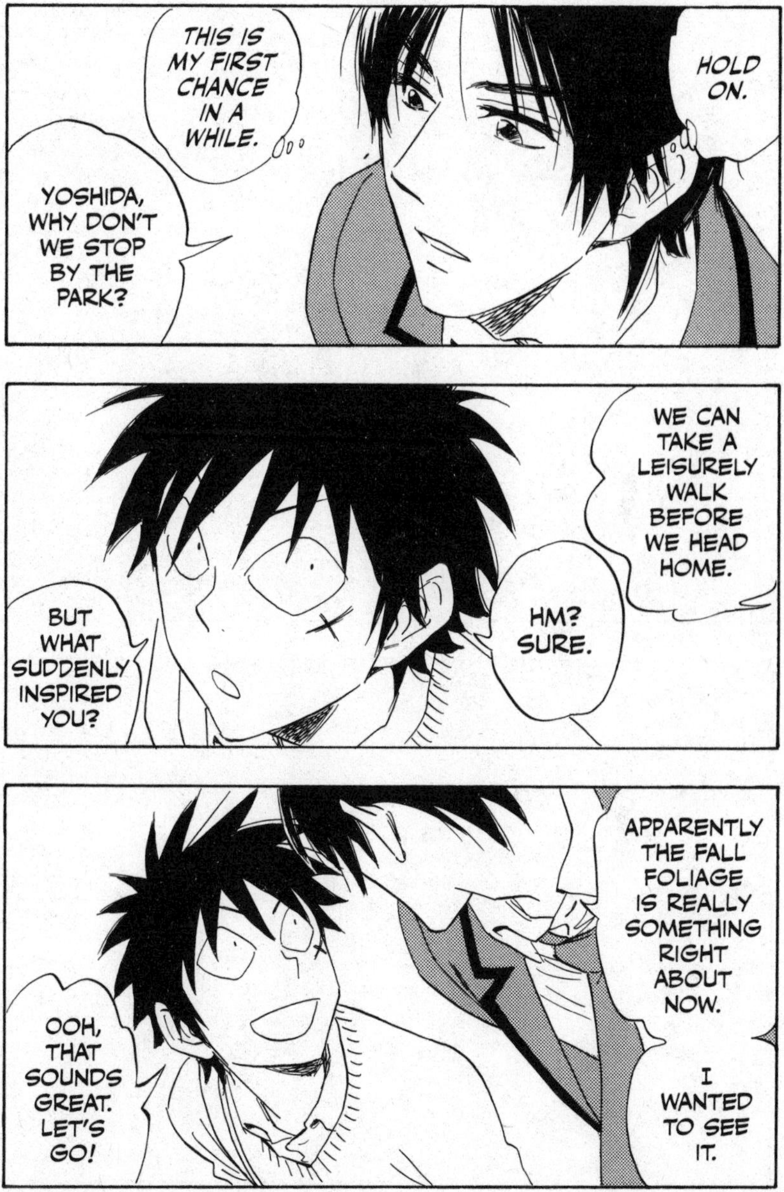
HOLD ON.
THIS IS MY FIRST CHANCE IN A WHILE.
YOSHIDA, WHY DON'T WE STOP BY THE PARK?
WE CAN TAKE A LEISURELY WALK BEFORE WE HEAD HOME.
HM? SURE.
BUT WHAT SUDDENLY INSPIRED YOU?
APPARENTLY THE FALL FOLIAGE IS REALLY SOMETHING RIGHT ABOUT NOW.
I WANTED TO SEE IT.
OOH, THAT SOUNDS GREAT. LET'S GO!

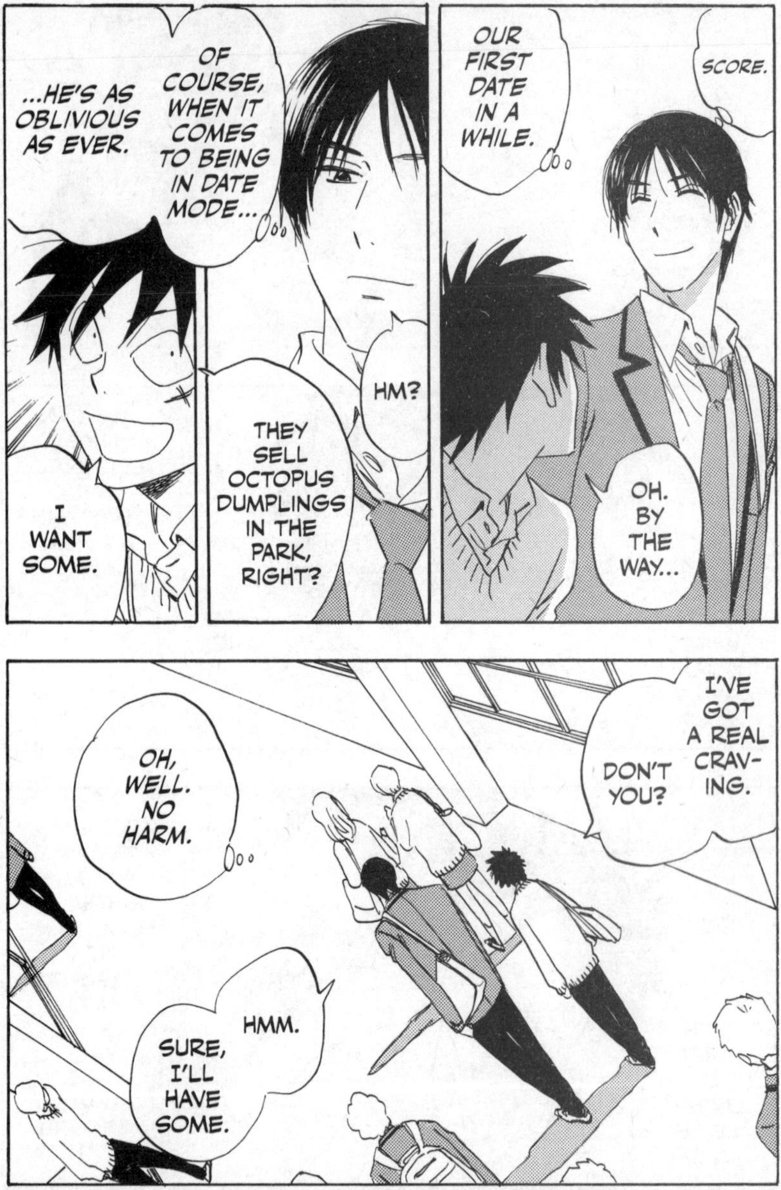
SCORE.
OUR FIRST DATE IN A WHILE.
OH. BY THE WAY...
HM?
THEY SELL OCTOPUS DUMPLINGS IN THE PARK, RIGHT?
I WANT SOME.
OF COURSE, WHEN IT COMES TO BEING IN DATE MODE...
...HE'S AS OBLIVIOUS AS EVER.
I'VE GOT A REAL CRAV-ING.
DON'T YOU?
HMM.
SURE, I'LL HAVE SOME.
OH, WELL. NO HARM.

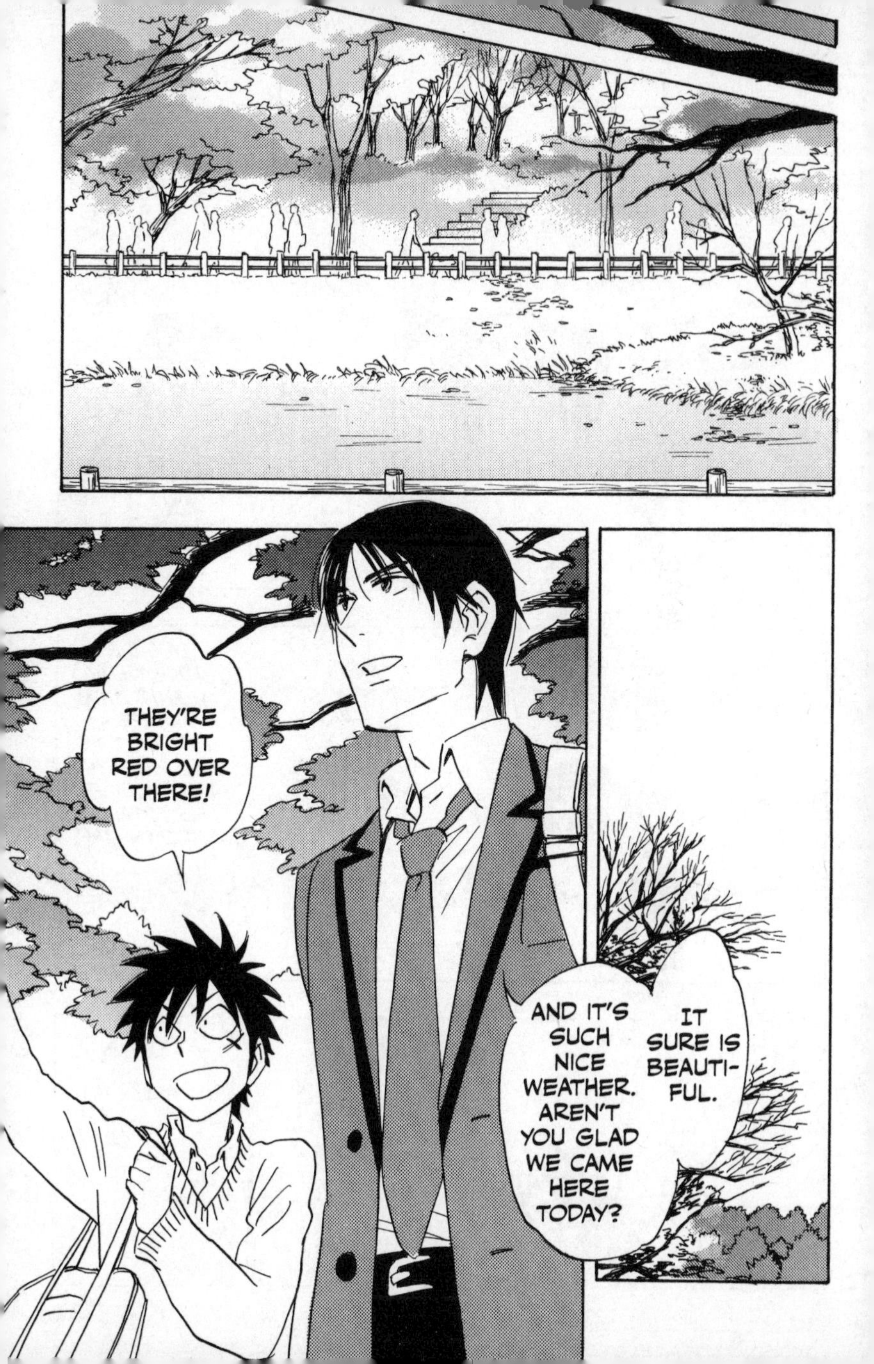
THEY'RE BRIGHT RED OVER THERE!
IT SURE IS BEAUTI-FUL.
AND IT'S SUCH NICE WEATHER. AREN'T YOU GLAD WE CAME HERE TODAY?

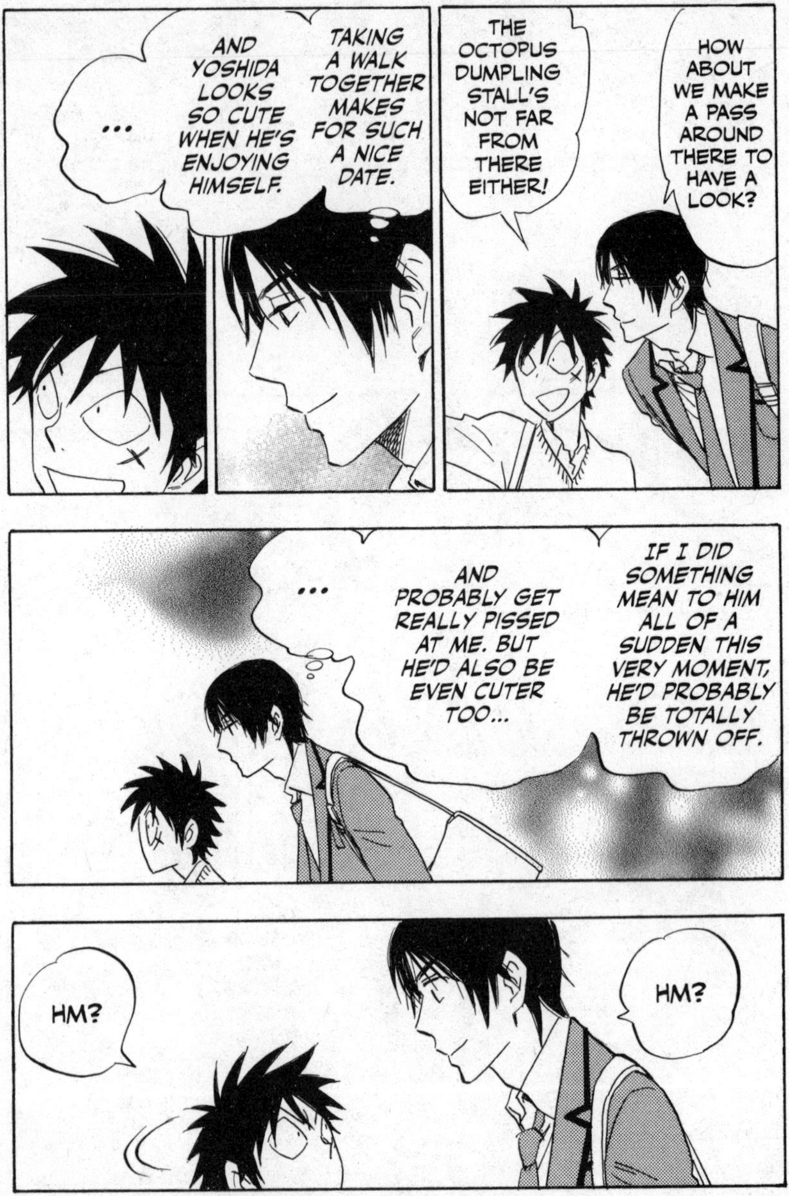
HOW ABOUT WE MAKE A PASS AROUND THERE TO HAVE A LOOK?
THE OCTOPUS DUMPLING STALL'S NOT FAR FROM THERE EITHER!
TAKING A WALK TOGETHER MAKES FOR SUCH A NICE DATE.
AND YOSHIDA LOOKS SO CUTE WHEN HE'S ENJOYING HIMSELF.
...
IF I DID SOMETHING MEAN TO HIM ALL OF A SUDDEN THIS VERY MOMENT, HE'D PROBABLY BE TOTALLY THROWN OFF.
AND PROBABLY GET REALLY PISSED AT ME. BUT HE'D ALSO BE EVEN CUTER TOO...
...
HM?
HM?

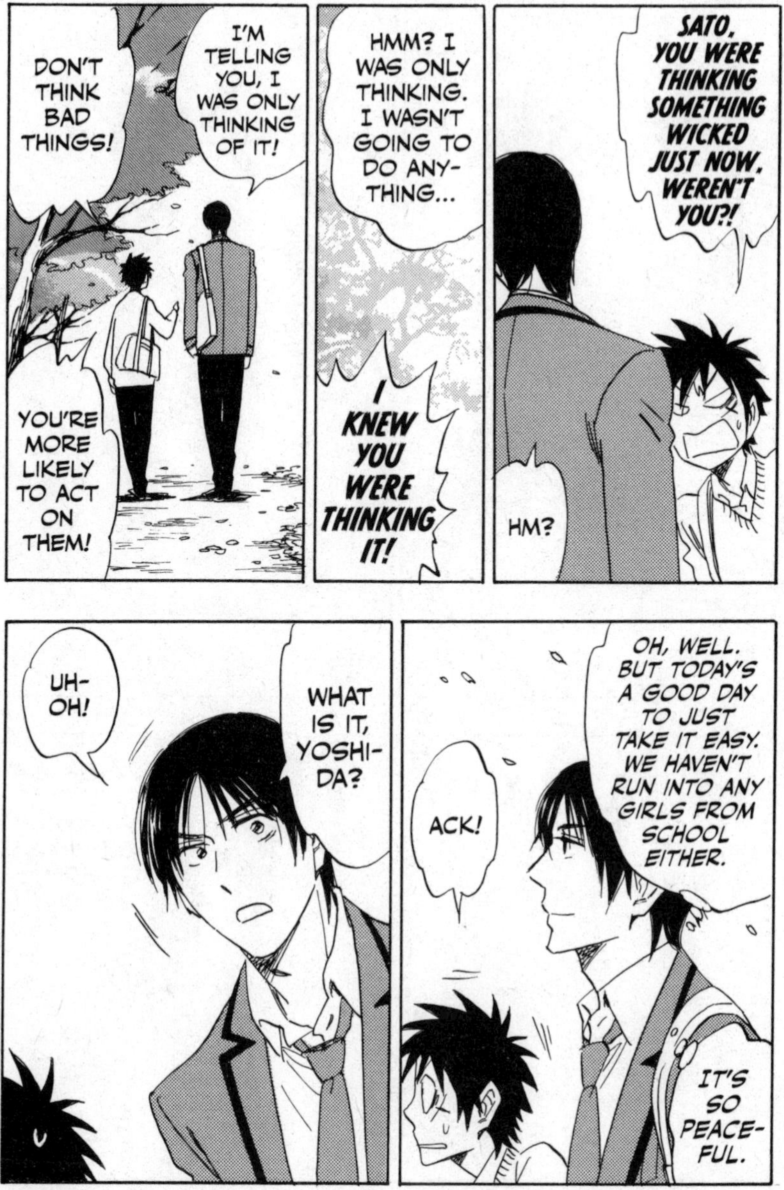
SATO. YOU WERE THINKING SOMETHING WICKED JUST NOW, WEREN'T YOU?!
HM?
HMM? I WAS ONLY THINKING. I WASN'T GOING TO DO ANYTHING...
I KNEW YOU WERE THINKING IT!
I'M TELLING YOU, I WAS ONLY THINKING OF IT!
DON'T THINK BAD THINGS!
YOU'RE MORE LIKELY TO ACT ON THEM!
OH, WELL. BUT TODAY'S A GOOD DAY TO JUST TAKE IT EASY. WE HAVEN'T RUN INTO ANY GIRLS FROM SCHOOL EITHER.
ACK!
IT'S SO PEACEFUL.
WHAT IS IT, YOSHIDA?
UH-OH!

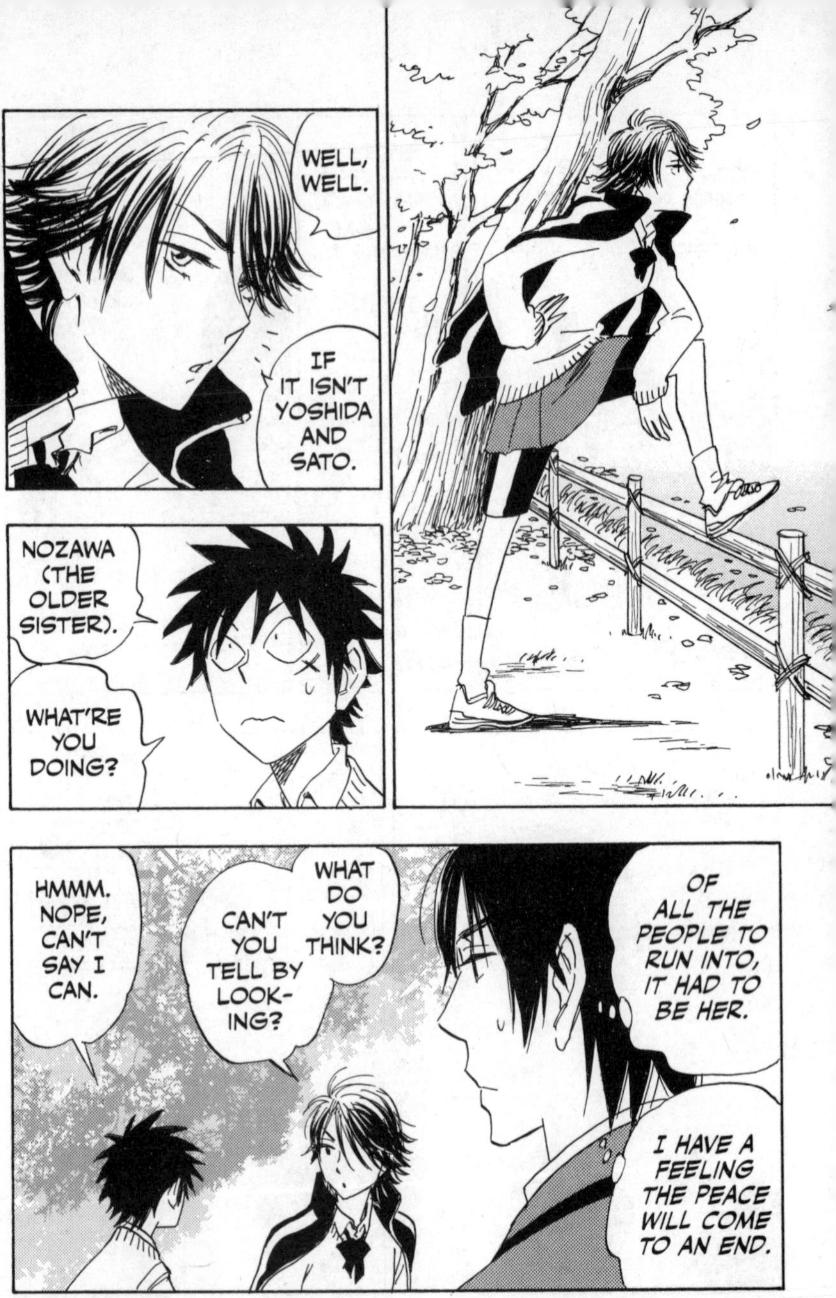
WELL, WELL.
IF IT ISN'T YOSHIDA AND SATO.
NOZAWA (THE OLDER SISTER).
WHAT'RE YOU DOING?
OF ALL THE PEOPLE TO RUN INTO, IT HAD TO BE HER.
I HAVE A FEELING THE PEACE WILL COME TO AN END.
WHAT DO YOU THINK?
CAN'T YOU TELL BY LOOKING?
HMMM. NOPE, CAN'T SAY I CAN.

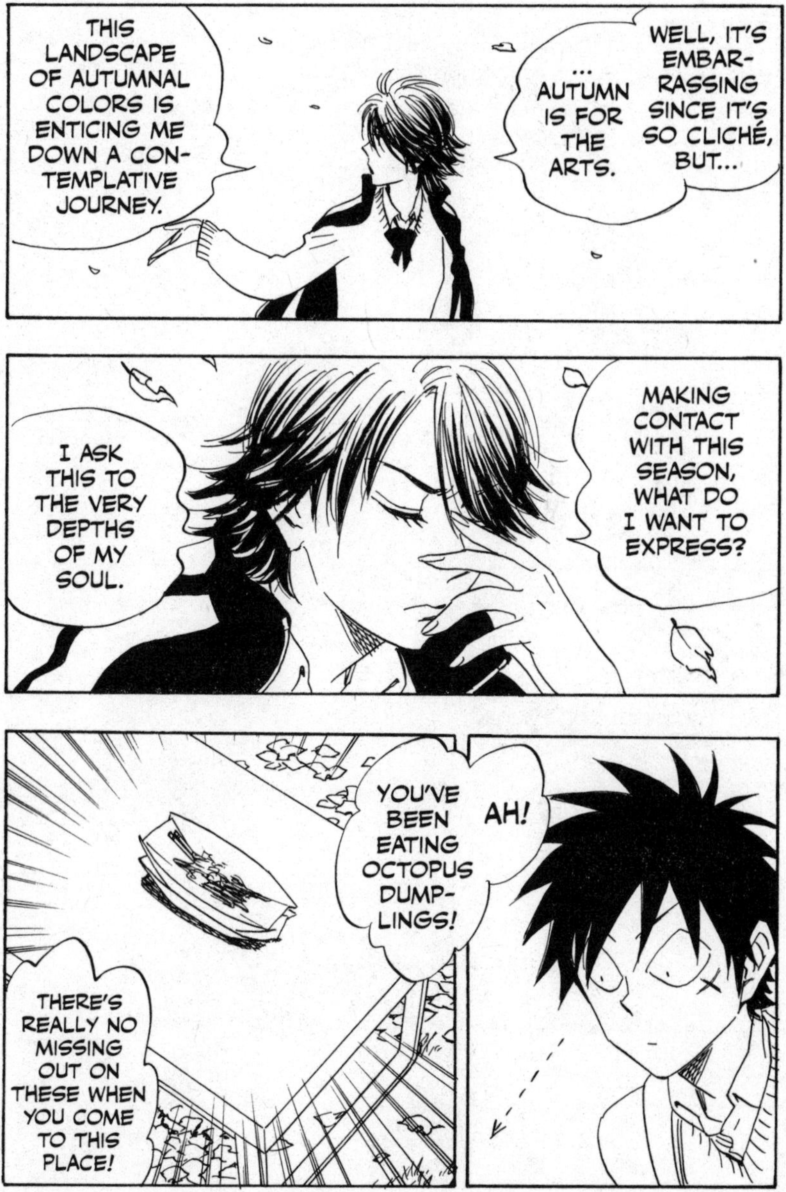
WELL, IT'S EMBARRASSING SINCE IT'S SO CLICHÉ, BUT...
... AUTUMN IS FOR THE ARTS.
THIS LANDSCAPE OF AUTUMNAL COLORS IS ENTICING ME DOWN A CONTEMPLATIVE JOURNEY.
MAKING CONTACT WITH THIS SEASON, WHAT DO I WANT TO EXPRESS?
I ASK THIS TO THE VERY DEPTHS OF MY SOUL.
AH!
YOU'VE BEEN EATING OCTOPUS DUMPLINGS!
THERE'S REALLY NO MISSING OUT ON THESE WHEN YOU COME TO THIS PLACE!

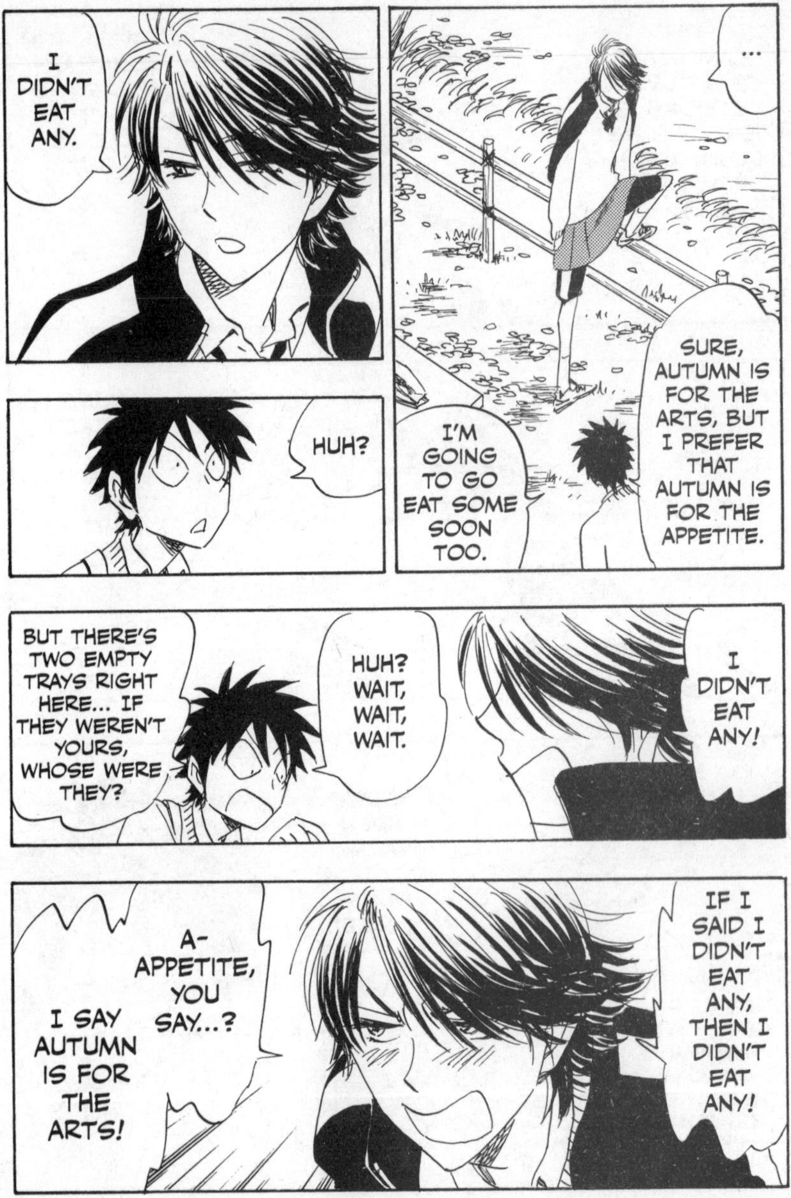
...
SURE, AUTUMN IS FOR THE ARTS, BUT I PREFER THAT AUTUMN IS FOR THE APPETITE.
I'M GOING TO GO EAT SOME SOON TOO.
I DIDN'T EAT ANY.
HUH?
I DIDN'T EAT ANY!
HUH? WAIT, WAIT, WAIT.
BUT THERE'S TWO EMPTY TRAYS RIGHT HERE... IF THEY WEREN'T YOURS, WHOSE WERE THEY?
IF I SAID I DIDN'T EAT ANY, THEN I DIDN'T EAT ANY!
A- APPETITE, YOU SAY...?
I SAY AUTUMN IS FOR THE ARTS!

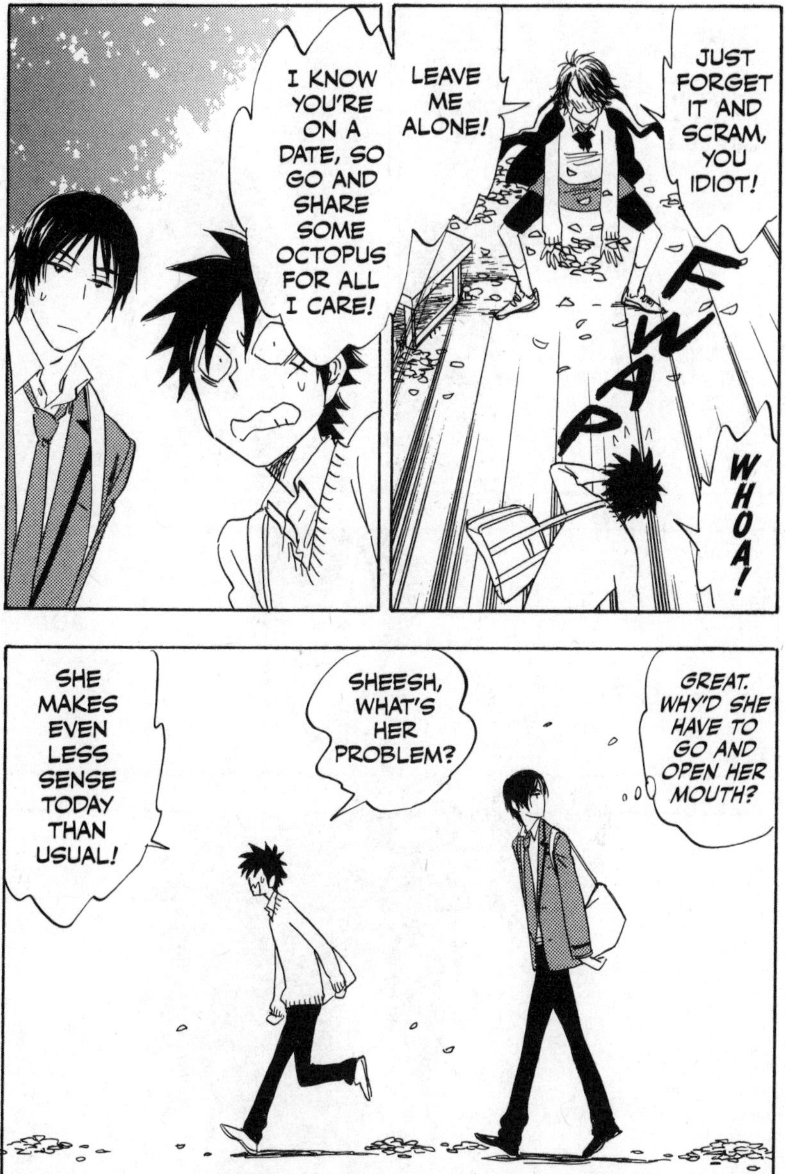
JUST FORGET IT AND SCRAM, YOU IDIOT!
LEAVE ME ALONE!
FWAP
WHOA!
I KNOW YOU'RE ON A DATE, SO GO AND SHARE SOME OCTOPUS FOR ALL I CARE!
GREAT. WHY'D SHE HAVE TO GO AND OPEN HER MOUTH?
SHEESH, WHAT'S HER PROBLEM?
SHE MAKES EVEN LESS SENSE TODAY THAN USUAL!

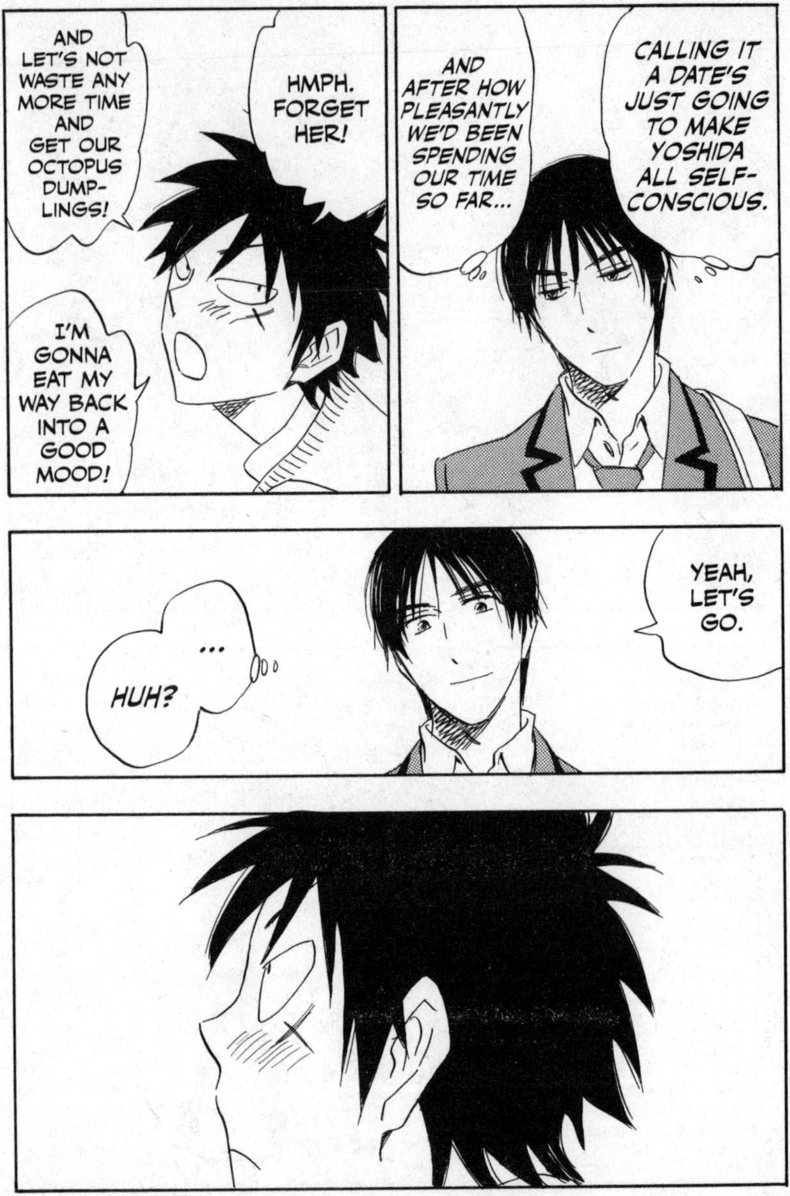
CALLING IT A DATE'S JUST GOING TO MAKE YOSHIDA ALL SELF-CONSCIOUS.
AND AFTER HOW PLEASANTLY WE'D BEEN SPENDING OUR TIME SO FAR...
HMPH. FORGET HER!
AND LET'S NOT WASTE ANY MORE TIME AND GET OUR OCTOPUS DUMP-LINGS!
I'M GONNA EAT MY WAY BACK INTO A GOOD MOOD!
YEAH, LET'S GO.
...
HUH?

COULD THIS MEAN ...

...THAT HE'D ALWAYS BEEN CONSIDERING THIS OUTING A DATE?

?!

AAAH! IT'S THERE!!

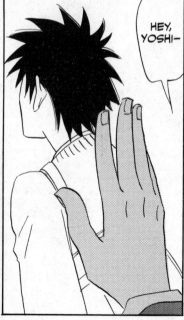

HEY, YOSHI—

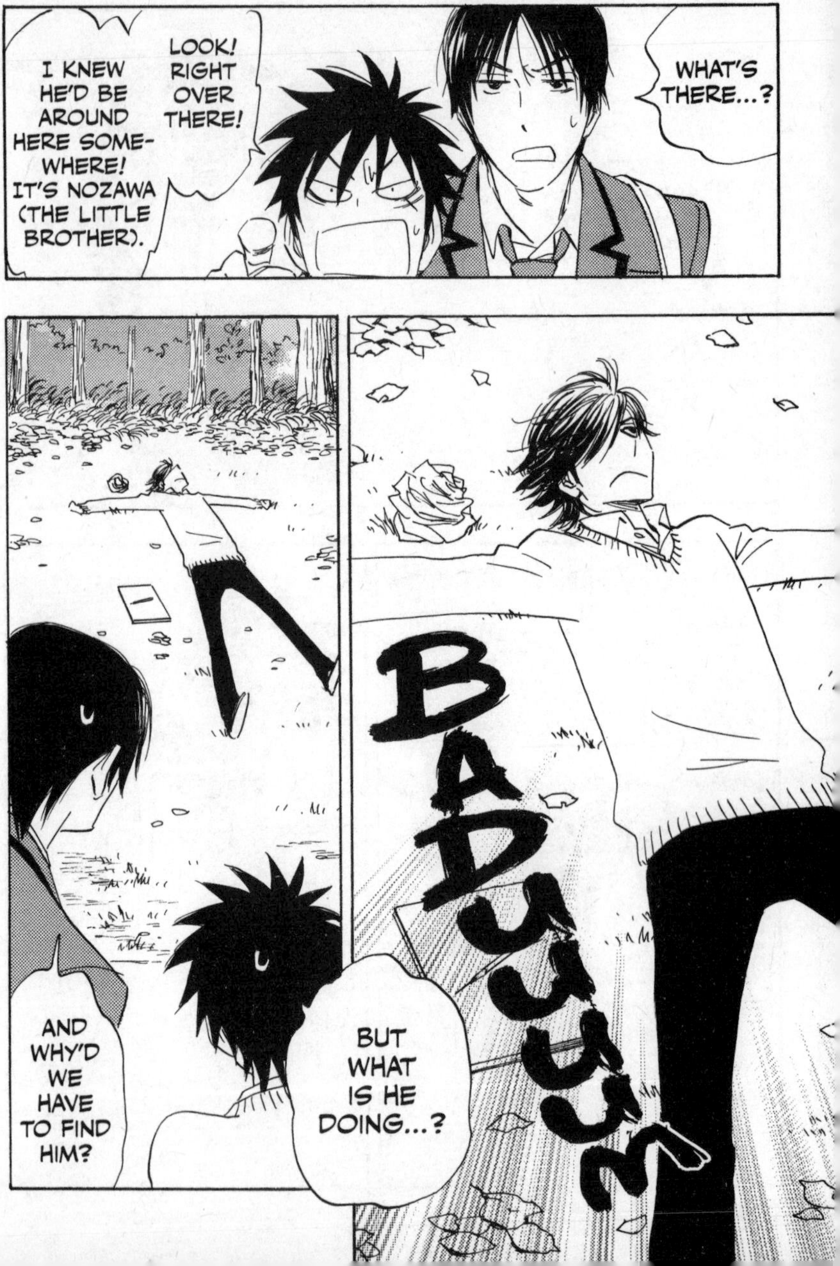
WHAT'S THERE...?
LOOK! RIGHT OVER THERE!
I KNEW HE'D BE AROUND HERE SOMEWHERE! IT'S NOZAWA (THE LITTLE BROTHER).
BADUUUM
BUT WHAT IS HE DOING...?
AND WHY'D WE HAVE TO FIND HIM?

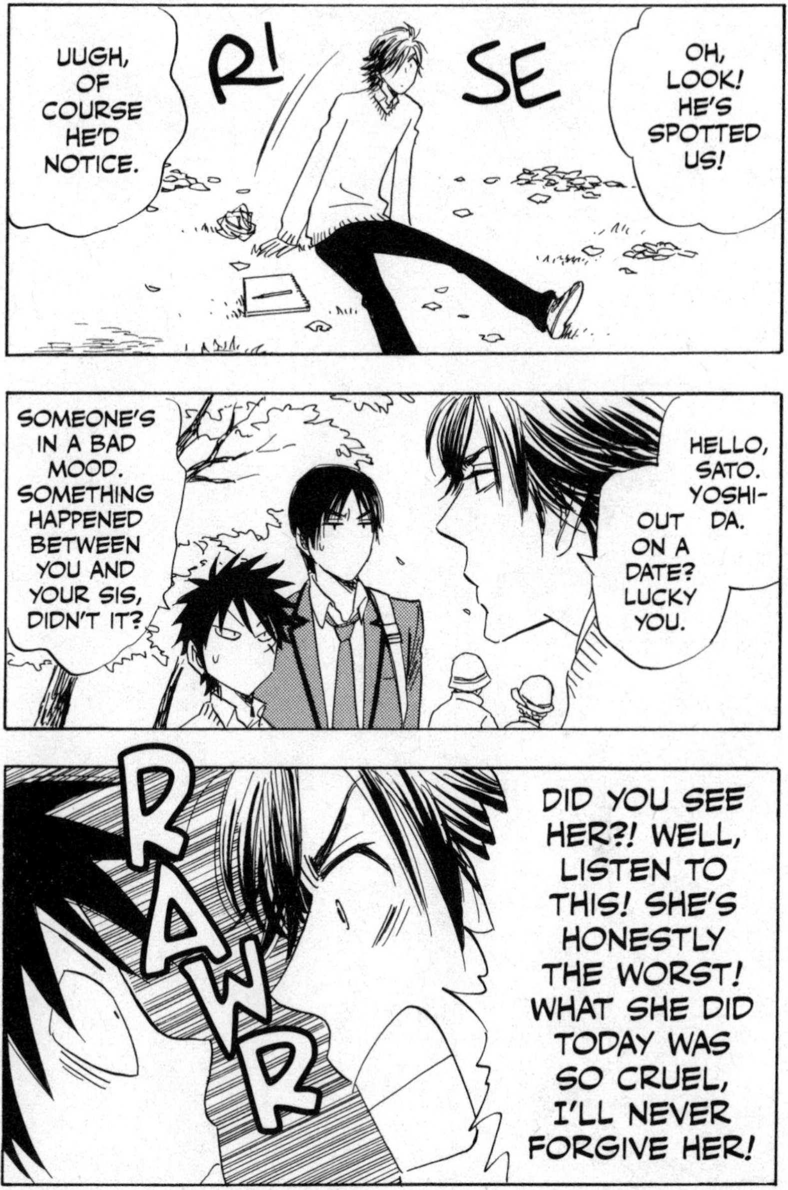
OH, LOOK! HE'S SPOTTED US!
RI SE
UUGH, OF COURSE HE'D NOTICE.
HELLO, SATO. YOSHIDA.
OUT ON A DATE? LUCKY YOU.
SOMEONE'S IN A BAD MOOD. SOMETHING HAPPENED BETWEEN YOU AND YOUR SIS, DIDN'T IT?
DID YOU SEE HER?! WELL, LISTEN TO THIS! SHE'S HONESTLY THE WORST! WHAT SHE DID TODAY WAS SO CRUEL, I'LL NEVER FORGIVE HER!
RAWR

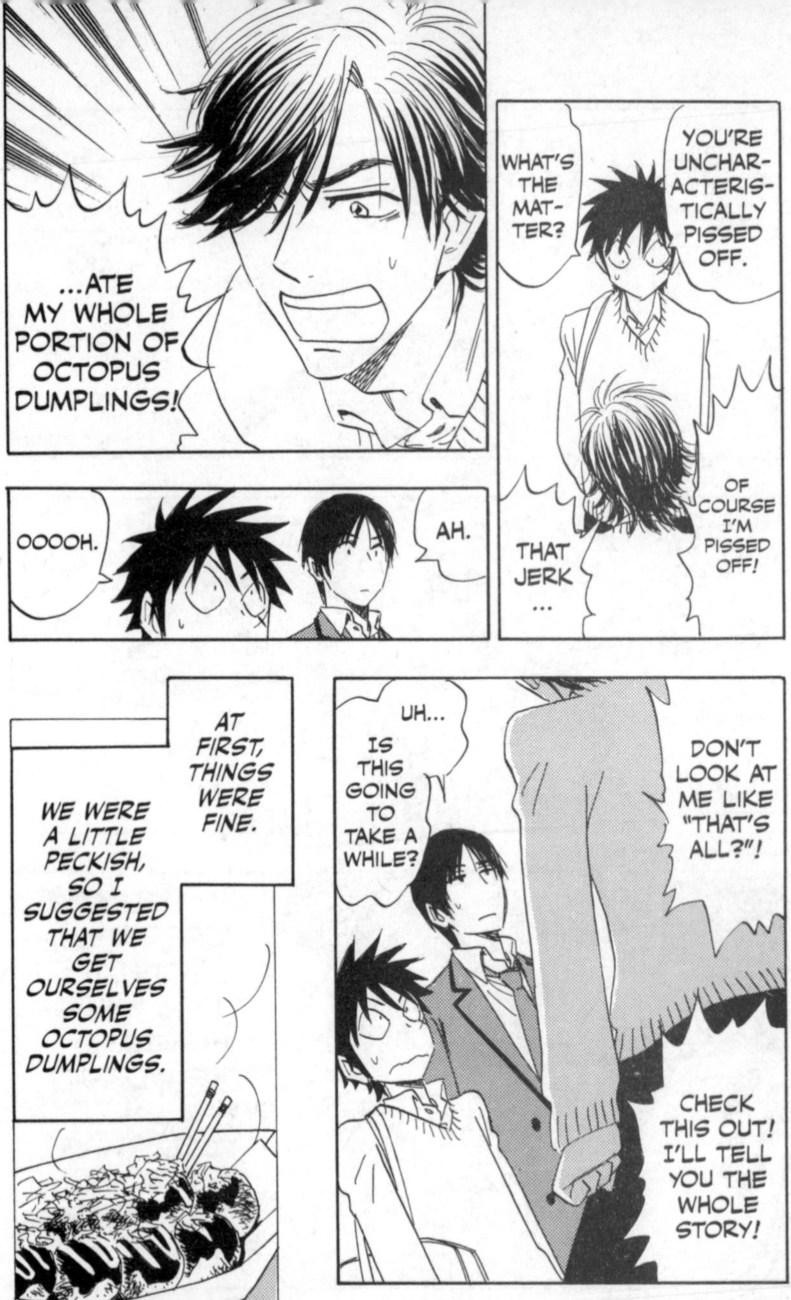
WHAT'S THE MATTER?
YOU'RE UNCHARACTERISTICALLY PISSED OFF.
OF COURSE I'M PISSED OFF!
THAT JERK...
...ATE MY WHOLE PORTION OF OCTOPUS DUMPLINGS!
AH.
OOOOH.
DON'T LOOK AT ME LIKE "THAT'S ALL?"!
UH...
IS THIS GOING TO TAKE A WHILE?
CHECK THIS OUT! I'LL TELL YOU THE WHOLE STORY!
AT FIRST, THINGS WERE FINE.
WE WERE A LITTLE PECKISH, SO I SUGGESTED THAT WE GET OURSELVES SOME OCTOPUS DUMPLINGS.

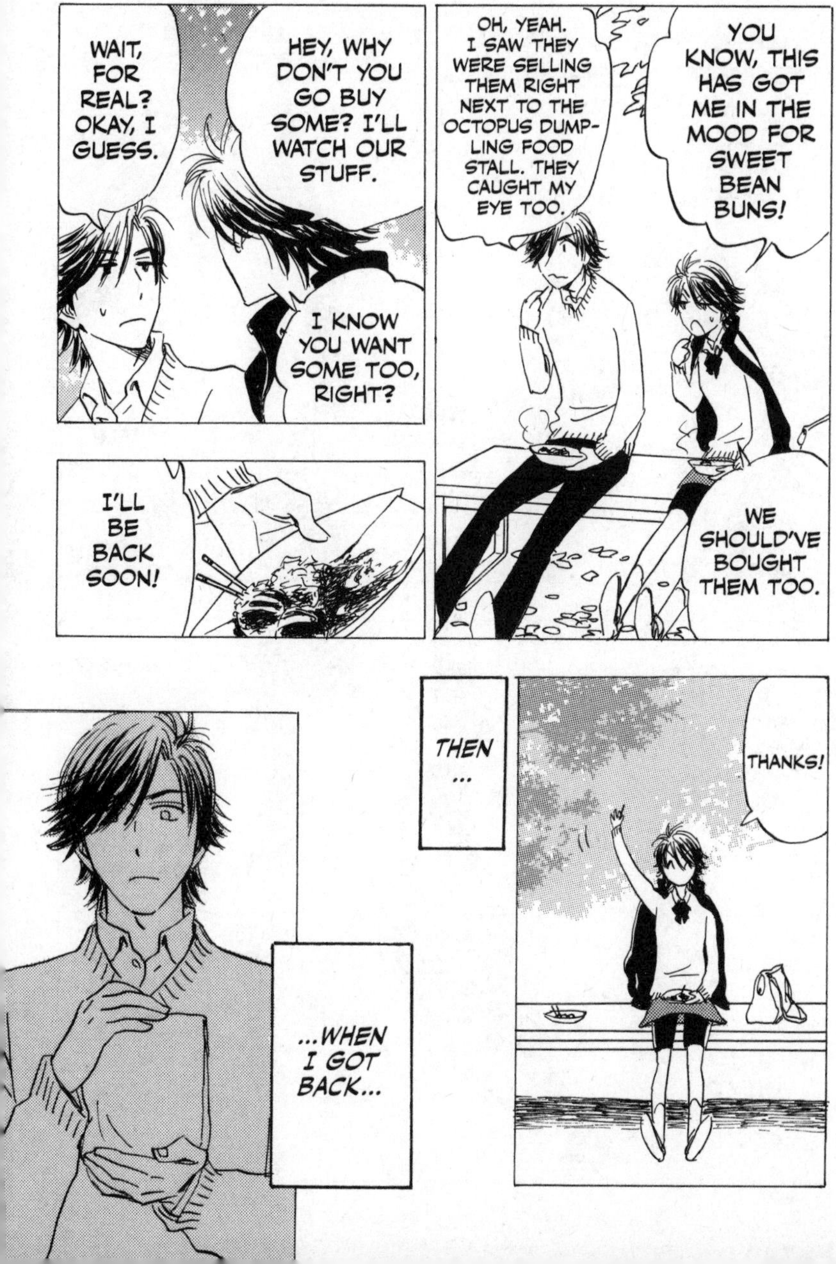
YOU KNOW, THIS HAS GOT ME IN THE MOOD FOR SWEET BEAN BUNS!
OH, YEAH. I SAW THEY WERE SELLING THEM RIGHT NEXT TO THE OCTOPUS DUMP-LING FOOD STALL. THEY CAUGHT MY EYE TOO.
WE SHOULD'VE BOUGHT THEM TOO.
HEY, WHY DON'T YOU GO BUY SOME? I'LL WATCH OUR STUFF.
WAIT, FOR REAL? OKAY, I GUESS.
I KNOW YOU WANT SOME TOO, RIGHT?
I'LL BE BACK SOON!
THANKS!
THEN ...
...WHEN I GOT BACK...

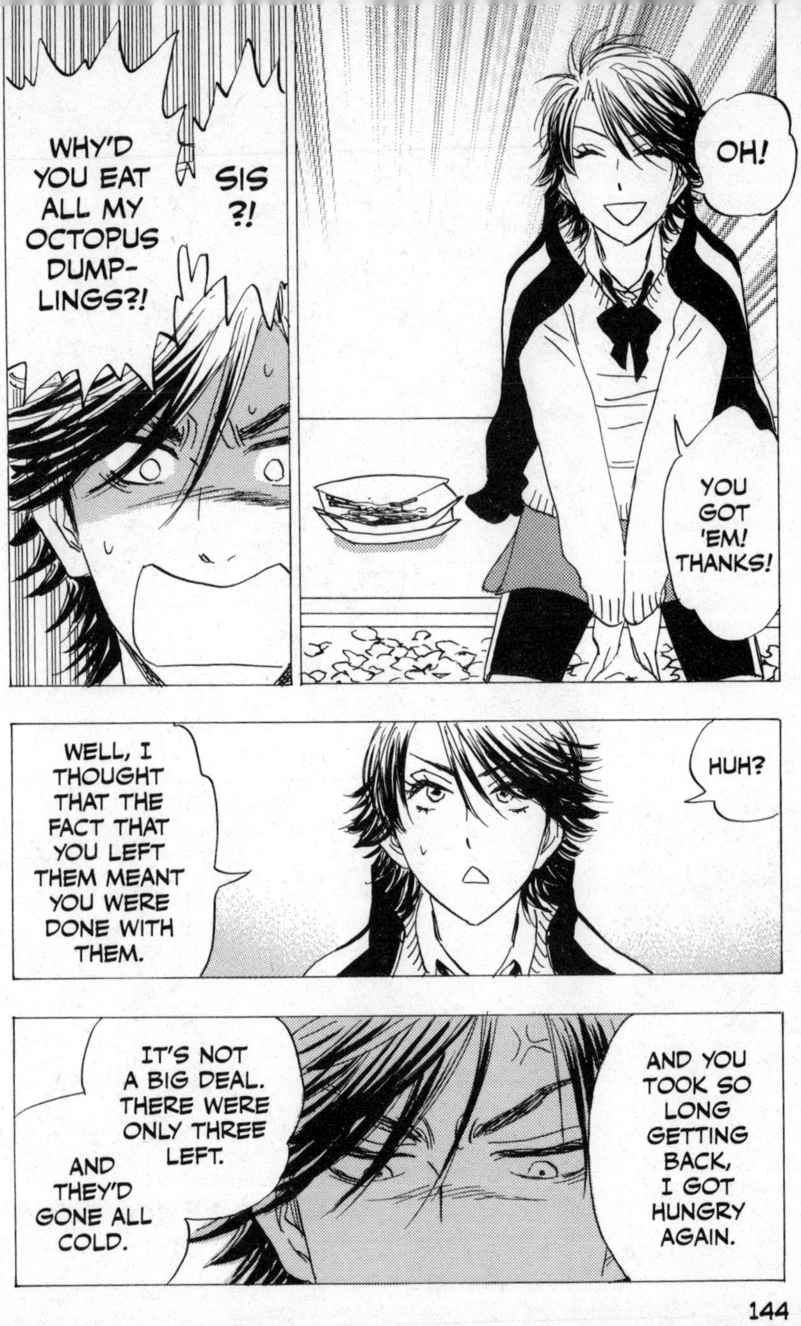
OH!
YOU GOT 'EM! THANKS!
SIS?!
WHY'D YOU EAT ALL MY OCTOPUS DUMP-LINGS?!
HUH?
WELL, I THOUGHT THAT THE FACT THAT YOU LEFT THEM MEANT YOU WERE DONE WITH THEM.
AND YOU TOOK SO LONG GETTING BACK, I GOT HUNGRY AGAIN.
IT'S NOT A BIG DEAL. THERE WERE ONLY THREE LEFT.
AND THEY'D GONE ALL COLD.

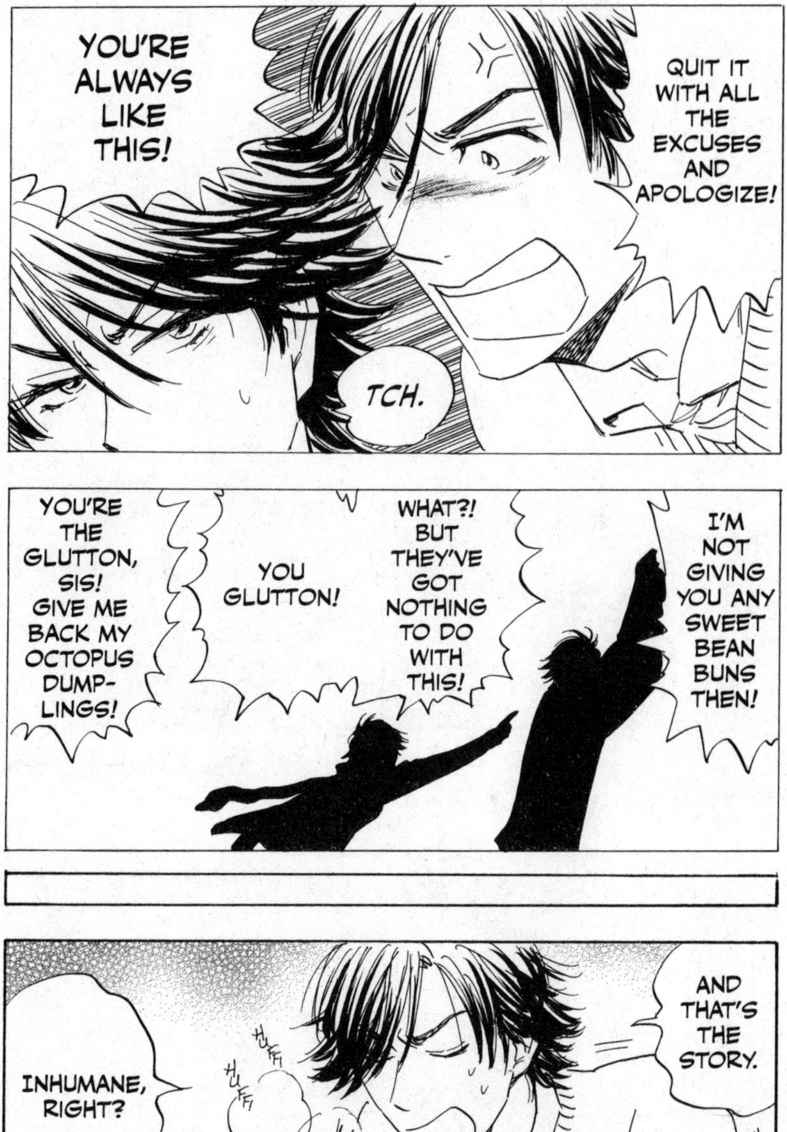
QUIT IT WITH ALL THE EXCUSES AND APOLOGIZE!
YOU'RE ALWAYS LIKE THIS!
TCH.
I'M NOT GIVING YOU ANY SWEET BEAN BUNS THEN!
WHAT?! BUT THEY'VE GOT NOTHING TO DO WITH THIS!
YOU GLUTTON!
YOU'RE THE GLUTTON, SIS! GIVE ME BACK MY OCTOPUS DUMP-LINGS!
AND THAT'S THE STORY.
HUFF!
HUFF!
INHUMANE, RIGHT?

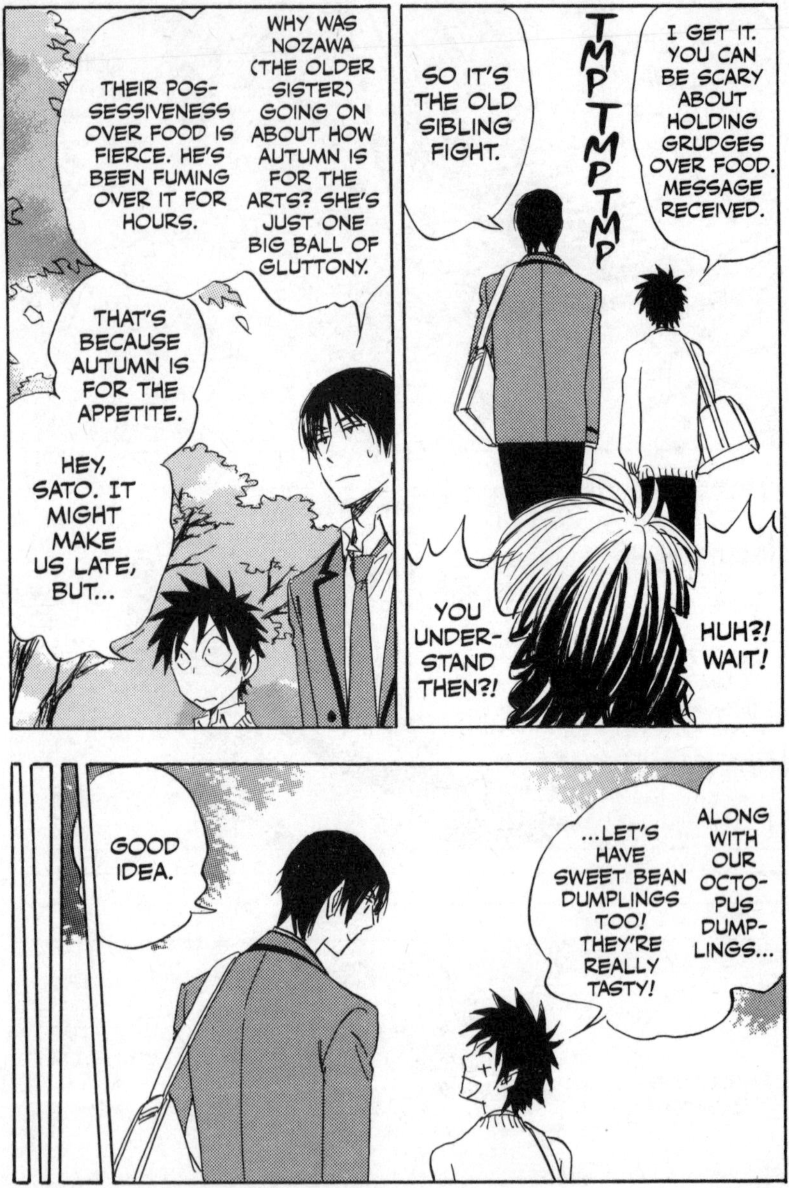
I GET IT. YOU CAN BE SCARY ABOUT HOLDING GRUDGES OVER FOOD. MESSAGE RECEIVED.
TMP TMP TMP TMP
SO IT'S THE OLD SIBLING FIGHT.
HUH?! WAIT!
YOU UNDERSTAND THEN?!
WHY WAS NOZAWA (THE OLDER SISTER) GOING ON ABOUT HOW AUTUMN IS FOR THE ARTS? SHE'S JUST ONE BIG BALL OF GLUTTONY.
THEIR POSSESSIVENESS OVER FOOD IS FIERCE. HE'S BEEN FUMING OVER IT FOR HOURS.
THAT'S BECAUSE AUTUMN IS FOR THE APPETITE.
HEY, SATO. IT MIGHT MAKE US LATE, BUT...
ALONG WITH OUR OCTOPUS DUMPLINGS...
...LET'S HAVE SWEET BEAN DUMPLINGS TOO! THEY'RE REALLY TASTY!
GOOD IDEA.

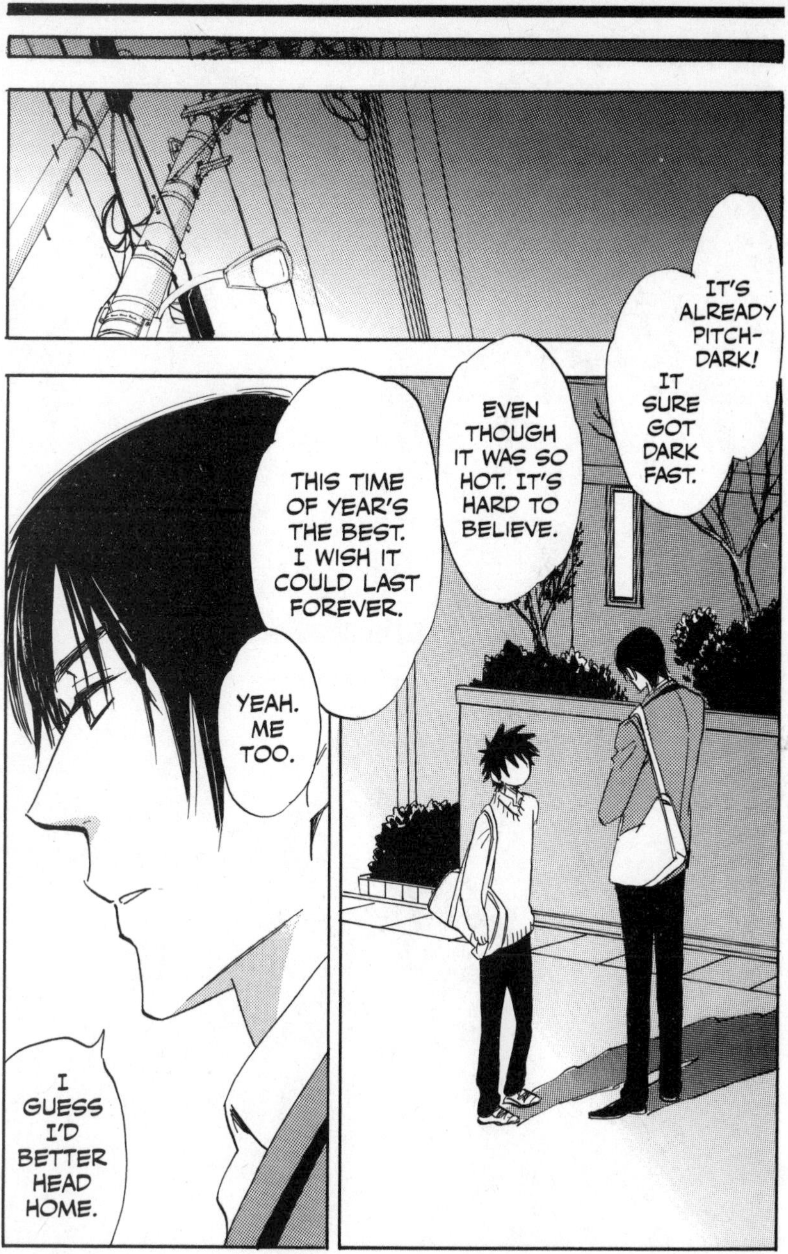
IT'S ALREADY PITCH-DARK!
IT SURE GOT DARK FAST.
EVEN THOUGH IT WAS SO HOT. IT'S HARD TO BELIEVE.
THIS TIME OF YEAR'S THE BEST. I WISH IT COULD LAST FOREVER.
YEAH. ME TOO.
I GUESS I'D BETTER HEAD HOME.

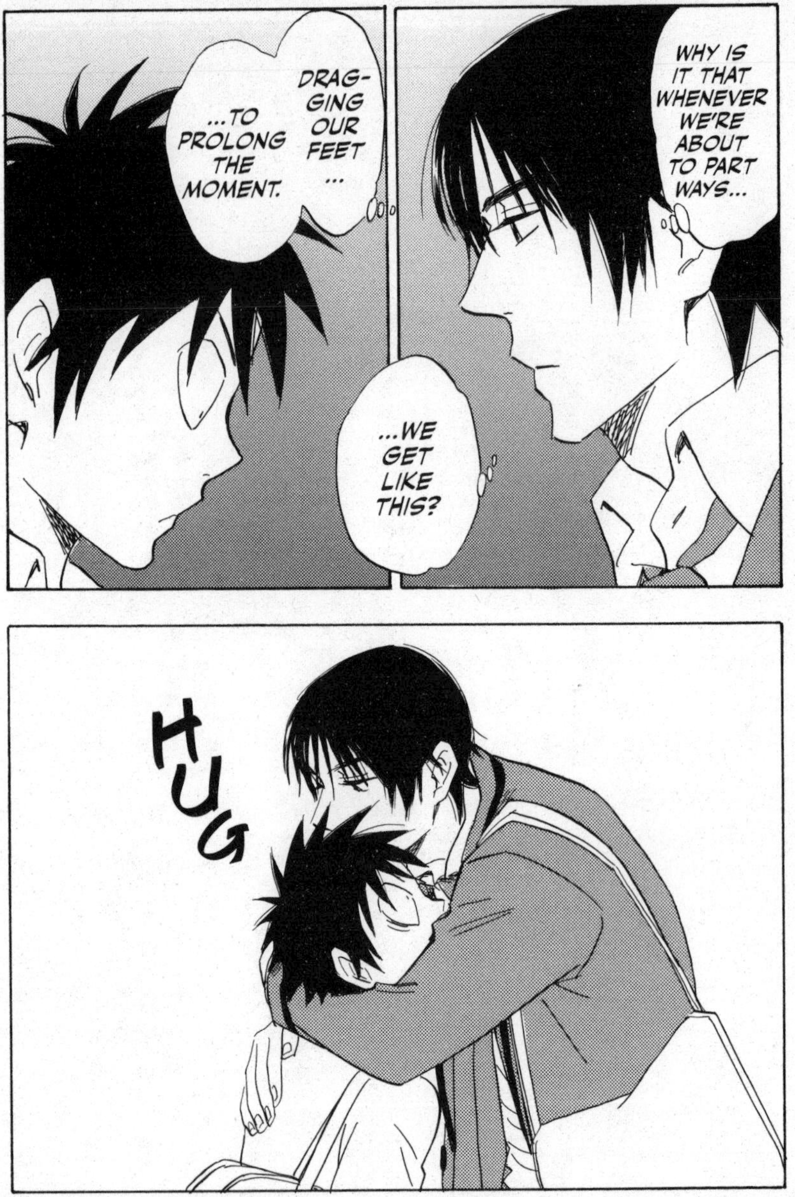
WHY IS IT THAT WHENEVER WE'RE ABOUT TO PART WAYS...
...WE GET LIKE THIS?
DRAG-GING OUR FEET ...
...TO PROLONG THE MOMENT.
HUG

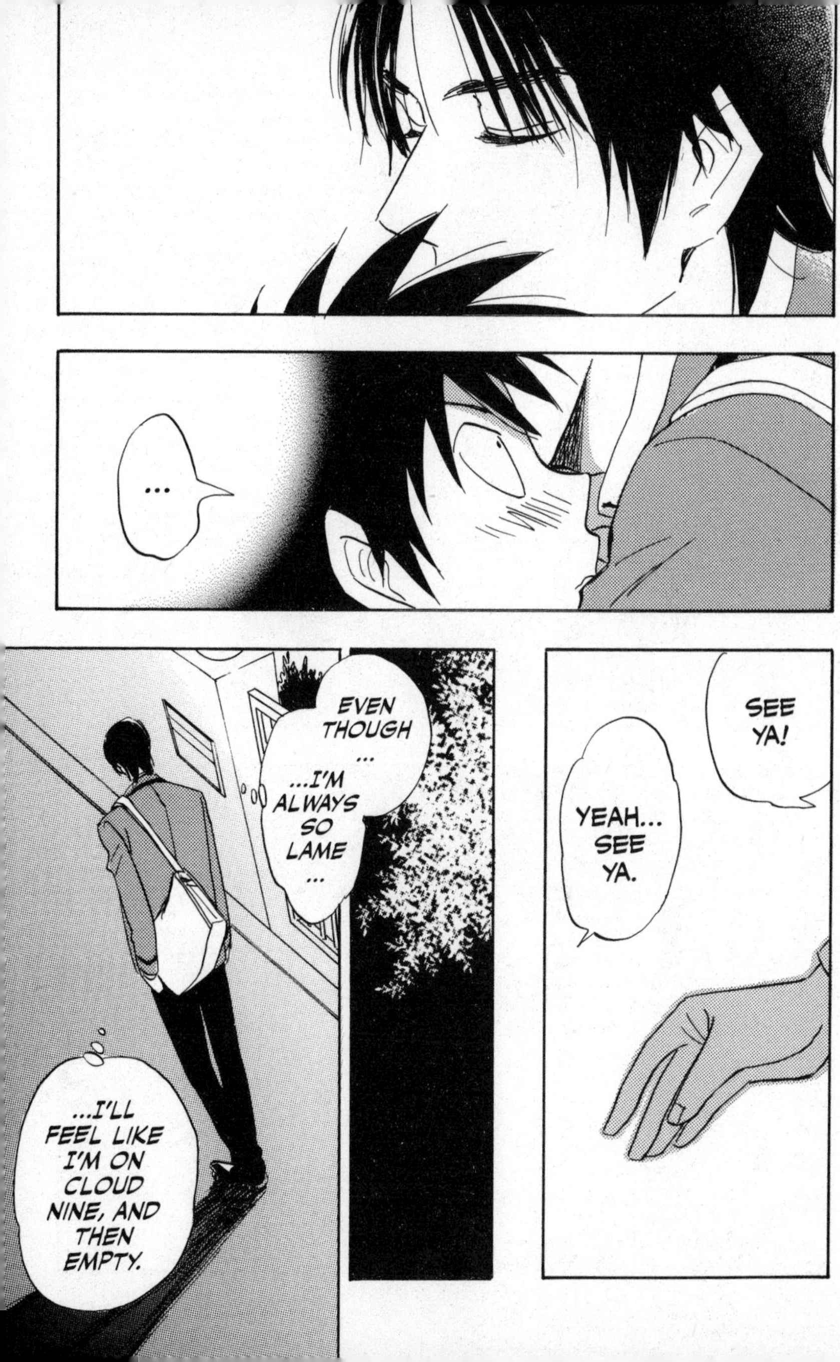
...
SEE YA!
YEAH... SEE YA.
EVEN THOUGH ... ...I'M ALWAYS SO LAME ...
...I'LL FEEL LIKE I'M ON CLOUD NINE, AND THEN EMPTY.

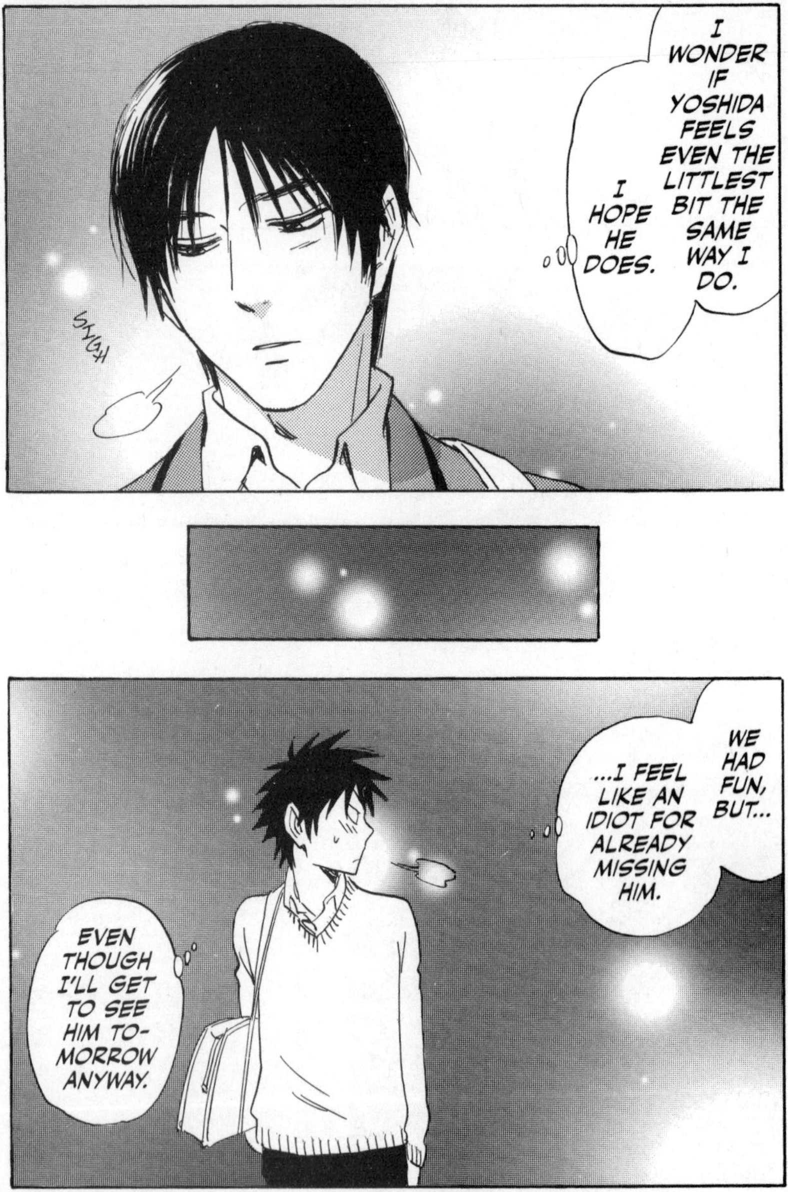
I WONDER IF YOSHIDA FEELS EVEN THE LITTLEST BIT THE SAME WAY I DO.
I HOPE HE DOES.
SIGH
WE HAD FUN, BUT...
...I FEEL LIKE AN IDIOT FOR ALREADY MISSING HIM.
EVEN THOUGH I'LL GET TO SEE HIM TO-MORROW ANYWAY.

ACT. 54 / END

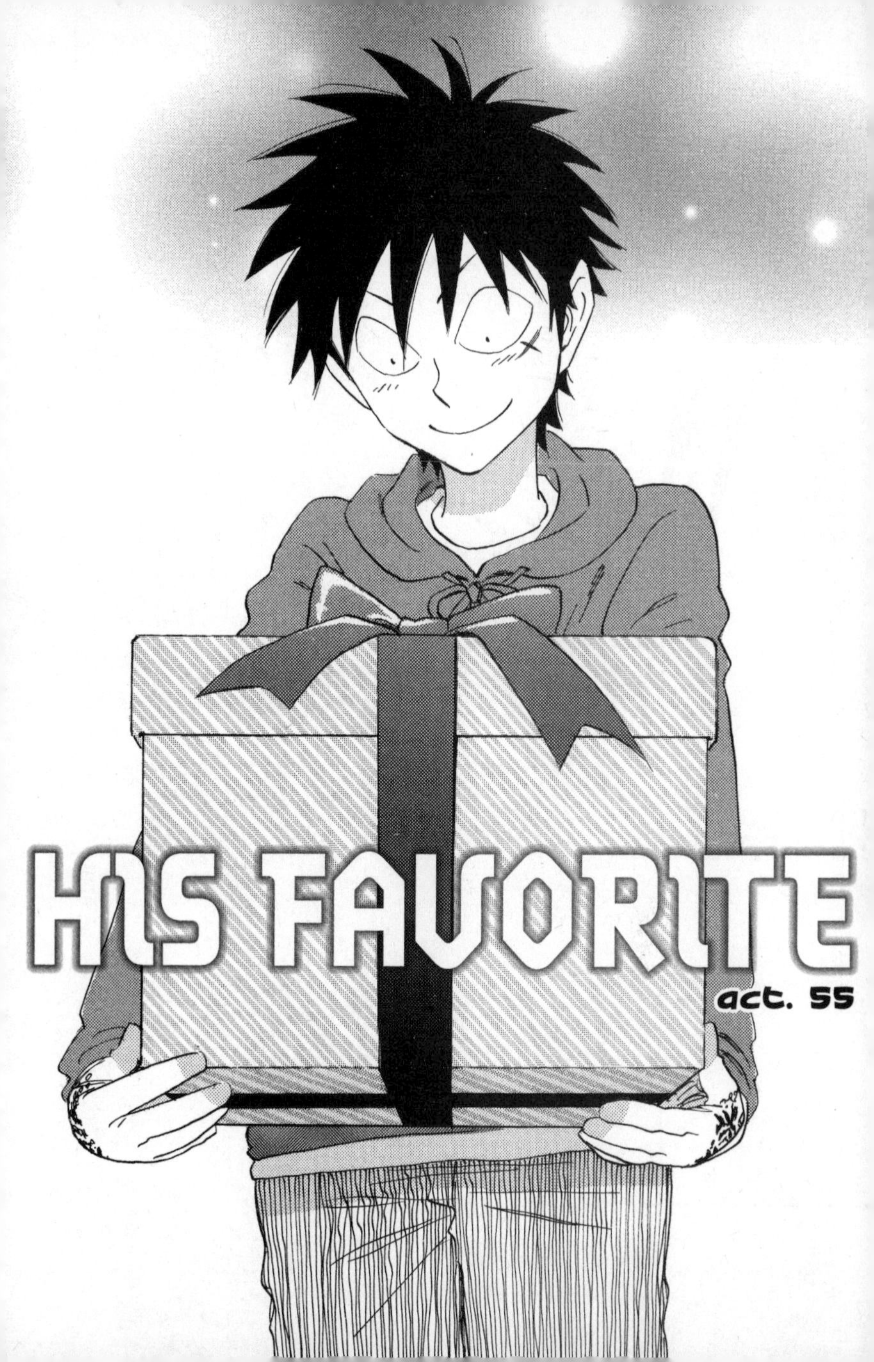
HIS FAVORITE
act. 55

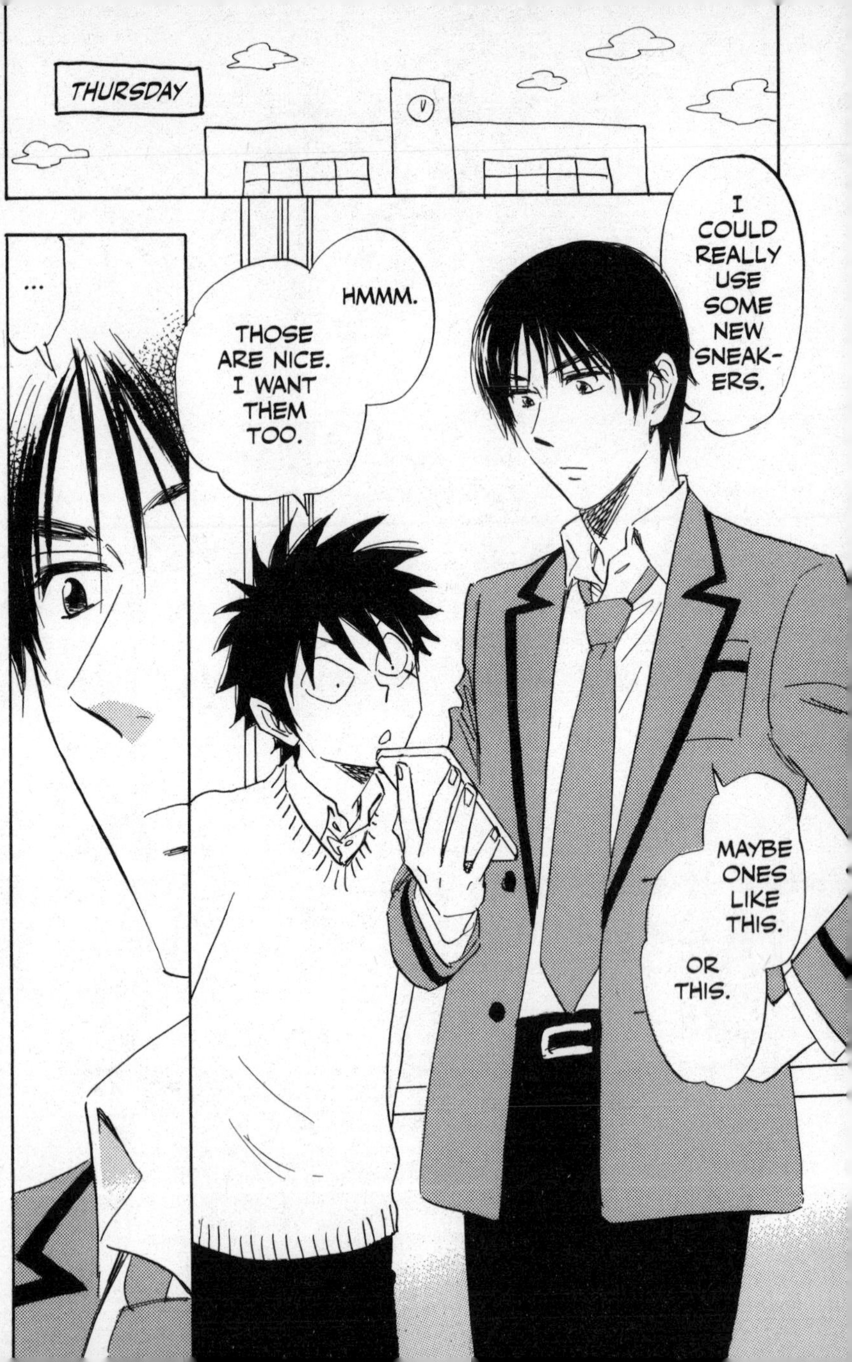
THURSDAY
I COULD REALLY USE SOME NEW SNEAKERS.
HMMM. THOSE ARE NICE. I WANT THEM TOO.
MAYBE ONES LIKE THIS. OR THIS.
...

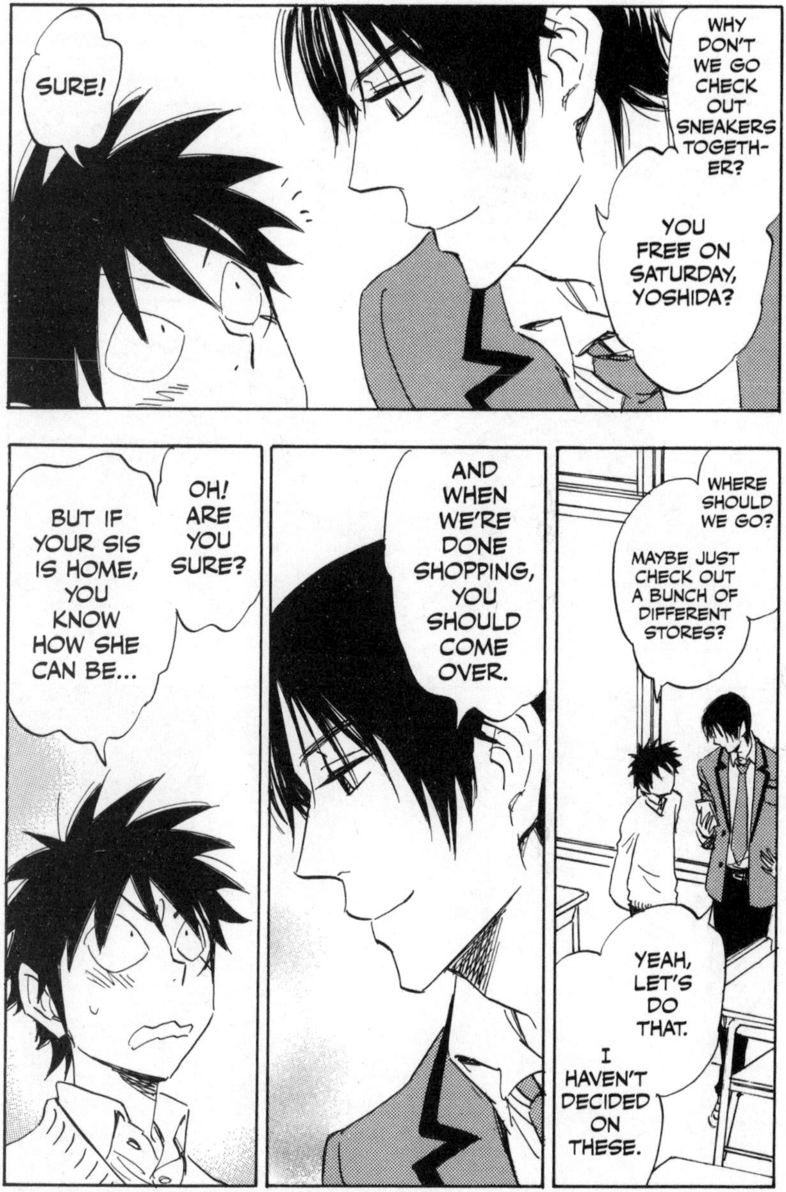
WHY DON'T WE GO CHECK OUT SNEAKERS TOGETH-ER?
YOU FREE ON SATURDAY, YOSHIDA?
SURE!
WHERE SHOULD WE GO?
MAYBE JUST CHECK OUT A BUNCH OF DIFFERENT STORES?
YEAH, LET'S DO THAT.
I HAVEN'T DECIDED ON THESE.
AND WHEN WE'RE DONE SHOPPING, YOU SHOULD COME OVER.
OH! ARE YOU SURE?
BUT IF YOUR SIS IS HOME, YOU KNOW HOW SHE CAN BE...

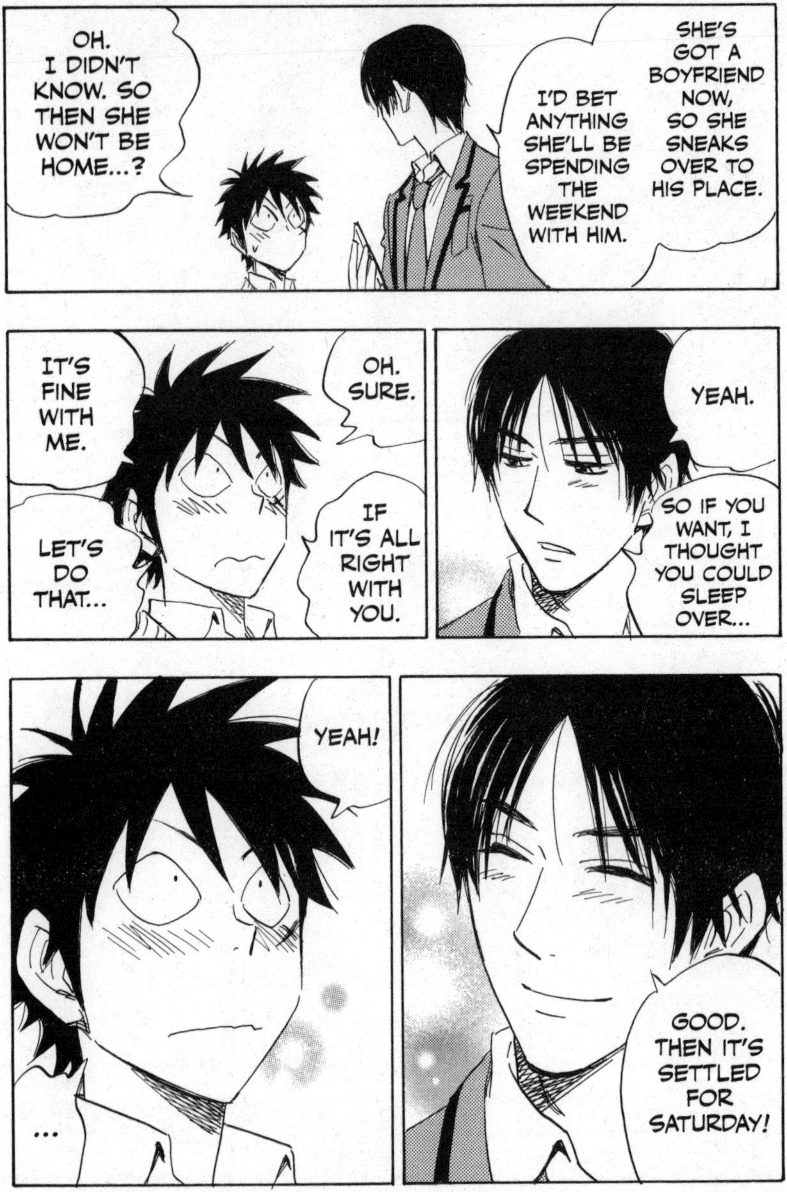
SHE'S GOT A BOYFRIEND NOW, SO SHE SNEAKS OVER TO HIS PLACE.
I'D BET ANYTHING SHE'LL BE SPENDING THE WEEKEND WITH HIM.
OH. I DIDN'T KNOW. SO THEN SHE WON'T BE HOME...?
YEAH.
SO IF YOU WANT, I THOUGHT YOU COULD SLEEP OVER...
OH. SURE.
IT'S FINE WITH ME.
IF IT'S ALL RIGHT WITH YOU.
LET'S DO THAT...
GOOD. THEN IT'S SETTLED FOR SATURDAY!
YEAH!
...

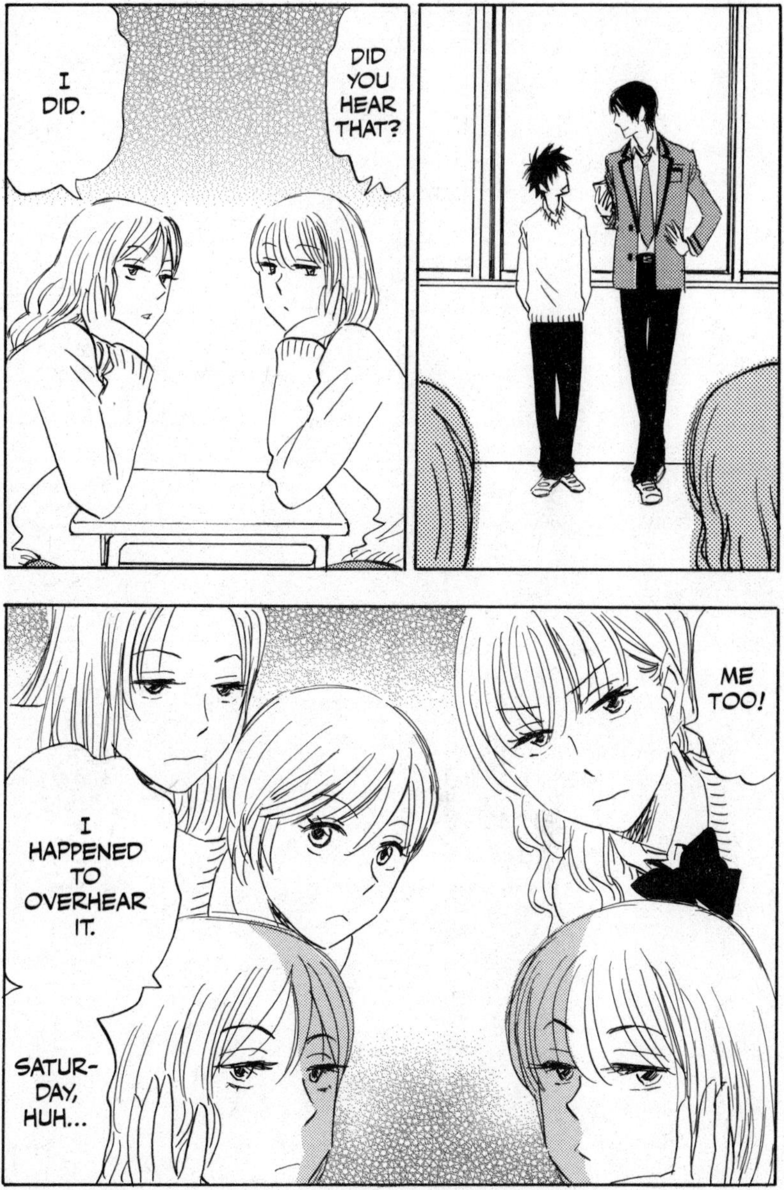
DID YOU HEAR THAT?
I DID.
ME TOO!
I HAPPENED TO OVERHEAR IT.
SATUR-DAY, HUH...

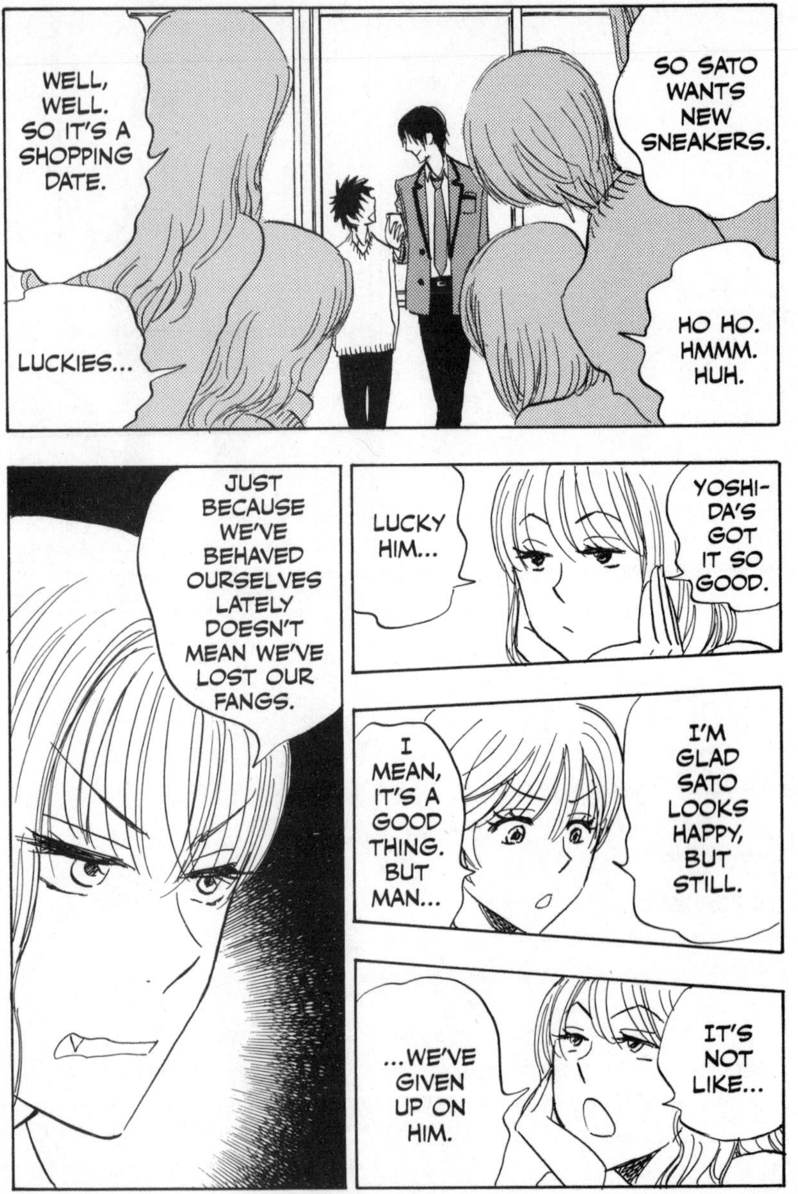
SO SATO WANTS NEW SNEAKERS.
WELL, WELL. SO IT'S A SHOPPING DATE.
HO HO. HMMM. HUH.
LUCKIES...
YOSHI-DA'S GOT IT SO GOOD.
LUCKY HIM...
I'M GLAD SATO LOOKS HAPPY, BUT STILL.
I MEAN, IT'S A GOOD THING. BUT MAN...
IT'S NOT LIKE...
...WE'VE GIVEN UP ON HIM.
JUST BECAUSE WE'VE BEHAVED OURSELVES LATELY DOESN'T MEAN WE'VE LOST OUR FANGS.

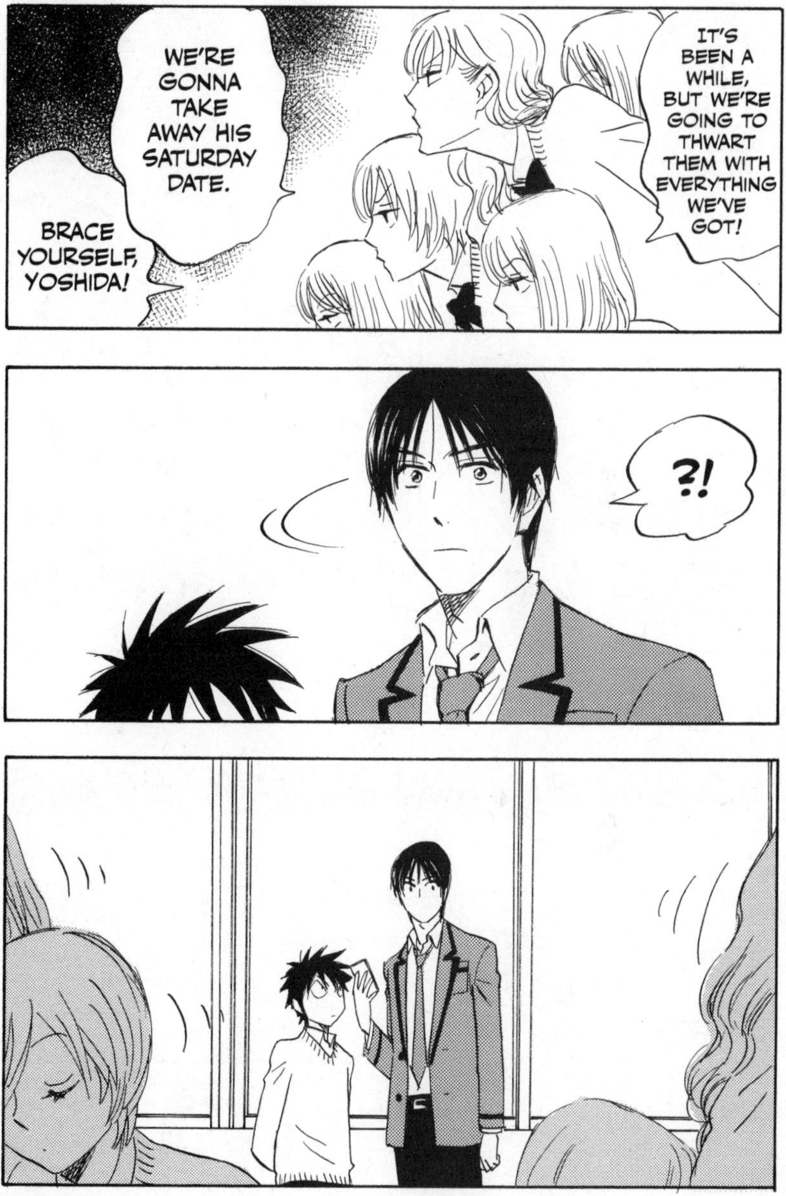
IT'S BEEN A WHILE, BUT WE'RE GOING TO THWART THEM WITH EVERYTHING WE'VE GOT!
WE'RE GONNA TAKE AWAY HIS SATURDAY DATE.
BRACE YOURSELF, YOSHIDA!
?!

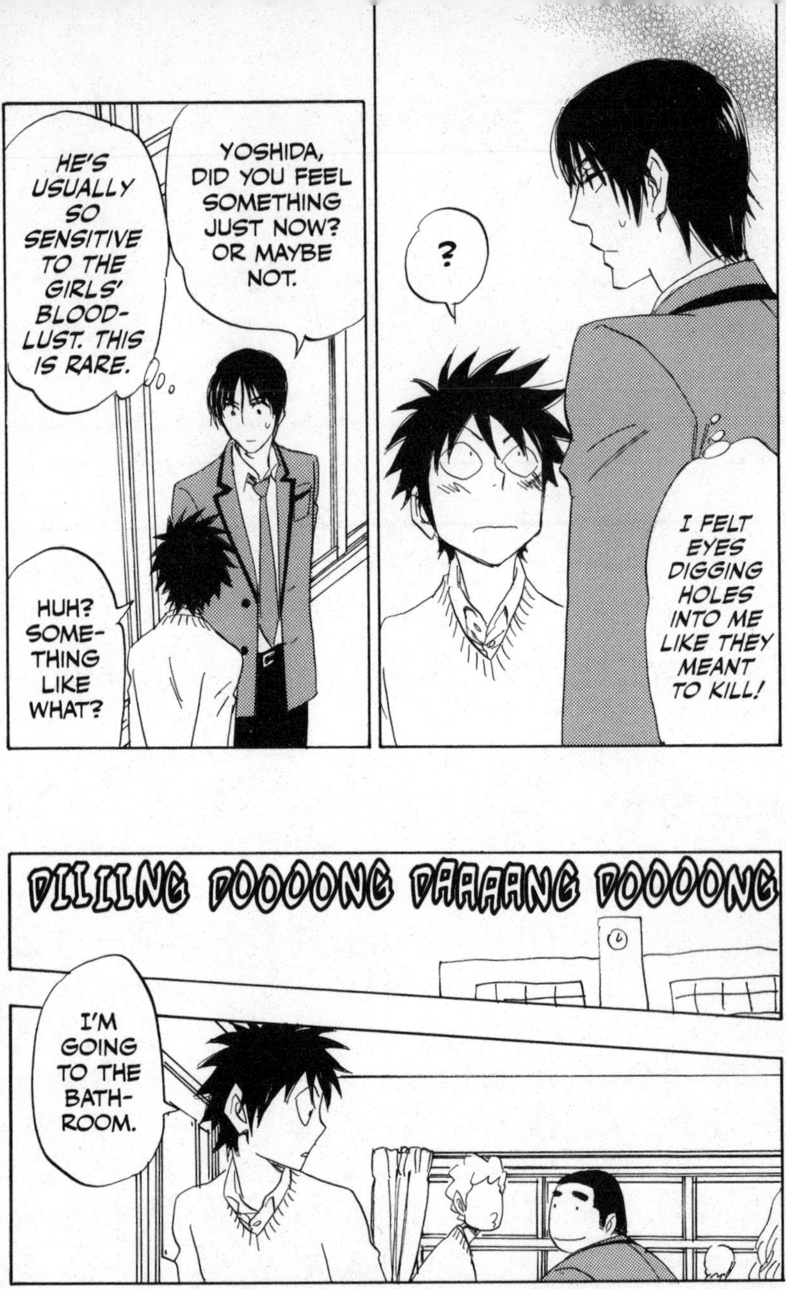
?
I FELT EYES DIGGING HOLES INTO ME LIKE THEY MEANT TO KILL!
YOSHIDA, DID YOU FEEL SOMETHING JUST NOW? OR MAYBE NOT.
HE'S USUALLY SO SENSITIVE TO THE GIRLS' BLOOD-LUST. THIS IS RARE.
HUH? SOME-THING LIKE WHAT?
DIIIING DOOOONG DAAAANG DOOOONG
I'M GOING TO THE BATH-ROOM.

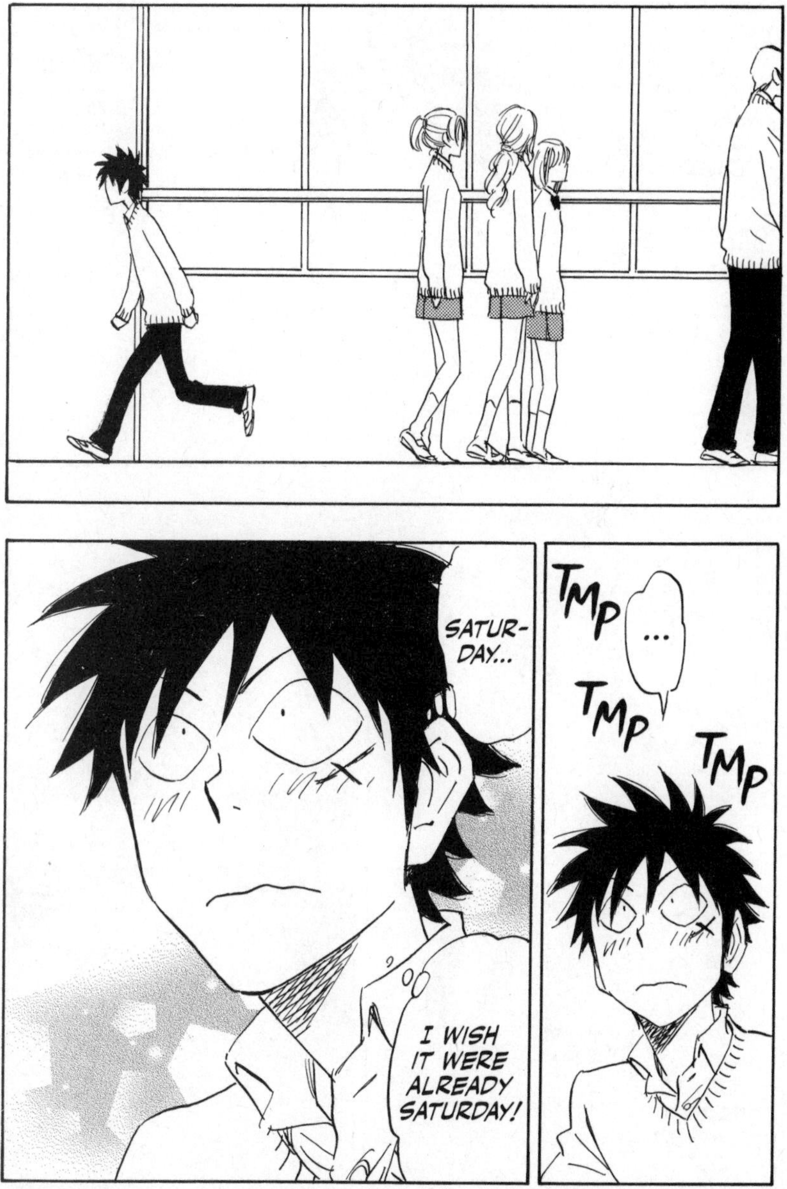
TMP
...
TMP
TMP
SATUR-DAY...
I WISH IT WERE ALREADY SATURDAY!

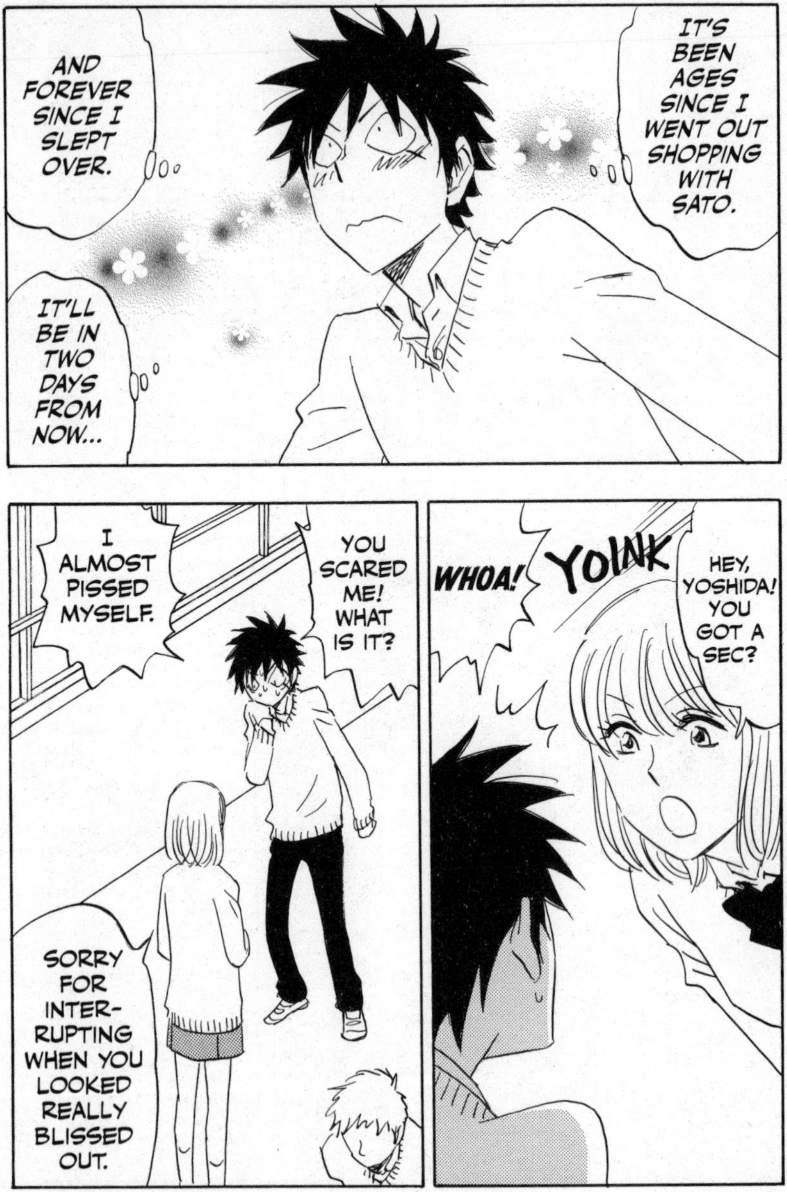
IT'S BEEN AGES SINCE I WENT OUT SHOPPING WITH SATO.
AND FOREVER SINCE I SLEPT OVER.
IT'LL BE IN TWO DAYS FROM NOW...
HEY, YOSHIDA! YOU GOT A SEC?
YOINK
WHOA!
YOU SCARED ME! WHAT IS IT?
I ALMOST PISSED MYSELF.
SORRY FOR INTER-RUPTING WHEN YOU LOOKED REALLY BLISSED OUT.

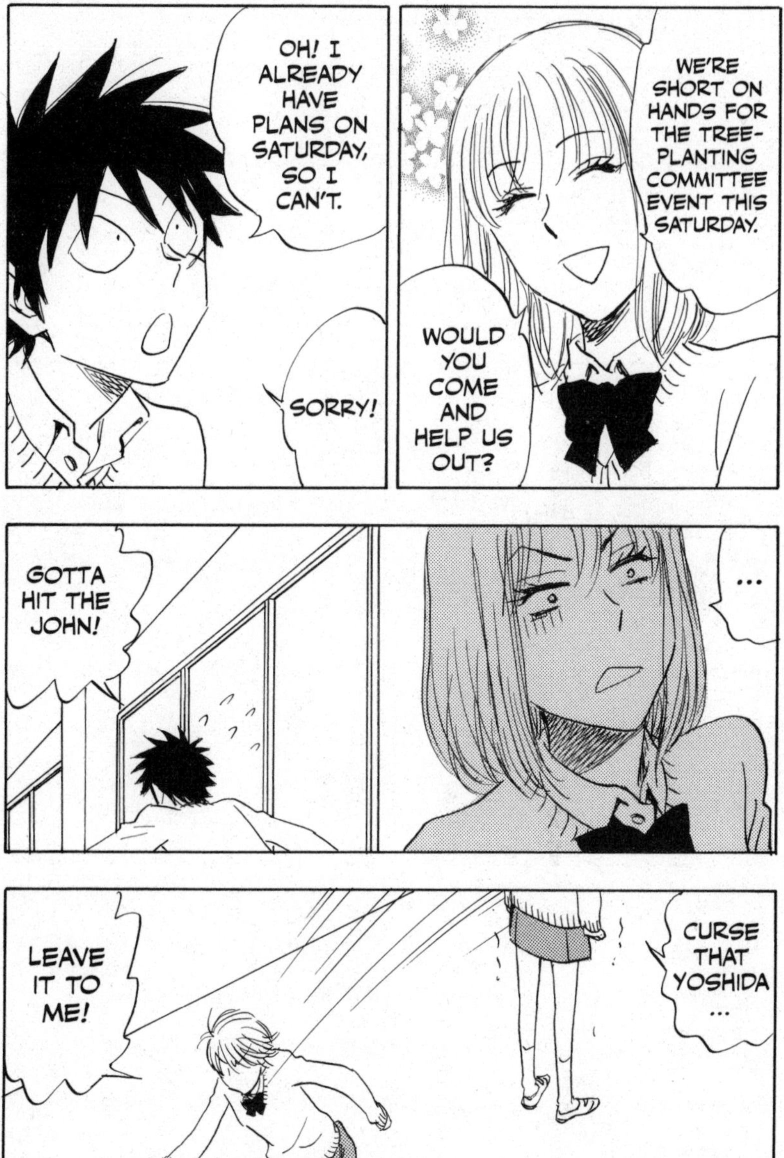
WE'RE SHORT ON HANDS FOR THE TREE-PLANTING COMMITTEE EVENT THIS SATURDAY.
WOULD YOU COME AND HELP US OUT?
OH! I ALREADY HAVE PLANS ON SATURDAY, SO I CAN'T.
SORRY!
...
GOTTA HIT THE JOHN!
CURSE THAT YOSHIDA ...
LEAVE IT TO ME!

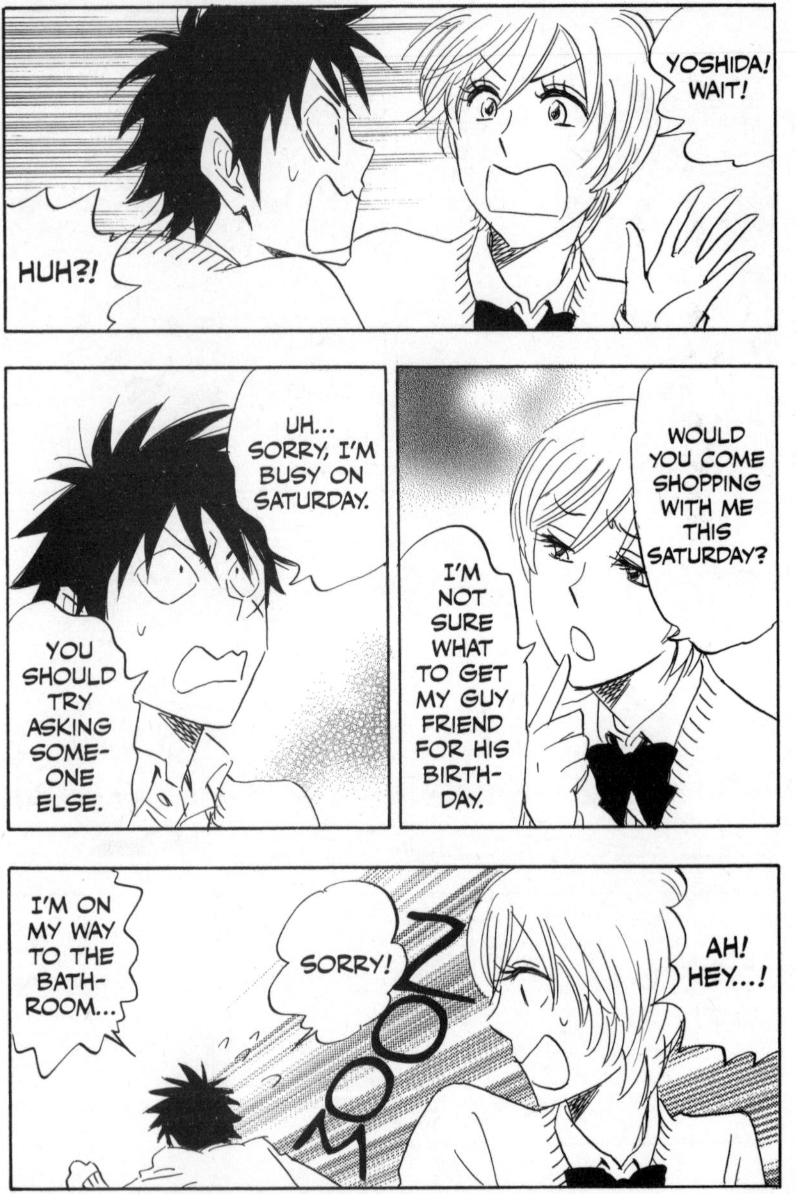
YOSHIDA! WAIT!
HUH?!
WOULD YOU COME SHOPPING WITH ME THIS SATURDAY?
I'M NOT SURE WHAT TO GET MY GUY FRIEND FOR HIS BIRTH-DAY.
UH... SORRY, I'M BUSY ON SATURDAY.
YOU SHOULD TRY ASKING SOME-ONE ELSE.
AH! HEY...!
ZOOM
SORRY!
I'M ON MY WAY TO THE BATH-ROOM...

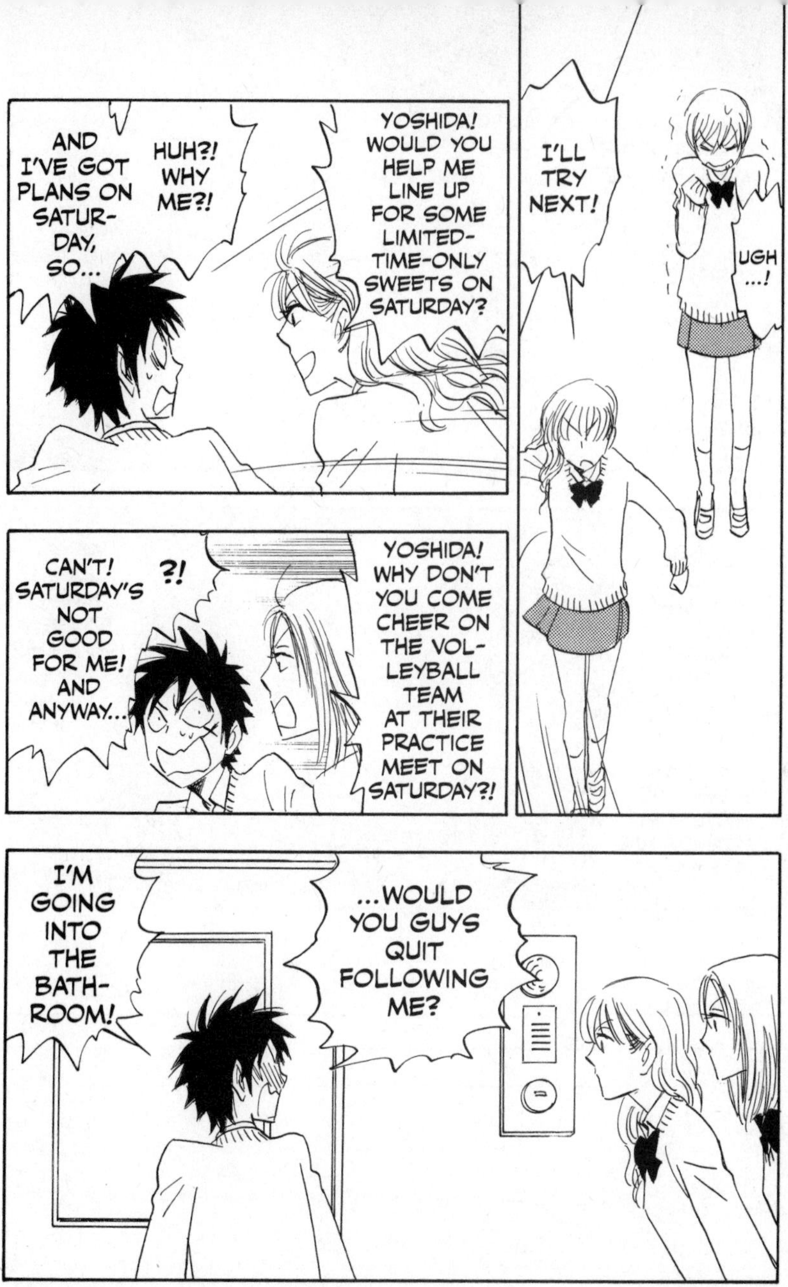
I'LL TRY NEXT!
UGH...!
YOSHIDA! WOULD YOU HELP ME LINE UP FOR SOME LIMITED-TIME-ONLY SWEETS ON SATURDAY?
HUH?! WHY ME?!
AND I'VE GOT PLANS ON SATURDAY, SO...
YOSHIDA! WHY DON'T YOU COME CHEER ON THE VOLLEYBALL TEAM AT THEIR PRACTICE MEET ON SATURDAY?!
?!
CAN'T! SATURDAY'S NOT GOOD FOR ME! AND ANYWAY...
...WOULD YOU GUYS QUIT FOLLOWING ME?
I'M GOING INTO THE BATHROOM!

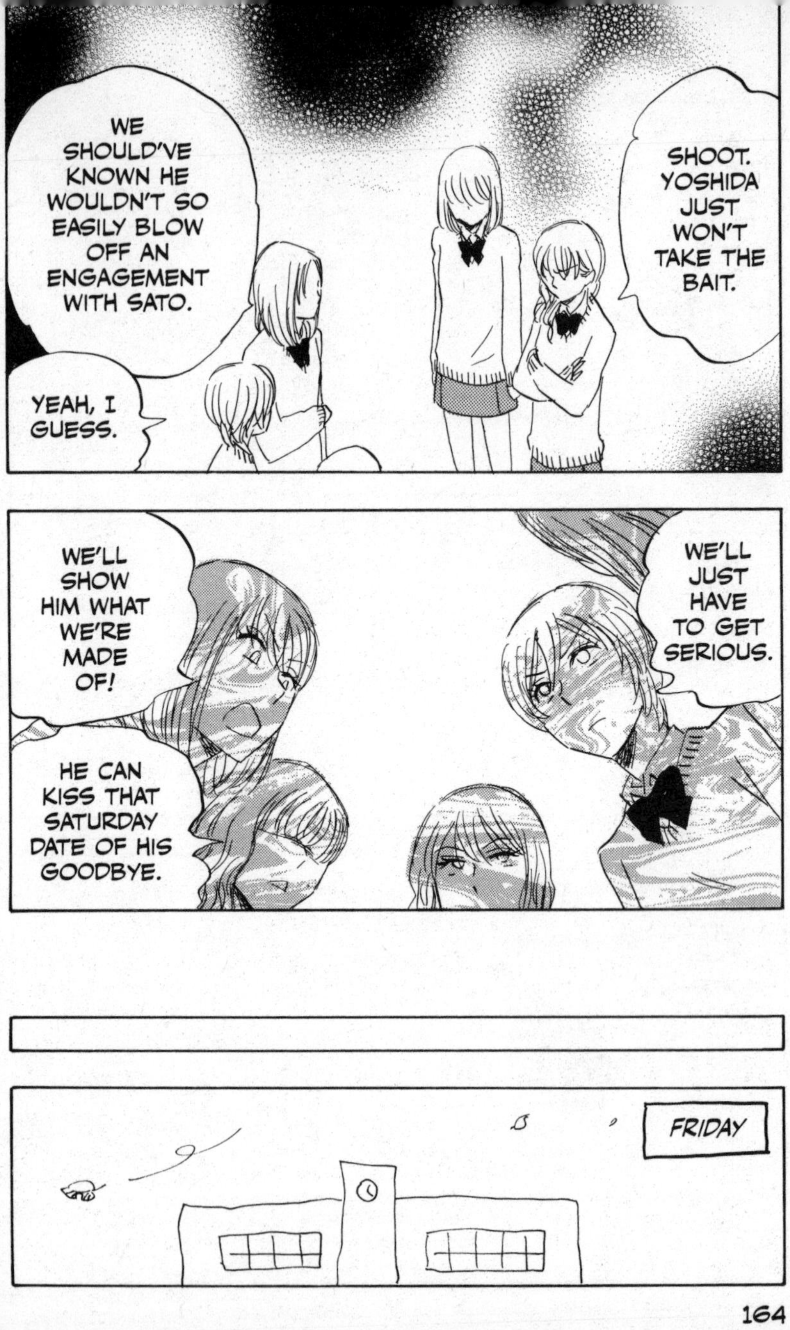
SHOOT. YOSHIDA JUST WON'T TAKE THE BAIT.
WE SHOULD'VE KNOWN HE WOULDN'T SO EASILY BLOW OFF AN ENGAGEMENT WITH SATO.
YEAH, I GUESS.
WE'LL JUST HAVE TO GET SERIOUS.
WE'LL SHOW HIM WHAT WE'RE MADE OF!
HE CAN KISS THAT SATURDAY DATE OF HIS GOODBYE.
FRIDAY

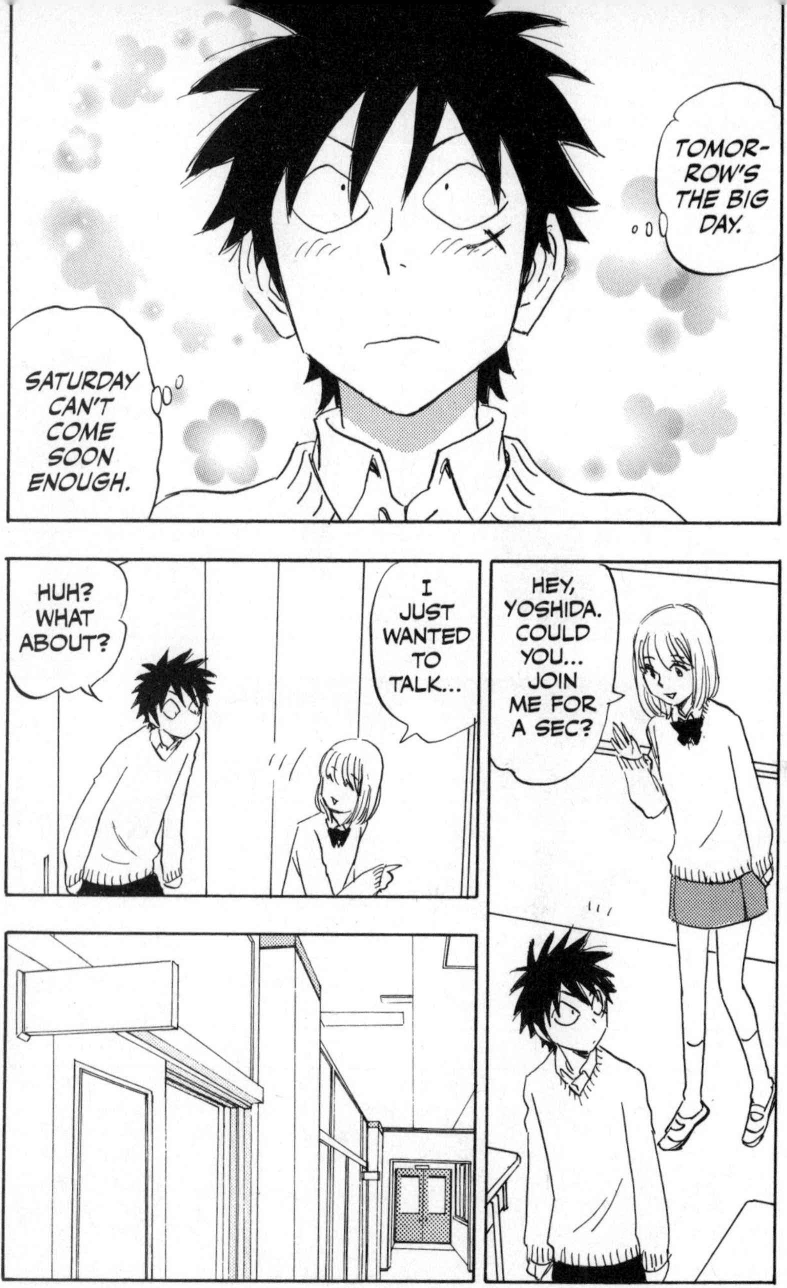
TOMORROW'S THE BIG DAY.
SATURDAY CAN'T COME SOON ENOUGH.
HEY, YOSHIDA. COULD YOU... JOIN ME FOR A SEC?
I JUST WANTED TO TALK...
HUH? WHAT ABOUT?

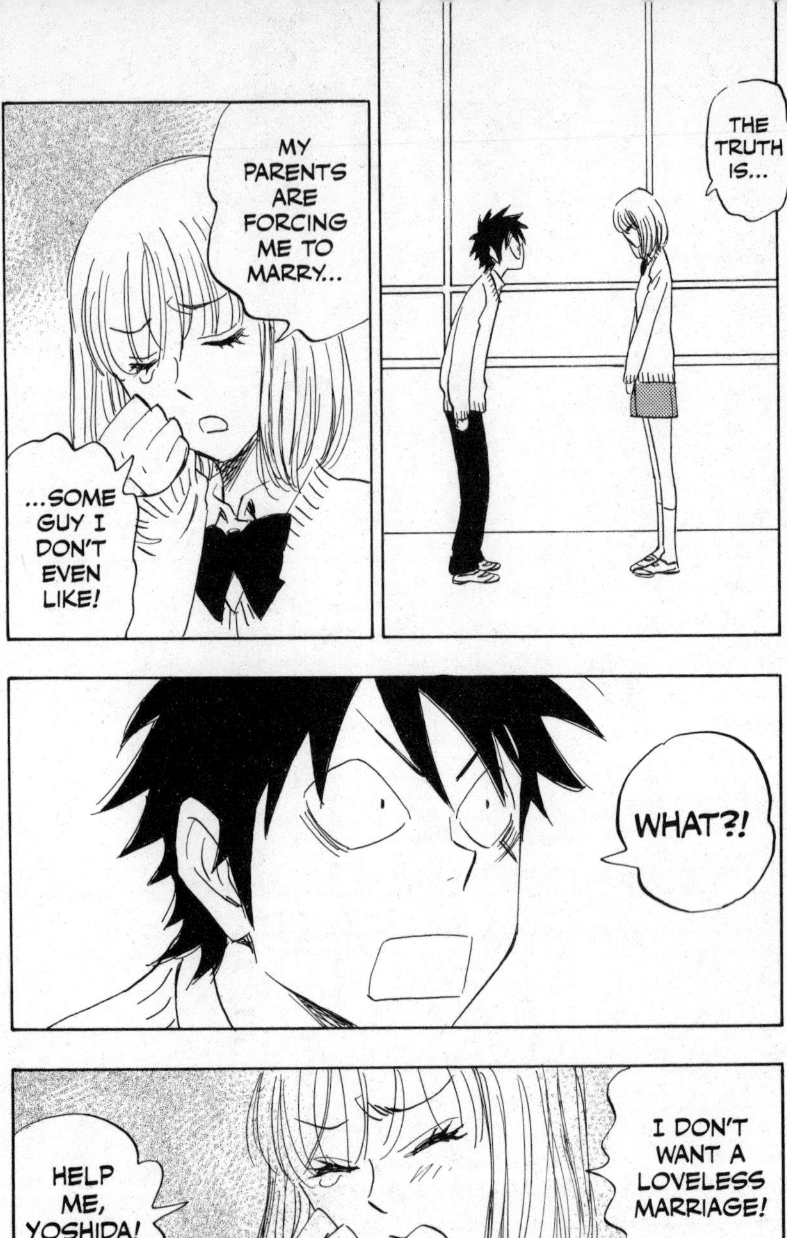
THE TRUTH IS...
MY PARENTS ARE FORCING ME TO MARRY...
...SOME GUY I DON'T EVEN LIKE!
WHAT?!
I DON'T WANT A LOVELESS MARRIAGE!
HELP ME, YOSHIDA!

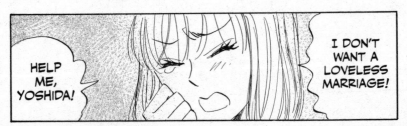

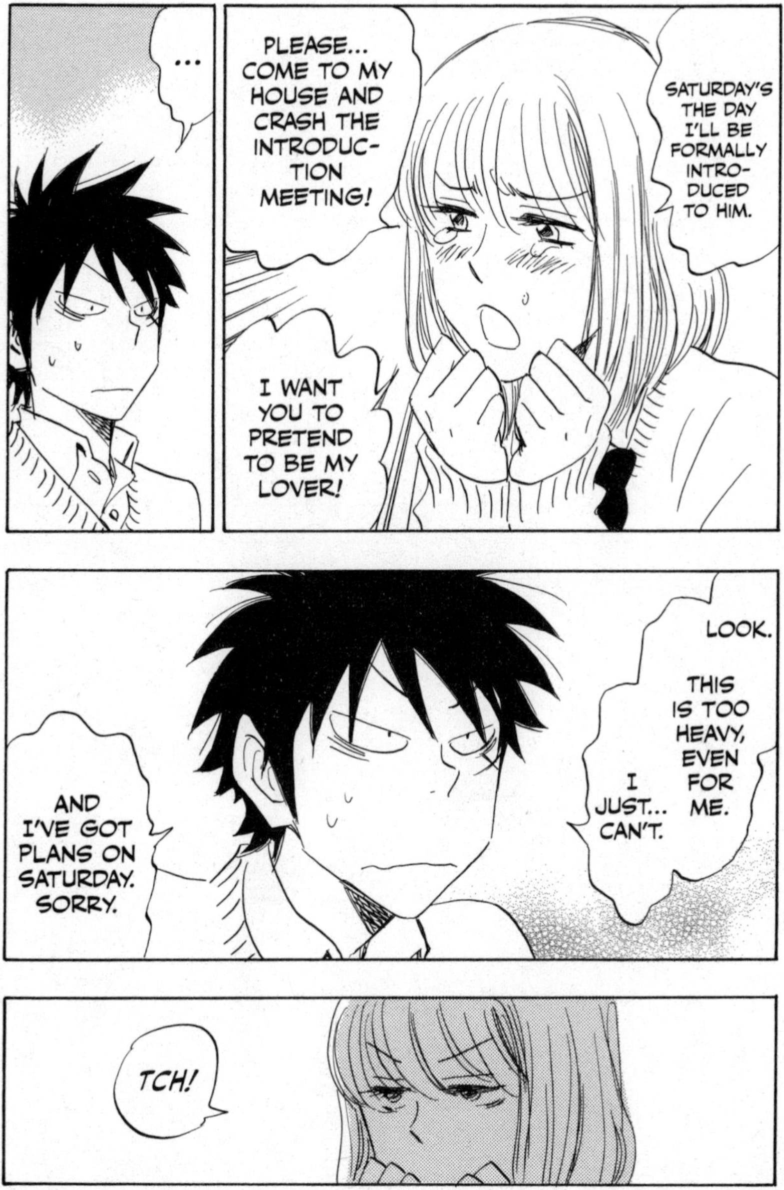
SATURDAY'S THE DAY I'LL BE FORMALLY INTRODUCED TO HIM.
PLEASE... COME TO MY HOUSE AND CRASH THE INTRODUCTION MEETING!
I WANT YOU TO PRETEND TO BE MY LOVER!
...
LOOK.
THIS IS TOO HEAVY, EVEN FOR ME.
I JUST... CAN'T.
AND I'VE GOT PLANS ON SATURDAY. SORRY.
TCH!

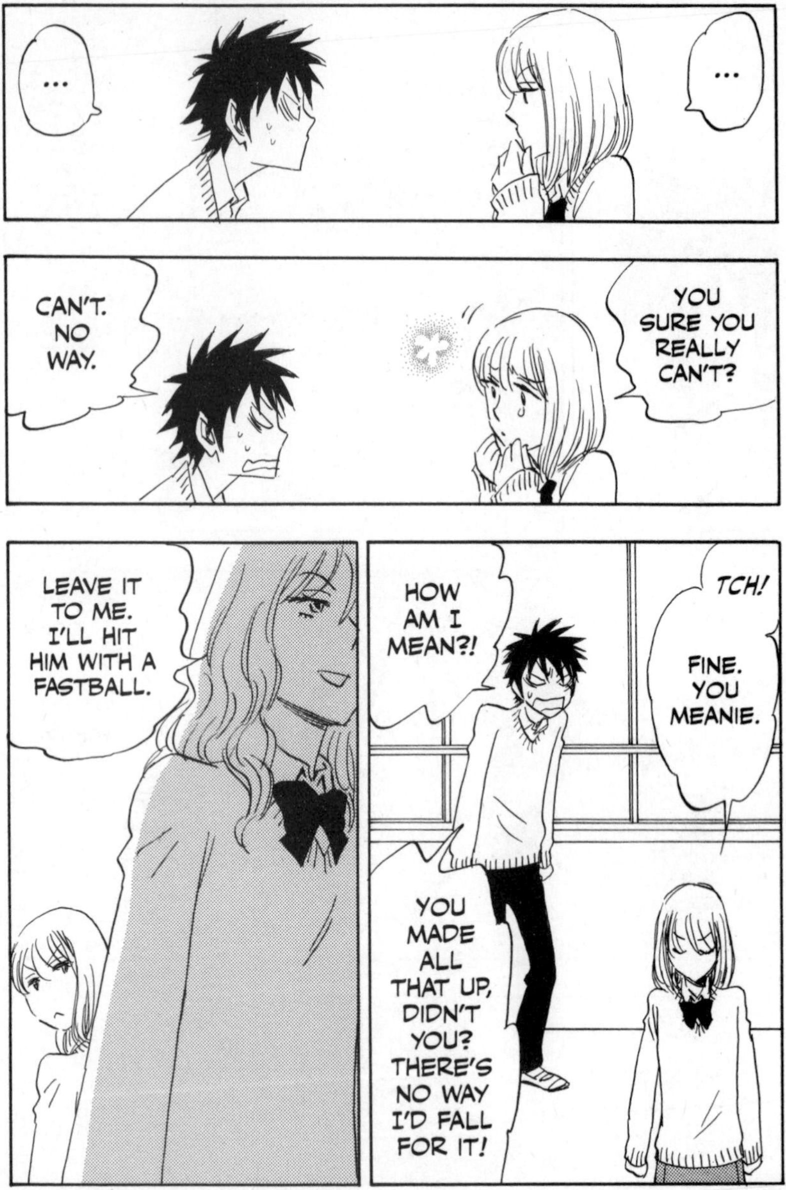
...
...
YOU SURE YOU REALLY CAN'T?
CAN'T. NO WAY.
TCH! FINE. YOU MEANIE.
HOW AM I MEAN?!
YOU MADE ALL THAT UP, DIDN'T YOU? THERE'S NO WAY I'D FALL FOR IT!
LEAVE IT TO ME. I'LL HIT HIM WITH A FASTBALL.

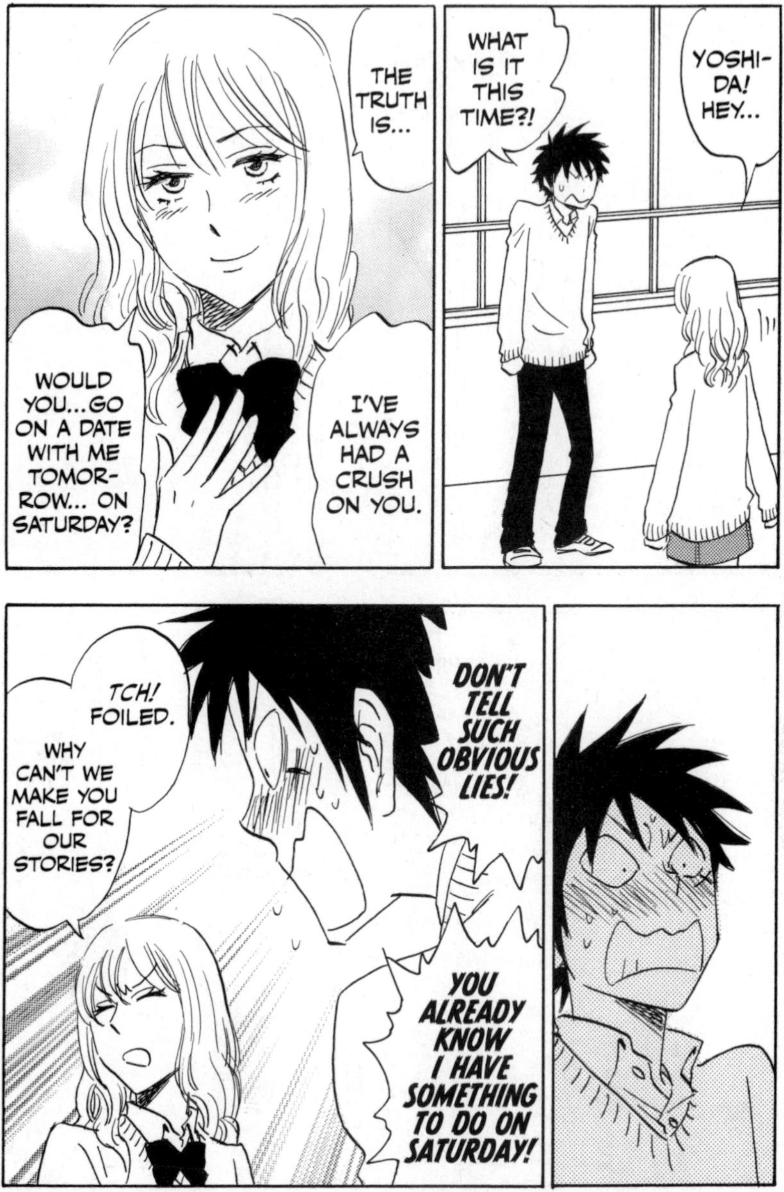
YOSHI-DA! HEY...
WHAT IS IT THIS TIME?!
THE TRUTH IS...
I'VE ALWAYS HAD A CRUSH ON YOU.
WOULD YOU...GO ON A DATE WITH ME TOMOR-ROW... ON SATURDAY?
DON'T TELL SUCH OBVIOUS LIES!
TCH! FOILED.
WHY CAN'T WE MAKE YOU FALL FOR OUR STORIES?
YOU ALREADY KNOW I HAVE SOMETHING TO DO ON SATURDAY!

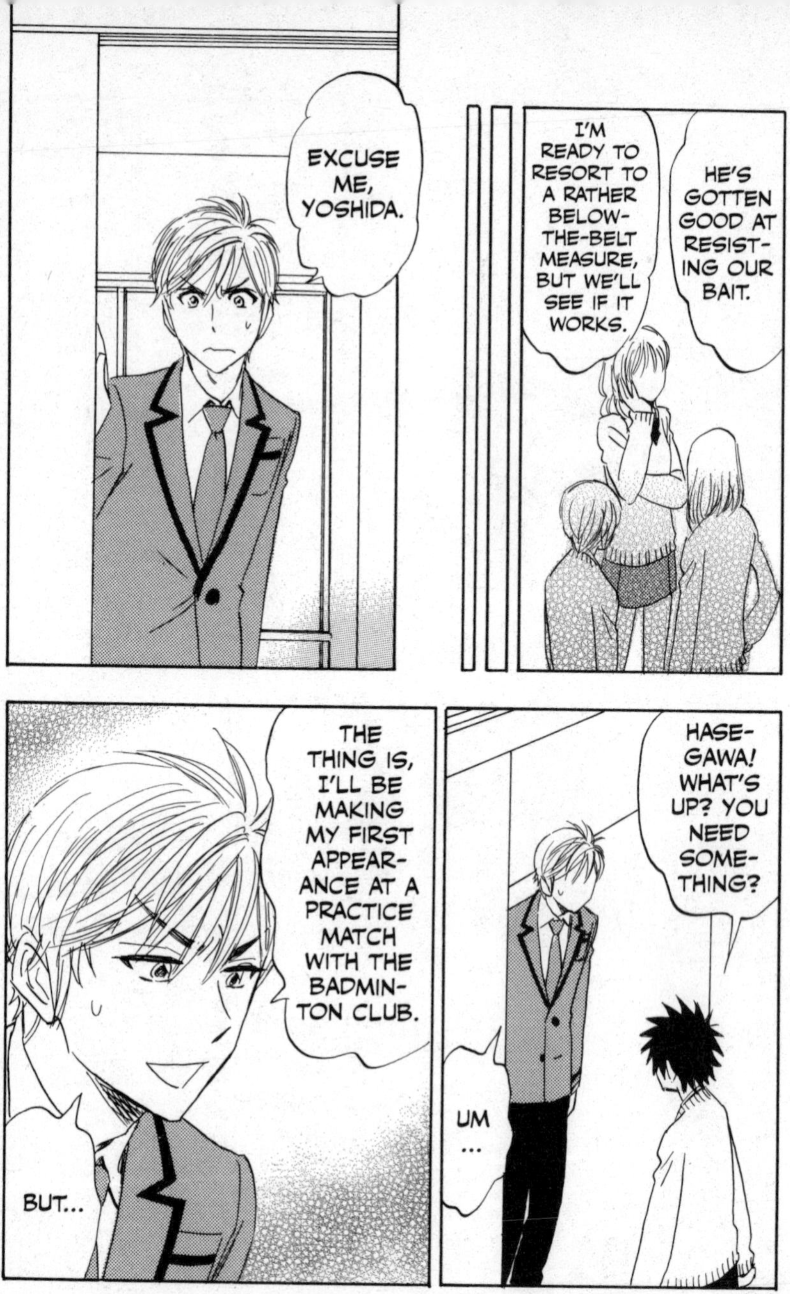
HE'S GOTTEN GOOD AT RESISTING OUR BAIT.
I'M READY TO RESORT TO A RATHER BELOW-THE-BELT MEASURE, BUT WE'LL SEE IF IT WORKS.
EXCUSE ME, YOSHIDA.
HASEGAWA! WHAT'S UP? YOU NEED SOMETHING?
UM...
THE THING IS, I'LL BE MAKING MY FIRST APPEARANCE AT A PRACTICE MATCH WITH THE BADMINTON CLUB.
BUT...

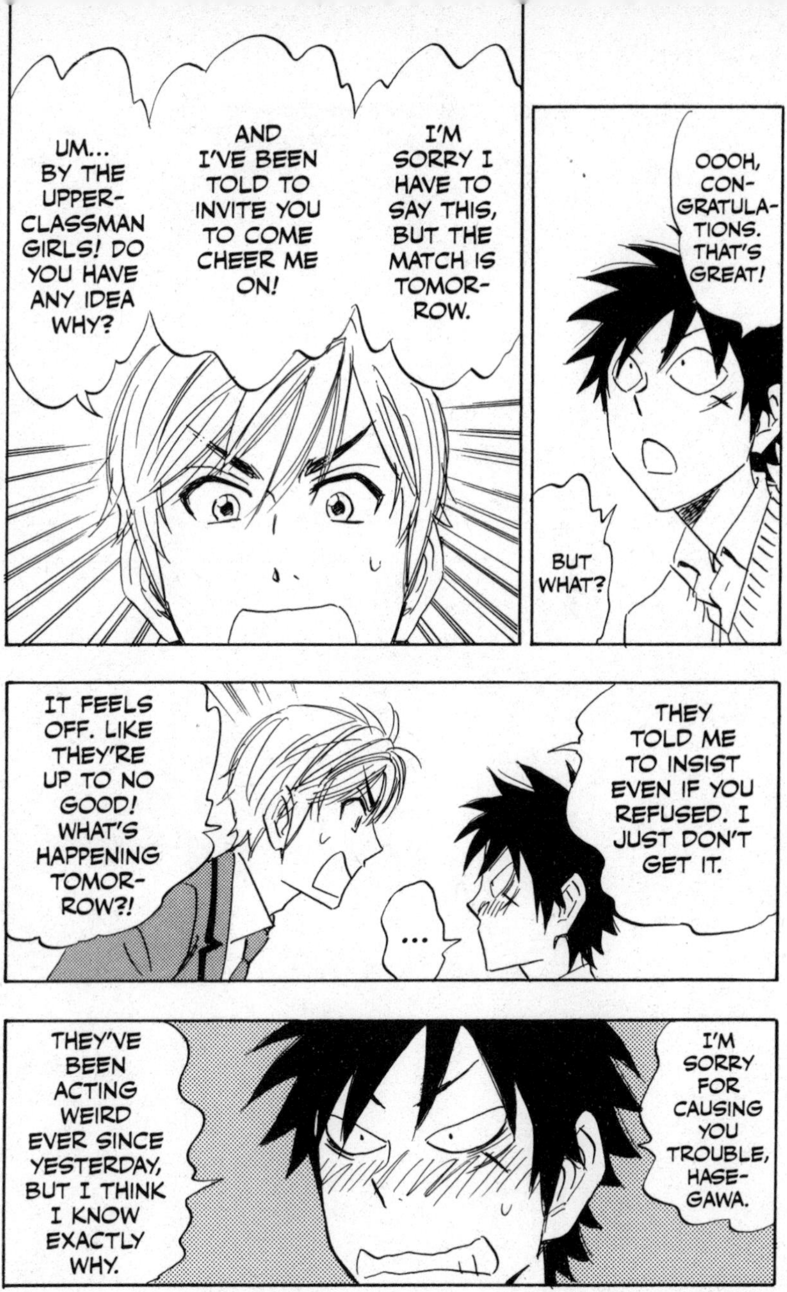
OOOH, CON-GRATULA-TIONS. THAT'S GREAT!
BUT WHAT?
I'M SORRY I HAVE TO SAY THIS, BUT THE MATCH IS TOMOR-ROW.
AND I'VE BEEN TOLD TO INVITE YOU TO COME CHEER ME ON!
UM... BY THE UPPER-CLASSMAN GIRLS! DO YOU HAVE ANY IDEA WHY?
THEY TOLD ME TO INSIST EVEN IF YOU REFUSED. I JUST DON'T GET IT.
...
IT FEELS OFF. LIKE THEY'RE UP TO NO GOOD! WHAT'S HAPPENING TOMOR-ROW?!
I'M SORRY FOR CAUSING YOU TROUBLE, HASE-GAWA.
THEY'VE BEEN ACTING WEIRD EVER SINCE YESTERDAY, BUT I THINK I KNOW EXACTLY WHY.

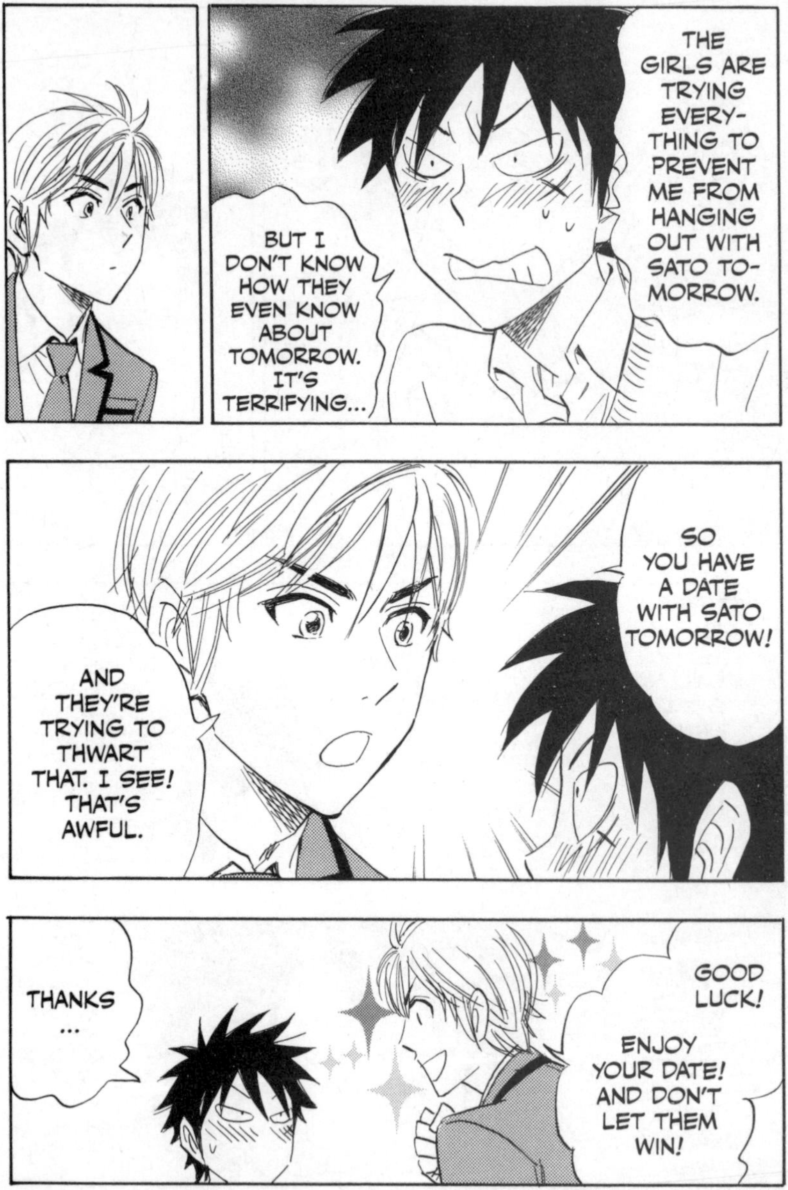
THE GIRLS ARE TRYING EVERYTHING TO PREVENT ME FROM HANGING OUT WITH SATO TOMORROW.
BUT I DON'T KNOW HOW THEY EVEN KNOW ABOUT TOMORROW. IT'S TERRIFYING...
SO YOU HAVE A DATE WITH SATO TOMORROW!
AND THEY'RE TRYING TO THWART THAT. I SEE! THAT'S AWFUL.
GOOD LUCK!
ENJOY YOUR DATE! AND DON'T LET THEM WIN!
THANKS ...

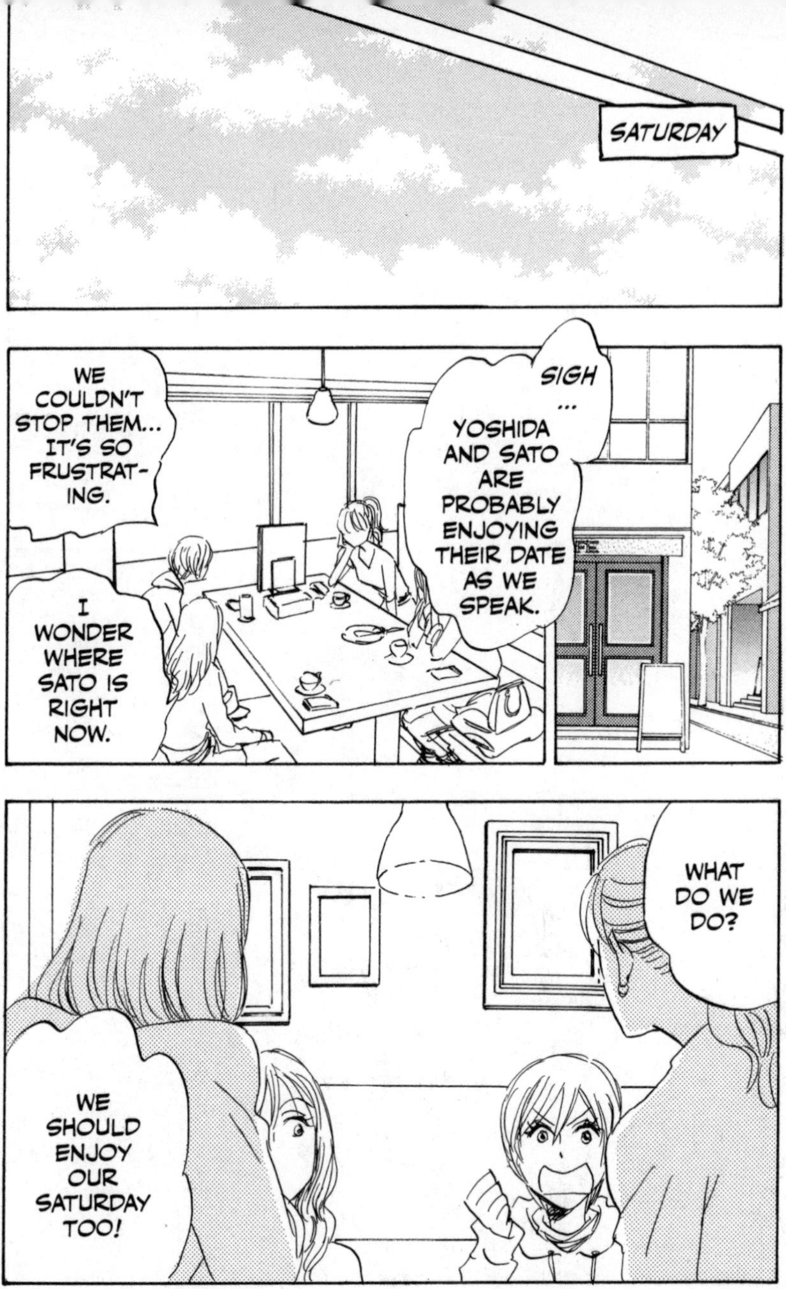
SATURDAY
SIGH ... YOSHIDA AND SATO ARE PROBABLY ENJOYING THEIR DATE AS WE SPEAK.
WE COULDN'T STOP THEM... IT'S SO FRUSTRAT-ING.
I WONDER WHERE SATO IS RIGHT NOW.
WHAT DO WE DO?
WE SHOULD ENJOY OUR SATURDAY TOO!

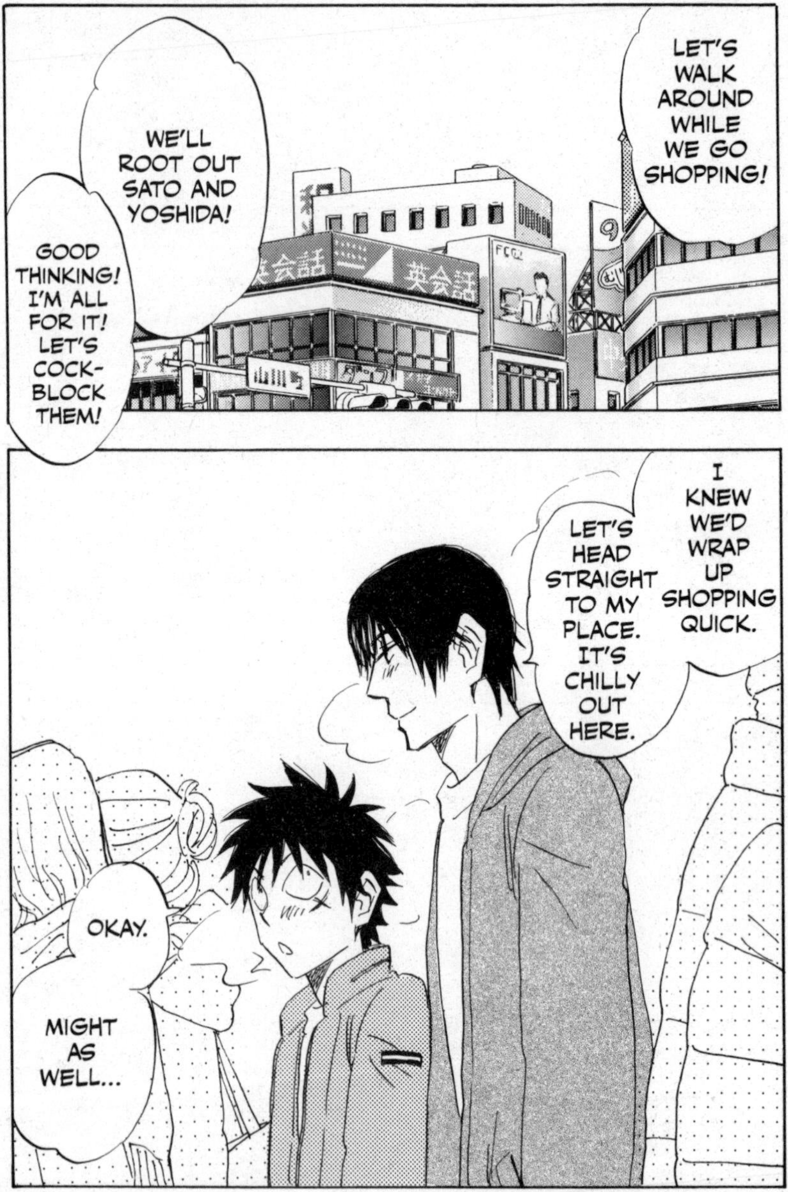
LET'S WALK AROUND WHILE WE GO SHOPPING!
WE'LL ROOT OUT SATO AND YOSHIDA!
GOOD THINKING! I'M ALL FOR IT! LET'S COCK-BLOCK THEM!
I KNEW WE'D WRAP UP SHOPPING QUICK.
LET'S HEAD STRAIGHT TO MY PLACE. IT'S CHILLY OUT HERE.
OKAY.
MIGHT AS WELL...

HIS FAVORITE

HIS
FAVORITE

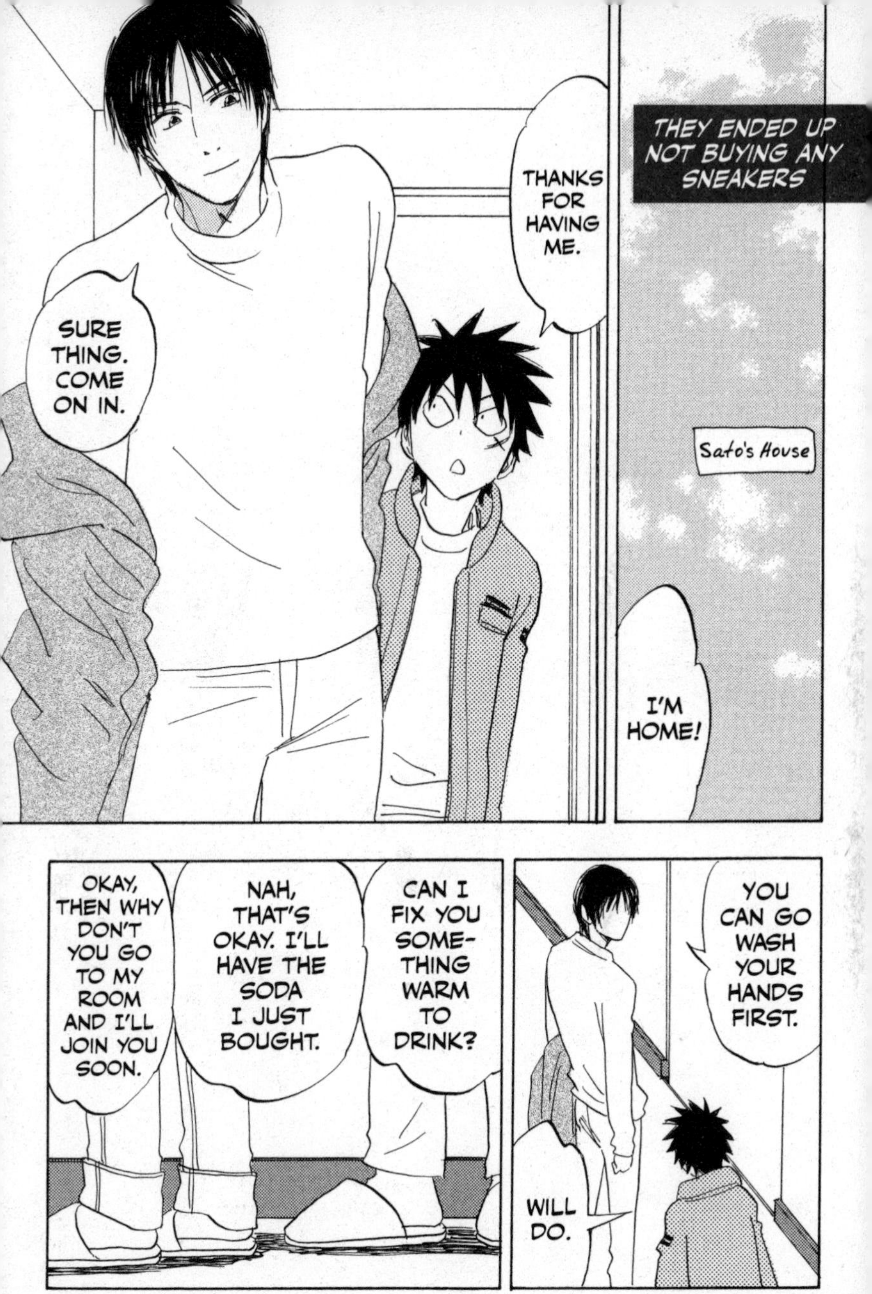
THEY ENDED UP NOT BUYING ANY SNEAKERS
Sato's House
I'M HOME!
THANKS FOR HAVING ME.
SURE THING. COME ON IN.
YOU CAN GO WASH YOUR HANDS FIRST.
WILL DO.
CAN I FIX YOU SOME-THING WARM TO DRINK?
NAH, THAT'S OKAY. I'LL HAVE THE SODA I JUST BOUGHT.
OKAY, THEN WHY DON'T YOU GO TO MY ROOM AND I'LL JOIN YOU SOON.

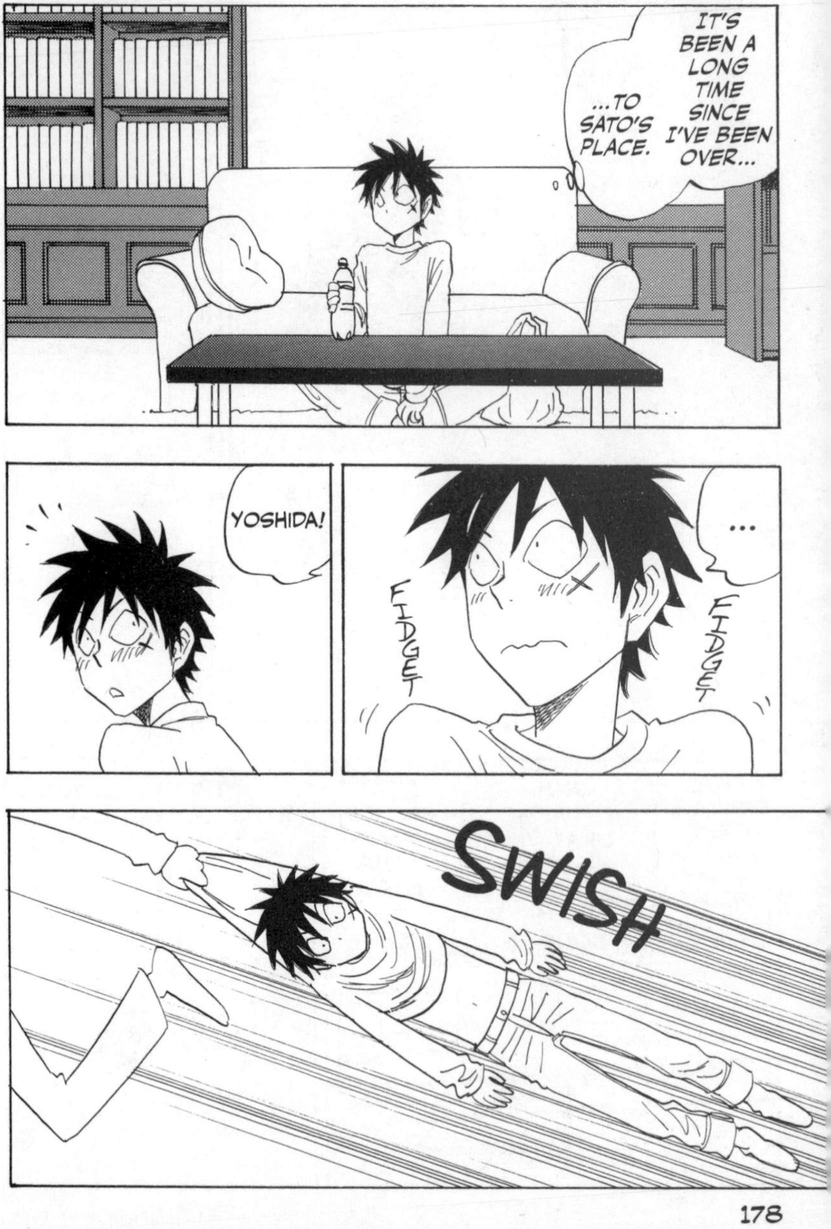
IT'S BEEN A LONG TIME SINCE I'VE BEEN OVER...
...TO SATO'S PLACE.
...
FIDGET
FIDGET
YOSHIDA!
SWISH

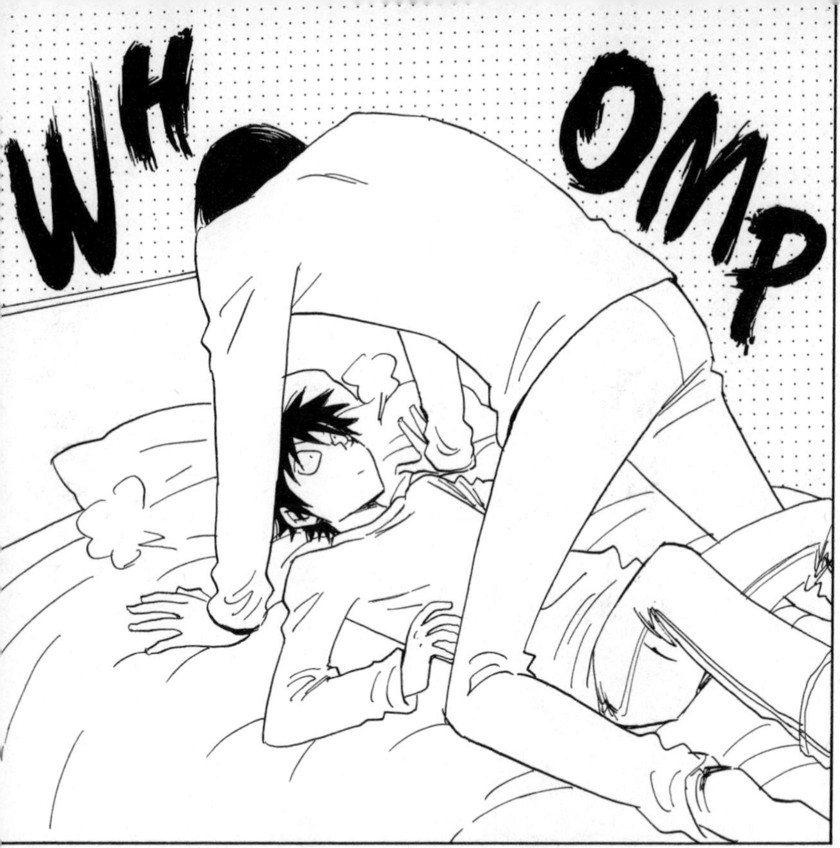
WHOMP

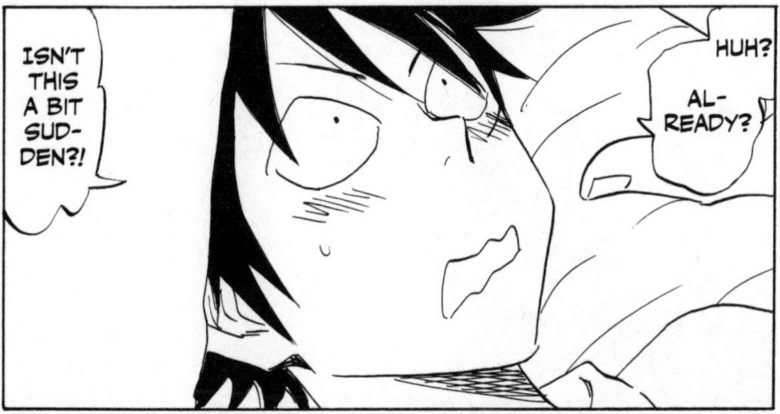
HUH?
AL-READY?
ISN'T THIS A BIT SUD-DEN?!

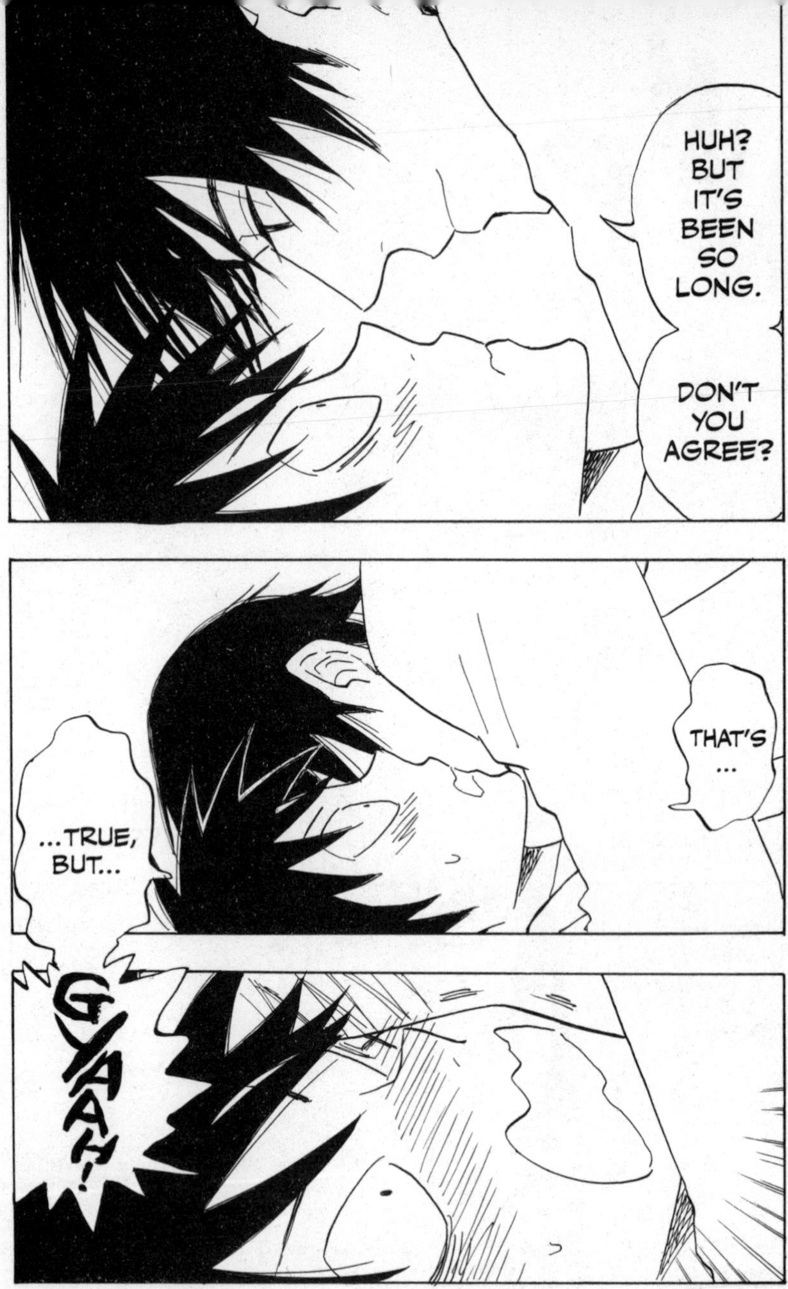
HUH? BUT IT'S BEEN SO LONG.
DON'T YOU AGREE?
THAT'S ...
...TRUE, BUT...
GYAAH!

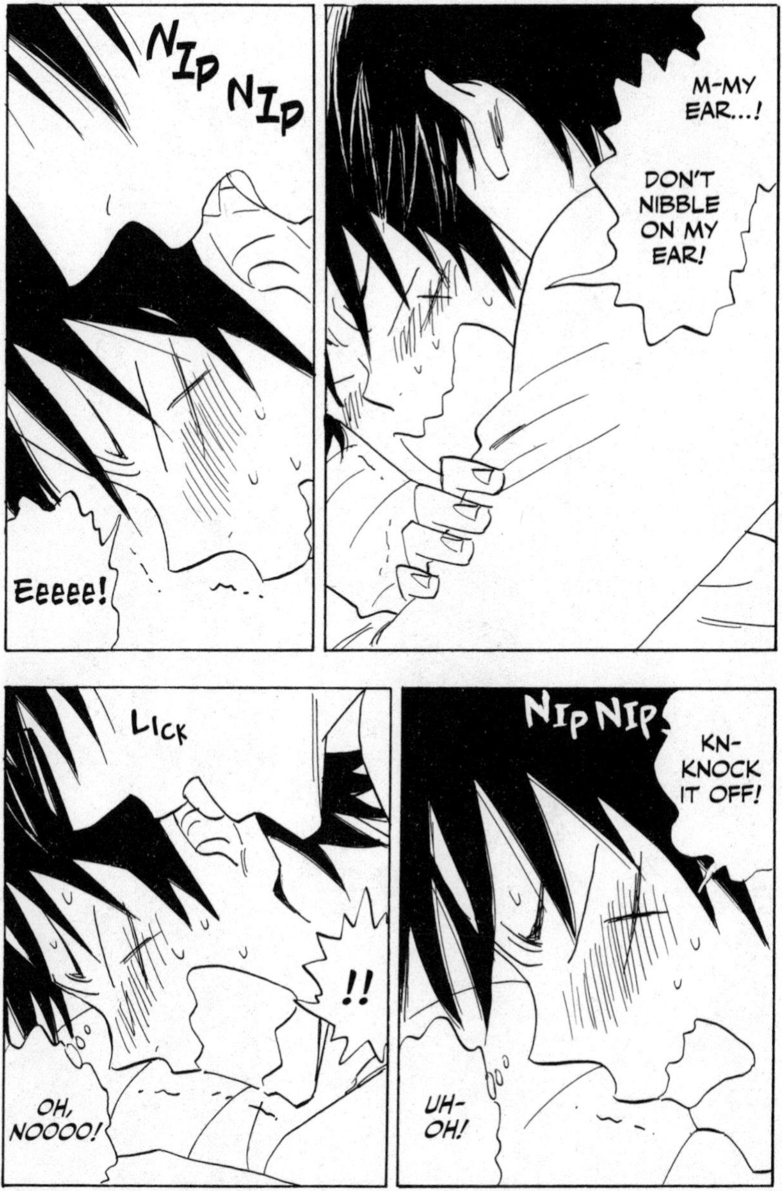
M-MY EAR...!
DON'T NIBBLE ON MY EAR!
NIP NIP
Eeeee!
NIP NIP
KN-KNOCK IT OFF!
UH-OH!
LICK
!!
OH, NOOOO!

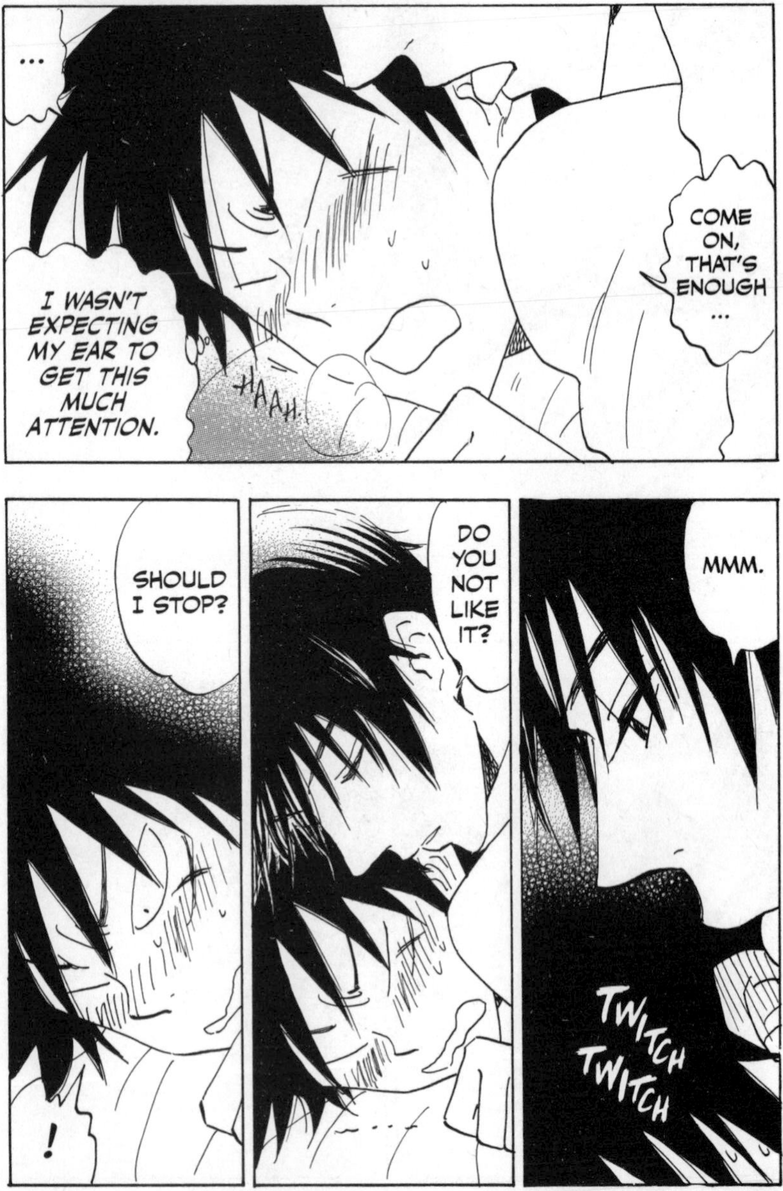
COME ON, THAT'S ENOUGH ...
...
I WASN'T EXPECTING MY EAR TO GET THIS MUCH ATTENTION.
HAAAH...
MMM.
TWITCH TWITCH
DO YOU NOT LIKE IT?
...
SHOULD I STOP?
!

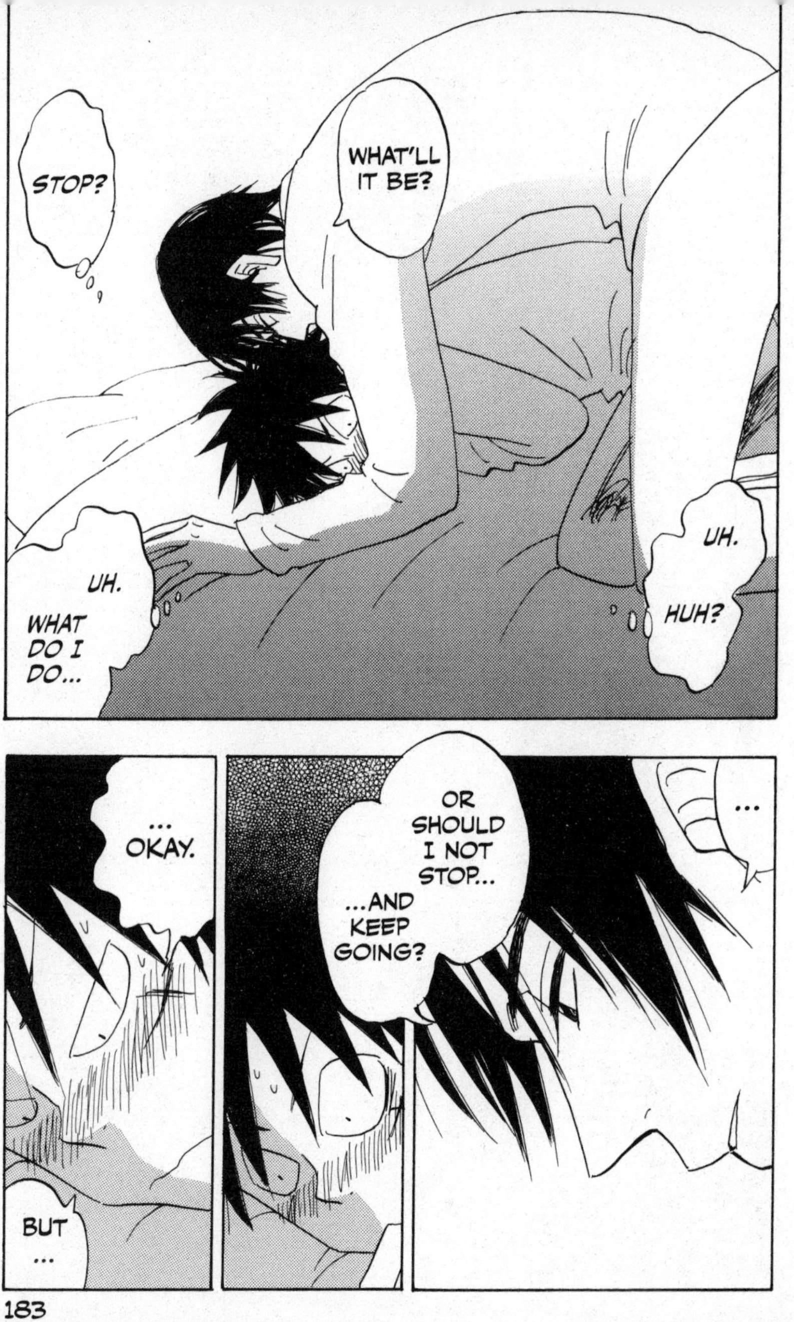
WHAT'LL IT BE?
STOP?
UH.
HUH?
UH.
WHAT DO I DO...
...
OR SHOULD I NOT STOP...
...AND KEEP GOING?
... OKAY.
BUT ...

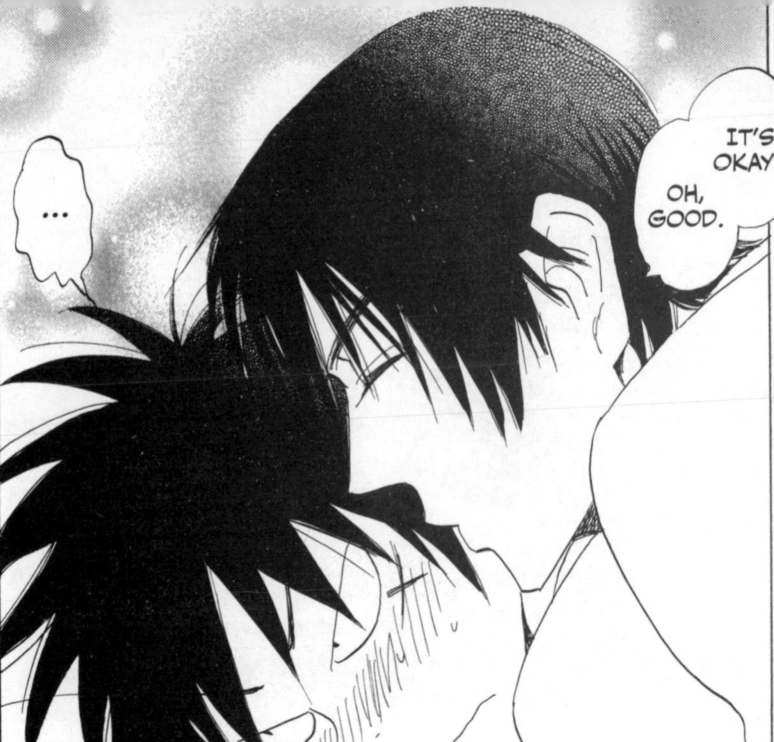
IT'S OKAY?
OH, GOOD.
...

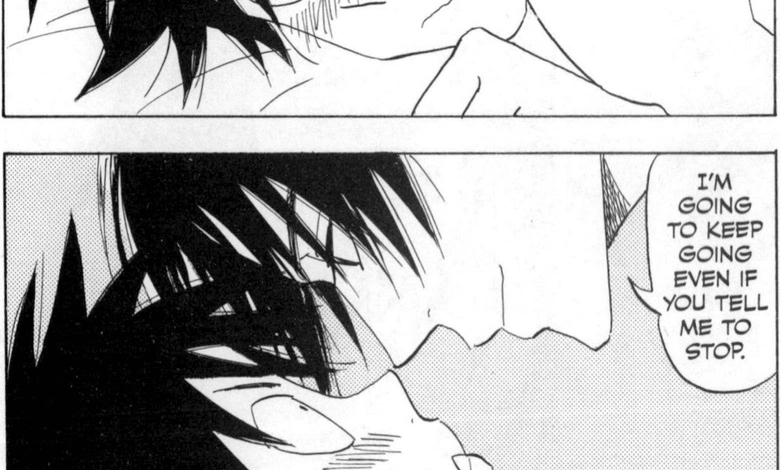
I'M GOING TO KEEP GOING EVEN IF YOU TELL ME TO STOP.

END

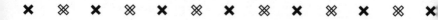

AFTERWORD

THANK YOU SO MUCH FOR READING ALL THE WAY
TO THIS LAST PAGE. THANKS TO ALL YOUR SUPPORT,
WE'VE REACHED THE 12TH VOLUME! THE FIRST CHAP-
TER IN THIS VOLUME WAS CREATED AT THE START OF
2020 (THE JANUARY ISSUE) AND WE TOOK ONE LAP
AROUND THE CALENDAR WITH ITS FINAL CHAPTER
BEING RELEASED IN THE FOLLOWING
JANUARY ISSUE. BUT THIS PAST YEAR TURNED OUT
TO BE A WILD TIME NOBODY COULD HAVE EVER
PREDICTED. THROUGH IT ALL, I'VE BEEN SUPPORTED
BY MY TWO EDITORS (WHOM I CAUSE TONS OF
TROUBLE FOR) AND I AM TERRIBLY GRATEFUL TO
ALL MY READERS FOR ALWAYS READING. THIS TITLE
TAKES ITS SWEET TIME MORE THAN MY STORIES
USUALLY DO, SO I HOPE YOU'RE ALSO ENJOYING
THE MORE LAID-BACK PACE.

SEE YOU LATER!

SUZUKI TANAKA

HIS
FAVORITE

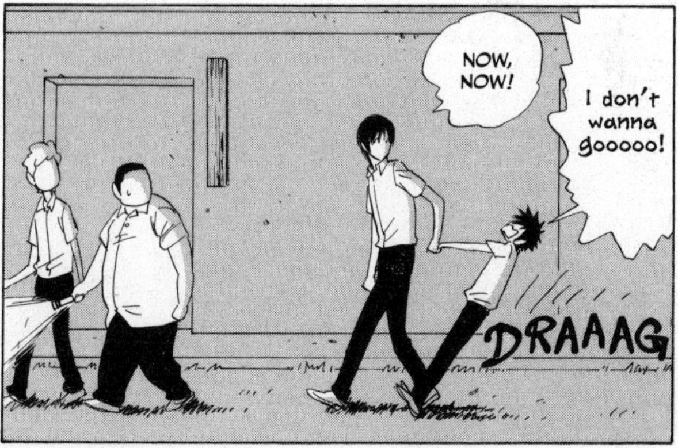
I don't wanna gooooo!
NOW, NOW!
DRAAAG

Date of Birth: March 12.
Pisces. Blood type B.

We have a volume 12! This is
thanks to everyone who has
read this far and supported
the series. Thank you!!

About the Author

Known for her engaging stories
and characters drawn with strong
lines, **Suzuki Tanaka** has garnered
plenty of attention for her latest hit,
His Favorite. After taking first place in
the 2009 Boys Love watch list book
Kono BL ga Yabai! 2009, the series
exploded in popularity and led to the
reprint of her earlier work, *Menkui*.

His Favorite
Volume 12
SuBLime Manga Edition

Story and Art by **Suzuki Tanaka**

Translation—**Christine Dashiell**
Touch-Up Art and Lettering—**Annaliese Christman**
Cover and Graphic Design—**Alice Lewis**
Editor—**Alexis Kirsch**

libre

Printed in the U.S.A.

Published by SuBLime Manga
P.O. Box 77010
San Francisco, CA 94107

10 9 8 7 6 5 4 3 2 1
First printing, May 2022

T+ OLDER TEEN

PARENTAL ADVISORY
HIS FAVORITE is rated T+ for Older Teen and is recommended for ages 16 and up. This volume contains suggestive themes.

SUBLIME
SuBLimeManga.com

For more information

on all our products, along with the most up-to-date news on releases, series announcements, and contests, please visit us at:

 SuBLimeManga.com

 twitter.com/**SuBLimeManga**

 facebook.com/**SuBLimeManga**

 instagram.com/**SuBLimeManga**

 SuBLimeManga.tumblr.com

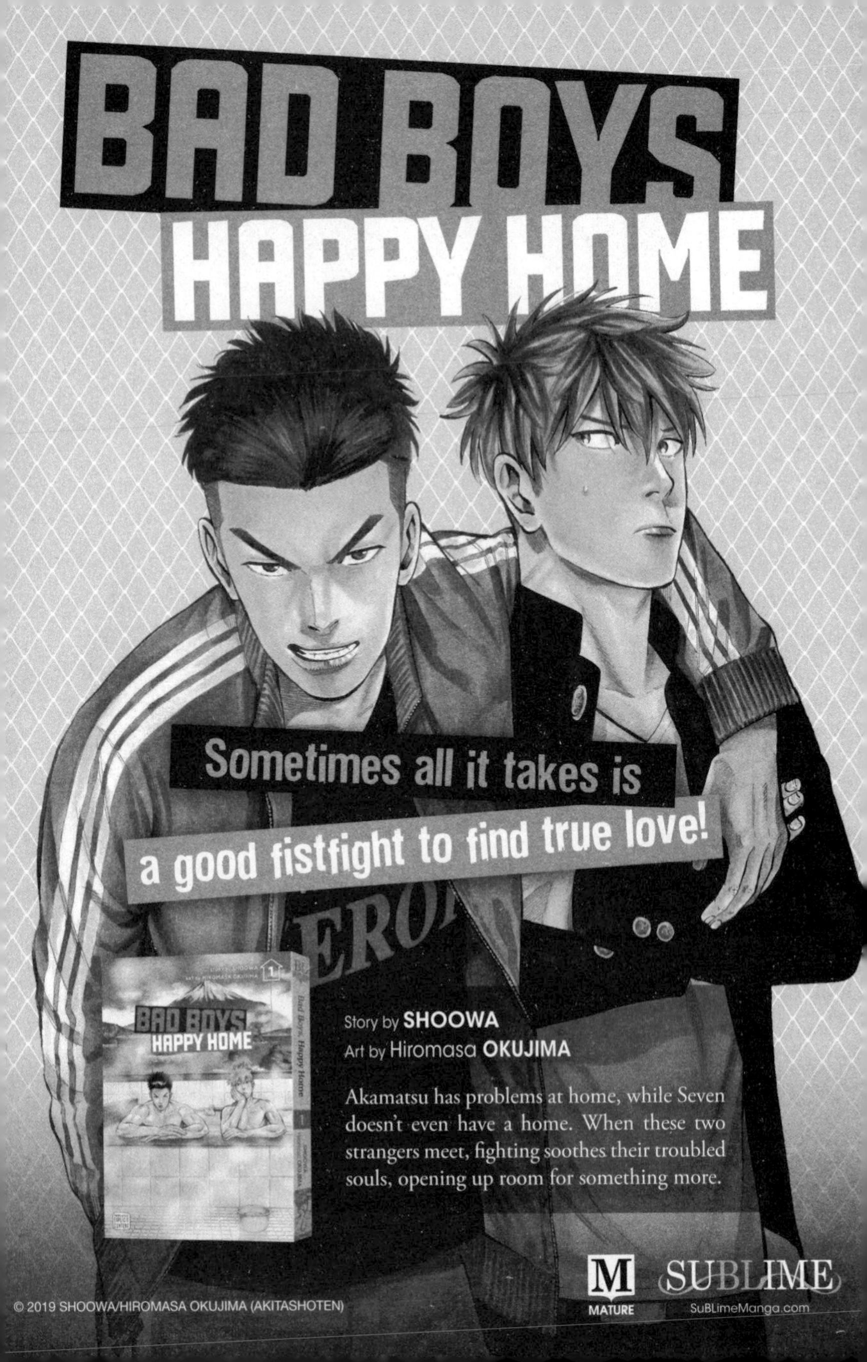
BAD BOYS
HAPPY HOME
Sometimes all it takes is
a good fistfight to find true love!
Story by SHOOWA
Art by Hiromasa OKUJIMA
Akamatsu has problems at home, while Seven doesn't even have a home. When these two strangers meet, fighting soothes their troubled souls, opening up room for something more.
M
MATURE
SUBLIME
SuBLimeManga.com
© 2019 SHOOWA/HIROMASA OKUJIMA (AKITASHOTEN)